It is enormously encouraging to read a book on mission that consistently puts God and God's mission first, that applies the grand biblical framework of creation, fall, redemption and new creation thoroughly and repeatedly across almost every issue it addresses, and which tackles some very controversial areas with grace, wisdom, and biblical thoroughness. Here is a book that will richly reward all who patiently digest it, but will especially nourish teachers and practitioners of the mission that God has entrusted to His church.

Christopher J. H. Wright
International Director, The Langham Partnership International
Author of *The Mission of God*

Evangelical Christians are in urgent need of assistance in knowing how to understand all the obligations of the gospel and to maintain a very clear conversionist understanding of the gospel of the Lord Jesus Christ. In this new volume, some of the best thinkers in evangelical life address the need for a theologically driven missiology. I am thankful for this book and for the contribution it will make to our evangelical conversation.

R. Albert Mohler, Jr.
President, The Southern Baptist Theological Seminary

The good news of Jesus Christ is more than just a story. It is a divine drama, the gripping and miraculous four-act story of creation, fall, redemption, and restoration. This collection of essays, written by scholar/practitioners, first builds a strong theological foundation and then offers practical application for taking the gospel to the world. This intentional direction—theology that drives missiology—makes this book a necessary addition to your library. Read it, study it, pray through it, and let it compel you to the nations.

Charles Lawless
Vice President for Global Theological Advance
International Mission Board, SBC

Theology without mission is abstract theory and powerless. Mission without theology is abstract activity and powerless. This book challenges the church to remember that what God has joined together, let no one tear asunder. Don't just contemplate the arguments here; let them spark you to worship and to mission.

Russell D. Moore
Dean, The Southern Baptist Theological Seminary

Whereas we sometimes experience a tension between theory and practice, the Bible knows no such tension. Our call to make disciples requires a faithful understanding of both the theology behind our mission and the practice of manifesting it. *Theology and Practice of Mission* helps us to do just that through a thorough examination of the most crucial missiological issues, articulated by some of the brightest scholars and practitioners currently serving the kingdom. The result is a volume that helps us all to understand how to obey more faithfully Christ's command to make disciples in light of the grand biblical narrative in which God made that possible.

Ed Stetzer
President, LifeWay Research

The postmodern world is built on rapidly shifting paradigms. Sociologically, it is flattened because adherents of world religions, traditional localized ones, and growing secularism blend into various pluralisms in unparalleled ways. Opportunities abound for Christ's ambassadors to witness to and engage the nations. The reader should carefully examine this book's view of human cultures in relation to God's created intent, its present form, and future restoration. The editor incorporates voices from the "Edge," where the most unreached and unengaged peoples reside. These insights bring frontline reconnaissance to current conversations in theology and missiology. The reader will be challenged and inspired.

Keith Eitel
Dean, Roy Fish School of Evangelism & Missions

THEOLOGY
AND
PRACTICE
OF
MISSION

GOD, THE CHURCH,
AND THE NATIONS

This Book Belongs To:

BRUCE RILEY ASHFORD
EDITOR

B&H
ACADEMIC
NASHVILLE, TENNESSEE

Theology and Practice of Mission: God, the Church, and the Nation
Revised Edition

Copyright © 2011 by Bruce Ashford

All rights reserved.

ISBN: 978-0-8054-6412-2

Published by B&H Publishing Group
Nashville, Tennessee

Dewey Decimal Classification: 269.2
Subject Heading: MISSIONS \ DOCTRINAL THEOLOGY \
EVANGELISTIC WORK

Printed in the United States of America

3 4 5 6 7 8 9 10 • 16 15 14 13 12

Contents

DEDICATION

For my wife, Lauren
"The heart of her husband trusts in her."
(Proverbs 31:11)

For my daughters, Riley Noelle
and Anna Katherine
"Children are a heritage from the Lord."
(Psalm 127:3)

For my parents, Bruce and Bobbi Ashford
"Honor your father and your mother."
(Exodus 20:12)

Acknowledgments

I wish to thank Brad Waggoner, Jennifer Lyell, and the editorial staff at B&H for their commitment to this project. I further wish to thank Jerry Rankin, Clyde Meador, Gordon Fort, and the leadership team of the Southern Baptist Convention's International Mission Board, without whose initiative and encouragement this project would never have been birthed. I also express gratitude to the many overseas workers and teachers, most of them missionaries with the International Mission Board, from whom I have learned so much over the years. In particular I wish to mention John B., Doug Coleman, Don D., Keith Eitel, Steve E., J. D. Greear, Phil Hopkins, John L., Nik Ripken, and Zane Pratt.

I also wish to express appreciation to Penny Keathley, Kristen Bell, and Claire Hilliard for all of their help with this project over the past three years. I am grateful to Ed Pruitt and Greg Mathias for their encouragement and counsel in the initial stages of this project, and to Danny Akin and David Nelson. Danny Akin is the visionary leader who took Paige Patterson's mantle at Southeastern Baptist Theological Seminary and furthered its reputation as a Great Commission seminary. I do not know any person who cares more deeply about the church's mission to the nations than President Akin. David Nelson is a friend and former colleague who was very involved in the initial stages of this project, and with whom I have had countless profitable discussions about things theological, missiological, and philosophical.

Finally, I wish to acknowledge my wife Lauren who is in every way a godly woman. She is a constant reminder of God's grace and love. During the first two years of our marriage, when the majority of the work for this book was done, she took care of our home, discussed the content of the book, and encouraged me in the project even when I worked evenings and weekends and spent weeks at a time overseas. Most importantly, I am thankful for how she has loved and cared for our daughters while Daddy was at work or out of the country. Her character is well-summarized by Proverbs 31:10–11, "Who can find a capable wife? She is far more precious than jewels. The heart of her husband trusts in her, and he will not lack anything good."

Bruce Riley Ashford
Christmas 2010

INTRODUCTION

T he purpose of this volume, *Theology and Practice of Mission: God, the Church, and the Nations*, is to provide a biblical-theological framework for understanding the church's mission to the nations. Toward this end, the book is divided into four parts: God's Mission, the Church's Mission, the Church's Mission to the Nations, and Concluding Challenges.

The first part, "God's Mission," contains two foundational chapters.[1] The first chapter argues that God's mission is to redeem for himself a people who will be a kingdom of priests to the praise of his glory, who will bear witness to his gospel and advance his church, and who will dwell with him forever on a new heavens and earth. This mission is communicated to us in the Bible's overarching narrative that unfolds in four movements: creation, fall, redemption, and restoration. The authors conclude by reminding us that we now live "between the times," between the first and second comings of the King, and find ourselves called to be ambassadors for the God who created us and purchased us with the blood of his Son. Chapter 2, "The Triune God: The God of Mission," is an investigation of what it means to say that God is the agent of missions. It defines *missio Dei* (the mission of God), delineates the missional character of God by arguing that God's nature is the *foundation* of the mission and that his triune life is the *pattern* of the mission, and deals with creation and redemption as missional acts of God.

The second part, "The Church's Mission," treats the mission of God's people in light of the mission of God.[2] Although the two are not synonymous,

---

[1] In using the concept of *missio Dei* or God's mission, this book is not identifying itself with various non-evangelical conceptions of missiology that also use *missio Dei* in order to define and delimit mission. In particular, the approach of this book does not resonate with the approaches taken by the World Council of Churches in Uppsala (1968) or Canberra (1999), approaches which identify revolutionary social movements with God's kingdom mission and which approvingly speak of God's mission in society being implemented by individuals and institutions outside of his redeemed people.

[2] Part 2, therefore, treats mission as "broadly conceived." The church's mission, broadly conceived, encompasses everything that God through Christ sends his people into the world to do (John 20:21). This mission, as mentioned above, embraces all of the various ways in which God's church seeks to give him glory, in all of the various contexts in which it finds itself.

the church's mission is framed by God's mission, seen upon the backdrop of God's mission, and understood in the light of God's mission. The church takes its cues from God himself and therefore is committed to his mission, seeking to increase his renown, proclaim his gospel, advance his church, and bear witness to the truth of his Word. This mission includes not only evangelism and church planting, but also discipleship and gospel witness in every dimension of human culture and across the fabric of human existence. It includes faithfulness in the various callings of the Christian life—our calling to glorify God in family, church, workplace, and community, as well as in Christian socio-cultural interaction—our dealings in the arts, the sciences, education, business, and the public square. The church's mission is also comprehensive in geographic scope, in that it refers not only to our local ministries, but also to regional and international ministries.

The chapters in part 2, therefore, provide an initial understanding of the church's role in proclaiming and embodying God's gospel for the furtherance of his kingdom mission. Chapters 3–5 give treatments of the Christian doctrines of humanity, redemption, and church. From the doctrine of humanity, we learn that God invites his image-bearers to join him in winning worshippers from every nation and reclaiming everything for his glory. Although God does not call every believer to live overseas, he does give all believers a part to play in his global mission. From the doctrine of redemption, we learn that Christ is the heart of God's redemptive mission. Only by his life, death, resurrection, and ascension may lost sinners be saved. Saving faith is consciously focused on Jesus Christ. Therefore, we are called to proclaim Christ and his gospel until the day he returns. From the doctrine of the church, we learn that the church is the community of God's mission, enlivened by his Spirit, appealing for the coming of his kingdom and seeking to live his will on earth as it is in heaven.

Chapters 6–9 deal with four of the issues that continually arise in relation to Christian mission: evangelism, social responsibility, culture, and lifestyle. Chapter 6 argues that God has commissioned his people to be master storytellers—proclaimers of the grand biblical narrative centering on Christ, his cross, and his resurrection. In so doing, we are able to treat the whole canon of Scripture as God's sacred gospel story and at the same time allow our audience the opportunity to find their place in that same story through repentance in Christ, so that they may become faithful storytellers as well. Chapter 7 treats our responsibility to the poor, arguing that a gospel-shaped life issues forth in care for the weak, the lowly, the oppressed, and the hurting. With joy-filled love for our God, we lay down our own lives in love, anticipating his Kingdom, lived out on a new heavens and earth, where there will be no spiritual or material poverty. Chapter 8 speaks of the God who created his image-bearers with the capacity to create culture, who inspired the Scriptures that were written in the midst of human culture, and who calls us to proclaim the gospel in the midst of such culture. This same God claims sovereignty over all of his creation and directs church's mission to extend across all of creation. For this reason, he calls his church to proclaim the gospel across the fabric of human existence and in every dimension of human culture, and to do so in a way that upholds his gospel, builds his church, and advances his kingdom. Chapter 9 encourages us to live missionally by leaving all of our resources at God's disposal, to use for the sake of his kingdom, thereby subverting the spirit of the age.

The third part, "The Church's Mission to the Nations," treats the cross-cultural and cross-linguistic outworking of the church's mission.[3] This mission to the nations has most often been relegated exclusively to international missionaries who must cross cultural divides and overcome daunting linguistic barriers in order to share the gospel. We must not overlook, however, that those who minister in the United States now must often cross cultures and subcultures and overcome linguistic barriers in their efforts to advance the kingdom. It is our contention that the North American church must come to terms with its missional calling, just as its international missionaries come to terms with theirs. Part 3, therefore, provides a basic starting point, a trajectory, and some parameters for conceiving the church's mission to all people groups and cultural contexts.

Chapter 10 sets forth the Hebrew Bible's treatment of "the nations," focusing on the Pentateuch, the Psalms, and the Prophets. Chapter 11 argues that "the nations" is a central theme of the New Testament, that the gospel is both *for* and *to* the nations, and that God always pursues his mission by choosing a specific person or group of people to accomplish his mission to fill the whole earth with his worshipers. Chapter 12 gives a historical treatment of the concept of "people groups" and then proceeds to argue that the church's mission to "the nations" involves more than mission to every country or geo-political entity. It involves preaching the gospel to all tribes, tongues, and languages, indeed from all people groups.

Chapter 13 makes the case for Christian mission as an enterprise which involves both reaching and teaching. The church is not called merely to make professions of faith, but to make disciples by teaching them all things Christ has commanded. Chapter 14 argues that church planting is central to the church's mission to the nations. God has commanded us to make disciples, the New Testament reveals that disciples are made through God's church, and therefore church multiplication is part of the mission of God until Christ comes again. Chapter 15 treats mission and suffering, arguing that all who desire to live godly lives in Christ Jesus will be persecuted, that God gives grace to his people in their time of suffering, and that he uses the suffering of

---

[3] Part 3, therefore, treats mission as "strictly conceived." This is the primary sense in which evangelicals speak of mission, missions, and missionaries; it refers to God's call for his church to cross national, cultural, and linguistic boundaries in order to make disciples. This sense of the word *mission* is compatible with the more broadly-conceived notion in part 2, in that evangelical missionaries make disciples and plant churches (across national, cultural, and linguistic boundaries) that are themselves intended to live out a mission that includes not only evangelism and church planting, but also discipleship and gospel witness in every dimension of human culture and across the fabric of human existence.

his people to build his kingdom. Chapters 16–20 treat mission to Muslims, Hindus, Buddhists, Animists, and Postmoderns. Each of these religion-world-view complexes seek to provide a sort of salvation and to explain ultimate reality, humanity, and the cosmos, and each is antithetical to the gospel. The Christian gospel alone is the power of God unto salvation and the biblical narrative alone explains God, humanity, and the world.

The fourth part consists of two concluding challenges. The first conclud-ing challenge, "A Theologically-Driven Missiology," provides a concise exposition of the major loci of Christian theology, showing how each locus of Christian theology should shape the church's missiological practice. This chapter serves to complement the first chapter, "The Story of Mission," in two ways. First, it complements the first chapter by exploring the same ter-rain, the canon of Christian Scripture, but by doing so from a different angle: the first chapter is narrative while the present chapter is systematic. Taken together, the narrative and systematic approaches provide the church with the solid theological framework necessary for fostering a healthy evangeli-cal missiology. Second, "A Theologically-Driven Missiology" draws upon both the narrative and systematic approaches in order to show how those two approaches help us to be biblically faithful as we craft a faithful twenty-first-century missiology which will in turn foster faithful methods and practices. The second concluding challenge, "A Challenge for our Churches," encour-ages our churches and mission agencies to continue their focus on mission and challenges them to work hard to forge missiological theory and practice that is driven by sound biblical theology, thereby based upon God's mission and centered on the gospel, and focused not only on this nation but also on all the *ethne* of the world.

We have carefully chosen authors who embrace and embody the neces-sary connection between orthodoxy and orthopraxy, between theology and mission, between theory and practice. Several of the contributors are profes-sors, several of them are pastors in the United States, but the majority of the chapters are written by international church planters. The chapters are penned by men and women whose ministry contexts vary geographically, including authors who serve or have served in the United States, South America, North Africa, the Middle East, Central Asia, South Asia, the Pacific Rim, and Sub-Saharan Africa. All of them, however, share the conviction that our mission must be driven by Christian Scripture and sound theology, and that theology disconnected from mission is not *Christian* theology at all.

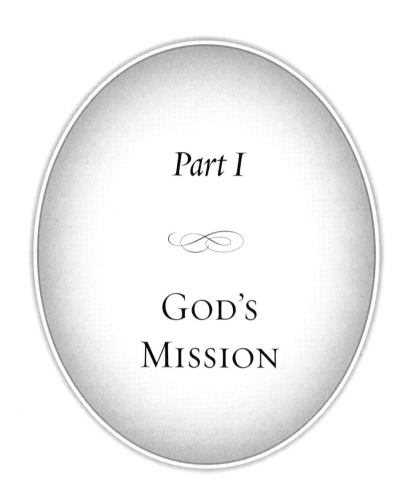

Part I

GOD'S
MISSION

Chapter One

THE STORY OF MISSION: THE GRAND BIBLICAL NARRATIVE

Bruce Riley Ashford

INTRODUCTION

In order to build a biblical-theological framework for understanding God's mission, the church's mission, and the church's mission to the nations, one must first understand the unified biblical narrative, including its four major plot movements—creation, fall, redemption, and restoration.[1] In creation, we learn that this world is a created world made by the uncreated triune God, a good world that God intends to fill with people made in his image whom he will make a kingdom of priests. God's world is a world that reflects his glory and points continually to the beauty and goodness of the Creator. In the fall, however, man and woman rebelled against God and in doing so alienated themselves from him, from each other, from themselves, and from the rest of the created order. As a result, God's good creation is marred by the ugliness of sin, and that sin has a far broader impact than we might typically imagine. In redemption, we see God's response to sin and

---

[1] Delineating Christian doctrine as narrative or drama is not unique and is evidenced in many recent proposals written by a diverse array of theologians such as N. T. Wright, Kevin Vanhoozer, and Michael Goheen, philosophers Albert Wolters and Craig Bartholomew, and biblical scholar Christopher Wright. See N. T. Wright, *The New Testament and the People of God* (London: SPCK, 1992), 139–43; Kevin Vanhoozer, *The Drama of Doctrine* (Louisville: Westminster John Knox, 2005); Craig G. Bartholomew and Michael W. Goheen, *The Drama of Scripture* (Grand Rapids: Baker, 2004); Albert M. Wolters, *Creation Regained* (Grand Rapids: Eerdmans, 2005); Christopher J. H. Wright, *The Mission of God* (Downers Grove: IVP, 2006).

rebellion. We learn that following man's rebellion, God promises to send One through whom he will redeem the nations and the world. The whole of Scripture speaks of this One, the Messiah, and the salvation he accomplished. The biblical narrative concludes with the restoration of the world God made, the establishment of the new heavens and new earth, foretold in the prophets, and inhabited by the redeemed of the nations who dwell eternally with their God.

This chapter expounds these four plot movements, focusing on the mission of God, and providing the starting point, trajectory, and parameters for this book's discussion of God's mission, the church's mission, and the church's mission to the nations.

CREATION

Creation and the God/world distinction. The biblical doctrine of creation is sometimes misunderstood because of a failure to appreciate the appropriate God/world distinction. The Scriptures teach that God is distinct from the created order, yet he is intimately involved with it. Not only has God created the world, but he sustains the world through his providential care. This distinction must be affirmed in order to maintain a truly Christian view of the world. But that is not all: A truly Christian view of the world recalls the goodness of the creation. While the cosmos has been genuinely affected by sin, the cosmos is not essentially evil; it is essentially good.[2] An appropriate view of the God/world distinction maintains both truths—God relates to the world, but the world is not God; God's world is good, but it is marred by the effects of human rebellion. Not only do we struggle with these truths about the God/world distinction, but we sometimes overlook or minimize the God/world distinction by erecting another distinction, one that is unbiblical, but unfortunately too common among believers. That distinction is what we call the soul/world distinction, in which Christians divide the creation into the "good" and the "bad" where the material is "bad" and the immaterial is "good." Our bodies are essentially "bad," according to this flawed view, while our souls are essentially "good."[3]

---

[2] For further reading on the inherent goodness of God's creation, see David P. Nelson, "The Work of God: Creation and Providence," in Daniel L. Akin, ed., *A Theology for the Church* (Nashville: B&H, 2007), 244–45, 262; Wayne Grudem, *Systematic Theology* (Grand Rapids: Zondervan, 1994), 272–73; Albert Wolters, *Creation Regained: Biblical Basics for a Reformational Worldview* (Grand Rapids: Eerdmans, 1985), 72–95; and Michael Wittmer, *Heaven Is a Place on Earth: Why Everything You Do Matters to God* (Grand Rapids: Zondervan, 2004), 37–49. Grudem's and Nelson's are brief treatments, valuable because they are standard evangelical systematic texts. Wolters' and Wittmer's texts are more comprehensive treatments of creation and culture, well-researched but accessible to interested lay people. Wolters speaks of creation being structurally good and directionally bad, while Wittmer speaks of it being ontologically good and morally corrupt.

[3] Trichotomists would paint a somewhat different picture, viewing body and soul as typically bad, while the spirit is basically good. We think this is precisely the same theological error, only accomplished with an unnecessary and unhelpful theological construct.

The goodness of creation. The goodness of creation is a fundamental
teaching of the Scriptures. Not only is this doctrine repeatedly affirmed in the
creation narrative in Genesis 1, but it is for the apostle Paul a teaching with
significant implications for the Christian life, as he affirms that "everything
created by God is good" (1 Tim. 4:4). This doctrine of the good is an important consideration in the doctrine of the incarnation. Athanasius made this
connection is his classic work *On the Incarnation*. In that work, he affirmed
that the goodness of God's creation is directly related to the incarnation and,
therefore, to Christian redemption.[4] That the Son would redeem by means
of assuming human flesh indicates that the material is not itself evil. That
the Son redeems by assuming human flesh indicates the value of the material—both human flesh (John 1:14) and the material cosmos (Rom. 8). To
argue otherwise is to undermine the gospel just as the Gnostics did with their
unbiblical dualism. Christians are not Gnostics, or at least they shouldn't be.
There are, to be sure, clear scriptural warnings about the "world" in the sense
of the evil powers of this age that set themselves up against the reign of God.
Thus we have instructions to "set your minds on things that are above, not on
things that are on earth" (Col. 3:2), and "Do not love the world or the things
in the world" (1 John 2:15). What does John mean, that we are to "not love
the world" that "God so loved" (John 3:16)? It is evident that John and other
biblical writers used the term *cosmos* in different ways,[5] and this helps us better understand the matter. We are also aided in our understanding by recalling
that John 3:16 does not stand in isolation. The truth that "God so loved the
world, that he gave his only begotten Son, that whosoever believeth in him
should not perish, but have everlasting life" (KJV) is followed by an explanation of God's incarnational mission: "For God did not send his Son into
the world to condemn the world, but in order that the world might be saved
through him" (John 3:17). We are to love God's world because it is his good
gift; we are not to love "the world" in the sense of loving the moral corruption
that pervades it since the fall.

Humanity and the created order: **anthropos** *and* **cosmos.** Human beings
are made in the image and likeness of God, and salvation includes being
remade into the image of our Creator (Col. 3:10), by being conformed to
the image of the Son (Rom. 8:29), who is himself the perfect image of God
(Col. 1:15). The doctrine of the *imago Dei* is central to biblical anthropology.
The first statement in Scripture about the creation of humanity indicates that
humans are made in the image and likeness of God, male and female alike.
The image of God is maintained, even after the fall, though the image is
surely marred. The writer of Genesis reminds us that Adam is made in God's
image (5:1), and Adam's sons are in Adam's image; that is, they too bear the
divine image though marred by Adam's fall. The existence of the image of

---

[4]   Athanasius, *On the Incarnation* (New York: St. Vladimir's, 1996), 4:2.

[5]   In John 3:16, for example, God loves the cosmos, while in 1 John 2:15, we are told to "love
not the cosmos." In the former case, cosmos refers to the world God created, while in the latter
reference, John apparently is referring to the spirit of the age that is opposed to God.

God in man is affirmed after the flood (Gen. 9:6), and the value of human life itself is tied to the reality that man bears the image of the Creator.

Indeed the first two chapters of Genesis reveal the significance that God gives to humanity. In the first chapter (which is devoted to showing the goodness of God's creation), the narrative centers on and pays the most attention to man and woman. Indeed, at each point along the way God calls his work "good," but when he creates man and woman he calls his work "very good." Man's unique nature and calling involve at least four relationships; he is made in the image of God as a relational being, and as such, it is *not good* for him to be alone. God is a God of love, and man created in his image is created to love. To these four relationships we now turn.

A love for God. If God created us, it makes sense that our purpose in life stands in direct relation to him. Not only does Scripture repeatedly inform us of this; God's creation also tells us. Many passages (Ps. 145:10,21; 148; 150:6) say that the creation already praises God. Romans 1:19–20, in particular, makes clear that since creation all men (even those without access to the Scriptures) know of God's existence and of his attributes, and they are held accountable to worship him. Indeed man's highest call is to love the Lord God (Deut. 6:5; Matt. 22:37; Mark 12:30; Luke 10:27).

A love for one another. Also in the opening narrative the Lord God says that it is "not good" for man to be alone and that he would make a helper for Adam, one who is "fit" for him, one who would "hold fast" to him, and him to her. Again, we see that God's handiwork is made to flourish in its divinely intended interdependence, which is a reflection of his own Trinitarian being; in this case, it is man and woman depending upon one another, as they both depend upon God. The movement from loving God to loving others is not uncommon in the Bible. When Jesus spoke of loving God, he spoke of the second command like it, to love neighbor (Matt. 22:39; Mark 12:31; Luke 10:27). When Paul gives his exhortation for Christians, in view of God's rich mercy, to love God by presenting themselves as living sacrifices in Romans 12, he then proceeds to instruct them to love others by using gifts to build up the church, to love even enemies, to submit to civil authorities, to avoid judgmentalism, and to avoid causing a brother to stumble, all of which is an expression of love owed to every man. Such love for others is definitive of what it means to be "Christian" (John 13:34–35; 15:12–17; 1 John 3–4).

A love for oneself. But not only is man to love God and others; he is also to love himself by seeing himself the way God sees him and by becoming who God wants him to become. The command to love neighbor as self (Matt. 22:39; Mark 12:31; Luke 10:27) calls for a proper response to all humanity, oneself included. Only Christian theism can properly explain humanity; other worldviews, philosophies, and religions tend either to denigrate man or to enthrone him, viewing him as nothing more than mere matter, on the one hand, or as the pinnacle of all that exists, on the other hand. But the Christian Scriptures make clear that man is neither mere matter nor a god. Man's great dignity is that he is created in the image of God, able to image forth the Creator himself, and his great humility is that he must submit to God and indeed owes his very existence to God.

A love for God's creation. In the creation narrative, the biblical writer notes that there was not yet a man to work the ground (Gen. 2:5), and then immediately tells us that God created such a man (Gen. 2:7–15). God thought it good to create a man who would work the very soil that God had made. The reader should note that God is asking man to change, and even enhance, the good creation that God has given! It is good for man to work; it is good for him to shape, form, and develop God's good creation. Moreover, the narrative tells us that God gives man stewardship over the whole of the created order (Gen. 1:26–30), so they may flourish in their mutual interdependence.

THE FALL

Everything God created was good; nothing he created was bad. In fact, all of man's relationships at this time were rightly ordered; they were good. Man was in right relationship with God, with the world, with others, and with himself. There existed a harmony and universal flourishing, as God intended. The narrative, however, takes a dramatic turn as Adam and Eve choose to rebel against their good Creator.

Out of all the trees in the garden, out of all God's good creation, there was only one tree whose fruit was forbidden—the tree of the knowledge of good and evil. God had given to Adam and Eve the tree of life, whose fruit was good for man, and the tree of the knowledge of good and evil, whose fruit would lead to death. Both trees were attractive, but one would lead to destruction. Nobody knows exactly why Adam and Eve chose to rebel on this particular occasion when they had not sinned before, but they did, choosing to partake of the tree of the knowledge of good and evil. Eve listened to the serpent, choosing the serpent's word over God's word. She offered the fruit to Adam, who also ate. In so doing, they rejected their dependence upon God and sought to make themselves autonomous, to elevate themselves to the position of "arbiter" of good and evil, and to seize for themselves power and happiness.

Adam and Eve's sin resulted not only in their fall from God's good will, but in the fall of the entire created order. The harmony and holistic flourishing of God's good creation was broken; man's relationships would from this point on be broken and distorted. He would suffer in his relationship to God, to the world, to others, and to himself.

A broken relationship with God. First, and most importantly, Adam and Eve's sin resulted in a broken relationship with God. Rather than being in loving fellowship with God, they became enemies of God, competing with him in an attempt to be Lord over his universe. Their sin was as much a "great folly" as it was a "great wickedness."[6] Because of it, they were separated from

---

[6]   John H. Sailhamer, *The Pentateuch as Narrative* (Grand Rapids: Zondervan, 1995), 103–4.

the God whose love and care for them extended to every aspect of life. Now things were not as they were created to be. Adam and Eve sought goodness and happiness on their own, apart from God, but when they ate of the fruit and their eyes were opened, they did not see goodness and happiness; rather, what they saw was their own nakedness. They were naked before him and unable to clothe themselves, not just physically but in every respect: physically, spiritually, morally, intellectually, and emotionally.

A broken relationship with others. The writer of Genesis further points out that man's relationship with others would be marked by strife. Adam and Eve could not limit the consequences of their sin to themselves alone. This is seen as Adam and Eve's own child Cain murdered his brother Abel, as Cain's descendent Lamech committed murder, and as man's wickedness on the earth became "great" (Gen. 6). The writer of Genesis prefaces the Noah narrative by saying of man that, "Every intention of the thoughts of his heart was only evil continually" (Gen. 6:5). This wickedness is seen not only in the pages of Scripture; it is manifest and evident across the landscape of human history and in every fiber of man's existence. Man must now deal with such interpersonal evil as murder, rape, divorce, and adultery, and such societal evil as ethnocide, child slavery, and terrorism.

A broken relationship with himself. Further, man's relationship with himself is broken. His love for himself is inordinate. He is in love with himself rather than with God, worshipping the creature rather than the Creator. Man is *incurvatus se* (as Luther put it) and, thus, is not "man fully alive" (Irenaeus).[7] Because of sin, man is less than fully human. The image of God was marred. This brokenness can be seen in every dimension of his humanness, as man becomes a slave to his own sin rather than to God. In his rational dimension, he has difficulty knowing the true, the good, and the beautiful. In his moral dimension, he has difficulty discerning good and evil. In his social dimension, he exploits others and loves himself inordinately. In his creative dimension, man's imagination leads to idolatry rather than the worship of the true God.

A broken relationship with the created order. The Genesis narrative tells us that because of Adam and Eve's sin, they would be removed from the land of blessing and sent into exile. Creation itself was affected by man's sin (Gen. 3:17–18), marring God's design that man and the rest of the created order flourish in their mutual interdependence. Man's work would now be marked by strife rather than by delight. Indeed, Adam and Eve's great folly resulted in a broken relationship with the rest of the created order, and the outworking of this brokenness can be seen throughout the pages of Scripture and the

---

[7] Luther argues that man is *incurvatus se*, "curved in on his own understanding." See Jaroslav Pelikan, ed. *Luther's Works* (St. Louis: Concordia, 1955–1986), 25:426. For Irenaeus, there is no "complete" or "perfect" man without the Spirit. Christ, through his incarnation, bestows the Spirit and enables man to be truly alive. See Dominic Unger, trans., *Against Heresies* (New York: Paulist Press, 1992), 5.6.1 and 5.9.2. Indeed there is only one man who is fully man. That is the Lord Jesus Christ, whose righteousness is not simply an expression of divinity, but also is an expression of his full humanity.

world. Man's interdependence with the rest of God's creation was marred; there would be floods, earthquakes, famines, and the like. Rather than unbroken harmony and delight, there would be fragmentation and pain.

God's common grace. Because of sin, the world is in a bad way. But it is not as bad as it could be. God, in his common grace toward man, has restrained the world from being an utter and complete horror.[8] Without those graces, the world would be intensively and extensively painful, ugly, unjust, and unhappy. In fact, unbelievers often don't believe they need the Savior, clinging instead to idols they have fashioned from the good things in God's creation.

REDEMPTION

The Genesis narrative plots the movement from creation to fall to redemption in three short chapters. Within the story of the fall in Genesis 3, God gave the promise of redemption amidst the very curse that he pronounced upon the serpent, the woman, and the man. That there is life yet to come in spite of Adam's sin is evident in the name Adam gave to the woman God made for him. He called her "Eve, because she was the mother of all living" (Gen. 3:20). This is a remarkable act on Adam's part. He was previously warned that the consequence for rebellion would be death (Gen. 2:17). After eating the forbidden fruit, God inquired of Adam and cursed him and the woman. Yet Adam named his wife in light of life to come and God provided for the continuance of human life in part by means of the death of other creatures (Gen. 3:20). What could possibly have given Adam such confidence in light of such inevitable consequences?

Adam had heard not only a promise of death (Gen. 2:17); he had also heard a promise of life (Gen. 3:15). The woman would bear children (her labor will be painful, but she will indeed bear children), and though the serpent would bruise the heel, the woman's "offspring" would crush the serpent's head. In this, Adam understood that life would be sustained by God's gracious provision. Life is here associated with the promise of an offspring. The apostle Paul understood these promises to point ultimately to Christ (Gal. 3:16), who is God's Son, "born of a woman" (Gal. 4:4). John's account of Jesus Christ similarly rehearses the association of sonship and salvation, stating that "For God so loved the world, that he gave his only Son, that whoever believes in him should not perish but have eternal life. For God did not send his Son into the world to condemn the world, but in order that the world might be saved through him" (John 3:16–17). The biblical story is a redemptive story, the story of God redeeming his image-bearers. Indeed all of creation awaits its freedom from bondage to corruption, which will be accomplished with the revealing of God's sons (Rom. 8:18–25).

Redemption of **anthropos** *and* **cosmos***.* At the center of God's redemptive purpose is the salvation of man, the creature made in the image and likeness of

---

[8]   For further reading on common grace, see Richard J. Mouw, *He Shines in All That's Fair: Culture and Common Grace* (Grand Rapids: Eerdmans, 2002).

God. God does not, however, simply save an individual; he redeems a people for himself, a people for his own possession (1 Pet. 2:9). This people of God is the body of Christ (Eph. 4:16) and the temple of the Holy Spirit (1 Cor. 6:19), whom God will make into a kingdom of priests (Exod. 19) to serve him and glorify him forever. Through this redeemed community and its proclamation (Matt. 28:18–20; Rom. 10:14–17) and spiritual ministries (Acts 2:42–47), God unleashes his gospel on the world. The Bible unfolds this grand redemptive narrative from Genesis to Revelation. Jesus Christ is the Redeemer, and the gospel is the good news that Jesus is the Savior of the world.

That Jesus is the Savior of the world does not mean that he redeems only humans. "In the beginning God created the heavens and the earth" (Gen. 1:1), and in the end God will redeem the world he made, forming what the Scriptures call "a new heaven and a new earth" (Isa. 65:17; Rev. 21:1). The redemptive work of Christ extends through God's people to God's *cosmos*, so that in the end "creation itself will be set free from its bondage to corruption and obtain the freedom of the glory of the children of God" (Rom. 8:21). The good end of God's redemptive purpose is a world in which the new heavens and new earth are formed, a world "in which righteousness dwells" (2 Pet. 3:13), thus restoring God's good order for his world.

Reversal of alienation (2 Cor. 5). Unredeemed man is under condemnation. As Paul puts it, man is "separated from Christ, alienated from the commonwealth of Israel and strangers to the covenants of promise, having no hope and without God in the world" (Eph. 2:12). This sense of separation and alienation is constitutive of condemnation. To be without God is to be without hope. To be alienated is to be cut off from relationship with God. To be saved is to have hope, to be restored to relationship with God.

Man's alienation from God is spoken of not only in terms of distance or separation, but also in terms of hostility and enmity. In Ephesians 2 Paul speaks of the gospel in terms of the reconciling work of God in Christ by which enmity between man and God, as well as enmity between Jews and Gentiles, is overcome. The apostle Paul tells us that God has "through Christ reconciled us to himself" and given us "the ministry of reconciliation" (2 Cor. 5:18). Man, by his sin and rebellion, became the enemy of God; Christ, by his death and resurrection, has brought peace between man and God. Those who have been reconciled to God in Christ are now ministers of reconciliation. Followers of Christ experience God's reconciliation both in this age and in the future (Heb. 11:16). We live between the times of the first coming of Christ (incarnation) and his second coming (the triumphant return). Our lives during this age, then, are lived with a certain purpose, one that aims to please the God of reconciliation (2 Cor. 5:8) and takes seriously Paul's instruction "that those who live might no longer live for themselves but for him who for their sake died and was raised" (2 Cor. 5:15). The effects of God's redemptive and reconciliatory ministry in Christ are immense, enabling the restoration of fractured relationships with God and others.

Redemption in man's relationship with God and others. That the atoning sacrifice of Jesus Christ restores a person's relationship with God is at
the heart of the gospel, but the effects of the cross go beyond the divine-
human relationship. The power of the reconciliatory ministry of the cross
heals relationships with oneself, with others, and with the cosmos itself. In
2 Corinthians 5:16 we learn that God's reconciling work in Christ redefines
one's relationships with others: "From now on, therefore, we regard no one
according to the flesh. Even though we once regarded Christ according to
the flesh, we regard him thus no longer." As Paul's relationship with God has
changed by Christ's ministry, so, by that same ministry, his relationship with
other people has changed. It is our natural course of action to treat others
"according to the flesh," that is in terms of fallen human nature. According to
my fallen nature, I may see those other than myself as competitors, as beneath
me, and even as my enemy. But the cross of Christ dispels such animus. In
fact, such hostility is destroyed by the blood of Christ (Eph. 2:16), redefining
the way I must look at others, to whom I now owe Christian love (Rom. 13:8)
and the gospel itself (Rom. 1:14).

Redemption in man's relationship with himself. Likewise, the reconciling ministry of the cross affects one's relationship with oneself. As the work
of Christ reconciles me to God, it brings healing effects in the soul, making
the corrupt sinner a "new creation" (2 Cor. 5:17). Just as in Christ I must look
at other people differently, now I must look at myself differently. What is old
(corrupt man) has become new (redeemed man). We sinful humans are being
transformed into the image of Christ (Rom. 8:29; 2 Cor. 3:18) as we undergo
the sanctifying work of Christ by the Spirit of God. Not only are we being
changed within; we also have new aims for life (2 Cor. 5:8). We live for something, for someone, beyond ourselves (2 Cor. 5:15), and we understand that
Christ's ministry of reconciliation to us has made us ministers of reconciliation to others; as ambassadors of Christ we plead for others to be reconciled
to God (2 Cor. 5:18–21).

Redemption in man's relationship to the created order. The reconciling
work of Christ also affects one's relationship to the world itself. The fall made
man's relationship with the earth one of struggle and turmoil (Gen. 3:17–19).
The cosmos has been distorted by the fall of Adam and the work of Satan and
his fallen angels. These organized powers and principalities (Eph. 6:12) are
committed to hostility with God. We ourselves walked in accord with these
(Eph. 2:1–3), but we are, as followers of Christ, no longer to do so. Instead,
we are to set our affections upon God and to align our allegiance with him and
to share in his reconciling ministry. This ministry is, first, the gospel ministry
of reconciling others to Christ, but it also includes the good work of performing our God-given ministry within whatever cultural context God places us as
his image-bearers (Gen. 1:26–31). If our goal for our work in God's world is
aligned with God's mission, we will see that his good end is to make anew the
heavens and earth and to see it populated with adoring angels and the saints
who are a kingdom and priests to our God (Rev. 5:8–10; 21–22).

RESTORATION

God's work of redemption will reach its goal in the end, as God saves for himself a people and restores his good creation. The entire biblical narrative moves toward this end. "All of Christian theology," writes Russ Moore, "points toward an end—an end where Jesus overcomes the satanic reign of death and restores God's original creation order. . . . In Scripture the *eschaton* is not simply tacked on to the gospel at the end. It is instead the vision toward which all of Scripture is pointing—and the vision that grounds the hope of the gathered church and the individual believer."[9] Scripture's final plot movement provides a broad and comprehensive vision of divine redemption and restoration, including three significant themes: the great divide, the redemption of the nations, and the new creation.

The great divide. The Scriptures teach that, in the end, man's relationship with God will be finalized. Those who die apart from Christ will receive eternal torment (Matt. 5:22; 8:12), while those who die in Christ will receive eternal life (Rev. 21:2–4). This is a difficult doctrine, but a necessary one as it is taught clearly in the Scriptures. Furthermore, it is a great motivator for Christians, as we hold three truths in tension: that there is no name other than Christ by which men are saved, and all men who die apart from Christ abide in eternal torment; that there are approximately two billion people who have practically no access to the gospel, and another two billion who have very little access; and that we, as believers, have a calling and responsibility to proclaim to them the good news.

The redemption of the nations. The Scriptures also teach that God will win worshippers unto himself from all tribes, tongues, peoples, and nations. Perhaps the most explicit teaching of our Lord, to this effect, is Matthew 24:14: "And this gospel of the kingdom will be proclaimed throughout the whole world as a testimony to all nations, and then the end will come." A striking picture of this is found in Revelation 5, where John was given a vision in which there were worshippers from all nations gathered around the throne, singing to our Lord: "You are worthy . . . for You were slain, and have redeemed us to God by Your blood out of every tribe and tongue and people and nation" (NKJV).

The ingathering of the nations is a deep and pervasive theme in Christian Scripture. The central promise in the Scriptures is that God would send a Redeemer, and tightly riveted to it is an additional promise that the Redeemer would win the nations unto himself. This promise is at the heart of God's covenant with Abraham that through his seed the nations would be blessed. God offered his Son as a sacrifice to purchase the nations (Rev. 5, 7).[10] Further, the ingathering of the nations is not something to be whispered about in

---

[9] Russell D. Moore, "Personal and Cosmic Eschatology," in Akin, *A Theology for the Church*, 858.

[10] Sinful humans killed the Son of God, but it is also true that God the Father's plan was to put his Son on the cross.

a corner. It is something to be proclaimed: Our God is not a tribal deity; he is the Creator of the nations and we will not know him in his full splendor until we know him as the King of the Nations.[11]

The new heavens and earth. The Scriptures, in both Old and New Testaments, contain God's promise of a new heavens and earth. In Isaiah, we read, "For behold, I create new heavens and a new earth, and the former things shall not be remembered or come into mind" (Isa. 65:17). In 2 Peter, we are told to "look for new heavens and a new earth in which righteousness dwells" (2 Pet. 3:13, NKJV).[12] In Revelation 21, John received a vision in which there was a new heaven and a new earth, where there remained no pain or tears. This is the doctrine of creation come full circle. The God who gave us the good creation recorded in the Genesis narrative is the God who will give us a new heavens and a new earth.

In this new universe, God's image-bearers will experience neither sin nor its consequences. No longer will we use our rational capacities to speak falsehoods or our creative capacities to construct idols. Never again will we use our relational capacities to suppress others and promote ourselves, our moral capacities to slander, rape, or murder. No longer will we live in an environment where tsunamis and floods destroy or where pollution poisons the ground and air. Never again will there be war or rumors of war. Instead, we will live in unbroken relation with God, with others, with the new universe, and with ourselves. We will be "man fully alive," man worshipping God in spirit and truth.

CONCLUSION

The Messiah who was promised in Genesis 3 has come, and he will return to win the nations unto himself and to reconcile all things unto himself. He will do this because he loves the world (John 3:16–17). In his first coming, he provided the firstfruits of that redemption, and in the second coming he will provide the consummation of it. We find ourselves living between those two comings, called to be ambassadors for the God who created us and purchased us with the blood of his Son.

---

[11]   A classic contemporary treatment of this theme is John Piper, *Let the Nations Be Glad: The Supremacy of God in Missions*, 3rd ed. (Grand Rapids: Baker, 2010). Also helpful is Wright, *The Mission of God*, 454–530.

[12]   The 1 Peter passage also speaks of the present heavens and earth being reserved for a fire on the day of judgment. Although some commentators take Peter to mean that the present universe will be consumed by fire, we believe that the fire referred to is a "purifying fire." Richard Bauckham's interpretation is compelling, in which he argues that the purpose of the fire in these verses is not the obliteration, but the purging of the cosmos. The cosmos will be purged of sin and its consequences, including its ecological consequences. Richard J. Bauckham, *2 Peter and Jude*, Word Biblical Commentary 50 (Waco, TX: Word, 1983), 316–22.

Chapter Two

THE TRIUNE GOD:
THE GOD OF MISSION

Keith Whitfield

INTRODUCTION

John Piper begins his book, *Let the Nations Be Glad*, with what has become a well-known statement. He says, "Missions exists because worship doesn't."[1] We argue in this chapter, "Mission exists because God exists." This twist on Piper's axiom is not an attempt to improve it. Actually, the concern of this chapter is consistent with the point that Piper seeks to make; namely, that "God is ultimate, not man." When the church understands that its mission is rooted in God's mission and is captured by the incredible privilege of participating in God's work for his name's sake, we believe the church will be energized and empowered to pursue its spiritual calling and purpose, namely, to make God's name known through making disciples to the ends of the earth (Matt. 28:18–20). If the church shapes and orients its mission around God's mission, it will not fail. We can be confident that God's mission can and will sustain the mission of the church, for it is God himself who empowers the church through his Spirit (Acts 1:8). And, God promised that "the forces of Hades will not overpower" his church and its mission (Matt. 16:18, HCSB). Thus, one of the goals for this chapter is, as David Wells put it, to "un-cage God" for the sake of God's mission and the church's role in that mission by describing his character and acts through the notion of the *missio Dei* (mission of God) and to orient the church to see its calling in light

---

[1] John Piper, *Let the Nations Be Glad! The Supremacy of God in Mission* (Grand Rapids: Baker, 1993), 11.

of God's mission. We will not be able to recover a vision and passion for missions until we recover the grandeur that God made us to know and worship him and to make him known throughout the whole earth.

The point of this chapter is to explore the contours of what it means to say that God is the agent of missions. To do this, we first define what we mean by *missio Dei*. In the second segment, we discuss the missional character of God by arguing that the nature of God is the *foundation* of the mission and that the life of God as triune is the *pattern* of the mission. The final section of this chapter deals with the missional acts of God in creation and redemption.

MISSIO DEI

Until the sixteenth century, the phrase *missio Dei* was used exclusively to refer to the doctrine of the Trinity, namely, the sending of the Son by the Father and the sending of the Holy Spirit by the Father and the Son.[2] Although it was used by some prior to the twentieth century to speak of spreading Christianity among non-Christians, it was not widely used to speak of the missionary enterprise until the twentieth century. Then it became widely acknowledged that biblically speaking the mission belongs to God, and as a corollary to this point, God's mission is bigger than the missionary activities of the church. The phrase *missio Dei* was used to capture this new perspective.[3]

Seeing missions as belonging to God rather than to the church came from two shifts that occurred in missions. First, it became clear that over-optimism in the capacity of humanity to change the world that characterized much of the Enlightenment and that shaped much of the missionary endeavors through the early part of the nineteenth century was ill founded. This recognition helped to develop the idea that missions belongs to God and is directed by his purposes.[4] The other impetus for understanding missions in this way was an uneasy posture toward missions in the church that came as a result of

---

[2]   David J. Bosch, *Transforming Mission: Paradigm Shifts in Theology of Mission* (Maryknoll, NY: Orbis Books, 2005), 1.

[3]   Previously, mission was understood in a variety of ways. Bosch says, "Sometimes it was interpreted primarily in soteriological terms: as saving individuals from eternal damnation. Or it was understood in cultural terms: as introducing people from the East and the South to the blessings and privileges of the Christian West. Often it was perceived in ecclesiastical categories: as the expansion of the church (or of a specific denomination). Sometimes it was defined salvation-historically: as the process by which the world—evolutionary or by means of a cataclysmic event—would be transformed into the kingdom of God" (*Transforming Mission*, 389). Darrell Guder observes, "Certainly the reduction of mission in Western theology has to do with the so-called Christianization of Western culture." See Guder, "The Church as Missional Community," in *The Community of the Word: Toward an Evangelical Ecclesiology,* eds. Mark Husbands and Daniel J. Treier (Downers Grove: IVP, 2005), 118.

[4]   See Jan A. B. Jongeneel, *Philosophy, Science, and Theology of Mission in 19th and 20th Centuries: Part 1* (Frankfurt am Main: Peter Lang Press, 1997), 60.

colonialism. Coinciding with this unease were significant developments in Trinitarian studies connecting missiology with ecclesiology.[5]

German missiologist Karl Hartenstein coined the phrase *missio Dei* for its contemporary usage in 1934 as he responded to the work of Karl Barth and his emphasis on the "actions of God." The ideas behind this phrase gained traction at the 1952 Willingen Conference, which started a decisive shift in mission theology in the ecumenical movement. Then, in 1958, Georg Vicedom published a book entitled *The Mission of God*, which ignited the popularity of this term.[6] Since this time, *missio Dei* has been used widely by ecumenicals and evangelicals, but not with consensus on what it means and how to use it. This confusion and some sub-biblical applications of it have led many people to suggest that it is largely an unhelpful concept. With the diverse usages of this concept, even among evangelicals, this conclusion is understandable.

We, however, are not ready to surrender the concept. It seems reasonable that this concept remains useful because a biblically constructed theology of mission must be based upon the nature and the life of the triune God. God is the basis of everything. The theology of mission must be shaped by all of God's actions in history: creation and redemption. The divine design and purpose for God's acts of creation and redemption are revealed in the narrative of Scripture. The Bible is a book about a mission, and that mission is the mission of the triune God. As Charles Taber helpfully captured,

> The very existence of the Bible is incontrovertible evidence of the God who refused to forsake his rebellious creation, who refused to give up, who was and is determined to redeem and restore fallen creation to his original design for it . . . . The very existence of such a collection of writings testifies to a God who breaks through to human beings, who disclosed himself to them, who will not leave them unilluminated in their darkness, . . . who takes the initiative in re-establishing broken relationships with us.[7]

If the mission of the church is to be rooted in and directed by God's mission, then we need to understand what God's mission is. There have been a number of ways that the *missio Dei* has been conceived. Below, we summarize these views in four broad and descriptive categories.[8] Also, we will list some proponents for each of the frameworks. We are not suggesting that the proponents agree on every point of mission theology. In fact, the very

---

[5]   Craig Van Gelder, "From Corporate Church To Missional Church: The Challenge Facing Congregations Today," *Review and Expositor* 101 (2004): 438.

[6]   This was the German edition. Later in 1965, it was translated into English.

[7]   Charles R. Taber, "Missiology and the Bible," *Missiology* 11 (1983): 232.

[8]   These categories are built off of an observation made by Michael Goheen. He characterized the shift in mission theology that took place in 1961 when the WCC adopted the paper entitled "The Missionary Structure of the Congregation" as a shift from "Christocentric-Trinitarian" to "Cosmocentric-Trinitarian." See Michael W. Goheen, "As the Father has sent me, I am sending you:" J. E. Lesslie Newbigin's missionary ecclesiology, http://igitur-archive.library. uu.nl/dissertations/1947080/inhoud.htm, accessed 16 June 2010, 117.

details of the frameworks vary from one proponent to the next. The point of these categories is to demonstrate that there are a number of different conceptual models by which to conceive of the *missio Dei*. The fourth model is the one adopted in this chapter. Though we are appreciative of the respective advocates listed under the fourth model, we differ at various points with their biblical and theological presuppositions and conclusions.[9] The remaining sections of the chapter are an attempt to unpack that framework from *our* biblical and theological perspective.

God who restores the world for the world's sake. This approach is eschatological in that it articulates that God's mission aims to affect the outcome of all of history. However, this eschatological vision is cosmocentric. By this, we are referring to a view of God's purpose for the world that focuses upon redeeming and reconstructing the world itself within its social, political, and economic dimensions, and God uses secular history to accomplish this mission. Redemption is defined by a return to *shalom* in the world. The work of mission, therefore, is the development of society. This approach is Trinitarian because each person of the Trinity is involved in God's mission. The mission is designed and initiated by God the Father. The Son offers the model of kingdom living through his messianic life and reign that should be followed by all mankind, and the ongoing establishment of the kingdom *shalom* is aided by the Spirit. This position follows the aspiration of the social gospel,[10] but is now set within a new missiological framework, the *missio Dei*. J. C. Hoekendijk was the first to set forth this vision for the mission of God. His views were evident at the 1952 Willigen Conference. However, his model received more serious attention in 1961, when it was adopted and was used to shape "The Missionary Structure of the Congregation."[11] More recently, Brian McLaren has articulated a similar vision.[12]

God who sends. What some people are describing with *missio Dei* are the redemptive activities of God, using this phrase to refer to the "sending of God." They do not deny that God sends with a purpose, but they emphasize the sending aspect of mission, for it reflects the definition of the Latin root *mitto*, which means "to send." What is often being considered when the phrase is taken this way is that God the Father sends the Son into the world; the Father and Son send the Spirit into the world; and the Father, Son, and the Spirit send the church into the world. With this understanding, the design

---

[9] For example, we differ with Lesslie Newbigin on at least three important points: his view on the nature of Scripture, his modified inclusiveness, and his incomplete understanding of the atonement.

[10] See Walter Rauschenbusch, *A Theology for the Social Gospel* (New York: Macmillan Co., 1917). See also, Bosch, *Transforming Mission*, 320–25, 382–84.

[11] J. C. Hoekendijk, "The Church in Missionary Thinking," *International Review of Mission* 39 (1952): 332, and J. C. Hoekendijk, "Notes on the Meaning of Mission (-ary)," in *Planning for Mission*, ed. Thomas Wieser (New York: U. S. Conference for World Council of Churches, 1966), 42, 44.

[12] Brian McLaren, *Everything Must Change: Jesus, Global Crises, and Revolution of Hope* (Nashville: Thomas Nelson, 2007).

and operation of the *missio Dei* is located after the fall of man. Those who advocate this approach tend to define mission by the act of sending. This model is Christocentric because the person and work of Jesus Christ are at the center of God's sending activities, vis-à-vis, the Son, the Holy Spirit, and the church. Karl Barth, John Stott, Francis Dubose, and Ed Stetzer view the mission of God according to this framework.[13]

God who saves from sins. Rather than the aim of God's mission encompassing all of history, this vision of God's mission sees the aim as the salvation of individual souls. Thus, we characterize it as soteriological rather than eschatological. The mission of the Son of God, his life and death, are at the center of God's fulfilling his soteriological mission. It is Trinitiarian, for it was God the Father's plan to send the Son, and the Holy Spirit was sent to apply the salvation accomplished by the Son. This approach has been articulated by St. Augustine, Georg Vicedom, and Stephen Holmes.[14]

God who redeems and restores for his sake. This model is eschatological, because God's mission is conceived as encompassing all of history. Some proponents of this view are Lesslie Newbigin, Christopher Wright, and Timothy Tennent.[15] Unlike the first model above, at the center of it is the person and work of Jesus Christ. The point here is that Jesus Christ in his coming, in his death, and in his resurrection changed something about the world. He defeated sin and death, both its power in the world and its effects upon people. It is the case that not everyone who articulates this framework has the same view on exactly what Jesus Christ accomplished on the cross. The fact that some do not ascribe to penal substitution does not invalidate this model. However, it seems to us that a very lively debate could be had on whether the model even works without ascribing to penal substitutionary atonement, though some have tried.

We would describe this forth model as *eschatological-Christocentric-Trinitarianism.* This model is the view of the *missio Dei* proposed in this chapter, for we affirm, "Meaningful action in history is possible only when there is some vision of a future goal."[16] We follow Christopher Wright's

---

[13] See Karl Barth, *Church Dogmatics* I/2, *The Doctrine of the Word of God*, 2nd ed., trans. G. W. Bromiley, ed. G. W. Bromiley and T. F. Torrence (Edinburgh: T&T Clark, 1975); John Stott, *Christian Mission in the Modern World* (Downers Grove: IVP, 1974); Francis Dubose, *God Who Sends: A Fresh Quest for Biblical Mission* (Nashville: Broadman & Holman, 1983); and Ed Stetzer, *Planting Missional Churches* (Nashville: B&H, 2006), 28.

[14] St. Augustine, *The Trinity* (Washington, DC: Catholic University of America Press, 1963); Georg Vicedom, *The Mission of God: An Introduction to Theology of Mission*, trans. Gilbert A. Thiele and Dennis Hilgendorf (St. Louis, MO: Concordia Publishing House, 1965); and Stephen Holmes, "Trinitarian Missiology: Towards a Theology of God as Missionary," *International Journal of Systematic Theology* 8 (2006): 72–90.

[15] Lesslie Newbigin, *The Gospel in a Pluralistic Society* (Grand Rapids: Eerdmans, 1989); Lesslie Newbigin, *The Open Secret: Sketches for a Missionary Theology* (Grand Rapids: Eerdmans, 1978); Christopher J. H. Wright, *The Mission of God: Unlocking the Bible's Grand Narrative* (Downers Grove: IVP Academic, 2006); and Timothy Tennent, *Invitation to World Missions: A Trinitarian Missiology for the Twenty-First Century* (Grand Rapids: Kregel, 2010).

[16] Newbigin, *The Gospel in a Pluralistic Society*, 114.

helpful refinement to viewing the mission of God as primarily God's sending activities. He says the mission of God is the commitment of God to make himself known to his creation.[17] This view of God's mission is consistent with the biblical witness, for what we find when we read the Scriptures is that God's ultimate purpose is for his creation to know him as the Lord. We find this in demonstrative statements such as "I am the LORD" (cf. Gen. 15:7; Exod. 6:2,6; 12:12). We also discern this in the indicative statements that no one compares to him (cf. 2 Sam. 7:22; Ps. 89:6–8; Jer. 10:6–7). Finally, this is made clearest when God in fact tells us that he is doing something to be known (cf. Exod. 5:22–6:8). Being known and worshipped is God's purpose in creation and is his purpose in redemption. God accomplishes his mission to be known through making a covenant with his people, and ultimately, in the life, death, and resurrection of Jesus Christ (John 8:19; 14:6–7). "For God . . . has shone in our hearts to give us the light of the knowledge of God's glory in the face of Jesus Christ" (2 Cor. 4:6).

This perspective offers a slight refocusing on what mission is, from activity to purpose.[18] It is also a shift from the mission being *primarily* the salvation of souls to the worship of God. We agree with this shift, not to distract us from evangelizing the lost, but to remind us that in our evangelistic tasks and in offering salvation, we are seeking to see people reconciled to God that they may know him, worship him, and enjoy him.

We argue that God's mission is to make himself known to his creation and that this is the driving plan for God's purpose for all of history. We intend to show that the sending activities are shaped by the nature, life, and purpose of the triune God.

There are two benefits in understanding the mission of God in these terms. First, it involves seeing God's purpose in redemption as concordant with God's purpose in creation. God, in both of these acts, is making his name known to his creation. Second, this approach offers a more thorough understanding of the relationship between the mission of God and the mission of the church. Missions includes our efforts to plan and go, but it does not primarily depend on our activity and initiation. Missions is from our point of view the privileged participation in God's mission to make himself known. Christopher Wright says,

> So all our missional efforts to make God known must be set within the prior framework of God's own will to be known. We are seeking to accomplish what God himself wills to happen. This is both humbling and reassuring. It is humbling inasmuch as it reminds us that all our efforts would be in vain but for God's determination to be known. We are neither the initiators of the mission of making God known to the nations nor does it lie in our power to

---

[17] Wright, *The Mission of God*, 62–64, 75–135.
[18] The use of "mission" over "missions" is one way to demonstrate this refocusing. Mission refers to the purpose and goal of the activity, whereas missions refers to the activities. Both of these terms are appropriate to use in reference to missiology and in reference to God. This chapter focuses more attention on the "mission" rather than "missions."

decide how the task will be fully accomplished or when it may be deemed to be complete. But it is reassuring. For we know that behind all our fumbling efforts and inadequate communication stands the supreme will of the living God, reaching out in loving self-revelation, incredibly willing to open blind eyes and reveal his glory through the treasures of the gospel delivered in the clay pots of his witnesses. (2 Cor. 4:1–7)[19]

THE MISSIONAL CHARACTER OF THE TRIUNE GOD

This section begins our exploration of the missionary character of God. We do this because the *foundation* and *pattern* for the mission is God himself.[20] In this section, we survey briefly the nature and the life of the triune God that reflect God's missional character. God's mission is directed by his nature and character. The dynamic life within the triune God is a model for the mission of God. Thus, we come to our discussion of God as the agent of mission from a Trinitarian point of view. Timothy Tennent perceptually observes, "the Trinity enlivens all theological discussions, demanding that they be seen from a missional perspective."[21]

The doctrine of the Trinity teaches that "[t]he eternal triune God reveals Himself to us as Father, Son, and Holy Spirit, with distinct personal attributes, but without division of nature, essence, or being."[22] When the Trinity is discussed along with missions, it is common for people to give priority to either the immanent Trinity, which refers to the life of God within the triune God, or economic Trinity, which refers to the acts of God outside the triune God. We are unconvinced that giving priority is necessary. We follow the rule that who God is in his action is the same as who God is in eternity.[23] That is not to suggest that his actions are definitive of him, but it is to argue that we cannot distinguish between who God is and what God does, because God is known by his Word and by his acts. It seems appropriate that the immanent Trinity and economic Trinity both may be used to construct a robust view of the missionary character of God. The immanent Trinity offers the *foundation* and *pattern* for the mission of God. Economic Trinity, the acts of God in history, is the story of God's mission.

The Trinity and the foundation of the mission. The *foundation* of God's mission is built on the attributes of God. These attributes establish that God

---

[19]　Wright, *The Mission of God,* 129–30.

[20]　Cf. "The point here is simply this: if the God YHWH, who is rendered to us in these texts, is really God, then that reality (or rather *his reality*) authorizes a range of responses as appropriate, legitimate and indeed imperative. These include not only the response of worship but also of ethical living in accordance with this God's own character and will, and a missional orientation that commits my own life story into the grand story of God's purpose for the nations and for creation. Mission flows from the reality of this God—the biblical God. Or to put it another way: mission is authorized by the reality of this God." Wright, *The Mission of God,* 54.

[21]　Tennent, *Invitation to World Missions,* 74.

[22]　"Article Three: God," *The Baptist Faith and Message,* 2000.

[23]　Karl Barth, *Church Dogmatics* I/1, *The Doctrine of the Word of God,* 299.

is able to exercise a free and sovereign mission, and shape the very nature of the mission itself. Many attributes of God have missional implications, but in this section, we will limit ourselves to three aspects of God's nature as foundations for God's mission.

God has life in himself. This is an attribute that pertains to the nature of God's being. God is life itself. To speak of God as the "I am" is not just to say that God is eternal. It is to say that "God necessarily exists in an infinitely better, stronger, more excellent way."[24] God created humanity, and we exist in his image. God exists as God. He alone is the source of life. Because God is life, he has the freedom to accomplish his will in creation and in redemption. This attribute is a foundation of God's mission because if God was not self-sufficient, his mission would not ultimately be his. Further, because he is life, he cannot be stopped from accomplishing his will. John writes about the second person of the Trinity, the Son, "In him was life, and the life was the light of men" and the "darkness [did not] overcome it" (John 1:4–5).

God is good. The goodness of God speaks to more than God's good actions. To speak of God as good means that he is good in his character, in his purposes, and in his actions. God's goodness characterizes his benevolent role in all of his relationships. Since he is the good source of all things, he is characterized as being good for others. Herman Bavinck says, "God, as the perfect and blessed One, is the supreme good for his creatures. . . . No good exists in any creature except that which comes from and through him."[25] The goodness of God is expanded over all of creation (Ps. 36:6; 104:21; Matt. 6:26). Although only his people recognize that all good things come from God, he still sends his providential care to the ungodly and godly (Matt. 5:45; Luke 6:35). He does this as a witness to himself (Acts 14:15–17).

However, God's goodness is most supremely demonstrated in his redemptive love, because the redemptive goodness of God is experienced only through the knowledge of God's grace. Athanasius connects God's goodness and salvation in his book, *On the Incarnation.* He writes,

> It was unworthy of the goodness of God that creatures made by Him should be brought to nothing through the deceit wrought upon man by the devil; and it was supremely unfitting that the work of God in mankind should disappear, either through their own negligence or through the deceit of evil spirits. As, then, the creatures who He had created reasonable, like the Word, were in fact perishing, and such noble works were on the road to ruin, what then was God, being Good, to do?[26]

Athanasius' observation is right. God loves us because we derive our value from him and from his purpose for us. He demonstrates his goodness

---

[24] Wayne Grudem, *Systematic Theology: An Introduction to Biblical Doctrine* (Grand Rapids: Zondervan, 1994), 162.

[25] Herman Bavinck, *God and Creation*, vol. 2 of *Reformed Dogmatics* (Grand Rapids: Baker, 2004), 212.

[26] St. Athanasius, *On the Incarnation,* rev. (Crestwood, NY: St. Vladimir's Seminary Press, 1996), 32.

in love and mercy for sinners, so that we might know him and give praise to his "glorious grace" (Eph. 1:3–6; 2:4–8). The redemptive goodness of God is experienced and enjoyed only through the knowledge and praise of God's grace. In knowing God and praising him, we know our great good, God himself. Richard Bauckham echoes this point when he writes, "The good of God's human creatures requires that he be known to them as God."[27]

God is one. The oneness of God is a key attribute of the triune nature of God, and the foremost challenge to the doctrine of the Trinity is how to articulate that God is both one and yet three persons. The oneness of three persons is not the only significant point for Christian theology when we speak of God as one. This doctrine relates also to the fact that God is the one true living God. He is uniquely God. There is no other God.

In Deuteronomy 6:4, Moses said, "Hear, O Israel: The LORD our God, the LORD is one." This statement is the classic text for monotheism. An examination of the larger context of this text reveals that Moses was preparing the Israelites to obey and to be solely committed to the Lord their God. He did this by making the case that the God of Israel is the only true God (see Deut. 4:33–35). Finally, Moses instructed the Israelites that the proper response to the oneness of God is, "You shall love the LORD your God with all your heart and with all your soul and with all your might" (Deut. 6:5). The call for the Israelites to love and obey their God comes from the reasoned conclusion that there is no other God besides their God. He is one, and he alone is God. The intent of Israel's confession and their devotion to God was that they would make their God's name known among the nations.

Monotheism is a part of the foundation of mission because this truth claims that there is something particular about all of reality. Monotheism asserts that there is a God from whom all things come and for whom all things exists. Because of this, it is right for all of creation to acknowledge God's glory and honor him (Rom. 1:19–23; Rev. 4:11). Thus, Wright says, "Monotheism is missional because it generates praise and also because it globalizes praise—the praise of the one true living God, known through his grace, his judgment, and above all his Messiah."[28] The one, true, living God does not share his glory with another (cf. Isa. 48:11). His uniqueness as God establishes him as the rightful authority and ruler of the universe (Ps. 47:7–8).

The Trinity and the pattern of God's mission. In this section, we focus on the relational nature of the triune God as the *pattern* of God's mission. By pattern, we are suggesting that what occurs within the life of the triune God is the model for what takes place outside the triune life. In the triune relationship, each of the persons of the Godhead is committed to the same purpose, and this is demonstrated in their *perfect knowledge of one another, unity of will*, and *expression of love*.

---

[27] Richard Bauckham, *Bible and Mission: Christian Witness in a Postmodern World* (Grand Rapids: Baker, 2004), 37, emphasis added.
[28] Wright, *The Mission of God*, 134.

The persons of the triune God are known by one another. What we seek to emphasize here is that within the triune relationship, there is full and complete knowledge of one another. It is a divine mystery as to how the triune persons know each other. Jesus declares that he has come to make known the Father (John 1:18). He is only able to do this because he knows the Father himself. Jesus says that he speaks only what he has seen while with the Father (John 8:38), and he "learned from my Father" what he makes known on the earth (John 15:15, NIV). Jesus as the Word of God also suggests that there is communication between the Father and the Son.[29] Timothy George echoes this point, saying, "Self-expression is constitutive of God's very being, as we can see from the name the Bible gives to the eternal Son: Logos."[30] The Spirit also knows the Father and the Son. Paul says the "Spirit searches everything, even the depths of God . . . no one comprehends the thoughts of God except the Spirit of God" (1 Cor. 2:10–11).

The missional significance of this point is profound. Because God knows himself, he possesses the means to make himself known. God communicates perfectly his glory to himself within the divine life, prior even to creating. Without such ability to communicate *within* the triune God, there would not be a way for God to make himself known *outside* the triune life. John Frame helps us to communicate the importance of this point for God's mission. He says,

> God knows himself exhaustively. We creatures do not have perfect knowledge. In our hearts, souls, and bodies there are hidden depths that we do not understand. Often our thoughts and actions . . . surprise us; often they reveal things about ourselves that we have not known and would perhaps just as soon not have known. But there are no unexplored depths in God's nature. He does not surprise himself. He is word. His word exhaustively expresses his being to himself, among the persons of the Trinity. Our God has perfect knowledge of who he is and of what he does.[31]

Herman Bavinck also makes the missional connection in his book *In the Beginning*. There, he argues, "If in an absolute sense God could not communicate himself to the Son, he would be even less able, in a relative sense, to communicate himself to his creatures. If God were not triune, creation would not be possible."[32] So, because each of the persons of the triune God knows each other comprehensively, God is able to communicate to his creation perfect knowledge of himself. We might not comprehensively know God, but that is a deficiency in the reception of the message on our part and not the messenger's ability to communicate.

---

[29] John Frame, *The Doctrine of God*, vol. 2 of *A Lordship Theology* (Phillipsburg, NJ: P&R Publishing, 2002), 473–75.

[30] Timothy George, "The Nature of God: Being, Attributes, and Acts," in *A Theology for the Church*, ed. Daniel Akin, 176–241 (Nashville: B&H, 2007), 199.

[31] Frame, *The Doctrine of God*, 475.

[32] Herman Bavinck, *In the Beginning: Foundations of Creation Theology*, ed. J. Vriend and J. Bolt (Grand Rapids: Baker, 1999), 39.

The persons of the triune God are committed to a unity of purpose. Though distinct in person, the orthodox teaching on the Trinity affirms that there is a harmony among the three persons in all that they do. The persons of the triune God are in agreement as to what their purpose is and how this purpose is accomplished. This is demonstrated biblically by observing that each person of the Trinity seeks to glorify the other persons of the Trinity. This is called "mutual glorification," which Gregory of Nyssa describes poetically,

> You see the revolving circle of the glory moving from Like to Like. The Son is glorified by the Spirit; the Father is glorified by the Son; again the Son has His glory from the Father; and the Only-begotten thus becomes the glory of the Spirit. For with what shall the Father be glorified, but with the true glory of the Son: and with what again shall the Son be glorified, but with the majesty of the Spirit? In like manner, again, Faith completes the circle, and glorifies the Son by means of the Spirit, and the Father by means of the Son.[33]

Mutual deference to one another in the Trinity expresses unity of purpose. Jesus came from heaven to do the will of his Father (John 6:38). What he taught to his disciples was not his own message, but it came from the Father who sent him (John 7:16). Jesus even said it stronger at one point. He said that the Father "commanded him what to say" (see John 12:49). Jesus was on a mission that the Father sent him on, and his mission was to execute all that the Father sent him to do. This is true also of the Spirit. Jesus said the Spirit will come not on his own authority or to teach his own message, but he will teach what he hears. What the Spirit teaches comes from the Father and the Son (John 16:12–15). Therefore, there is one mission shared by each person of the Trinity to glorify the triune God. Because the Trinity is the ground of all reality, the mission of the triune God is the mission for everything. The church is redeemed for this purpose, and the church's mission is to participate in this God-glorifying mission.

Mutual glorification also displays a divine order for the fulfillment of the divine mission. The Son is sent to make the Father known. The Spirit is sent to make the Son known, and by making the Son known, the Spirit makes the Father known. This order rules out any view of salvation that excludes personal and conscious knowledge of the Son. Some have tried to argue that the Spirit can work in areas where the gospel of Jesus Christ has not been proclaimed. In this view, the Spirit guides people to live for God in their culture. This view goes against what the Bible teaches regarding the unity of purpose within the Trinity. The Spirit comes to glorify God by making the Son known.

God is defined by love. When we speak of God being defined by love, it highlights the fact that there is love within the triune God. Love assumes that there are at least two persons in relationship. Love is a self-giving action toward another person. The Father loves the Son. The Son loves the Father.

---

[33] Gregory of Nyssa, *Dogmatic Treatises*, in *NPNF2*, 5:324, http://www.ccel.org/ccel/schaff/npnf205.viii.iii.html, accessed 18 June 2010.

This love existed between the person of the Trinity before creation (John 17:24). This love binds them together in one mission. Anyone who loves the Father will love the Son (John 5:42–43), and if anyone loves the Son, the Father will love them (John 14:23). The love within the divine life is a form of self-love, because it is God loving God. While humanity is unable to both love ourselves and love in self-giving action, God can, because God's love for himself is self-giving love.

Self-giving love is at work in the very act of creation. The Father loves the Son and gives him everything (John 3:35). In the beginning, God created, but he created through the Son, and this creation was a gift to the Son (Col. 1:16). The Son loves the Father in self-giving action when he says, "not my will, but yours, be done" (Luke 22:42). At the end of this age, the Son will demonstrate his love for the Father again when he delivers to the Father the kingdom (1 Cor. 15:24).

Jesus spoke again of the love between the Father and the Son in the Gethsemane prayer; "I made known to them your name, and I will continue to make it known, that the love with which you have loved me may be in them, and I in them" (John 17:26). He introduces the missional goal for the love he has for the Father. He wants to share the love they have for one another with humanity. He wants his disciples to know the Father, so that the love between the triune persons might be in them. The love within the divine life is then the pattern for the love of God expressed in the mission of God to redeem and restore humanity. The connection between the love among the persons of the Trinity and the love God demonstrates to us in redemption is made even more explicit in John 15:9: "As the Father has loved me, so have I loved you." Paul says, "In love, [the Father] predestined us for adoption as sons through Jesus Christ" (Eph. 1:4–5). This love is demonstrated in that while we were sinners the Father sent the Son to die for us (cf. Rom. 5:8; 1 John 4:10).

THE MISSIONAL ACTS OF THE TRIUNE GOD

In this section, we will unpack the idea of God as the initiator and primary agent of his mission. From this perspective, we will discuss three main aspects of God's mission: (1) the missional acts of God in creation, (2) the missional acts of God in salvation, and (3) the missional acts of God in the new creation.

The Trinity and the mission of creation. There is a danger to suggesting that God is missional by nature. The danger is that it might lead to the conclusion that creation is necessary to God. We have already in some ways addressed this challenge, particularly in our discussion on God being self-existent. We also dealt with this challenge as we observed that God's desire to be known is fully accomplished within the life of the Trinity. What we want to continue to affirm is that the only necessary thing about God is that God be God.

God was free to create (or not to create). He was free to create the world according to his plan. He could have created a world that is very different than the world that he created. However, whatever world(s) God would create must have the following two qualities:

1. The world(s) must have the capacity to reflect and would reflect the glory of its Creator. The way creation reflects God's glory is through its beauty, its orderly design, and its righteous purposes (cf. Ps. 19:1–6), for creation is, in Augustine's words "the stamp of the triune God."[34] As the psalmist tells us, it does not bear the stamp of its Creator quietly. It proclaims the glory of God (Ps. 19:1; cf. Rom. 1:19–20).

2. The world(s) must have creatures with the capacity to know, love, and respond to their creator. This capacity is uniquely possessed by humanity, and is what the Bible calls being created in the image of God.[35]

The reason that creation must have these two qualities is that creation has a purpose. That purpose is to acknowledge the glory of its Creator. Creation does not add anything to God. It is, in Calvin's words, a "spectator" of the awesome works of God.[36]

---

[34] St. Augustine, *On the Trinity*, XI, 10.

[35] John Calvin makes a similar point while explaining what Paul meant by "what can be known about is plain to them" in Romans 1:19. He writes, "By saying, that God *has made it manifest*, he means, that man was created to be *a spectator of this formed world*, and *that eyes were given him, that he might, by looking on so beautiful a picture, by led to the Author himself.*" John Calvin, *The Epistle of Paul the Apostle to the Romans*, vol. 19 of *Calvin's Commentaries*, trans. and ed. John Owen (Grand Rapids: Baker, 1993), 70, emphasis original.

[36] Dorothy Sayers, in her book *The Mind of the Maker*, makes a helpful observation along these lines. She writes, "The Trinity abides and works and is responsive to itself 'in Heaven.'" Thus, "the creative act [of God] . . . does not depend for its fulfillment upon its manifestation in a material creation." However, she continues, "it is true that the urgent desire of the creative mind is towards expression in material form." She makes this point by explaining it from the vantage point of the work of a writer. She says, "The writer in writing his book on paper, is expressing the freedom of his own nature in the law of his being; and we argue from this that the material creation expresses the nature of the Divine Imagination. We may perhaps say that creation in some form or the other is necessary to the nature of God; what we cannot say is that this or any particular form of creation is necessary to Him. It is in His mind, complete, whether he writes it down or not. To say that God depends on His creation like a poet depends on His written poem is an abuse of metaphor . . . . To write the poem (or, of course, to give it material form in speech or song), is an act of love towards the poet's own imaginative act and towards his fellow-beings. It is a social act; but the poet is first and foremost his own society, and would be none the less a poet if the means of material expression were refused by him or denied by him." Sayers' analogy of the writer helps us to see that God did not create in order to glorify himself. Yes, he is glorified in his creation. But he was already fully known, loved, enjoyed, and thus glorified within his own triune existence before creation. What he did in creating was to make his glory known outside the divine life. There is an important distinction between making something glorious and recognizing that something is already glorious. God creates so that his creation will recognize his glory. See Dorothy Sayers, *The Mind of the Maker* (San Francisco: HarperCollins, 1979), 31–32.

In creation, God established a kingdom to display his glory.[37] He formed the world out of nothing, and he ordered it to manifest his glory and goodness. He formed and ordered a world in which the final act was to create human beings. He created a place for his people and called them to live life under his providential blessings and rule. God placed Adam and Eve in the garden and provided for them perfectly, and they related to him intimately. He was their God and they were his people. God had established his plan and promised his continual provision. By relying on God and trusting him, displaying their knowledge of God and their love for him, Adam and Eve enjoyed his blessing. At the end of creation, Adam and Eve were in the garden enjoying fully all of God's blessings.

Humanity has a unique role to play in God's kingdom. They are to participate in the fulfillment of God's creation by being fruitful, multiplying, and filling the whole earth. To fill the whole world with his image-bearers who know him, trust him, depend on him, and enjoy him was and is the mission of God in creation. God seeks to be glorified in the cultural mandate. Humanity is to order God's creation. We are to take what God created and use it for the purposes God ordained. These are the basics of culture—taking the resources that God gives and using them. God intended that all things would operate under his rule and for his purpose. His will was for there to be a God-ward culture(s).

Creation is therefore *eschatological* by the simple fact that there is a purpose for creation, and that purpose is for God to be known, enjoyed, worshipped, and glorified. Creation is also *Trinitarian,* for each person of the Trinity is involved in the acts of creation. The Scriptures tell us that the Son of God spoke all things into existence (John 1:1–3; Heb. 1:2) and he holds all things together by his own power (Heb. 1:3). The Spirit of God prepared the world for the human race (Gen. 1:2). The Holy Spirit is the One that gives life, the One who gives form and direction to our lives (Job 33:4; Ps. 104:30). Finally, creation is *Christocentric.* Paul says, referring to Jesus, in Colossians, "all things were created through him and for him" (Col. 1:16). After his death, burial, and resurrection, all things were placed under his rule and authority (Eph. 1:22). He claimed authority over all creation in the act of sending his disciples out to make more disciples for him, underscoring his rule by sending them to all the nations (Matt. 28:18–20).

The Trinity and the mission of redemption. God's purpose to make himself known in his creation was challenged in the serpent's temptation of Adam and Eve. The very nature, character, and purpose of God was called into question when the serpent asked, "Did God actually say . . . ?" (Gen. 3:1). Dietrich Bonhoeffer calls this the first theological discourse. He writes, "It is not common worship, a common calling upon God, but a speaking about God, about God in a way that passes over, and reaches beyond," for the serpent speaks about God "with an attitude of having a deep knowledge of the

---

[37] Vaughn Roberts, *God's Big Picture: Tracing the Storyline of the Bible* (Downers Grove: IVP, 2004).

secrets of God."[38] What the serpent actually did was question the knowledge that Adam and Eve had of God by questioning his generosity.

Although God's purposes were challenged by the lie of the serpent and the rebellion of Adam and Eve and all of their descendants, God's plan continued. In his redemptive plan, God effectively said, "The serpent does not know me. Let me tell you who I am." God's ultimate purpose in redemption is to be known and worshipped by his creation. There are many ways to point this out from the Scriptures. We will do it by looking first at God's redemptive activities in the Old Testament, and then by looking at what God does in sending his Son to accomplish his redemptive purpose.

After the fall, God's way of proceeding was to choose a particular people, give them land, and bless them and all humanity through them (Gen. 12:1–3). The particular community that God chose became a sign that God was on a mission and Israel was the instrument by which God sought to accomplish his mission. God chose and created the nation Israel to make himself known to all the nations. He did this by guiding them, providing for them, establishing an ordered life for them, protecting them, and judging them. Through the nation of Israel, God made preparations to reestablish his kingdom on the earth by calling them and covenanting to give them a land and to be their God. Whenever the mission through Israel seemed to be failing, God reaffirmed his promise that his kingdom would come by sending prophets to remind his people of his plan. God did all of this to make his name known in his creation.

One specific way that God pursued his mission was by making a covenant with his people in order to make himself known to them. He did this by revealing himself to his people and by regularly using his own name to build the Israelites' trust and confidence that he has the power to provide his covenant promises. After calling Abraham, promising to give him land, making him a great nation, and blessing all the nations of the earth through him, the word of the Lord came to Abraham, saying, "I am your shield; your reward shall be very great." Abraham responded to God with the question, "How can this be, for I am childless?" (Gen. 15:2, paraphrased). Then God reaffirmed his promise to Abraham to be his shield and provider, and he did so by revealing himself as his covenant provider with his covenant name. He said, "I am the LORD who brought you out from Ur of the Chaldeans to give you this land to possess" (Gen. 15:7c). With his name, God reaffirmed to Abraham that he is a covenant provider.

The same thing occurs throughout the Scriptures, particularly in the book of Exodus. The Lord sent Moses to the people of Israel to tell them that he had not forgotten the covenant that he had made with them. As Moses shared with the people, "I am the LORD, and I will bring you out from under the burdens of the Egyptians" (Exod. 6:6). And again, prior to giving Israel the law, God said, "I am the LORD your God, who brought you out of the land of Egypt, out of the

---

[38] Dietrich Bonhoeffer, *Creation and Fall: A Theological Exposition of Genesis 1–3, Dietrich Bonhoeffer Works: Vol. 3*, ed. John W. de Gruchy and trans. Douglas Stephen Bax (Minneapolis: Fortress Press, 1997), 111–12.

house of slavery" (Exod. 20:2). As the covenant promises were rehearsed and reaffirmed in the prophets, the sovereign rule and covenant provision of God were pronounced again and again. They were announced with a similar purpose, namely, to engender confidence in God's covenantal faithfulness. Isaiah prophesied that the Lord would send his servant, and the servant would come with the Spirit and to bring forth justice to all peoples (cf. Isa. 42:1–4). Then, to ratify these covenant promises, God said,

> "I am the LORD; I have called you in righteousness; I will take you by the hand and keep you; I will give you as a covenant for the people, a light for the nations, to open the eyes that are blind, to bring out the prisoners from the dungeon, from the prison those who sit in darkness. I am the LORD; that is my name; my glory I give to no other, nor my praise to carved idols. Behold, the former things have come to pass, and new things I now declare; before they spring forth I tell you of them." (Isa. 42:6–9)

"I am the LORD" is used in this context to confirm the covenant promises to the people of God. What is revealed in this statement is the *Godwardness* of the divine mission. As the God of the covenant reveals his covenant name and his sovereign rule, he guarantees the covenant provisions and blessings. What cannot be missed is that when God reveals himself in this way, he is calling for a personal response and commitment from his people. He says, "Trust me for my name's sake." He seeks the response, "I will trust you for your name's sake" (cf. Ps. 23:3).

What God began in Israel, he accomplished by sending his Son into the world. God decisively challenged the deception of the serpent when the Son became flesh to reveal the Father to the world (John 1:14,18). Through Jesus, God the Father accomplished his purposes for creation. The divine will to be universally known is carried out in the ministry of Jesus. The New Testament carefully demonstrates that Jesus shares in the identity and function of the Lord, the God of Israel. Jesus' identity with God may be demonstrated in a number of ways in the New Testament, but here we will note just three.

First, there are many passages where the acts of creation are attributed to Jesus, which reveals his divine identity and relationship with the God of Israel (John 1:1; Col. 1:15–17; Heb. 1:2). God's two great actions outside of the triune life, creation and redemption, are both accomplished through the Son. Thus, Athanasius concludes that there is no inconsistency between creation and salvation, because God ordained that his Son would be the agent for both.[39] Next, the pronouncements that declare Jesus' authority over all things identify him with the God of Israel (Eph. 1:20–23; Col. 3:1; Heb. 2:1–8). It was by his authority over heaven and earth that Jesus commissioned his followers to continue in the mission of God (Matt. 28:18–20). Finally, that Jesus will be worshipped at the end of time identifies him with the God of Israel, who alone is God and worthy of worship (Rev. 5:9). God himself promises to

---

[39] Athanasius, *On the Incarnation*, 26.

exalt the Son above every name, and at this name, every knee will bow and confess Jesus as Lord (Phil. 2:9–11).

Therefore, it is through Jesus that God the Father accomplishes his mission to be known by creation. God's mission is fulfilled in the life, death, and resurrection of Jesus Christ. He establishes the promised kingdom that is prophesied in the Old Testament. Jesus accomplished all that God sent him to do in his life and ministry (John 17:4). He has announced that the kingdom has come. He demonstrates the power and the presence of the kingdom in his actions. He declares that if someone knows him, they also would know the Father (John 14:7). It is through Jesus that God is known and worshipped in creation. Paul says, in our redemption, God delivers us from the kingdom of darkness and moves us to the kingdom of his beloved Son (cf. Col. 1:13–14).

One way to understand this transformation is the process of recovering spiritual sight and knowledge. When Jesus became a man, he began this process of recovering spiritual knowledge. It was not until death and resurrection that the knowledge of God's glory was fully revealed in Jesus Christ (2 Cor. 4:6). On the cross, God manifested his righteousness by demonstrating his covenant faithfulness and by satisfying his judgment toward sin in the atoning sacrifice of Jesus Christ (Rom. 3:21–26). This spiritual knowledge is revealed through the power and work of the Spirit of God, who knows the depth of God (1 Cor. 2:7–12). The apostle John actually defines salvation in terms of recovering spiritual knowledge. He says, "And this is eternal life, that they know you the only true God, and Jesus Christ whom you have sent" (John 17:3). The final stage of salvation, glorification, will be complete when we see Jesus face to face (1 John 3:2).

God's mission of salvation is *eschatological-Christocentric-Trinitarian*. Perhaps the best portrait of this framework is found in Ephesians 1:3–14, particularly verses 7–10.

> In him we have redemption through his blood, the forgiveness of our trespasses, according to the riches of his grace, which he lavished upon us, in all wisdom and insight making known to us the mystery of his will, according to his purpose, which he set forth in Christ as a plan for the fullness of time, to unite all things in him, things in heaven and things on earth. (Eph. 1:7–10)

In these verses, we see that Christians are redeemed by the atoning sacrifice of Jesus to accomplish God's great *eschatological* plan to unite all things underneath the authority of Jesus. This great act of God fulfills God's mission. These verses in Ephesians are the thesis of this New Testament letter, and not just for the Ephesians, but also for all of history. Everything is in view here. Paul intentionally stresses the phrase "all things." What God does in history, he does to work *all things according to His will* (cf. Eph. 1:9–10). These verses reveal to us the goal of history. "All things" here is personal, corporate, and cosmic. God predestined individuals for adoption as a significant part of his great plan for *all things*. God called a people together to be his church, to be the body of his Son. Summing up "all things" also includes the cosmos

(Col. 1:20). This Christ-centered plan is the Trinity's plan for accomplishing the goal of history.

God's plan is *Christocentric* in two significant ways. Jesus Christ is the means to accomplishing God's plan and the aim of God's plan. Through his atoning sacrifice, people are adopted as sons and receive forgiveness for their sins by the blood of Jesus (Eph. 1:5,7). The goal of this saving work is for those who are adopted to be united together under the rule and authority of Jesus Christ.

The structure of this passage reflects a carefully articulated *Trinitarian* salvation. The Father is praised for his will and purposes (Eph. 1:3–6). The Father's will is accomplished through redemption in the Son and forgiveness by his blood (vv. 7–10). The salvation is confirmed by the sealing work of the Holy Spirit (vv. 13–14). Summing up all things in Jesus is the way God accomplishes his mission in creation, and God does this so that all those who are redeemed would give praise to God for his glory (v. 12; cf. v. 7). Those who hope in Jesus Christ are sealed with the Holy Spirit as the guarantee of this salvation "to the praise of his glory" (vv. 13–14).

The Trinity and the mission of the new creation. The new creation was inaugurated by the life, death, and resurrection of Jesus Christ and by the sending of the Holy Spirit to seal the work of salvation upon those who believe in Jesus and to empower them for their missions. It is not realized fully until Jesus returns for his church, and God established the new heavens and new earth for his people. There is a reasonable tendency to see that when this takes place, God's mission is finished. What we argue is that just because God's mission is accomplished does not mean it is finished. God's mission is to gather to himself a people for his praise and glory, and God's people will live for God, worshipping him and enjoying him and his blessings. The painful effects of sin are not present in the new creation. There will be no mourning, death, or pain (Rev. 21:4). The new creation is designed to be a place where God dwells with his people (Rev. 21:3). This is God's purpose, and his actions flow from this. The new city has no need for a temple or the sun, for God is the temple and the glory of God is light that illuminates the city (Rev. 21:22–25).

Eschatological-Christocentric-Trinitarianism continues to characterize God's mission, even into the new creation. The new creation is the end of redemptive history and where God's mission is fully realized. Jesus is at the center of eternity, for he will be worshipped and will be seen face to face. His name will be written on the foreheads of his people (Rev. 22:4). The Lord God and the Son are present in the new creation (Rev. 21:22–25). While the Spirit's role in the new creation is not explicitly stated in Revelation 21–22, the Spirit plays a role in the preparation for the new creation, and because God is triune, the Spirit will surely have a role in the new creation.

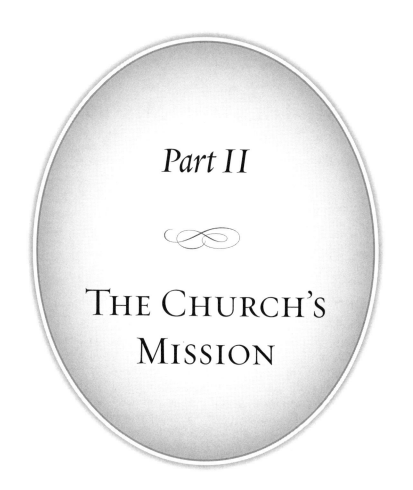

Part II

THE CHURCH'S
MISSION

Chapter Three

THE AGENTS OF MISSION: HUMANITY

Doug Coleman

INTRODUCTION

At a meeting of ministers in 1786, John Ryland Sr., an elder pastor, requested from his colleagues a topic for discussion, and the young William Carey proposed for consideration, "The duty of Christians to attempt the spread of the gospel among heathen nations." To this suggestion Ryland Sr. supposedly retorted, "Young man, sit down. When God pleases to convert the heathen, He will do it without your aid or mine!"[1] Although Carey's topic was tabled for the day, his growing passion for the conversion of the heathen abroad could not be squelched. Six years later, Carey published his "plan of action," *An Enquiry into the Obligations of Christians to Use Means for the Conversion of the Heathens*. One of the key elements in the genesis of the modern missions movement, the *Enquiry* rightly stressed the importance of humanity's role by arguing for the Great Commission's continuing validity.

Carey has been criticized for limiting the biblical foundation of the *Enquiry* to one single text.[2] While perhaps unfair to Carey given his purpose and context, the question of humanity's role in the mission of God warrants

---

[1] There is some disagreement regarding the historicity of Ryland's response, although George considers it reliable. Timothy George, *Faithful Witness: The Life and Mission of William Carey* (Worchester, PA: Christian History Institute, 1998), 53.

[2] See Christopher J. H. Wright, *The Mission of God: Unlocking the Bible's Grand Narrative* (Downer's Grove: IVP, 2006), 34.

a robust treatment. In other words, Carey was right to affirm the Great Commission's abiding force, but there is much more to the story. This chapter will consider the purpose of humanity within the biblical narrative, particularly his role as agent in the *missio Dei*.

CREATION

The story of man's role in the *missio Dei* begins not with the Great Commission, or even with the call of Abraham, but in the garden of Eden. While the creation account is relatively short, Genesis 1–2 reveals foundational truths about humanity's nature and role. After creating the world and all other creatures, God made man, "the culmination of [his] infinitely wise and skillful work of creation."[3] It was only after the creation of man that God declared everything "very good." Here we learn that man is a dependent creature, but one clearly different from all others. One of the first assertions made about man is that he—as male and female—is made in God's image (1:26–27). Although theologians have engaged in much discussion on the topic, Scripture provides no direct commentary on the nature of God's image in humanity.[4] At the most basic level, this indicates that we are like God in some way and possess an intrinsic worth and dignity other creatures lack.[5]

The creation account also reveals the distinctly relational nature of humanity. While animals possess gender, God created a special helpmate only for man and established marriage to designate a unique relationship. Although the creation account concludes before the multiplication of humanity, the later biblical record and human experience indicate that the potential for interpersonal harmony is far greater in human relationships than among animals.[6] Humanity's relational aspect extends to his unique interaction with God as well. The rest of creation obeys God's word and depends on him for existence, but man *fellowships* with God. The communication between God and humanity in the garden is portrayed as distinct from that of any other creatures.

Upon creating him, God placed man in a specially prepared garden (Gen. 2:8). As Sailhamer notes, since "Eden" means "delight" in the Hebrew Bible, "we may assume that the name was intended to evoke a picture of idyllic delight and rest."[7] There God provided all of man's needs—food to eat,

---

[3]   Wayne Grudem, *Systematic Theology: An Introduction to Biblical Doctrine* (Grand Rapids: Zondervan, 1994), 499.

[4]   For a short discussion of various aspects of the image of God in man, see Grudem, *Systematic Theology*, 445–49. For a more extensive treatment, see Anthony A. Hoekema, *Created in God's Image* (Grand Rapids: Eerdmans, 1986), 11–101. See also Millard J. Erickson, *Christian Theology*, 2nd ed. (Grand Rapids: Baker, 1998), 517–36; John M. Frame, *Salvation Belongs to the Lord: An Introduction to Systematic Theology* (Phillipsburg, NJ: P&R, 2006), 88–90.

[5]   John S. Hammett, "The Doctrine of Humanity," in *A Theology for the Church*, ed. Daniel L. Akin (Nashville: B&H, 2007), 352–53.

[6]   Grudem, *Systematic Theology*, 447.

[7]   John Sailhamer, *The Pentateuch as Narrative* (Grand Rapids: Zondervan, 1992), 98.

suitable human companionship, and even his own presence. Commentators have noted significant similarities between Eden and the Old Testament tabernacle and temple.[8] For example, Greg Beale records eleven different parallels and concludes that Eden was the first archetypal temple.[9] God placed Adam in this garden-temple as a priestly vice-regent, or priest-king.[10] Genesis 2:15 notes two specific responsibilities for the garden given to Adam: to cultivate and guard/keep it. According to Beale, when these two words appear together in the Old Testament they refer either to the Israelites' serving God and keeping God's word or to priests who keep the service of the tabernacle.[11] Therefore, it seems that Adam was both to tend to the garden and protect it from uncleanness, similar to the later functions of Israel's temple priests. Of course, all of this was to be done in the context of worshipful obedience to God.

To say that Eden was a place of idyllic delight and rest is not to say that it—or creation—was complete in every sense. God declared creation "very good" and rested on the seventh day, but there was still more to be done. Genesis 1:28 records additional responsibilities God gave humanity.[12] First, man is told to be fruitful and multiply. This clearly refers to procreation. As Calvin notes, God himself could have covered the earth with a multitude of men, but he chose to use the means of human reproduction. Second, man is told to fill the earth. Assuming the garden of Eden constituted an identifiable space, this implies that Adam and Eve were to extend its geographical boundaries until Eden covered the entire earth.[13] By subduing the earth and ruling over it—the final responsibilities mentioned in 1:28—humanity, as God's image-bearer, was "to spread God's luminescent presence by extending the boundaries of the original Edenic temple outward into the earth."[14]

This charge to humanity, often referred to as the cultural mandate, implies development. As John Frame states, "Creation is what God makes; culture is what man does with creation."[15] The Genesis account contains no reference to much that we associate with culture. There were no arts, sciences, or educational institutions. These, and much more, were yet to be developed, and God had given man the amazing capacity and privilege of doing so. In his excellent work *Creation Regained*, Albert Wolters explains:

---

   [8]   Ibid., 97–100.

   [9]   G. K. Beale, *The Temple and the Church's Mission: A Biblical Theology of the Dwelling Place of God* (Downers Grove: IVP, 2004), 66–80.

   [10]   Beale, *The Temple and the Church's Mission*, 66–70. Although he disagrees with Beale regarding the best translation of 2:15, Sailhamer agrees that Adam was to function as a priest, not merely as a worker and keeper of the garden. Sailhamer, *The Pentateuch*, 100–102.

   [11]   Beale, *The Temple and the Church's Mission*, 67.

   [12]   Some, like Sailhamer, interpret the English imperatives in 1:28 as blessing rather than command. Sailhamer, *The Pentateuch*, 96. Regardless, they represent responsibilities or roles that humanity is to fulfill.

   [13]   Beale, *The Temple and the Church's Mission*, 81–82.

   [14]   Ibid., 82.

   [15]   Frame, *Salvation Belongs to the Lord*, 98.

Creation is not something that, once made, remains a static quantity. There is, as it were, a growing up (though not in a biological sense), an unfolding of creation. This takes place through the task that people have been given of bringing to fruition the possibilities of development implicit in the work of God's hands. . . . We are called to participate in the ongoing creational work of God, to be God's helper in executing to the end the blueprint for his masterpiece.[16]

We must not misunderstand. Creation, and all of its possibilities, is God's handiwork. He is the Creator and in him all things hold together; however, in his sovereignty he has chosen to use human agents to actualize creation's inherent potential.

Man's position as vice-regent introduces one of the key themes of Scripture: mediation. The fall would necessitate a new kind of mediation, but even in creation God employed human agents to fulfill his purpose of covering the earth with his glory. By subduing and ruling over the Earth man was to reflect God's kingly character. As we have seen, caring for and keeping the garden were priestly functions. Even in naming the animals, God used Adam as a mediate agent.

Before moving on to the fall, a final observation from creation is in order. One of the most fundamental assertions about man is that he is a created person.[17] As with the rest of creation, his creaturely status renders him ultimately dependent on God. Even the pagan poets whom Paul referenced in Athens recognized via general revelation that "in him we live and move and have our being" (Acts 17:28). Yet man is also a person, an assertion that implies responsibility. God clearly affirms this responsibility in his command to Adam regarding the tree of the knowledge of good and evil. Here already—even before the fall—a tension arises that we must carefully balance. As Hoekema states, "To be creatures means that God is the potter and we are the clay (Rom. 9:21); to be persons means that we are the ones who fashion our lives by our own decisions (Gal. 6:7–8)."[18] In regard to the *missio Dei*, we must continually affirm that the mission is God's and he alone can bring it to completion. On the other hand, he has created us as responsible human agents—responsible not only in our individual relationship to him, but also to fulfill our God-given role in relation to the world around us.

FALL

God created the cosmos for his own glory. As part of that cosmos, man, the only creature made in God's image, was assigned an important task. Beale writes, "God's ultimate goal in creation was to magnify his glory throughout the earth by means of his faithful image-bearers inhabiting the world in

---

[16] Albert M. Wolters, *Creation Regained: Biblical Basics for a Reformational Worldview*, 2nd ed. (Grand Rapids: Eerdmans, 2005), 43–44.

[17] Hoekema, *Created in God's Image*, 5–10.

[18] Ibid., 6.

obedience to the divine mandate."[19] Yet, apparently a short time after creation, the story takes a grievous turn. Encouraged by the serpent, Adam and Eve made one of the most baffling decisions of history—they rejected God's authority and suffered devastating consequences.

With the fall, almost everything changed, and the terrible results are immediately evident. Adam and Eve's eyes were opened and they knew nakedness. They began to hide from one another and from their Creator. Guilt, shame, and fear entered the world. In short, man was now faced with his archenemy—sin and death.

While every human wrestles with the reality of sin in daily life, theologians have long contemplated its origin. But ultimately it is unfathomable. Herman Bavinck describes it well:

> When all is said and done, sin proves to be an incomprehensible mystery. We know neither whence it is nor what it is. It exists, but has no right to exist. It exists, but no one can explain its origin. Sin itself came into the world without motivation, yet it is now the motivation for all human thought and action. From an abstract point of view, it is nothing but a privation, yet concretely it is a power that controls everyone and everything. It has no independent principle of its own, yet it is a principle that devastates the whole creation. It lives off the good, yet fights it to the point of destruction. It is nothing, has nothing, and cannot do anything without the entities and force God has created, yet organizes them all into rebellion against him. With everything that belongs to God, it opposes everything that belongs to God. It is the will of a weak, finite creature in its revolt against the Creator. It is dependence at war with the Independent One and striving for its own independence. It is impermanent becoming in a struggle with him who exists eternally. It is the greatest contradiction tolerated by God in his creation, yet used by him in the way of justice and righteousness as an instrument for his glory.[20]

All of creation was now terribly damaged. Man, the pinnacle of that creation, became sinful and separated from his Creator. Banished from the garden, the pleasure of fulfilling his priestly duty of cultivating God's sanctuary was now altered by sin. Although the image of God in man was not completely eradicated, his basic orientation toward God, his fellow man, and the world around him changed.[21]

But all was not entirely lost. Even as God the judge pronounced sentence on rebellious man, evidence of his grace shone through. He would not give up on his creation. In Genesis 3:15, the *protoevangelium* or "first gospel,"

---

[19]   Beale, *The Temple and the Church's Mission*, 82.

[20]   Herman Bavinck, *Reformed Dogmatics: Sin and Salvation in Christ*, vol. 3, ed. John Bolt, trans. John Vriend (Grand Rapids: Baker Academic, 2006), 145.

[21]   Even Calvin who strongly affirmed the pervasive depravity of man claimed that the image was not entirely lost in the fall. He states, "Therefore, even though we grant that God's image was not totally annihilated and destroyed in him, yet it was so corrupted that whatever remains is frightful deformity." John Calvin, *Institutes of the Christian Religion*, vol 1, ed. John T. McNeill (Philadelphia: Westminster, 1960), 208.

God revealed the initial hint of redemption. Here it is immediately clear that humanity, as the seed of the woman, will participate in God's plan. It is through her seed that the head of the serpent will be dealt a fatal blow. In other words, humanity becomes both *object* and *agent* of mission.

REDEMPTION

Beginning with man's fall and banishment from Eden in Genesis 3 to the unveiling of the new heavens and earth in Revelation 21, Scripture narrates the story of God's plan for redemption. This record contains both implicit and explicit testimony of humanity's role in the process. At every major turning point God uses humanity in his mission to glorify himself through redemption.[22]

A brief review of redemption history. Already in Genesis 4 the difficulty of life outside the garden becomes painfully manifest. Cain cannot master his sin and ultimately murders his own brother. As generations progress, so does man's wickedness, until "every intent of the thoughts of his heart [is] only evil continually." So desperate is the situation that God resorts to drastic measures in the form of a catastrophic flood. However, he again refuses to abandon his creation entirely. One man, Noah, finds favor in God's sight. God not only commissions Noah to build the ark, but also to preach righteousness to his generation. Through the cooperation of a human agent God saves Noah, his family, and the animals, and he rescues humanity from total annihilation. As God instructs Noah to leave the ark, he commissions Noah with a phrase that harkens back to Adam's original mandate, "Be fruitful and multiply on the earth" (Gen. 8:17).

Generations later, after humanity defied his Creator at Babel, we reach another major turning point in salvation history. God called Abram and began the long process of establishing a people who will play a major role in his mission. In spite of his advanced age, God promised Abraham offspring that would eventually constitute a great nation. This people of God would be the means by which blessing would come to all the families of the earth.[23]

After several more generations and a migration to Egypt, Israel indeed constituted a populous nation. However, as God had foretold, they suffered under the hand of oppressors in a land that was not theirs. Again God called a man, Moses, who played a critical role in their deliverance, their journey to the Promised Land, and the establishment of their worship system. Moses served as God's mediator before Pharaoh and to the nation of Israel.

---

[22] As Beale states, commentators have noticed that the commission given to Adam in the garden was passed on to Noah, Abraham, and his descendants, although altered as a result of sin's entrance into the world. Beale, *The Temple and the Church's Mission,* 93–121.

[23] For excellent treatments of the role of Abraham in the *missio Dei,* see Andreas J. Köstenberger and Peter T. O'Brien, *Salvation to the Ends of the Earth: A Biblical Theology of Mission,* New Studies in Biblical Theology, ed. D. A. Carson, no. 11 (Downers Grove, IL: InterVarsity, 2001), 28–32; Wright, *The Mission of God,* 194–221.

As Moses passes from the scene, the fulfillment of the Abrahamic covenant progresses with Israel's entry into the Promised Land. Throughout
Israel's history in the Old Testament, God uses human agents to further his
mission—judges, prophets, kings, and even pagan nations. In spite of Israel's
repeated failure to keep her covenant, God remains faithful and preserves a
remnant from his people.

In the fullness of time, through this remnant, God would send forth his
Son, the God-man, to redeem mankind, destroy the works of the devil, and
reverse the effects of the fall. The incarnation, the ultimate example of mediation, reveals humanity's participation in the *missio Dei* in astonishing terms.
Through Jesus' life, death, and resurrection, the kingdom breaks into the
present, although it is not yet fully come. The preparation of the disciples
constitutes a major focus of Jesus' earthly ministry. Through them and their
disciples, as they are empowered by the Holy Spirit, the inaugurated kingdom extends its territory, primarily through God's new covenant people, the
church.

The ultimate scope of salvation history is universal—nothing other than
all nations and all of creation. Beginning with the call of Abram, God makes
known his intention to bless all nations. Throughout Israel's history Scripture emphasizes her universal redemptive purpose.[24] In his final commission,
Jesus explicitly defines its scope as encompassing all nations, and Revelation
7:9–10 gives us a glimpse of its fulfillment.

Observations and implications. From this brief review of salvation history we can make some important observations regarding humanity's role in
the *missio Dei*. As mentioned previously, at every turn Scripture records the
significant role of humanity. While God occasionally operates immediately
or directly, he most frequently employs human agents to accomplish his purposes, whether in the building of a boat, delivering a message to Pharaoh, or
even bringing judgment on his own people via pagan nations. Perhaps the
most striking evidence of God's commitment to human agency is found in
the conversion of Cornelius.

As Cornelius was praying, God spoke to him in a vision by means of
an angel. Although the angel could have easily, and perhaps more power-
fully, delivered the content of the gospel, he instructed Cornelius to dispatch
men to Joppa to summon Peter. Likewise, God communicated with Peter in
a supernatural way. However, neither through the vision nor by the Spirit did
God instruct Peter to visit Cornelius; that task he reserved for human messengers. At several points in Cornelius' conversion, it seems that God went
out of his way to preserve an essential role for man. God clearly employed
extraordinary means to connect Peter and Cornelius, but the responsibility of
delivering the gospel message he reserved for a human agent.

Several well-known passages record even more explicit evidence
of man's essential role. First, immediately prior to his ascension, Jesus

---

[24] For a helpful discussion of Israel and the nations, see Wright, *The Mission of God*,
467–500.

expressly assigned his followers the task of continuing his mission. Paul defines redeemed humanity's mediatorial role as "ambassador" (2 Cor. 5:20), and stresses the essential role of man in Romans 10:14: "How then will they call on Him in whom they have not believed? How will they believe in Him whom they have not heard? And *how will they hear without a preacher?*" (NASB, emphasis added). Certainly the preacher's going is a response to being sent, but he still performs a critical God-given task. Proclamation of the gospel—by human agents—is the means God has ordained for the salvation of the nations.

Second, salvation history reveals a key theme of Scripture: the people of God. Through his covenant with Abraham, God begins the process of creating a distinct people whose very existence contained a missional purpose.[25] This purpose sees its clearest expression in Exodus 19:5–6 in which God specifically identifies Israel as a kingdom of priests and a holy nation. At various places in the Old Testament, her purpose as a testimony to the nations features prominently in Israel's history. Although she was given no cross-cultural mandate, Israel was to relate to the nations historically through incorporation and eschatologically through ingathering.[26] As we are sometimes painfully aware, Israel's failure resulted in a shift to fulfillment of redemption through the faithful remnant.[27] Out of this remnant and the line of David the suffering servant would emerge.

After Jesus' resurrection and ascension, focus shifts to the church. The relationship between Israel and the church has engendered great debate and is beyond the scope of this chapter.[28] However, as the New Testament people of God the church features prominently in the *missio Dei*. As Wolters notes:

> [I]n making provision for the communication of the good news to many different cultures in the succeeding centuries, Jesus did not (like Mohammad) write a book. Rather, he formed a *community* to be the bearer of this good news. The identity of that community is formed by its mission—it's being *sent* by Jesus—to make known the good news of the kingdom.[29]

The church does not constitute the kingdom, but it is "the concrete display of the 'already/not yet' of the Kingdom."[30] Therefore, the church is currently the primary human means through which God is accomplishing his mission.

Third, the atonement must be repeatedly affirmed as the central act of all redemption and its focus must be steadfastly maintained in the *missio Dei*.

---

[25] This is not to suggest that mission was the singular purpose of Israel's existence. Her ultimate purpose was God's glory. For more on Israel's missionary role, see Köstenberger and O'Brien, *Salvation to the Ends of the Earth*, 32–36; Wright, *The Mission of God*, 24–25.

[26] Köstenberger and O'Brien, *Salvation to the Ends of the Earth*, 35.

[27] Ibid., 37.

[28] Hammett notes both continuity and discontinuity, John S. Hammett, *Biblical Foundations for Baptist Churches: A Contemporary Ecclesiology* (Grand Rapids: Kregel, 2005), 32–33.

[29] Wolters, *Creation Regained*, 122.

[30] Russell D. Moore, *The Kingdom of Christ: The New Evangelical Perspective* (Wheaton, IL: Crossway, 2004), 173.

In the words of Wolters, "We return to creation through the cross, because only the atonement deals with sin and evil effectively at their root."[31] All of salvation history prior to Calvary points forward to the cross, while all of salvation history afterward is rendered possible only because of it. The cross and the resurrection constitute the central foundation of man's participation in the *missio Dei*.

Finally, if the scope of redemption history is all nations, mission necessarily includes a cross-cultural element. Debates about the grammatical structure of Matthew 28:18–20 notwithstanding, the *missio Dei* cannot be accomplished without an intentional effort to cross linguistic, cultural, and geographic boundaries. Nowhere does Scripture demonstrate or imply that God intends to accomplish this mission to all the nations without the involvement of human agents.

The nature of humanity's role. With the fact of man's God-given responsibility well established, another question warrants brief consideration. What is the nature of humanity's role? What activities constitute his sphere of responsibility? This is a question that has occupied theologians and missiologists and sometimes spawned debate and disagreement. We will not be able to fully resolve the issue here, but some general parameters can be established.

First, if sin is the root cause of the curse, then the gospel—in its narrow sense—is the fundamental solution. The salvation of man constitutes a central feature of God's mission. Therefore, proclamation of the gospel is ultimate. Christopher Wright explains well the difference between primacy and ultimacy, "Mission may not always *begin* with evangelism. But mission that does not ultimately *include* declaring the Word and the name of Christ, the call to repentance, and faith and obedience has not completed its task" (emphasis original).[32] Ultimately, our responsibility extends beyond evangelism, however. In his final pre-ascension commission, Jesus defined his followers' task as making disciples, a more comprehensive assignment that includes teaching believers to obey all that Christ commanded. In biblical or theological terms, the aim is sanctification and conformation to the image of Christ. Anthropologically stated, this involves total worldview transformation.[33]

Second, the clear precept and practice of the New Testament affirms the church's importance and, therefore, argues for church planting as a central element of man's role in the *missio Dei*, particularly in pioneer areas. Although Jesus himself never started *a* church, he clearly intended to establish *the* church (Matt. 16:18). He is its cornerstone (Eph. 2:20) and head (Col. 1:18). He purchased it with his own blood (Acts 20:28), and it is his bride (Eph. 5:25–27; Rev. 19). The covenant relationship of church life is the God-appointed context for disciple-making. The "one another" commands of the New Testament are best fulfilled through the regular interaction and

---

[31] Wolters, *Creation Regained*, 83.

[32] Wright, *The Mission of God*, 319.

[33] Paul G. Hiebert, *Transforming Worldviews: An Anthropological Understanding of How People Change* (Grand Rapids: Baker, 2008). See especially 265–333.

accountability of committed believers assembling together in mutual submission to each other and to Christ. Evangelism and even serious attempts at discipleship that neglect the vital focus of the church fail to honor Christ and his bride and fall short of God's intent.

Third, to affirm the ultimacy of proclamation and the importance of church planting is not to deny the present validity of the cultural mandate. As John Frame states, a comprehensive gospel "is a message that will both save sinners and transform cultures, so that the Great Commission fulfills the cultural mandate."[34] Just as the whole creation was affected by the fall, redemption involves the reclamation of all creation in Christ.[35] While the death of Jesus Christ, the second Adam, secures the salvation of the world, redeemed humanity participates in its renewal. Since Christ is the reconciler of all things and has entrusted us with the ministry of reconciliation, "we have a redemptive task wherever our vocation places us in this world."[36]

Cross-cultural efforts at cultural transformation may sometimes be possible and appropriate. However, the wisest and most effective application of the cultural mandate will most often come from indigenous believers and churches. In many parts of the world, direct efforts by foreign missionaries will likely be perceived as cultural, religious, or even political imperialism. However, by teaching a robust biblical theology and worldview, cross-cultural church planters can set in motion the processes that lead to transformation induced by the gospel and its implications for life. Perhaps the apostle Paul serves as the best biblical example of such an approach. As D. A. Carson writes, "The brilliant little letter to Philemon, though it carefully avoids any hint of advocating the overthrow of slavery, nevertheless lays the groundwork for its destruction."[37]

RESTORATION

As in the original creation, the ultimate purpose of restoration is God's glory displayed through the reconciliation and restoration of all things (Isa. 65:17; Acts 3:21; Rom. 8:20–22; Col. 1:20; Rev. 21:5). This restoration culminates in the new heavens and earth and the final state in which the effects of sin are completely eradicated. God alone can fully accomplish this final restoration. However, the kingdom has broken into the present and the process has already begun. Currently this renewal is most often conceptualized in the salvation of man and his being restored in the image of God (Rom. 8:28; 2 Cor. 3:18; Col. 3:10). Even here God calls us to participate in our

---

[34] Frame, *Salvation Belongs to the Lord*, 98.

[35] Much of the rest of this paragraph is from Wolters, *Creation Regained*, 72–73.

[36] Wolters, *Creation Regained*, 73. This raises the fundamental question of the definition and scope of mission. A full treatment of this issue is not possible here. Proposals tend to emphasize Jesus or Paul as the appropriate model for mission. For a discussion of the implications of these models, see David J. Hesselgrave, *Paradigms in Conflict: 10 Key Questions in Christian Missions Today* (Grand Rapids: Kregel, 2005), 141–65.

[37] D. A. Carson, *Christ and Culture Revisited* (Grand Rapids: Eerdmans, 2008), 170.

own sanctification, instructing us to work out our salvation (Phil. 2:12–13). Of course, this process will only see completion when we inherit glorified bodies.

Our participation in the restoration of all things extends beyond personal salvation, however. If the scope of God's plan is all creation, this draws us back to the garden and God's original intention for humanity to participate in extending his glory throughout the earth as culture builders. A comprehensive view of redemption encompasses all of life, including all the various elements of human culture—personal relationships, family life, education, arts, sciences, entertainment, etc. This is not a utopianism that assumes humanity can usher in God's kingdom on earth. Scripture seems clear that evil will persist until Christ's return and that the final coming of the kingdom will be the result of more cataclysmic events. However, if the church is intended to be a concrete, albeit preliminary, display of the kingdom in the present age, that display should manifest itself both in the church and in the world, in our relationship with the body of Christ and with the broader culture in which we live. It is Christ who has established a beachhead in this present age, but he "calls on his subjects to press his claims even further in creation."[38]

The fate of the present creation and its relationship to the new heavens and earth has generated much discussion, particularly as described in 2 Pet. 3:10–13. Regardless of how one resolves the question, it is difficult to assert that the two will be entirely discontinuous. If God's original purpose for man, even before the fall, was to glorify him by developing the inherent possibilities of creation, including culture, it seems reasonable to believe that a fully redeemed humanity will continue to glorify his Creator in the new heavens and earth in similar ways. In other words, the Great Commission will be complete, but the cultural mandate, issued prior to the fall, will continue. In his book *Heaven*, Randy Alcorn suggests that in the new heavens and earth humanity will continue to learn, create, design and entertain.[39]

CONCLUSION

Regardless of our particular calling, God assigns us a responsibility in the *missio Dei*. Whether in our vocation, family, or other spheres of influence, God calls us to honor him by reclaiming everything for his glory. However, God's plan to extend salvation to the ends of the earth is the major focus of Scripture from beginning to end.[40] God intends for the knowledge of his glory to cover earth as the waters cover the sea (Hab. 2:14).

In his *Enquiry*, Carey estimated the population of the world at 731 million, 420 million of which were unconverted. Carey summarized the situation thusly: "It must undoubtedly strike every considerate mind, what a vast

---

[38] Wolters, *Creation Regained*, 74. Here Wolters uses the term "creation" in a more comprehensive sense, not just to refer to the physical world.

[39] Randy Alcorn, *Heaven* (Carol Stream: Tyndale, 2004).

[40] Köstenberger and O'Brien, *Salvation to the Ends of the Earth*, 263.

proportion of the sons of Adam there are, who yet remain in the most deplorable state of heathen darkness, without any means of knowing the true God, except what are afforded them by the works of nature; and utterly destitute of the knowledge of the gospel of Christ, or of any means of obtaining it."[41] In its 2008 assessment of the status of world evangelization, the Joshua Project estimated that two billion people still have had virtually no exposure to the gospel message.[42] Furthermore, approximately 6,700 of the world's estimated 16,300 ethnic people groups are less than 2 percent evangelical or 5 percent Christian.[43] Some of these are probably totally unreached or even unengaged.

The question is not whether God will accomplish his mission. The knowledge of his glory *will* cover the earth as the waters cover the sea. Every tongue, tribe, people and nation *will* be represented among the redeemed before God's throne. The question is whether we will know the joy of obedience and participation. Not everyone is called to move overseas, learn another language, and plant a church in a foreign country, but all redeemed humanity has a part to play.

Perhaps no one has described the connection between love for God and love for the nations better than John Piper:

> God is pursuing with omnipotent passion a worldwide purpose of gathering joyful worshipers for himself from every tribe and tongue and people and nation. He has an inexhaustible enthusiasm for the supremacy of his name among the nations. Therefore let us bring our affections into line with his, and, for the sake of his name, let us renounce the quest for worldly comforts, and join his global purpose. If we do this, God's omnipotent commitment to his name will be over us like a banner, and we will not lose, in spite of many tribulations (Acts 9:16; Rom. 8:35–39).[44]

---

[41] William Carey, *An Enquiry into the Obligations of Christians to Use Means for the Conversion of the Heathens* (Leicester: by Ann Ireland, 1792), 62–63. Can be accessed from http://www.wmcarey.edu/carey/enquiry/anenquiry.pdf.

[42] Joshua Project, "Status of World Evangelization—2008," http://www.joshuaproject.net/download.php, accessed on 15 February 2009.

[43] Ibid.

[44] John Piper, *Let the Nations Be Glad! The Supremacy of God in Missions* (Grand Rapids: Baker, 1993), 40.

Chapter Four

THE HEART OF MISSION: REDEMPTION

Zane Pratt

INTRODUCTION

What is the point of mission? What is its goal? In the contemporary Western church, the word *mission* has come to cover essentially everything the church does outside its own walls. That may include helping the poor, healing the sick, caring for drug addicts, campaigning for peace and justice, loving on children, or a whole host of other activities. Many of these may be good things in and of themselves, and many are things that Christians ought to be doing. However, they address the symptoms of a fallen world rather than the heart of the matter. The mission of God goes deeper than just alleviating the symptoms of evil. Because the world is fallen, the goal of God's mission is nothing less than full redemption: redemption of a people for God's own possession, and redemption of the entire creation from the curse brought on it by humanity's disobedience. The universal narrative of biblical Christianity is creation, fall, redemption, restoration. Redemption leading to restoration is the goal of God's mission.

Even this, however, needs to be put in a wider perspective. Redemption is indeed the goal of mission, but it is a penultimate goal, because creation itself is a penultimate concern. God is ultimate. In order to safeguard ourselves against the very real temptation to see ourselves as the point of the redemptive mission of God, we need to set that mission in the context of the supreme concern of biblical Christianity—the glory of God.

THE ULTIMATE GOAL: GOD'S GLORY

The glory of God is the ultimate goal of everything. God created the world for his own glory. Everything he made reflects the glory of his being and his character. "The heavens declare the glory of God, and the sky above proclaims his handiwork" (Ps. 19:1). The angels in Isaiah's vision of God cried out, "Holy, holy, holy is the LORD of hosts; the whole earth is full of his glory!" (Isa. 6:3). God designed the human race to glorify him. "Ascribe to the LORD, O families of the peoples, ascribe to the LORD glory and strength! Ascribe to the LORD the glory due his name" (Ps. 96:7–8).

Indeed, God created men and women in his own image, and human sin is fundamentally a failure to live up to the glory of that image and to give God the glory that naturally belongs to him. "For all have sinned and fall short of the glory of God" (Rom. 3:23). Idolatry is the foolish exchange of the true glory of the living God for the shoddy false glory of man-made gods: "They . . . exchanged the glory of the immortal God for images resembling mortal man and birds and animals and creeping things" (Rom. 1:22–23). God manifests his glory in his judgment against sin and wickedness. "And I will set my glory among the nations, and all the nations shall see my judgment that I have executed, and my hand that I have laid on them" (Ezek. 39:21).

The final objective of the work of the triune God in redeeming fallen people, Paul argues, is "the praise of his glory" (Eph. 1:3–14). Those who are redeemed are commanded to live entirely for God's glory: "whether you eat or drink, or whatever you do, do all to the glory of God" (1 Cor. 10:31). The missionary message of the people of God is a declaration of the glory of God as revealed in his saving acts: "Declare his glory among the nations, his marvelous works among all the peoples!" (Ps. 96:3). Ultimately, the destiny of creation is universal knowledge of the glory of God: "For the earth will be filled with the knowledge of the glory of the LORD as the waters cover the sea" (Hab. 2:14). The mission of God has the glory of God as its driving passion and as its ultimate goal, as God reveals the amazing spectrum of his glory in creation, judgment, redemption, and restoration.

Some have a hard time with the idea that God's ultimate passion is for his own glory. If we think of God in human terms, such a passion makes God look insecure or egotistical. However, as John Piper has pointed out, while it would be wrong for created human beings to seek their own glory, it would be idolatry for God to do anything else.

> Things are forbidden to us that are not forbidden to God precisely because we are not God and he is. The reason we are not to exalt our own glory, but God's, is because he is God and we are not. For God to be faithful to this same principle means that he too would exalt not our glory, but his. The unifying principle is not: don't exalt your own glory. The unifying principle is: exalt the glory of what is infinitely glorious. For us that means exalt God.

And for God that means exalt God. For us it means *don't* seek your own glory. For God it means *do* seek your own glory.[1]

When we think about redemption, it is critical that we maintain this focus on the glory of God as the chief end of all that God does. As fallen human beings, we are naturally inclined toward self-absorption. We tend to think more about ourselves than about anyone or anything else. We tend, sinfully, to put ourselves at the center of every story. As a result, our fallen human tendency is to think that the mission of God is mostly (or entirely) about us. It isn't. The fact that God, in his amazing grace, has decreed that our good should be linked to his glory should never lead us to the idolatrous notion that our good is primary. He does not exist for us; we exist for him. He is God and we are not. He is primary and we are subordinate. Self-absorbed religion, even self-absorbed evangelical Christianity, is fundamentally idolatrous and un-Christian. The mission of God has God himself as its center and focal point and consuming passion. "For from him and through him and to him are all things. To him be glory forever. Amen" (Rom. 11:36).

WHY REDEMPTION IS NECESSARY

God displayed the glory of his power and wisdom in amazing ways in the creation of the world and in his providential care of what he had made. However, God's good creation was marred by human sin. Adam and Eve were created in the image of God and given the task of serving God by ordering and caring for his creation. They had every advantage. They lived in a perfect world. They had no natural inclination toward sin. They knew God personally, and they had heard his voice directly. They faced only one prohibition: they were forbidden to eat the fruit of one tree, the tree of the knowledge of good and evil. They probably didn't have any real idea what that was (the knowledge of good and evil, that is), but they had every reason to trust in the goodness and wisdom of God.

Despite all these advantages, however, they believed the lie of Satan and disobeyed God. The consequences were immediate and disastrous. They were alienated from God, from one another, and from the rest of creation. They incurred the righteous judgment of God, which entailed immediate spiritual death, expulsion from the garden, and ultimate physical death. The marriage relationship, the process of childbirth, and physical labor all were marred by the rebellion of Adam and Eve. Creation itself was subject to futility and corruption (Rom. 8:19–22). The consequences of their sin didn't stop with them or with their day, either. Adam stood as the federal representative of the entire human race. When he fell, we all fell in him (Rom. 5:12–19). Except for Christ, every human being born since the fall of Adam has been born with a double curse. We are all guilty before God in Adam, and we are also all born with a corrupt nature that is now incurably bent toward sin. The

---

[1]   John Piper, *Let the Nations Be Glad* (Downers Grove: IVP, 1993), 24.

one original sin of Adam left a trail of destruction in its wake that mars God's good creation to this day.

The biblical picture of fallen humanity is not a pretty one. Sin, however, has left us both proud and deceived, and our tendency is to have a much higher opinion of ourselves than Scripture warrants. This is a lethal mistake. Much of the false religion that plagues the world is based on humanity's habitual underestimation of the effects of sin. So, too, is much of the heresy that has infected the church. Anselm's comment in the eleventh century is still applicable to most of the human race, and sadly even to many Christians: "You have not as yet estimated the great burden of sin."[2] According to Scripture, sin has affected every aspect of the human person. Every man and woman born into this world since Adam, other than Christ, is a fallen sinner (Rom. 3:23). Fallen people are blind to the gospel. "The god of this world has blinded the minds of the unbelievers, to keep them from seeing the light of the gospel of the glory of Christ, who is the image of God" (2 Cor. 4:4). Fallen people are unable to understand spiritual truth. "The natural person does not accept the things of the Spirit of God, for they are folly to him, and he is not able to understand them because they are spiritually discerned" (1 Cor. 2:14).

Fallen people are not free at all, but are slaves to sin (Rom. 6:17). Fallen people do not seek God: "no one understands; no one seeks for God" (Rom. 3:11). Fallen people cannot obey God or please God (Rom. 8:7–8). Fallen people justly fall under the wrath of God (Eph. 2:3). Fallen people are spiritually dead: "You were dead in the trespasses and sins in which you once walked" (Eph. 2:1–2). What a condition to be in! Fallen men and women are not spiritually well, or even spiritually sick. They are spiritually dead. Sick people can cooperate in their own healing, and indeed their cooperation and contribution are usually essential. Dead people, on the other hand, don't just need to be healed. They need to be resurrected. Unlike healing, resurrection is not a cooperative venture. Dead people contribute nothing to their own resurrection, because they are incapable of contributing anything.

This is the biblical picture of fallen humanity. By nature, fallen people are spiritually dead, enslaved to sin, unable to understand the things of God, unable to obey God, unable to please God, and unable to do anything about it. They are justly under the wrath of God and headed for an eternity in hell. They are not looking for God; they are looking to escape God. All human religion is an attempt to evade the true and living God in favor of a substitute god we can manipulate on our own terms. Left to ourselves, the condition of fallen humanity is terrible and hopeless.

The biblical picture of fallen humanity is unpopular news. At least in the West, secular society has managed to convince itself that people are really okay. A hundred years ago G. K. Chesterton lamented the widespread denial of original sin in his day, even though daily experience made the reality of

---

    [2]   Anselm, *Cur Deus Homo,* from *St. Anselm: Basic Writings,* trans. S. N. Deane (LaSalle: Open Court, 1962), 228.

universal sin and evil "plain as a pikestaff" and "the only part of Christian theology which can really be proved."[3] Two world wars, the Great Depression, and the Cold War dealt a severe blow to the optimistic liberalism of the nineteenth and early twentieth centuries, and yet this illusion of human goodness is even more deeply engrained in the popular mind today. The loss of a biblical worldview, and the loss of biblical knowledge, has resulted in the loss of anything to shatter the self-inflating delusion inflicted by sin. Without the mirror of God's law, we do not notice how dirty our faces are. However, the bad news about sin is the absolutely essential context for understanding the good news about the redemptive mission of God. Sin is universal, both in the sense that it infects every human being (other than Christ) who has ever lived, and in the sense that it corrupts every aspect of the human person. The wages of sin is death (Rom. 6:23), and God would be less than God if he didn't hate sin, judge it, and punish it.

THE BASIS OF REDEMPTION: GRACE

God is under no obligation to redeem fallen humanity. The human race is guilty, individually and collectively, and we deserve nothing but condemnation. Nor is God under any internal necessity to redeem us. God has no needs. God did not create the human race because he was lonely, or because there was any lack or need in him. He created us entirely out of the overflow of his infinite greatness. He therefore does not need to redeem us to make up for any loneliness or necessity in him. God was infinitely blessed and satisfied in the fellowship of the Trinity before the world was created, and he doesn't need our company to be blessed or satisfied now.

Furthermore, we can do nothing to earn redemption. "All our righteous deeds are like a polluted garment" (Isa. 64:6). Even the best things we do are filthy in the sight of God, because they are polluted by sin. There is nothing we can do to obligate God to redeem us, or even to make our redemption fair. Fairness is exhausted by hell. Just as God created the world, not out of need, but out of the overflow of his infinite greatness, so also he embarked on this glorious mission of redemption not out of any necessity, but entirely out of the overflow of his grace. Grace alone is the basis of the redemptive mission of God. At the conclusion of his devastating description of the extent and severity of sin, Paul says, "for all have sinned and fall short of the glory of God, and are justified by his grace as a gift" (Rom. 3:23–24). Only those who have grasped the fatal seriousness of sin can grasp the glorious riches of grace. Sinners can be saved by grace alone, neither by intrinsic merit nor by earned merit. Furthermore, this grace is not some impersonal commodity controlled and dispensed by the church or by any individual. Grace is an attribute of the character of God that expresses itself in the activity of God in

---

[3]   G. K. Chesterton, *Orthodoxy* (New York: Dodd, Mead & Co., 1908), 15.

doing good to those who deserve only judgment. The redemptive mission of God flows entirely from his free grace.

THE HISTORY OF REDEMPTION

God gave the first indication of his redemptive intentions in Genesis 3, in the context of his confrontation with Adam, Eve, and the serpent immediately after the fall. He did not destroy them on the spot, as they deserved. He actually ministered to their sense of shame by providing them with clothing made of animal skins. Even though their future life would be marked with suffering as a result of their rebellion, childbearing and fruitful labor would continue. Perhaps most intriguingly, in Genesis 3:15 God tells the serpent, "I will put enmity between you and the woman, and between your offspring and her offspring; he shall bruise your head, and you shall bruise his heel." This has long been understood to go beyond the physical enmity that exists between snakes and humans. The serpent, clearly, is serving as a vehicle for the voice of Satan. Not only will there be general conflict between the offspring of Satan (who, according to John 8:44, are unbelievers) and the believing offspring of Eve, the passage envisions an individual conflict between Satan/the serpent himself and a particular, individual offspring of Eve. It would not be an even match. Satan would bruise the heel of the offspring, but the offspring would crush Satan's head. This is the first, faint indication that there would one day be a redemptive victory over evil, fulfilled by the paradoxical victory won by Christ when he died on the cross.

From the fall of the human race in Genesis 3, things went rapidly downhill. Genesis 6:5 summarized the situation well: "The LORD saw that the wickedness of man was great in the earth, and that every intention of the thoughts of his heart was only evil continually." God displayed his justice and his holy hatred of evil in the universal flood, but he also displayed his mercy in rescuing Noah and his family through the ark. These hints of redemptive mercy began to take on concrete form in Genesis 12. Out of the mass of fallen humanity God, in sheer grace, chose one man and his family to be his people and to receive his blessing. However, God made it clear from the start that his intention in choosing Abraham was global: "In you all the families of the earth shall be blessed" (Gen. 12:3). The narrowing process continued for two more generations, as God chose only Isaac out of the sons of Abraham and only Jacob out of the sons of Isaac to inherit the promise given to Abraham. However, through this process God continued to declare the global scope of his redemptive plan. When he renewed his covenant promises to Isaac, he told him, "In your offspring all the nations of the earth shall be blessed" (Gen. 26:4). Similarly, when God appeared to Jacob in his dream of the ladder reaching into heaven, he promised Jacob, "In you and your offspring shall all the families of the earth be blessed" (Gen. 28:14). From Genesis to Revelation (Rev. 5:9, 7:9), God made it clear that his redemptive purposes extended to every nation and every family on earth. On another note, the covenant of circumcision (Gen. 17) marked the Old Testament people of God as unique and distinct, and intimated the fact that sinful people would have to put something off in order to be the people of a holy God. These themes would be repeated again and again. In the book of Genesis the foundations are laid for God's redemptive mission.

The redemptive purposes of God became even clearer in the exodus of Israel from Egypt. In the face of opposition and oppression from the greatest power in the fallen world of their day, God redeemed a people for himself out of slavery. In the process he showed himself faithful to his covenant promises made to Abraham, Isaac, and Jacob. He also showed himself sovereign over all nations as he judged and defeated the false gods of Egypt. Through the slaying of the Passover lamb, and through the sacrificial system subsequently instituted for Israel, he made it clear that without the shedding of blood there can be no deliverance and no forgiveness of sin (Heb. 9:22), pointing to the necessity of sacrifice for redemption to take place. Through a variety of ordinances given to Israel God pressed home the lesson that his people must be separate from the world around them and be clean and pure. God also revealed his holy character through his law. The law was not an arbitrary code of rules, nor again some standard higher than God himself, but rather a faithful reflection of his holy perfection. The law was thus the perfect tutor to show deceived, fallen humanity the reality of their sin and the depth of their need for redemption.

Through Melchizedek (Gen. 14:18–20) and through the office of Aaron and his descendants, God displayed the role of the priest, an anointed intermediary between a holy God and sinful men, doing the work of sacrifice and intercession. Through Moses and subsequent men like him, God similarly gave a model of what it meant to be a prophet, an anointed vehicle of the Word of God. Through David, God presented his designated picture of the anointed king, to defend his people and to rule them rightly. Just as God had made a covenant with Abraham, Isaac, and Jacob, to bless them and to bless all peoples through them, and just as God had made a covenant with Israel through Moses at Sinai, giving them his law and undertaking to be their God and to take them as his people, so also God made a covenant with David, a promise that the kingship would never depart from his house. In these three anointed offices—prophet, priest, and king—the essential elements of redemption were addressed. Fallen men and women are ignorant, deceived, and unable to understand the things of God. They need truth that they can never work out on their own. They need a prophet. Fallen people are guilty and in need of atonement. They are alienated and separated from God, and they need intercession. They need a priest. Fallen human beings are defenseless prey to the world, the flesh, and the devil. They are unable to rule themselves, much less to rule the world over which God placed them as stewards. They need a king. Yet Moses, Aaron, and David were mere men. They only imperfectly mirrored what God intended in each of their offices, and they all died. The law continued to reflect back to God's people their own inability to live holy lives consistent with the character of God. Through the anointed prophet, the anointed priest, and the anointed king of the Old Testament, God pointed forward to the perfect Anointed One (*Messiah* in Hebrew) who would be the ultimate prophet, priest, and King, while his law made it ever clearer to people just how desperately they needed such a Redeemer.

Through all of this, even with his focus on one nation, God continued to make it clear that his redemptive purposes were global. The Old Testament is full of references to God's heart for the nations. The Psalms declare that God has blessed his people in order that all nations might know him and worship him (Ps. 67), and the psalmist challenges his listeners to proclaim God's glory and deeds to all nations (Ps. 96). Isaiah, speaking of the Servant of the Lord, says, "I will make you as a light for the nations, that my salvation may reach to the end of the earth" (Isa. 49:6). The entire book of Jonah demonstrates God's compassion on nations outside of Israel and decries the parochial, self-absorbed racism of the people of Israel. God used Old Testament history to set the context for redemption by making clear the truth about who he is, who we are, what he requires of us, and what it will take to redeem us from our fatal predicament. He also used that time not only to prepare people to receive the good news of redemption, but also to prepare a people who could take that good news to the ends of the earth. God has always had all peoples—nothing less—as the intended recipients of his redemptive mission.

The history of Old Testament Israel makes for sad reading. Even with all the advantages of the law and the ordinances of God, the people of Israel kept rebelling against him and provoking him to judgment. Eventually, judgment came down hard on Israel, first through the Assyrians against the northern kingdom, and then through the Babylonians against Judah. Although a remnant returned to the land, the people of Israel were scattered and they never regained their former glory. However, God used even this national calamity to advance his redemptive mission in the world. The Jews learned a critical lesson, and after the Babylonian captivity they never again fell prey to the kind of unfaithfulness that characterized them before Jerusalem fell. They also carried the knowledge of the true God with them everywhere they went. Because of the judgment that fell on Israel, Jews were scattered all over the ancient world. It is true that not many Gentiles were willing to go through the difficult and painful process of conversion to rabbinic Judaism. However, around the synagogues of the Jewish dispersion, groups of God-fearing Gentiles began to emerge—people who were attracted to the God of Israel and to the beauty of his law. This network of synagogues and God-fearers was the perfect launching pad for God's redemptive good news to go global.

THE CENTER OF GOD'S REDEMPTIVE MISSION: CHRIST

All of God's redemptive purposes found their culmination and fulfillment in Christ. The very word *Christ* is simply a Greek translation of the Hebrew

Messiah, which means Anointed One. Jesus was the reality to which all Old Testament religion, and the Old Testament anointed offices, pointed. As the Messiah, Jesus was the ultimate prophet. He indeed spoke the Word of God, but even more, he *was* and *is* the Word of God. Jesus was the perfect revelation of God, because, in his own words, "Whoever has seen me has seen the Father" (John 14:9). Jesus the Messiah was also the ultimate priest. Animal sacrifices could never really atone for human sin (Heb. 10:4). Old Testament priests were guilty sinners who had to offer sacrifices for themselves before they could offer sacrifices for anyone else. They all eventually died and some other priest had to take their place. Jesus was sinless and eternal. The sacrifice he offered was not a symbolic bull or goat, but the infinitely worthy sacrifice of himself. He was both the only real priest and the only effective sacrifice, to which the Levitical priesthood and the temple sacrificial system simply pointed as types and shadows. As Intercessor, he is at the right hand of the Father, and he ever lives to make intercession for his people. Jesus the Messiah was also the ultimate King. All authority in heaven and on earth has been given to him (Matt. 28:18). He has the power to overcome the world (John 16:33). His yoke is easy and his burden is light (Matt. 11:30). He is King of kings and Lord of lords (Rev. 19:16). He has overcome death, and he will reign forever. He has the legitimacy, the authority, and the power to rule all things from our personal lives to the entire universe, and he has the wisdom, the goodness, and the love to rule them all perfectly. Jesus completely meets all the needs of a fallen world. He is the uniquely perfect Redeemer.

In Jesus, God himself became a man in order to redeem his creation back to himself. Because God created the material world as intrinsically good, a good God could take on flesh without compromise of his infinite goodness, and because man himself was created in God's image, there was a basic compatibility between God and humanity that allowed God to express his character as a man. Indeed, Christ is called the second Adam—Adam as he should have been, and the founder of a new, redeemed human race (1 Cor. 15:45). In Christ, God in flesh, the image of God was perfectly displayed.

The heart of Christ's redeeming work was sacrificial substitution. First, in our place Christ lived the life we should have lived. Then, on the cross he died the death we deserved to die. As a real, flesh and blood human, he was qualified to take the place of humans. As a perfect man, he owed no debt for his own sins, and he qualified as the spotless sacrifice God requires. As God, his worth was infinite and more than sufficient to pay for sin. When Jesus died on the cross, he dealt with our guilt by bearing the punishment we deserved for our rebellion against God. He bore on himself the righteous wrath of God against our sin. All of Old Testament religion pointed to this one infinitely worthy sacrifice, and from this one infinitely worthy sacrifice flowed all of redemption.

In his resurrection the sacrifice of Jesus was vindicated and confirmed. In rising from the dead Jesus also slew death and became the firstfruits of the resurrection of his people. He anticipated and modeled the restoration that will come to the redeemed. When he ascended into heaven, he took up a ministry of intercession for his people, and he sent his Holy Spirit to apply his redeeming work to them. At the end of the age, the work of redemption will be brought to completion when Jesus returns, the dead are raised, all people are judged based on their relationship with Jesus Christ, the old heavens and earth pass away, and all things are made new.

TRINITARIAN REDEMPTION

The work of redemption was and is the work of all three persons of the Trinity. God the Father chose to save us and gave his Son to redeem us (John 6:37–39; 17:6; Eph. 1:3–11); God the Son accomplished our redemption through his perfect life, his atoning death, and his victorious resurrection (Isa. 53:5–6; Rom. 3:21–26; 4:25; 5:6–11); God the Holy Spirit now applies the redeeming work of Christ to our lives. He does this by making us alive in Christ (John 3:1–8), sealing us for the day of redemption (Eph. 1:13–14), baptizing us into the body of Christ (1 Cor. 12:13), putting sin to death in us (Rom. 8:13), creating the character of Christ in us (Gal. 5:22–23), and gifting and empowering us for service (1 Cor. 12:4–11). His work in our lives is both a promise and a foretaste of the restoration that will come to the adopted children of God.

THE DIMENSIONS OF REDEMPTION

The redeeming work of the triune God addresses every aspect of humanity's fallen condition. Through Jesus' propitiatory sacrifice on the cross, God can forgive sins and remain just at the same time (Rom. 3:26). With sin forgiven, the barrier between God and men is removed, so that we are reconciled with God. In fact, redeemed sinners not only cease to be his enemies, but God also adopts them as his children. In his life, death, and resurrection, Jesus the triumphant King delivered his people from the power of the world, their own flesh, and the devil. Based on the completed work of Christ, the Holy Spirit takes people who were dead in their trespasses and sins and makes them alive in Christ through the glorious work of regeneration. The Holy Spirit indwells the adopted children of God, progressively puts to death the misdeeds of the sinful nature, and remakes them in the image of Christ through the work of sanctification. The Holy Spirit also opens their minds to understand the things of God through the illumination of the Scriptures. Even the physical consequences of the fall are undone by the redeeming work of God. Although believers still experience sickness, pain, and death in this life, the promise of the gospel is not some amorphous disembodied eternal existence, but the resurrection of the body in an eternal state of glory like the resurrected body of Jesus.

The redeeming mission of God has had social consequences as well. One of the results of sin was alienation of people from one another, manifesting itself immediately in the marriage relationship between Adam and Eve and degenerating quickly to the point of murder between their first two sons. Christ has broken down the dividing walls of hostility that separated groups of people from one another (Eph. 2:14–16). He has taken estranged sinners and made them a family, uniting them to each other in his body even as he reconciles them to himself. The church is an intrinsic and essential component of the redeeming mission of God. It is a countercultural miracle that testifies to the wisdom of God in his work of redemption (Eph. 3:10), and it serves as an indispensable tool in the hands of the Holy Spirit as he grows believers into maturity in Christ (Eph. 4:1–16).

Finally, there is a cosmic dimension to the redeeming mission of God. Just as human redemption will culminate in the resurrection of the body, so also the climax of this present age will be new heavens and a new earth (2 Pet. 3:13). Paul tells us that the created world groans under its present state of corruption, and that it too will one day be set free from its bondage to decay (Rom. 8:19–22). When the history of this present age is finally complete, every consequence of human rebellion will have been addressed and defeated.

THE APPLICATION OF REDEMPTION

The redeeming work of Christ is appropriated by sinful men and women only through repentance from sin and faith in Jesus Christ, which are themselves gifts of God through the work of the Holy Spirit (Acts 11:18, Eph. 2:8–9). God has ordained that repentance and faith should come in response to the proclamation of the Word of Christ (Rom. 10:17). The Holy Spirit uses the Word of God and the people of God to draw men and women to salvation in Christ. In this age, the triune God's redemptive mission is being carried out by the Holy Spirit through the church, as the church worships God, proclaims the gospel to the ends of the earth, and disciples believers. Each of these components of the work of the church is essential if the church is to fulfill its role in the redemptive mission of God.

We must first recognize that God himself must be the focus of our proclamation. He is primary, and his glory is the goal of all things. The mission of the church is to worship God and to summon others to join in worshipping him and giving him the glory due his name (Ps. 96). Evangelistic proclamation is itself a form of worship, as the content of the gospel message is the glory of God's character and the glory of his saving deeds. Evangelism is declaring his glory among the nations; it is proclaiming the excellencies of him who called us out of darkness into his marvelous light (Ps. 96:3, 1 Pet. 2:9). Second, the scope of the proclamation must be gobal . We have already seen in the Old Testament that God's redeeming intentions extended to every nation and family. The New Testament is no less expansive, and from the Great Commission in Matthew to the vision of the throne in Revelation, God's clear purpose is to redeem a people to himself from every tribe, tongue, people, and nation. Third, the summons of the proclamation must be a summons to discipleship. In the Great Commission, Jesus commands his followers to make disciples, not merely to ask for decisions. The mission of God has every consequence of sin in its sights. The proclamation of the people of God can aim at no less. Evangelistic decisions that do not result in a life of discipleship are not real gospel fruit. When discipleship does not ensue, it is legitimate to question whether rebirth has actually happened.

IMPLICATIONS AND APPLICATIONS

By his grace and for his glory, God is on a mission of redemption in this fallen world. The story of this mission is the theme of Scripture, with the person and work of Christ as its center point. Several implications and applications flow from God's redemptive mission.

The ultimate goal of the mission of God is the glory of God. Therefore, as the church participates in the mission of God, it must remain resolutely God-focused. The message it proclaims must be a message about the character and deeds of God and not be reduced to a mechanistic formula for escaping hell. All that it does must be done as a form of worship to God. The way in which the church goes about its mission must glorify God as much as the message itself. He must be the church's all-consuming passion.

The proximal goal of the mission of God is redemption. That must be the goal of the people of God as well. There are a lot of good things that churches and believers can do, but unless the church commits itself to the mission of redemption, it is doing little more than putting a bandage on cancer. The evils of the world flow from the sinfulness of the human heart. Only redemption addresses both the root and the symptoms of our problem.

Sin characterizes every human being and corrupts every aspect of human life. Sin has left people enslaved, uncomprehending, blind, and dead. No amount of human persuasiveness, cleverness, technique, or manipulation will bring a spiritually dead sinner to life. Only the Spirit of God, using the word of God, can save anyone. With Paul, we have every reason to renounce manipulative methods or to distort or dilute the message (2 Cor. 4:2). Understanding the severity of the problem helps to safeguard us from compromising the integrity of our methods. We are called to proclaim the unvarnished gospel and to live lives that commend it. The Holy Spirit saves sinners.

Christ is the heart of God's redemptive mission. His life, his death, his resurrection, his ascension to the right hand of his Father, and his return in glory are the basis for all the benefits that flow to God's people and the answer to all the tragic consequences of sin. For this reason, the church in its mission must major on Christ. The world dislikes the exclusivity of a Christ-centered message and pressures the church to soften its tone. However, there is absolutely no redemption apart from the full biblical Jesus. With courteous but firm boldness, the church must proclaim Christ in all the glory of his deity, his propitiatory death, his historical resurrection, and his physical return.

Chapter Five

THE COMMUNITY OF
MISSION: THE CHURCH

Jedidiah Coppenger

O ne of the great tragedies in evangelicalism has been the separation
of our ecclesiology from our missiology. It is difficult to talk about
the mission of God without people thinking we are talking about
missions for God. Of course, the difference between missions and mission is
significant. The former is an activity of the church, and the latter is the reason
we have a church. Missions are rooted in our ecclesiology, while our ecclesiology should be rooted in mission.

While the reasons for this separation are undoubtedly many, perhaps the
most significant reason is our neglect of the kingdom of God. Sure, evangelicals have not denounced the notion of kingdom per se; we have simply
deserted it, leaving it to be found on our prophecy charts or in our footnotes.
But the kingdom of God was no footnote in Jesus' ministry; it was his central
message. Long before he started building his church, he placed the church
within the overarching kingdom mission of God. In so doing, he provided the
conceptual resources needed for the church to reach the nations in all of their
diversity (Matt. 28:18–20).

In order for evangelicals to recover a missional ecclesiology, they must
grasp how the church fits into the overarching kingdom mission of God. This
chapter contends that God's kingdom mission is the storyline of Scripture,
and it is rooted in his nature. His kingdom is inaugurated in Christ's first
coming, although it awaits consummation in the new creation. The church
is composed of those who have repented of their sins and placed their faith
in Christ. Yet, in the "already" of the kingdom, Christ rules his subject in
kingdom outposts, where baptized believers regularly assemble and faithfully

infiltrate in a particular culture. Every aspect is to be understood in light of God's kingdom mission for his glory among the nations.

THE NATURE OF GOD AND THE MISSION OF GOD

Before we address the mission of God, we need to examine the nature of God. Darrell Guder rightly observes, "The theology of the *missio Dei* is making clear that our ecclesiology, if it is truly to be a doctrine for the church that is continuing the apostolic witness, must be rooted in God's nature, purpose and action."[1] Without a proper understanding of God's trinitarian nature, our *missio Dei* formulations lack the foundation needed to actually join the mission.[2] Thus, God's nature reveals both the goal and pattern of the mission of God.

The church has long believed in a trinitarian God: The Father, Son, and Holy Spirit are three persons, although, as one God, they have one essence and one name (Matt. 28:18). God's eternal existence, then, has been in community. Community is fundamental to the mission of God because it is fundamental to God. As it were, God is God-the-community. Since God's nature is communitarian, we cannot understand his mission without seeing it as a divine community effort.

But what was the community of God like when all that existed was God-the-community? While the Scriptures do not give us a comprehensive or detailed picture of the immanent trinitarian life, we do know that God was a place of joy, love, and glory (Ps. 16:11). God-the-community existed eternally for the glory of God (John 17:5). God has always been central to God; otherwise he would be an idolater and cease to be God (Exod. 20:3).[3]

A cursory reading of Scripture shows us God's continued commitment to his glory. God tells us that he created us for his glory (Is. 43:6–7), predestined and adopted us for his glory (Eph. 1:5–6), sent Jesus to die on the cross for his glory (John 12:27–28; 17:1), calls his followers to do good deeds for his glory (Matt. 5:16), sends his Spirit to bring himself glory (John 16:14), plans on filling the earth with his glory (Hab. 2:14), designs everything to bring himself glory (Rom. 11:36), and will ultimately fill the earth with his glory (Rev. 21:23). Christopher Wright accurately observes that "there is one God

---

[1]　Darrell Guder, "The Church as Missional Community," *The Community of the Word: Toward an Evangelical Ecclesiology*, ed. Mark Husbands and Daniel Treier (Downers Grove: InterVarsity, 2005), 125.

[2]　David Bosch identifies the modern emphasis and formulation of the mission of God coming out of the nature of God as starting at the Willingen Conference of the IMC in 1952. He writes, "It was here that the idea (not the exact term) *missio Dei* first surfaced clearly. Mission was understood as being derived from the very nature of God. It was thus put in the context of the doctrine of the Trinity, not of ecclesiology or soteriology. The classical doctrine on the *missio Dei* as God the Father sending the Son, and God the Father and the Son sending the Spirit was expanded to include yet another 'movement': Father, Son, and Holy Spirit sending the church into the world." David Bosch, *Transforming Mission: Paradigm Shifts in Theology of Mission* (Maryknoll: Orbis, 1991), 390.

[3]　For a succinct articulation of this view, see John Piper, *Let the Nations Be Glad: The Supremacy of God in Missions* (Grand Rapids: Baker, 2003), 20–28.

at work in the universe and in human history, and that this God has a goal, a purpose, a mission that will ultimately be accomplished by the power of God's Word and *for the glory of God's name*. This is the mission of the biblical God."[4] Guder concurs: "The purpose of God's mission is ultimately the acknowledgement and enjoyment of the glory of God."[5]

The church as the community of God has to see its existence within the mission of God-the-community. As Lesslie Newbigin writes, "The mission of the Church is to be understood, can only be rightly understood, in terms of the trinitarian model."[6] When this is done, we understand that "the church's mission began as the radioactive fallout from an explosion of joy. When it is true to its nature, it is so to the end. Mission is an acted out doxology. That is its deepest secret. Its purpose is that God may be glorified."[7] The mission of God–the-community for his glory, then, provides the pattern and goal of the church's mission.

THE MISSION OF GOD AND THE KINGDOM OF GOD

By placing the mission of God within the nature of God, we are able to see the reason behind God's formation of the community of mission. An evangelical ecclesiology nimble enough to make its way off the beaten path and into the countless nameless villages throughout our globe, will need to position itself within the overarching mission of God. And when the church sees itself as a part of the *missio Dei*, it sees itself as a part of God's kingdom—because God's kingdom is the means by which God pursues his glory on earth. Therefore, an evangelical, missional ecclesiology must be a kingdom ecclesiology.

God's kingdom purposes are most fully seen in Christ. Indeed, the New Testament teaches us that Jesus' ministry has to be understood in light of the kingdom of God. The angel told Mary that Jesus would "reign over the house of Jacob forever, and His kingdom will have no end" (Luke 1:33). Jesus began his ministry by proclaiming the kingdom of God (Matt. 4:23). He went from town to town, village to village, synagogue to synagogue, preaching the gospel of the kingdom (Matt. 9:35). He told parables of the kingdom (Matthew 13; 20). He performed miracles that pointed to the presence of the

---

[4]   Christopher Wright, *Mission of God: Unlocking the Bible's Grand Narrative* (Downers Grove: InterVarsity, 2006), 64, emphasis added. Echoing this, Treier and Lauber write, "The love of God lived out and expressed in the context of the eternal community of love gives rise to the missional character of God, who seeks to extend the love shared by Father, Son and Holy Spirit into the created order." Daniel J. Treier and David Lauber, eds., "God Is Love: The Social Trinity and the Mission of God," in *Trinitarian Theology for the Church: Scripture, Community, Worship* (Downers Grove: InterVarsity, 2009), 119.

[5]   Darrell Guder, "The Church as Missional Community," 128.

[6]   Lesslie Newbigin, *The Gospel in a Pluralistic Society* (Grand Rapids: Eerdmans, 1989), 118.

[7]   Ibid., 127.

kingdom (Matt. 12:28). Jesus was consumed with the kingdom of God. The central motif of Jesus' ministry was the kingdom of God.[8]

Yet, long before Jesus' stepped onto the earth with the gospel of the kingdom, God's intentions for a kingdom had been made clear. Although the "kingdom of God" phraseology is not present in the Old Testament as it is in Jesus' ministry, the kingdom is present. The kingdom of God is, simply put, God's rule of God's people in God's place.[9] God's mission from creation to fall, redemption, and restoration is to be glorified through a people in a place under his righteous rule. Before we can see the place of the church in the overarching kingdom mission of God, we need to quickly trace its four major plot movements.

Kingdom in creation. The creation of the world was the creation of a kingdom. Here, we see God's people, Adam and Eve, in God's place, the garden of Eden, under God's rule. God's kingdom is created and ruled by his word. Adam and Eve would glorify God as they obeyed his word in their rejection of the fruit of tree of the knowledge of good and evil, and in their expansion and dominion over all of the earth (Gen. 1:28; 2:17). Greg Beale rightly observes, "Adam was to widen the boundaries of the Garden in ever increasing circles by extending the order of the garden sanctuary into the inhospitable outer spaces. The outward expansion would include the goal of spreading the glorious presence of God."[10] Interestingly, there is a point where God does not have a people, but only has a person, namely Adam, to carry out his mission. After God proclaims the goodness of his creation repeatedly, he declares that the singularity of humanity is not good (Gen. 2:18). God desires a unified people, not just individuals, to worship him and join him in his kingdom mission. Beale observes, "God's ultimate goal in creation was to magnify his glory throughout the earth by means of his faithful image-bearers inhabiting the world in obedience to the divine mandate."[11]

Kingdom in the fall. Almost as quickly as the kingdom is spoken into existence, the biblical narrative shows us that it falls apart. Every aspect of the kingdom splinters. God's kingdom mission seems in jeopardy. Instead of submitting to God's word, the people of God submitted to the serpent. Rather than rule over the serpent as God had intended, Adam and Eve were deceived by the serpent and became his subjects (Gen. 1:26). God's unified people rejected God's righteous rule, which led to their removal from God's place

---

[8]   Hans Kung rightly notes, "The 'reign of God' to which Jesus refers does not mean the constant universal reign of God, which is a consequence of the creation and which Jesus in his message takes for granted on the basis of the Old Testament. It means the eschatological, that is the fully realized, *final and absolute reign of God at the end of time, which as an event is now 'at hand'* (Mk. 1:15): it has 'come upon you' (Mt. 12:28; Lk. 11:20), it will 'come' (Lk. 22:18; cf. Mk. 14:25, Mt. 26:29), 'come with power' (Mk. 9:1)." Hans Kung, *The Church* (New York: Sheed and Ward, 1967), 47–48.

[9]   Graeme Goldsworthy, *According to Plan: The Unfolding Revelation of God in the Bible* (Downers Grove: InterVarsity, 1991), 95, 99; and Vaughan Roberts, *God's Big Picture: Tracing the Storyline of the Bible* (Downers Grove: InterVarsity, 2002), 2.

[10]   Greg Beale, *The Temple and the Church's Mission: A Biblical Theology of the Dwelling Place of God* (Downers Grove: InterVarsity, 2004), 85.

[11]   Ibid., 82.

(Gen. 3:23). The community was no longer on mission with God, and their community disintegrated. Humanity's relationships to God, to one another, and to the earth were all fractured. Instead of Adam and Eve's extending God's righteous rule throughout the earth, the ground was cursed (Gen. 3:17). Instead of a relationship characterized by perfect unity and diversity, Adam and Eve's relationship was contaminated by sin (Gen. 3:16). Instead of enjoying eternal life, Adam and Eve would die (Gen. 3:19). The kingdom of life had become a kingdom of death at the fall, but the story did not end here.

Kingdom redemption. The story of redemption must be understood as the recovery of God's kingdom. Starting with Genesis 3:15, where God promised a son who would defeat the serpent, the Old Testament is the story of God's kingdom mission. God-the-community uses his word to redeem and rule a people so that he can bring them into his place. Yet, like Adam and Eve, a faithful community was not found—that is, until Christ came. Jesus ushered in the kingdom of God in his person, reversing the effects of sin and the curse. Although Adam and Eve and Israel rejected God's rule while in a land of plenty, Jesus was obedient in the wilderness (Matt. 4:4). Even though Adam and Eve and Israel disobeyed the word of God and were exiled from God's presence, Jesus' obedience to God's word led him into exile so that others could come back into God's presence (Heb. 13:12). Jesus won salvation for a people with his obedience and sacrifice, just as he won salvation for the cosmos by taking on its curse, signified by the crown of thorns that the cursed ground brought forth (Matt. 27:29; cf. Gen. 3:18).

The kingdom of God, then, is established in the person of Christ. He is the obedient people of God and he is the place where God's rule is present. Lesslie Newbigin rightly observes, "The whole point of the gospel is that the kingdom of God has drawn near, but it is quite different from what people, especially religious people, expected. It is Jesus, this man going his humble way from a stable in Bethlehem to a cross on Calvary, who is the presence of the kingdom. The reign of God is therefore no longer something about which we are free to develop our own ideas. It is no longer a doctrine or a programme which we are free to shape as we will. The kingdom of God, his kingly rule, now has a human face and a human name—the name and the face of Jesus from Nazareth."[12] God's kingdom redemption is brought about through the life, death, and resurrection of Christ. Therefore, "Any theology of mission that claims to be biblical must have at its core that which is at the very core of biblical faith—the cross of Christ."[13]

Kingdom restoration. Jesus inaugurated the kingdom of God with his first coming, but the kingdom awaits consummation. Indeed, Jesus "shed his blood to rescue the creation from the curse of sin. And the cleansing blood of Christ must reach not only into the hearts and lives of individuals, but

---

[12] Lesslie Newbigin, *Mission in Christ's Way* (Geneva: WCC Publications, 1987), 6–7.
[13] Wright, *The Mission of God,* 312.

into every corner of the creation which the curse has affected."[14] Yet, when Jesus ascended into the presence of the Father, Caesar still sat on his throne. The nations still rejected God's rule. The earth still groaned (Romans 8). And as Jesus' followers stared at the kingdom in the person of Jesus right before their eyes, he taught them to pray, "Your kingdom come" (Matt. 6:10). Jesus described his future kingdom as an end-time feast (Matt. 8:11–12) and a place where judgment will take place (Matt. 25:31–46). Thus, there is a future aspect to the kingdom. The consummation of the kingdom, which will take place at the second coming of Christ, will involve the renewal of the created order (Rev. 21:1–2). God will finally and fully have a people, since "God's dwelling is with humanity, and He will live with them. They will be His people, and God Himself will be with them and be their God" (Rev. 21:3). God will remove every threat to his glory in his kingdom, like the devil, sin, and death (Rev. 20–21). God's kingdom will be a place of joy, since God "will wipe away every tear from their eyes. Death will no longer exist; grief, crying, and pain will exist no longer" (Rev. 21:4). The consummated kingdom of God will be a place of sin-free culture and dominion, as we enjoy the glory of the nations and reign with God (Rev. 21:24; 5:10). God's kingdom mission is achieved. The work of Christ on the cross accomplishes all that it set out to do. This is where the storyline of Scripture ends, but life truly begins.

AN OUTPOST OF THE KINGDOM: THE CHURCH

Since the *missio Dei* aims for God's glory through Christ's kingdom, our missional ecclesiology must be a kingdom ecclesiology. While some might think ecclesiological considerations to be a hindrance to the mission of God, we would do well to listen to Stackhouse: "When we, the church, are confused about who we are and whose we are, we can become anything and anyone's."[15] This means that we must articulate the church's relationship to the kingdom and recast the nature and purpose of the church in light of the kingdom of Christ.[16] Jesus is building his church between the inauguration and consummation of his kingdom. He does this as the church serves as witnesses to the reality of the gospel of the kingdom in the power of the Spirit praying for the fullness of the kingdom to come (Matt. 6). Ladd notes, "The Kingdom is God's reign and the realm in which the blessings of his reign are experienced; the church is the fellowship of those who have experienced God's reign and entered into the enjoyment of its blessings. The Kingdom creates the church,

---

[14] Richard Mouw, *When the Kings Come Marching In: Isaiah and the New Testament* (Grand Rapids: Eerdmans, 2002), 110.

[15] John G. Stackhouse Jr., "Preface," in *Evangelical Ecclesiology: Reality or Illusion*, ed. John G. Stackhouse Jr. (Grand Rapids: Baker, 2003), 9.

[16] Although we could discuss the images the New Testament uses for the church or the way that churches should plant new churches (Acts 13:1–3), the limitations of space require us to overlook such important topics.

works through the church, and is proclaimed in the world by the church. There can be no Kingdom without a church—those who have acknowledged God's rule—and there can be no church without God's Kingdom; but they remain two distinguishable concepts: the rule of God and the fellowship of men and women."[17] Therefore, we see that the church is an outpost of the kingdom and not the kingdom himself. As communities of the kingdom, local churches consist of those who have responded in faith to the gospel of the king and have passed through the baptismal waters to join an accountable community that worships the king in regular assembly and in faithful cultural engagement for the glory of God.

THE KING'S ASSEMBLY

What should a church do, regardless of its location around the world? As an outpost of the kingdom, the place where Christ's kingly rule is visible, church joins God's kingly mission for the glory of God among the nations. While some have reduced the life of the church to its assembly and others have denigrated the assembly for the sake of cultural infiltration, a kingdom ecclesiology recognizes that the King calls his church both to gather and scatter for the glory of God. God's kingdom mission calls people from every nation into local kingdom outposts that assemble around his Word. The word *ekklesia* supports the importance of gathering, since it means "assembly." The apostle Paul assumes as much, stating, "Whenever you come together . . ." (1 Cor. 14:26). The writer of Hebrews states that Christians should not forsake the church's "worship meetings, as some habitually do . . ." (Heb. 10:25). It was the practice of New Testament churches to meet on the first day of the week to commemorate the resurrection of King Jesus, praying that Christ's kingdom would come (Acts 20:7; John 20:1; Matt. 6:10). These local assemblies joined the heavenly assembly of the firstborn with myriads of angels in festive gathering (Heb. 12:22–23). And they are a foreshadowing of the future assembly of the King that worships him from every tribe, tongue, people, and land (Rev. 4–5). Therefore, we should start local churches where believers assemble regularly to hear God's Word, baptize, enjoy the Lord's Supper, and hold one another accountable.

The King's gospel. At the heart of this gathering is the glorious gospel of the kingdom. The gospel is the good news that King Jesus paid the penalty for our sin and destroyed the power of our sin by absorbing God's wrath in our place on the cross (1 Cor. 2:2; 15:3–5). Or, in short, Christ has died for our sins. Jesus lived the obedient life we have all failed to live, died the death we all justly deserve, and was raised from the dead, providing a way for the forgiveness of sins and reconciliation with God. All those who turn from their sins and place their faith in Christ as their Savior and Lord will receive

---

[17] George Eldon Ladd, *A Theology of the New Testament*, rev. ed. (Grand Rapids: Eerdmans, 1993), 117.

the benefits of Christ's work (Phil. 3:9; Rom. 3:22). This good news is at the heart of the kingdom of community

The gospel is at the heart of the church's gathering because it was at the center of Jesus' ministry. Matthew writes, "Jesus was going all over Galilee, teaching in their synagogues, preaching the good news of the kingdom, and healing every disease and sickness among the people" (Matt. 4:23). After Pentecost, the Apostles' preaching was characterized by the gospel of the kingdom of Christ, since they proclaimed the one whom God has made "both Lord and Messiah" (Acts 2:36). Also, for the last two years of the apostle Paul's life, "he welcomed all who visited him, proclaiming the kingdom of God and teaching the things concerning the Lord Jesus Christ with full boldness and without hindrance" (Acts 28:30–31). The proclamation of the kingdom of God was central to the early church as it expanded throughout the nations.[18] In fact, their preaching caused riots and prompted opposition by the Jewish leaders, since they were "all acting contrary to Caesar's decrees, saying that there is another king—Jesus!" (Acts 17:7).

The proclamation of the gospel is the proclamation of God's Word. By his Word, God creates, sustains, rebukes, and trains his people in righteousness (2 Tim. 3:16). Indeed, he builds the church by strengthening or creating faith, since "faith comes from what is heard, and what is heard comes through the message about Christ" (Rom. 10:17). The apostle Paul directs Timothy to give himself to the public reading, exhortation, and teaching of the Word (1 Tim. 4:13). He also passionately exhorts him to "proclaim the message; persist in it whether convenient or not; rebuke, correct, and encourage with great patience and teaching" (2 Tim. 4:2). Timothy is to do this for the sake of the kingdom (2 Tim. 4:1). As Ligon Duncan writes, we are to "[r]ead the Bible, preach the Bible, pray the Bible, sing the Bible and see the Bible."[19] And it is necessary for every proclamation of the gospel to make sense within a particular culture, which is a serious challenge. Lesslie Newbigin observes, "Everyone with the experience of cross-cultural mission knows that there are always two opposite dangers, the Scylla and Charybdis, between which one must steer. On the one side there is the danger that one finds no point of contact for the message as the missionary preaches it, to the people of the local culture the message appears irrelevant and meaningless. On the other side is the danger that the point of contact determines entirely the way that the message is received, and the result is syncretism. Every missionary path has to find the way between these two dangers: irrelevance and syncretism. And if one is more afraid of one danger than the other, one will certainly fall into the opposite."[20] God's Word and God's gospel, therefore, are at the center of the community's gathering.

---

[18]   The proclamation of the kingdom always included the proclamation of the cross of Christ, which is why the apostle Paul's teaching could be summarized both as kingdom and cross proclamation (Acts 20:25; 1 Cor. 2:2).

[19]   J. Ligon Duncan, "Foundations for Biblically Directed Worship," in *Give Praise to God: A Vision for Reforming Worship*, ed. P. G. Ryken, D. W. H. Thomas, and J. L. Duncan III (Phillipsburg: P & R, 2003), 65.

[20]   Lesslie Newbigin, *A Word in Season* (Grand Rapids: Eerdmans, 1994), 67.

The King's baptism. We enter the kingdom assembly through baptism. Baptism, which means "immersion," is made a priority of the kingdom mission of the church by the king (Matt. 28:18–20). Following the New Testament teaching and pattern, all believers, and only believers, are to pass through the waters of God's judgment into God's kingdom, Jesus was baptized by John the Baptist before he began proclaiming the good news of the kingdom (Matt. 3:15–16). At the church's creation in Pentecost, the 3,000 believers who were added all passed through the baptismal waters (Acts 2:41). The apostle Paul tells the early church that there is "one baptism" (Eph. 4:5). In the Old Testament, God's people passed through the waters of God's judgment on their way to new life. Noah and his family came through the flood waters, leaving behind the old world and stepping onto a new creation (Gen. 8; 2 Pet. 3:6). Moses led the people of God through the waters of the Red Sea. The apostle Paul writes that Israel was "baptized into Moses in the cloud and in the sea" (1 Cor. 10:2). Baptism has consistently been a means by which the people of God enter the place of God. Just as Jesus identifies the baptism of all baptisms, believers are to be baptized into his death and resurrection, since he is our life (Col. 3:4). Therefore, the apostle Paul writes, "we were buried with Him by baptism into death, in order that, just as Christ was raised from the dead by the glory of the Father, so we too may walk in a new way of life" (Rom. 6:4). "Baptism," writes Russell Moore, "is a matter of inaugurated eschatology, considered by Paul as a sign, not only of union with Christ in the present, but also of resurrection in Him in the eschaton (Rom. 6:1–11)."[21] Since it is the King's assembly, we should follow the King's instructions and make baptism a part of our assemblies.

The King's feast. God's people have always been a feasting people. God's feasts are a sign of God's blessing and presence. From the fruit-filled garden of Eden, to the land flowing with milk and honey, God has always laid a feast before his people. Of course, after God's kingdom fell in the garden of Eden, God's feast contained symbols of kingdom redemption. At the heart of Israel's redemption from the Egyptians was the Passover meal. Here, the meal points the people of God to the means by which God is redeeming them (Exod. 12:1–28). Similarly, the Lord's Supper points the church's attention towards its salvation, which is found in the life, death, and resurrection of Christ. Therefore, the Lord's Supper points our attention backwards to the inauguration of the kingdom through the King's sacrifice. As we partake of his body and blood, we are declaring that Jesus' sacrifice and life are ours (John 6:54–56). We signify that Jesus' life is our life, since his life is symbolized in the blood (Lev. 17:14).

The Lord's Supper points our attention backwards to Christ's sacrifice, but it also directs our attention toward a future kingdom feast (Rev. 19:6-10). Indeed, Jesus focuses his followers' attention on this future feast, since he tells them that he will not eat or drink the fruit of the vine "until the kingdom of God comes" (Luke 22:16,18). In the meantime, as we look forward to

---

[21] Russell Moore, *The Kingdom of Christ: The New Evangelical Perspective* (Wheaton: Crossway, 2004), 163.

sitting around the feasting table with our crucified and risen King in his consummated kingdom, we are to feast in the presence of our enemies, enemies not made of flesh and blood (Ps. 23:5; Eph. 6:12). It is a key part of the kingdom assembly, since it is a means of proclaiming "the Lord's death until He comes" (1 Cor. 11:26). The Lord's Supper, therefore, takes place in the assembly of the people of God both as a reminder of Christ's sacrifice on the community's behalf and as a reminder of Christ's future kingdom banquet.

King's subjects. God's kingdom people have always been discernible. They are those who are under God's rule. In the garden of Eden, Adam and Eve constituted God's people, since they were under God's rule. Out of all of the nations, Israel was placed under God's rule. And as we move to the New Testament, we see Christ assembling a people who have submitted to his reign in their lives. Once God's image-bearers repent of their sins and identify with Christ, they place themselves under his righteous rule. They are effectively the King's subjects. Each kingdom outpost, then, is to be composed of those who have submitted and are submitting to Christ's kingship.

This means that each local assembly of the King will identify those who are and are not a part of their gathering. While the manner of this identification might be in some way unique depending upon historical and cultural context, God's church always identifies the members of a local assembly. After all, the Scriptures indicate that someone was keeping track of who and who was not joining the church at Jerusalem, since they added 3,000 people to their small group of 120 (Acts 1:15; 2:41). The church at Corinth did this, since they had to know when they were assembled and when they were not (1 Cor. 5:4). Tracking the membership of the King's subjects, or church membership, in a particular place at a particular time can be achieved without becoming intoxicated with numbers like much of the Western evangelical church. Each number represents a person over whom heaven rejoices (Luke 15:7).

The church is charged with the task of discerning who is a part of the kingdom and who is not. That is, the church has been given the responsibility to discern whether a professed follower of the King is genuinely converted.[22] The church at Corinth was not supposed to judge those outside of their assembly, since God judges them (1 Cor. 5:13). Instead, they were to judge those in their assembly, putting "away the evil person from among yourselves" (1 Cor. 5:12–13). This is what it means for the church to have the "keys of the kingdom of heaven" (Matt. 16:19). The binding and loosing that are executed by the church are focused on discerning the subjects of the King. After all, Jesus employs the same language of binding and loosing only a few chapters later in reference to the removal of a member from their midst (Matt. 18:15–18). Of course, our assemblies can and should welcome unbelievers

---

[22] Russell Moore convincingly states, "If inaugurated Kingdom blessings are received by those who 'see the Kingdom of God' through the new birth (John 3:3), then it would seem that the church, as an initial manifestation of the Kingdom, must reflect in its membership those who have experienced this new birth and are participants in the Kingdom blessings of the new covenant" (Moore, *The Kingdom of Christ*, 162).

into their assembly. But the kingdom outpost should not include people who claim to be believers but live godlessly (1 Cor. 5:11). With our church membership, we are saying to the world, repentant sinners who have turned from their sin to identify with Christ will inherit the kingdom of God. And by excluding false professors of Christ, we are saying with the apostle Paul, "No sexually immoral people, idolaters, adulterers, or any kind of homosexual no thieves, greedy people, drunkards, verbally abusive people, or swindlers will inherit God's kingdom" (1 Cor. 6:9–10). But without corrective discipline, the church communicates the exact opposite. Therefore, it is imperative that each kingdom outpost takes the discerning of the King's subjects seriously for the sake of the kingdom and the good of the person (1 Cor. 5:5).

The King's leaders. Leadership has always been critical to God's kingdom mission, since God's kingdom is designed like God's nature. That is, within the Godhead there is equality between all three persons of the Trinity, yet distinction between each of their roles. The Father sends the Son. The Son does not send the Father. The Spirit is sent by the Father and the Son, and not vice versa. The Son does everything the Father tells him, not the other way around. There is distinction, then, in each person's role in God-the-community, and it does not come at the expense of equality.[23] Each person of God-the-community is equal in essence, even as each plays a diverse role in kingdom mission.

So it is in the kingdom of God. In the beginning, God created Adam and Eve equally in his image and likeness (Gen. 1:27). Yet, their equality was not monolithic; Adam and Eve had distinct roles in the kingdom. Eve was to help Adam as he led. This is seen in the way that God created Adam before Eve, in Adam's naming of Eve, and in the way that God held Adam accountable for the failed kingdom project (Gen. 2–3).[24] In the wisdom of God, then, God's kingdom was designed to advance through a community that was equal yet diverse. And this pattern is seen in the kingdom of God in Israel. While both men and women are still made in God's image, God calls qualified men to lead his people. The consistent practice in the kingdom of God is to have men as the kings, prophets, and priests. Without denigrating women, the Old Testament outlines a clear structure for leadership in the kingdom of God.

In light of the Old Testament background, we should not be surprised to find similar leadership structures in Christ's kingdom outpost. The church is led primarily by pastors and served through qualified deacons. Even in the church's early stages, the New Testament shows a great concern with identifying the proper leadership. The New Testament very clearly identifies several characteristics of elders. They are to be men who are "above reproach, the husband of one wife, self-controlled, sensible, respectable, hospitable,

---

[23] For a helpful and succinct treatment of this, see Bruce Ware, *Father, Son, and Holy Spirit: Relationships, Roles, and Relevance* (Wheaton: Crossway, 2005).

[24] For a substantive and extensive articulation of this view, see Wayne Grudem and John Piper, eds., *Recovering Biblical Manhood and Womanhood: A Response to Evangelical Feminism* (Wheaton: Crossway, 1991).

an able teacher, not addicted to wine, not a bully but gentle, not quarrelsome, not greedy—one who manages his own household competently, having his children under control with all dignity. . . . He must not be a new convert. . . . He must have a good reputation among outsiders" (1 Tim. 3:2–4,6–7; cf. Titus 1:7–9). Deacons are to be characterized by all of these qualities, except they do not have to be able to teach (1 Tim. 3:8–13).

Leadership issues are not unimportant in God's kingdom mission. After all, God has designed his kingdom to advance as qualified men train "the saints in the work of ministry, to build up the body of Christ, until we all reach unity in the faith and in the knowledge of God's Son, growing into a mature man with a stature measured by Christ's fullness" (Eph. 4:12–13). This is why early on in the life of the church, the apostles divided responsibilities between those who ministered the Word through teaching and prayer and those who focused more on deeds (Acts 6:2–4). Rather than performing most of the ministry, as in the Western church, the church's leadership is to equip the saints for their ministry. When effective leadership like this is executed, a church flourishes, since "then we will no longer be little children, tossed by the waves and blown around by every wind of teaching, by human cunning with cleverness in the techniques of deceit" (Eph. 4:14). The leadership of the kingdom outpost is critical. These leaders need to be qualified, so that they do not "fall into disgrace and the Devil's trap" (1 Tim. 3:7). Indeed, as Michael Goheen puts it, "as the leadership and structures of the church are directed toward nurturing the new life of Christ, the church can be a missional body in the midst of the world."[25] The King has designed his kingdom outposts, therefore, to follow qualified male leadership for the glory of God.

THE KING'S REPRESENTATIVE

As outposts of the kingdom of Christ, local churches gather intentionally for the glory of Christ. But we cannot reduce the life of the kingdom to the gathering of church. The King's people must also understand that kingdom life can flourish as they are scattered throughout our villages, towns, and cities. As the church lives life in its respective communities, it needs to focus on being a people who witness to the kingdom in word and deed. Grenz rightly argues, "the church is the 'eschatological company,' the body of those who bear testimony by word and deed to the divine reign, which Christ will consummate at his return and hence will be present throughout the cosmos."[26] Thus, the kingdom outpost gathers for worship of their King and instructions on how to live for his glory in their culture.

Kingdom words. God's kingdom people infiltrate their respective cultures with God's Word. As they live life, they are to use God's Word for believers and unbelievers. Among believers, God's Word is an instrument of edification.

---

[25] Michael Goheen, *A Light to the Nations: The Missional Church and the Biblical Story* (Grand Rapids: Baker, 2011), 198.

[26] Grenz, *Theology for the Community of God*, 478.

One of the key ways that this takes place in the New Testament is through Spirit-filled fellowship. This is fellowship that is Word-saturated and -focused. Believers within a church are called to "build each other up," "live in harmony with each other," "spur one another on toward love and good deeds," "accept one another," and "teach and admonish one another." This command is radical in nature, and it is this aspect of its nature that is often missed by the Western church. The first-century church (as well as have many contemporary churches outside of the West) understood this command in its pointed power: God is calling people who fought against each other outside of the church to love one another and serve one another within the community of Christ. Sinclair Ferguson writes, "The whole of the Christian life then, with its deep roots in the love of the Father and its foundation in the grace of Christ, is characterized by what Paul calls the *koinonia* of the Holy Spirit (2 Cor. 13:14; Phil. 2:1).[27] "The church displays the firstfruits of the forgiven and forgiving people of God who are brought together across the rubble of dividing walls that have crumbled under the weight of the cross. It is the harbinger of the new humanity that lives in genuine community, a form of companionship and wholeness that humanity craves."[28] Therefore, as the kingdom community is scattered, they are to use God's Word to bring life to their fellow believers' lives.

The scattered community should also speak God's Word into a lost world. It is true that as kingdom people, the church joins God's kingdom mission to renew all things. The necessary way in which the church joins God in his kingdom renewal is by sharing the gospel. We share the gospel of the kingdom because it is through this gospel witness that the nations will come to faith in Christ. And when the nations come to faith in Christ, God will renew the creation completely. The apostle Paul writes, "For I consider that the sufferings of this present time are not worth comparing with the glory that is going to be revealed to us. For the creation eagerly waits with anticipation for God's sons to be revealed. For the creation was subjected to futility—not willingly, but because of Him who subjected it—in the hope that the creation itself will also be set free from the bondage of corruption into the glorious freedom of God's children. For we know that the whole creation has been groaning together with labor pains until now. And not only that, but we ourselves who have the Spirit as the firstfruits—we also groan within ourselves, eagerly waiting for adoption, the redemption of our bodies" (Rom. 8:18–23).

This glorious passage shows us a cursed creation that awaits its renewal. This renewal does not come about because of the church's work. Instead, it will be "revealed to us" by God, after all of God's sons have been revealed (Rom. 8:18–19). So God does indeed reconcile the creation to him, but it starts with men and women being reconciled to God in Christ (2 Cor. 5:18–21). Our role as ambassadors of reconciliation focuses on the delivery of the "message of reconciliation" (2 Cor. 5:19–20), which involves pleading

---

27 Sinclair Ferguson, *The Holy Spirit* (Downers Grove: InterVarsity, 1996), 175.
28 Darrell L. Guder, ed., *Missional Church: A Vision for the Sending of the Church in North America* (Grand Rapids: Eerdmans, 1998), 103.

"on Christ's behalf, "Be reconciled to God'" (2 Cor. 5:20). Mark Dever rightly notes, "The church's vertical purpose to worship God mandates its horizontal purpose: working to evangelize and edify those made in God's image. The church itself then is a means of grace, not because it grants salvation apart from faith but because it is the God-ordained means his Spirit uses to proclaim the saving gospel, to illustrate the gospel, and to confirm the gospel."[29] Therefore, the reconciliation of the cosmos is accomplished in the cross and advanced through its proclamation (2 Cor. 5:20; Col. 1:20).

Kingdom deeds. As kingdom people, the scattered church is also known by their deeds for believers and unbelievers. Outside of the assembly of the King, the church is called to live for the kingdom in their respective cultures. Members of the kingdom community will see their whole life as service to the King. As stated, they are a people who have the responsibility to communicate the gospel of the kingdom to their communities. But they must also show what kingdom life looks like. This means that they will take their work seriously in obedience to the apostle Paul's command, "Whatever you do, do it enthusiastically, as something done for the Lord and not for men" (Col. 3:23). God is glorified when his people do everything to his glory (1 Cor. 10:31), and this glorification includes even the seemingly mundane tasks in our human existence. After all, one of the most spiritual things Adam could do in the garden of Eden was to name animals and expand the garden (Gen. 2). God loves to see humanity work for his glory. And God will continue to delight in humanity's God-glorifying work as we reign and rule with Christ over a new creation throughout eternity (Matt. 25:29; Rev. 5:10; 22:5). And as kingdom people, the church will be known as a people of love, joy, peace, patience, kindness, goodness, and self-control (Gal. 5:22–23). We will be a people who are forgiving, since God has forgiven us in Christ (Eph. 4:32). The kingdom mission of the church includes training and equipping the kingdom people to live God-glorifying lives in their families, work, and every other aspect of life.

A major area of living as Christ's representatives in a culture is working for the good of the people in the culture. Scripture indicates that God's kingdom mission involves the loving actions of his kingdom people for the good of our fallen creation. When Adam and Eve sinned and discovered that they were shamed, God did not simply speak words to them, although he did do that. God also met a physical need, covering them with the animal skins (Gen. 3:21). God intervened through Joseph so that there would be food for the nations in the midst of a massive famine (Gen. 41–44). As Israel made its way through the wilderness and established the kingdom, God continually cared for their physical needs. And while it is true that we are to do good works especially for those in our kingdom outposts, we must also be willing to lovingly and sacrificially serve those outside the household of faith. After all, Jesus and the apostles came in both word and deed. And many of the recipients of their actions did not believe in Christ.

---

[29] Dever, "The Church," 812.

Of course the specific tasks will vary from place to place, but the New Testament is clear that Christ's followers should evidence love towards the world. Richard Bauckham rightfully notes, the apostle Paul's "missionary policy becoming all things to all people was weighted in the direction to the poor."[30] For example, Jesus' brother James chastised the church for failing to take care of the orphans and widows who surrounded them (James 1:27). He warns of a faith that is all talk and no action (James 2:14–26). It should be noted, however, that the church should seek wisdom and discernment in their efforts to meet physical needs. The New Testament shows places where it is inappropriate for a church to meet certain physical needs (1 Tim. 5:16). Certainly we should avoid equating water purification projects in the third-world to the sharing of the gospel; both are significant, but evangelism is the highest priority, as it was in Paul's ministry. But we also need to avoid acting as though verbal proclamation were the only important aspect of mission. After all, God's mission was understood broadly enough to include a concern for God-glorifying eating and drinking (1 Cor. 10:31). A holistic approach to life is critical for the church to be salt and light in the world (Matthew 5). While verbal proclamation is central to the mission, so are the nonverbal aspects of our obedience and witness. Discipleship is a seamless endeavor, encompassing the whole of our lives, the entirety of Jesus' teaching (Matt. 28:18–20). Indeed, the Jewish leaders who passed the hurting person could have said that providing a helping hand like the Good Samaritan was outside the scope of God's mission and, therefore, their mission. Love of neighbor should compel the church to worldwide and holistic mission. Therefore, "flowing from its communal life are words and deeds that point to Christ, the source of this new life. The missional church is an evangelizing church that speaks the good news pointing to Christ. It also enacts the good news with deeds of mercy and justice. In all this, the messianic community follows Jesus, who made known the good news of the kingdom in his own words and deeds."[31] God's kingdom people will be known, therefore, as a people whose loving deeds impact both believers and unbelievers.

CONCLUSION

If evangelicals are going to join the *missio Dei*, we will have to join a community of mission. Any articulation of the *missio Dei* that fails to include the community of mission fails to understand the mission. And any ecclesiological formulation that fails to place itself in the mission of God fails to understand the church.[32] God's mission includes the community of mission,

---

[30]   Richard Bauckham, *Bible and Mission: Christian Witness in a Postmodern World* (Grand Rapids: Baker, 2003), 53.
[31]   Goheen, *A Light to the Nations*, 198.
[32]   "Mission," writes David Bosch, "is thereby seen as a movement from God to the world; the church is viewed as an instrument for that mission. There is church because there is mission, not vice versa" (Bosch, *Transforming Mission*, 390).

since God's mission has eternally had a community of mission, Father, Son, and Spirit. God's trinitarian nature not only shows us the necessity of community for God's mission; it also shows us the goal of God's mission, which is his glory. God's sending is never ultimate; his glory is. By understanding the goal of God's mission as the glory of God, we will be in a place where we can see that our *missio Dei* formulations must say more than God is a missionary God. As we see the goal of God's mission, we learn our goal. We must be more than a "sent people"; we must be sent for God's glory in Christ. And we pursue his glory in community because God-the-community creates a community to join him in his community mission for his glory.

A missional ecclesiology also understands that the *missio Dei* is a kingdom mission. God is glorified by a people in a place who are under his righteous rule. This kingdom is both present and future. It was inaugurated by the life, death, and resurrection of Jesus the Christ. It is entered into by repentance and faith in Christ, making his life, death, and resurrection our life, death, and resurrection. Even though we enter into Christ's kingdom immediately by faith, we are still in the present evil age. While the world stays under the control of the enemy, Christ is creating more and more kingdom outposts; he is creating local churches. Although the kingdom is not the church, the proclamation of the gospel of the kingdom creates and sounds forth from the church. The church, as the community of mission, is the community of the kingdom mission. And as a community of kingdom mission, the church is necessarily a kingdom community.

The distinctive mark of these kingdom communities is that they have come under Christ's rule.[33] As such, these kingdom communities are kingdom outposts. Kingdom outposts distinguish themselves from one another by holding one another accountable to be on mission with Christ in both word and deed. Their community life is shaped by Christ's rule, which requires the gathering and scattering of each local church. A missional ecclesiology that neglects the King's clear commands for assembling regularly and engaging the culture as Christ's representatives for the glory of God does not advance the *missio Dei*; it dilutes it. The community of mission cannot show the reality of the presence of the kingdom by ignoring the King's words. The kingdom community must be a community that is built on the gospel of the King, and the deeds of the kingdom flow from it. As God renews all of creation, the church must prioritize the verbal communication of his gospel. Deeds done for both believers and unbelievers proceed from an experience of the love of God in Christ and the love of neighbor. This is how God-the-community has been and will continue to be glorified, as we continue to pray for the King to return (Matt. 6:10).

---

[33] Russell Moore accurately argues, "The 'already' of the kingdom then has everything to do with the church. The church is where Jesus rules now (Eph. 1:22–23)" (Russell Moore, "Personal and Cosmic Eschatology," in *A Theology for the Church*, ed. Daniel Akin [Nashville: B&H, 2007], 868).

Chapter Six

THE GOSPEL AND EVANGELISM

George Robinson

W e were made to worship and commune with our Creator. The primary effect of the fall is not the presence of sin, but rather the absence of authentic worship. Thus, the primary goal of the gospel is the transformation of wicked sinners into awestruck worshippers. Anything less is reflective of our reductionist approach to communicating an otherwise comprehensive gospel message. If the gospel is indeed the greatest story ever told, it must be retold in a robust and compelling manner that elicits authentic, biblical worship.

THE STORY OF A MISSIONARY GOD

Most good stories follow a coherent theme from beginning to end. Plots may shift and different characters may take the story in unexpected directions, but the theme must remain consistent if any sense is to be made of the story. This volume started with a theme—our God is on a redemptive and restorative mission that originated in his divine character. God, not man, is the primary character in the biblical story. And so God, not man, is also the primary storyteller by virtue of biblical inspiration. In John Stott's words, the Bible is the story of a missionary God.[1] Christopher Wright adds that the term "mission of God," or in Latin *missio Dei*, "originally meant the sending of God—in the sense of a Father sending of the Son . . . . All human mission . . . (therefore) is seen as participation in an extension of this

---

[1]   John R. W. Stott, "The Living God Is a Missionary God," *Perspectives on the World Christian Movement,* 3rd ed., Ralph D. Winter and Steven C. Hawthorne (Pasadena, CA: William Carey Library, 1999), 3.

divine sending.”[2] And this mission in its totality is good news because it does not leave the outcome up to chance or speculation. What God started and intended from the beginning, he has been working toward and will certainly accomplish in the *telos* (end). Andreas Köstenberger and P. T. O'Brien add, "God's saving plan for the whole world forms a grand frame around the entire story of Scripture."[3]

Each part of God's mission—creation, fall, redemption, restoration—is not only God's plan, but it is also his story. This chapter will be dedicated to the dual theme of the gospel as a comprehensive story and evangelism as the faithful, contextual retelling of that story. We will examine how the whole canonical grand narrative is in reality *gospel*, or good news. We will also focus on how this missionary God has commissioned us to become master storytellers through the art of evangelism.

An Altogether Unique Story

God chose to bring his gospel to the world in the form of an unfolding story, so why then have we reduced it into an outline of propositional statements? In *The Convergent Church*, Mark Liederbach and Alvin Reid assert that North America has become virtually biblically illiterate. In light of that fact, they warn that "our approach to communicating the timeless truths of Scripture must change as well."[4] Rick Richardson adds that the lost will be reached, "not first through logic and proposition and dogma . . . (but) through the renewal of the Story."[5] In a world where relativism is the norm, it is apropos that we have unchanging and exclusive truth to communicate in the form of a story. Lists of propositional truths may come across impersonal and be quickly dismissed. We must recognize that God has chosen to write us into his story, and part of our role is to learn how to faithfully retell that story to the changing world around us.

Though the grand narrative shares some commonalities in its structure with other stories, it is altogether unique with regard to meaning and implication. As you will see later in this book, many world religions have their own story to tell that attempts to define reality. Hinduism has the Vedas and Upanishads, which contain their own creation epics. Islam has the Qur'an. Most cultures have their own narratives that attempt to explain where the world came from and where it is headed. When we talk about the gospel as story, however, we must understand that the Bible is not merely the chief among equals in the world of literature. The gospel is not *just another* explanation of reality. Instead, it is *the story*

---

2   Christopher J. H. Wright, *The Mission of God: Unlocking the Bible's Grand Narrative* (Downers Grove: IVP Academic, 2006), 63.

3   Andreas Köstenberger and P. T. O'Brien, *Salvation to the Ends of the Earth: A Biblical Theology of Mission* (Downers Grove: IVP, 2001), 263.

4   Mark Liederbach and Alvin L. Reid, *The Convergent Church: Missional Worshipers in an Emerging Culture* (Grand Rapids: Kregel, 2009), 231.

5   Rick Richardson, *Reimagining Evangelism: Inviting Friends on a Spiritual Journey* (Downers Grove: IVP, 2006), 86.

by which all other stories are to be evaluated. Though other stories may contain elements of truth, the Bible alone is the infallible word of God and thereby sets itself up as the standard for all truth (2 Tim. 3:16–17).

Augustine claimed that all truth is God's truth, meaning that when we read literature or other narratives, they are true only insofar as they accord with the Bible.[6] Kallenberg notes, "In deeming the gospel truth, Augustine was not only allowing the story of God to make sense of his past, he was also allowing it to shape his future by joining its storyline."[7] Bryan Stone makes application of this to us all by adding, "To become a Christian is to join a story and to allow that story to begin to narrate our lives."[8] Thus, evangelism must be characterized by more than a mental assent to abstract propositions. Biblical evangelism invites people into worshipful obedience as a part of God's story.

Lesslie Newbigin speaks of the unique and comprehensive nature of the biblical narrative in saying, "The Bible gives us the whole story of creation and of the human race and therefore enables us to understand our own lives as a part of that story."[9] Newbigin goes on to tell of a Hindu friend who once said to him regarding the biblical story:

> I can't understand why you missionaries present the Bible to us . . . as a book of religion . . . . [W]e have plenty of books of religion . . . (and) we don't need any more! I find in your Bible *a unique interpretation of Universal history* (emphasis mine), the history of the whole of creation and the history of the human race. And therefore (it is) a unique interpretation of the human person as a responsible actor in history. That is unique. There is nothing else in the whole religious literature of the world to put alongside it.[10]

Christians have a timelessly relevant and unique story to tell. God is by nature the master communicator, and he chose to use a narrative story as a means for disseminating the gospel. Our identity as Christians is tied to the faithful telling and retelling of the biblical story of redemption.[11] So what can we learn from God's methodology? Next we turn to look at how the Holy Spirit inspired the writers of the New Testament to tell the story of God by tying it to the Old Testament Scriptures.

ACCORDING TO THE SCRIPTURES

In his book *Introduction to Evangelism*, Alvin Reid notes that, "the noun form (of gospel) is *euangelion* and is found seventy-six times in the New

---

[6] Augustine, *De doctrina Christiana*, 2.2.

[7] Brad J. Kallenberg, *Live to Tell: Evangelism for a Postmodern Age* (Grand Rapids: Brazos, 2002), 37.

[8] Bryan Stone, *Evangelism After Christendom: The Theology and Practice of Christian Witness* (Grand Rapids: Brazos Press, 2007), 39.

[9] Lesslie Newbigin, *A Walk Through the Bible* (Vancouver: Regent College Publishing, 1999), 82.

[10] Ibid., 4.

[11] Kallenberg, *Live to Tell*, 38.

Testament. It can be translated 'gospel,' 'good news,' or 'evangel.' It emphasizes not just any good news but a specific message . . . that Jesus died and
rose again."[12] We have a story to tell, and there is a bloody cross at the center of that story. Many well-meaning evangelists, though, have unintentionally reduced the comprehensive message of the cross to only a few verses of
Scripture. Plenty of people died on a bloody cross throughout history, but
only one did so as a sacrifice of atonement for the sins of the world. My fear
is that the term "gospel" has often been communicated in a reductionistic
manner. The lost may in fact be skeptical about the gospel because we have
been telling only parts of the story, failing to provide adequate context that is
crucial to understanding. It is the identity of the One on the cross that makes
all the difference! Understanding that Jesus was no ordinary man, but rather
the creative force behind all that exists, provides a depth of meaning that is
not only helpful, but crucial. Chester and Timmis affirm that our message
"can be summarized in simple gospel outlines or even the three-word confession, 'Jesus is Lord.' Yet it is also a message that fills the entire Bible. It is the
story of salvation from creation to new creation."[13] In fact, when we look at
the grand narrative through the interpretive lens of the cross of Christ, we see
that it is the cross that not only makes sense of the story; it makes our part in
the story possible.

How did the New Testament writers tell the story of the gospel of God?
Paul wrote in 1 Corinthians 15:3–4, "For I delivered to you as of first importance what I also received: that Christ died for our sins *in accordance with the
Scriptures,* that he was buried, that he was raised on the third day *in accordance with the Scriptures"* (emphasis added). What Paul is communicating
here is the very heart of the gospel and must in no uncertain terms be told.
Notice, however, that the gospel that Paul mentioned is tied to the broader
story of the mission of God. Paul saw the triad of truths—that Christ died for
our sins, was buried, and was raised on the third day—all to be built upon the
foundation of "the Scriptures." The Scriptures that Paul was referring to was
most likely not the written Gospels of the New Testament canon, but rather
the Old Testament.[14] This implies that Paul's communication of the *kerygma*,
or content of the gospel message, was directly tied to the broader story of the
mission of God, which predated the crucifixion and resurrection. So here we
find that Paul inadvertently addresses our common problem of isolating the
events surrounding Jesus' sacrifice of atonement by giving the gospel deeper
biblical and historical moorings that reach back into earlier parts of the story.

What about the narrative accounts of Jesus' story—the four Gospels? Do
they follow a similar pattern to that which was documented by Paul as being

---

[12] Alvin Reid, *Introduction to Evangelism* (Nashville: Broadman & Holman, 1998), 10.

[13] Tim Chester and Steve Timmis, *Total Church: A Radical Reshaping around Gospel and
Community* (Wheaton: Crossway, 2008), 32.

[14] It is generally believed among evangelical scholars that Paul wrote 1 Corinthians c. AD 55
while in Ephesus. While it is possible that at least Matthew and Mark were written by this time,
it is highly unlikely that Paul is making reference to them here, but rather to the uncontested Old
Testament canon of his time.

a matter of first importance? Matthew, in addition to identifying Jesus as the very presence of God among men, the "Immanuel" of Isaiah 7:14 (Matt. 1:23), started his gospel by tracing the lineage of Jesus back to Abraham (Matt. 1:1).[15] Luke's precise historical account makes a similar assertion in tracing the genealogy of Jesus all the way back to God himself in addition to tying the birth of Jesus to several Old Testament promises (Luke 3:23–38). John's Gospel takes the story back even further stretching the mind of his readers into eternity past displaying Christ as Creator (John 1:1–3). If the Gospel writers saw the story of the good news reaching back like this, then we must acknowledge that what we commonly refer to as the "gospel" is more than the few truths that dot the landscape of the New Testament canon. The gospel is truly eternal and cosmic because the story of Jesus is eternal in scope and cosmic in its implications. In all, *Baker's Evangelical Dictionary of Biblical Theology* notes that there are at least 343 direct Old Testament quotations in the New Testament and at least 2,309 allusions.[16] This interrelatedness between the canons demonstrates that there is a single theme uniting all of Scripture—the story of the gospel. Wright adds:

> The New Testament, then, building on the massive foundations of Israel's faith in YHWH, their saving God, sees the climactic work of God's salvation in the person and work of Jesus. And since the mission of God could be summed up in that one comprehensive concept that so dominates Yahweh's character and intentions in the Old Testament—salvation—the identification of Jesus with YHWH puts him right at the center of that saving mission.[17]

Since the New Testament is the story of Jesus, and that story cannot be told by the apostles without providing Old Testament context, then why do we attempt to do so?

THE REST OF THE STORY

For the better part of the twentieth century, the airwaves (first by radio and later by television) carried the voice of legendary broadcaster Paul Harvey. After decades of experience documenting history in the making through retelling people's stories for a broader audience, Harvey created a new program called "The Rest of the Story." The purpose of the program was to tell the little known facts from the earlier years of those people who made headlines. Harvey thought that it would be helpful for America to learn about the lives of great men and women and the stories of how they became great.

---

[15] The importance of that lineage will be discussed at length later in this chapter.

[16] Walter A. Elwell, "Old Testament in the New Testament," *Evangelical Dictionary of Theology*, http://www.biblestudytools.net/Dictionaries/BakerEvangelicalDictionary/bed.cgi?number=T523, 1997.

[17] Wright, *The Mission of God,* 121.

What about Jesus? We have just seen that the New Testament writers often referred or alluded to the Old Testament with great frequency when telling the story of Jesus. Why? In order to understand the fullness of the gospel people need to hear the rest of the story. So now we will take a look at the grand narrative of Scripture and consider the importance and implications of each "act" with regard to the gospel message. You will note that every act in the divine drama points in the direction of the cross, which is itself the climax of all history. That being said, we must not think of redemption as being contained within a single act in God's mission. Rather, redemption transcends all of the acts with creation and fall looking forward to the full expression of God's divine love at the cross of Christ, and restoration looking back on all that Christ accomplished via his atoning sacrifice. So the cross is not merely one-fourth of the story—it *is* the story. But the cross cannot be fully understood apart from the rest of the story.

CREATION: WHERE DID WE COME FROM?

In the world of literature "exposition" usually comes at the beginning of the story where the author sets the stage or gives context for the audience. In this part of a story the main characters are normally introduced, providing further development of the plot. Exposition takes place in the first several chapters of Genesis with the creation account and subsequent fall. Packer notes, "We must know what it means to call God Creator before we can grasp what it means to speak of him as Redeemer."[18] It is fitting then that the Bible wastes no time in introducing the main character of history: "In the beginning, God!" By displaying God as the creator of all that exists, there is no questioning what his role in the story should be. And by virtue that we are told all things were declared "good" by him, we learn something of God's character by virtue of his expressive creation. That God created all things good and orderly indeed provides the setting for the story of all history.

For most of us the first few verses of the Bible, which document the creation account, are disinteresting because man is not around yet. The minor characters within the grand narrative, man and woman, are not introduced until the final verses of the creation account and owe their own existence to the creative will of the protagonist. Unfortunately, humanity in its current fallen state consistently attempts to rewrite the story. Our revisionist history is demonstrated in the fact that humans generally place themselves at the center of the story almost relegating God as a minor character on history's stage. Bob Sjogren demonstrates the human propensity for trying to upstage God by comparing the way we treat Scripture as if it were a high school yearbook.[19] What was the first thing you did when you received your yearbook? You probably went through scanning every page to find yourself. By the end of the

---

[18]   J. I. Packer, *Evangelism and the Sovereignty of God* (Downers Grove: IVP, 1991), 59.

[19]   Bob Sjogren and Gerald Robison, *Cat and Dog Theology: Rethinking Our Relationship with Our Master* (Colorado Springs: Authentic Books, 2005).

day you knew every page that your photograph was on. Sjogren's observation is both keen and cutting. When most of us read the Bible we are usually so busy looking for ourselves in the pages that we miss the main point: the God of glory. And interestingly enough, we normally read ourselves into the story as the hero. When we are taken back to Genesis 1 in the grand narrative, we are forced to accept that God, not man, is the protagonist in the Bible. Part of the gospel then is reminding humans that our purpose on the stage of history is not to make much of ourselves, but rather to make much of God. John Piper reminds us, "God is the absolute reality that everyone in the universe must come to terms with . . . . To ignore him or belittle him is unintelligible and suicidal folly."[20]

Genesis 1:28 provides the first command to the humans that God had just created, and thus his purpose in creating. "And God blessed them. And God said to them, 'Be fruitful and multiply and fill the earth and subdue it and have dominion over the fish of the sea and over the birds of the heavens and over every living thing that moves on the earth.'" Prior to the creation of man and woman he had declared his work to that point to be "good" (v. 25). But after making man in the *imago Dei* and giving this command, God declared created order to be "very good" (v. 31). So it is obvious that with man something unique was added to creation. Being *imago Dei*, man and woman had a unique ability to communicate with their Creator in a worshipful fashion. The command to "be fruitful and multiply and fill the earth" contained within it the implicit concept that the earth was to be filled with worshippers. This is man's primary reason for existence: to fill the earth with worship. This purpose is both reiterated and made conceivable as the fullness of the gospel mystery comes to light in the death, burial, and resurrection of Jesus. The very purpose of the gospel is to reconcile fallen humanity to God through repentance and faith in the finished atoning work of Christ on the cross. In short, the gospel makes worship possible. What we commonly refer to as the Great Commission is merely a restatement and clarification of that original Genesis 1:28 command to fill the earth with worshippers.

The Fall: What Went Wrong?

"Rising action" is the series of complications that sets up the central conflict between the main character and the antagonist of a story. In this part of the story tension builds, and the story works its way up to the point of climax. In the biblical narrative rising action begins with the introduction of the serpent as an embodiment of the antagonist in Genesis 3. The tension escalates from that point in the form of a tangled web of destruction that he spreads through all of creation. All the while as the tension builds, the mission of God continues to unfold like a scarlet cord that culminates at the cross of Christ. Thus, it is through a biblical understanding of what occurred at the fall of

---

[20] John Piper, *Let the Nations Be Glad* (Grand Rapids: Baker, 1993), 14.

humanity that we come to understand and appreciate what Jesus has accomplished in his redemptive work.

A people not fallen see no need for the cross. Of course, Paul reminds us that "all have sinned and fall short of the glory of God" (Rom. 3:23, HCSB). But fallen from what? What does it mean to be fallen? These questions can only be adequately addressed by going back first to creation and then to the entrance of original sin. There we find that our ability to communicate with and worship God was not just damaged, but destroyed. The fall and subsequent inherited sin nature have led humanity to embrace and love created things above the Creator. This eternally terminal condition is commonly known as *idolatry*. Idolatry did not burst on the scene in the explicit form of stone and wooden images. Instead it arrived in the form of a deceptively nuanced question. "Did God really say . . . ?" (Gen. 3:1, HCSB). This subtle but deadly question rings down through the annals of history making idolaters of us all. Thus, the emergence of sin created a massive tension because all of created order was thrown from being "very good" to being very bad. Unfettered worship devolved into brazen idolatry. Depravity spread through the human race like a plague and not one person went untouched by its viral sickness . . . until Jesus.

The fall in Genesis 3 enacted a devolution of worshipful intimacy between man and his Creator. Our Just God responded by declaring a fourfold curse that had ramifications for the serpent, woman, man, and himself. Genesis 3:15 is the basis of the latter. This verse is often referred to as the *proto-evangelium*, or first mention of the gospel. It reads, "I [God] will put enmity between you and the woman, and between your offspring and her offspring; he shall bruise your head, and you shall bruise his heel." An ensuing conflict begins that would not be resolved until one of Eve's offspring came to crush the head of Satan.

From that point, Genesis 3–11 illustrates the main thrust of how bad things could get with humans living without God as the conscious focus of their lives. Within that section of the fall narrative we see God grieved that "the wickedness of man was great in the earth, and that every intention of the thoughts of his heart was only evil continually" (Gen. 6:5) The flood is a vivid display of God's wrath against rebellious humanity. It amazes me that the story of Noah's ark makes it into all of the children's books. All of humanity comes under the wrath of almighty God and is destroyed, except Noah's family, but we focus on the cute animals making their way to the ark as if it were a day at the zoo. We have emasculated the message of Scripture to make it more marketable. Interestingly, as soon as Noah and his family got off of the ark, God restated his original command in 9:1,7: "be fruitful and multiply and fill the earth" with worshippers. One might think that from that point things would begin to improve, but they did not. In fact, just two chapters later we see the human race gathered on the plain of Shinar building a monument to their own self-sufficiency. God graciously scattered them to the ends of the earth confounding their languages so that they would be humbled (Gen. 11).[21]

Up to this point, the identity of the promised deliverer mentioned in Genesis 3:15 had been shrouded in mystery. A degree of clarification comes in Genesis 12:1–3 when God chose Abraham and promised to bless the nations through his offspring in what is known as the Abrahamic covenant. Ironically, the Talmud suggests that Abram was likely the son of an idol maker.[22] To our knowledge the earth was lacking much authentic worship and yet, "Abram believed the LORD, and He credited it to him as righteousness" (Gen. 15:6, HCSB). Beyond that, Paul identifies God's promise to Abram as carrying the very content of the gospel. "The Scripture foresaw that God would justify the Gentiles by faith, and announced the gospel in advance to Abraham: 'All nations will be blessed through you'" (Gal. 3:8, NIV). Christopher Wright adds, "Since it was by human hands that sin and evil have invaded life on Earth, it would be by human means that God would act to regress it. The declaration of blessing on Abraham and the anticipation of the inclusion of all kindred and nations in the blessing of Abraham answer the language of curse and exclusion in Genesis 3."[23] He continues,

> One of the reasons for the appalling shallowness and vulnerability of much that passes for the growth of the church around the world is that people are coming to some kind of instrumental faith in the God they see as powerful, with some connection to Jesus, but a Jesus as disconnected from his scriptural roots. They have not been challenged at the level of their deeper worldview by coming to know God in and through the story that is launched by Abraham.[24]

The remainder of the Old Testament traces the descendants of Abraham through Israel and documents the effects of the fall creating tension both within and surrounding Israel. Wright posits, "The whole Bible could be portrayed as a very long answer to a very simple question: What can God do about the sin and rebellion of the human race? Genesis 12 through to Revelation 22 is God's answer to the question posed by the bleak narratives of Genesis 3 through 11."[25] The identity of the Messiah who would embody God's answer to that question becomes the grand mystery that dots the landscape of the Old Testament. Hints are given throughout. The law was given to Moses as a tutor to direct people to the identity of the Messiah (Gal. 3:24). It is this mystery that feeds the tension right up to the point of climax. When would this Messiah come? Who is he?

---

[21] But as the story later unfolds it becomes evident that God would create a symphony from the emerging diversity by creating worshippers for himself from every tongue, tribe, language and nation (Matt. 28:18–20; Rev. 7:9).

[22] Louis Ginzberg, "Abraham, Apocalypse of," http://www.jewishencyclopedia.com/view.jsp?artid=361&letter=A, last accessed 13 February 2009.

[23] Wright, *The Mission of God,* 212.

[24] Ibid., 219.

[25] Ibid., 195.

From the time of the fall God displayed both kindness and judgment on humanity. There was mercy for Adam and Eve, and there was wrath for the animal whose skin provided their covering. There was mercy for Noah and his family, and there was wrath for the remainder of the earth's inhabitants. There was mercy for true Israel and there was wrath for idolatrous nations. Why is it important to communicate that God's response to sin entails both wrath and mercy? John Piper says that God is always speaking two languages at once: both wrath and mercy.[26] In wrath, there is always mercy. And in mercy, there is always wrath. These two languages became audible at the fall and culminated at the cross of Christ. The identity of the Messiah was none other than the Son of God clothed in flesh. So that which was spoken by God in Genesis 3:15 became visible at the incarnation of Christ. The offspring of woman had finally arrived to destroy the works of the devil (1 John 3:8). There at the cross the wrath of God was poured out upon Jesus because of our sins.[27] God had reserved the gravest consequence of sin for himself. And for those who put their faith in his finished atoning work, there is mercy. That is the gospel, and it makes more sense in light of the depth of depravity brought on humanity as a result of the fall.

REDEMPTION: WHAT HOPE IS THERE?

Schnabel reminds us, "Biblical narratives are paradigms that provide us with models for our own faithful and authentic response to God's revelation."[28] Within the biblical narrative it is no surprise then that the climax occurs at the cross of our Lord. "Climax" is the high point or crescendo of the entire story. It is at this turning point where the conflict between the protagonist and antagonist comes to a head. This is the most exciting point in the story—the point which gives meaning to all the previous other pages in the story.

As mentioned in the creation account, God created humans in his image that they might fill the earth with worshippers. However, when the fall of humanity occurred in the garden of Eden, it seemed as if the evil antagonist had won by convincing the man and woman to doubt God. But in Genesis 3:15 we saw that God was not taken by surprise and had a plan to overturn the works of the devil.[29] The serpent was warned that one of the woman's

---

[26] John Piper, "The Wrath of God Against Ungodliness and Unrighteousness" (August 30, 1998), http://www.desiringgod.org/ResourceLibrary/Sermons/ByDate/1998/1048_The_Wrath_of _God_Against_Ungodliness_and_Unrighteousness.

[27] This is what is meant by the term *propitiation*. God's wrath was satisfied as Christ bore the full brunt of punishment for our sins.

[28] Eckhard J. Schnabel, *Paul the Missionary: Realities, Strategies and Methods* (Downers Grove: IVP, 2008), 394.

[29] It should always be communicated that Satan is himself a created being, albeit one who has rebelled against God's authority. Many people are confused about good and evil and take a dualistic approach in explaining the presence of evil in the world. There is not a good God and a bad god. There is but one God existing in three persons—Father, Son, and Holy Spirit. It is

seed would come and crush his head. Even in the wake of this promise, it seemed as if the earth was destined to be filled with idolaters, rather than worshippers as God had intended. Instead of humans getting better, their sin nature only innovated and became more pervasive (Rom. 1:22–31). Then we were introduced to Abraham, with whom God made an eternal covenant, promising that through his lineage the nations would be blessed. And from that point the nation of Israel emerged and provided a microcosm of fallen humanity through which we have the benefit of watching the perseverance of God's redemptive nature. Then at just the right time (Rom. 5:6) God sent his only Son into the world to accomplish his redemptive purposes. Wright reminds us that "it is hardly going too far to say that salvation defines this God's identity."[30] The evangelistic intent of the incarnation is summarized by Wright, "The name . . . Jesus means Yahweh is salvation. Through the arrival of Jesus of Nazareth, God was bringing in the promised new era of salvation for Israel and for the world, because through Jesus God would deal with sin."[31]

Jesus obeyed the Father and laid down his own life as an atoning sacrifice for fallen humanity on a hill called Golgotha. At the cross we see the grandest and purest display of worship that there has ever been . . . or ever will be. God's plan at the cross was not merely to erase sin and defeat the devil. His plan had not deviated one bit from his original command back in Genesis 1:28. Jesus' act of ultimate worship served as an atoning sacrifice for our sins, but it also serves as the means by which Christ's righteousness is imputed to us by faith.

The redemptive work of Christ on the cross is first and foremost an act of unfettered and perfect worship. It stands at the climax of all history as just that. And we are invited into the benefits of the cross, not by means of following Christ's example alone, but first by means of going back to the garden per se and making that choice for ourselves. Will we trust God at his word and live as worshippers by putting our faith in Christ, allowing him to destroy our idols? Or will we question God once more and be deceived in our idolatry by worshipping something other than the Creator?

Many well-meaning Christians have an anthropocentric understanding of the gospel that stems from our idolatrous sin nature. We look to God only for what he can give us—things such as forgiveness, fulfillment, happiness, healing, and heaven. The problem is that we fail to see that those things are significant only in relation to how they bring us back to the God who made us for himself. We talk to people about being saved, but fail to communicate that salvation is not only from sin, but from the wrath of God upon sin. We

---

not clear how much time passed between creation in Genesis 1 and the fall in Genesis 3, but we can be assured it was time enough for the angel Lucifer to garner pride in his heart and initiate a disastrous rebellion against a sovereign God.

[30] Wright, *The Mission of God*, 118.

[31] Ibid.

talk about going to heaven but fail to communicate that the concept has more to do with a person than with a place.

John Piper has written extensively addressing these common errors in our understanding of the gospel. The title of Piper's book provides his simple, but not simplistic, understanding of the message that is our hope: *God Is the Gospel: Meditations on God's Love as the Gift of Himself.*[32] Elsewhere he elaborates that the gospel is the message that "Christ, the Son of God, died in our place—became our substitute—to pay the price for all our sins, and to accomplish perfect righteousness, and to endure and remove all of God's wrath, and rise from the dead triumphant over death for our eternal life and joy in his presence—and all of this offered freely through faith alone in Jesus Christ alone. That's the good news."[33] So the gospel is not *only* the tenets that Christ died, was buried, and raised on the third day. Christ's finished work on the cross is the crown jewel of the gospel making all other aspects imaginable. Through the gospel, we are saved *from God's wrath* and we are saved *for God's presence.* Salvation is God's work from beginning to end, and therefore, God himself *is* the gospel. The cross of Christ was not only necessitated by the fall of humanity; it is against the backdrop of a fallen world that the cross makes any sense at all.

In writing to the Romans, Paul stated, "But now a righteousness from God, apart from law, has been made known, *to which the Law and the Prophets testify.* This righteousness from God comes through faith in Jesus Christ to all who believe" (Rom. 3:21–22, NIV). Paul reaches back into salvation history and declares that this is the same gospel that was testified to by both the Law and the Prophets. Paul was making reference to act 2. So, in Christ's righteousness, we are once again enabled to worship the Father as we were created to do. What's more, we are enabled to participate in the *missio Dei* through the spread of the gospel so that worship might spread to the ends of the earth.

RESTORATION: WHAT DOES THE FUTURE HOLD?

Denouement is the point of closure at the end of a narrative where the conflict is resolved. The term comes from the French, meaning "to untie a knot," connoting that the tension that once existed has now been straightened out. With regard to the biblical grand narrative, the Revelation is God's *denouement* statement that his promises have been kept and his mission has been fulfilled.[34] Kallenberg notes, "the plotline of this single story races underneath the reader's feet and off into a future whose final end is the reconciliation of creation with Creator under the reign of King Jesus."[35] It is there in the last

---

[32] John Piper, *God Is the Gospel: Meditations on God's Love as the Gift of Himself* (Wheaton: Crossway, 2005).

[33] John Piper, *Finally Alive* (Great Britain: Christian Focus Publications, 2009), 169.

[34] Wright, *The Mission of God,* 356.

[35] Kallenberg, *Live to Tell,* 109.

few chapters of the Bible that all of creation is restored and God's people at last fill the earth with Christ-honoring worship.

Ephesians 2:15–17 explains that what was lost in the garden, fellowship with God and the ability to worship authentically, was regained through the reconciliation mediated in the body of Jesus on the cross. Something priceless was made accessible there at the cross. And on the new earth described in Revelation 21 and 22, we see the Tree of Life present once more. Only this time all of the inhabitants of the new earth are those who have been completely restored to God and are able to eat freely:

> On each side of the river stood the tree of life, bearing twelve crops of fruit, yielding its fruit every month. And the leaves of the tree are for the healing of the nations. No longer will there be any curse. The throne of God and of the Lamb will be in the city, and his servants will serve him. They will see his face, and his name will be on their foreheads. There will be no more night. They will not need the light of a lamp or the light of the sun, for the Lord God will give them light. And they will reign forever and ever. (Rev. 22:2–5, NIV)

The imagery given by John in this passage from Revelation 22 displays that eternal life is ever-present as there is not a season where the fruit of the tree of life is not available. And this life is not only made available to the ethnic nation of Israel. The nations that were scattered back in Genesis 11 because of their prideful self-sufficiency (a subtle, but deadly form of idolatry) are gathered, not around a self-made tower, but around the person of Jesus. Healing is theirs to be had. Also significant is that the curse that God enacted in Genesis 3 at the fall is removed. God himself once again becomes accessible as he dwells there in the city along with all of the redeemed. That we will be enabled to see his face will be the greatest gospel-bought blessing of heaven. It is a face that we will never tire of seeing. And if there were any doubt, God makes clear that all of humanity belongs to him by placing his name upon our foreheads. So even when we look at one another we will be reminded of our great and gracious God. The *Imago Dei* is fully restored. The original command from Genesis 1:28 to fill the earth with worshippers is accomplished. Yes, something priceless is restored in heaven. Newbigin speaks of the radical evangelistic implications of this eschatological vision for us today:

> That is the vision with which the Bible ends, and it is a vision that enables us to see the whole human story and each of our lives within that story as meaningful, and which therefore invites us through Jesus Christ to become responsible actors in history . . . . Each of us must be ready to take our share in all the struggles and the anguish of human history and yet with confidence that what is committed to Christ will in the end find its place in his final kingdom.[36]

---

[36] Newbigin, *A Walk Through the Bible,* 84–85.

EVANGELISM AS STORYTELLING

Seeing the gospel as story implies that evangelism becomes storytelling. Bartholomew and Goheen remind us, "The Biblical story is about what God is doing in the world, working toward the renewal of the whole creation. God chooses people to join with him and participate in his work . . . . [T]oday we too are invited to participate in what God is doing. If we are to understand our own calling, we must understand it in relation to those who have heard it before us."[37] Storytelling is an art form, and we can learn much from the "artists" who have gone before us. Good storytelling requires skill because no one wants to be guilty of ruining a good story. Gabriel Fackre points out, "The task of Christian Storytelling is to keep alive the set of counter-perceptions so the Church may be what it is and see what it is called to see, rather than be made over in the image of the regnant culture."[38] Unfortunately, we have listened to and observed the culture's attention deficit and have edited how we communicate the gospel. Some crucial parts of the story have been left on the cutting room floor in an attempt to get more people to hear our story. Bad publicity has plagued the church's evangelistic efforts, and the lost, in the Western hemisphere in particular, have dismissed the story in large part without even hearing it. This analysis is confirmed by the responses we get when asking lost people their understanding of why Jesus died on the cross. We have done such a poor job of communicating the gospel that most people who call themselves "Christian" would struggle to articulate the fundamental tenets of the gospel. So where do we go from here? How can we reeducate the saints and recapture the attention of sinners? We must refine our skills and tell the whole story.

There are no set biblical guidelines given for evangelistic methodology beyond calling for a response. The gospel in grand narrative form is different from other lesser stories in history in many ways, primarily of which is that the gospel demands a response. Packer asserts, "Since the divine message finds its climax in a plea from the Creator to a rebel world to turn and put faith in Christ, the delivering of it involves the summoning of one's hearer to conversion."[39] Beyond that, *how* we are to communicate depends upon a number of factors ranging from the worldview of our audience to the context of the conversation.

There are biblical guidelines for content; we are admonished to proclaim Christ crucified and risen (1 Cor. 1:23). Keep in mind that nearly all of the New Testament books reveal that the authors communicated Christ crucified and raised as an extension and fulfillment of the mission of God from the Old Testament. We must be careful not to assume that people will be able to understand the implications of the cross apart from the larger grand narrative

---

[37] Craig G. Bartholomew and Michael Goheen, *The Drama of Scripture: Finding Our Place in the Biblical Story* (Grand Rapids: Baker Academic, 2004), 198.

[38] Gabriel Fackre, *The Christian Story* (Grand Rapids: Eerdmans, 1978), 12.

[39] Packer, *Evangelism and the Sovereignty of God*, 41.

story. In some instances, the New Testament evangelists unfolded each of the acts within the grand narrative in a single message. In other instances they found that their audience already understood the foundational context of creation and fall and were able to go directly to redemption. Even so, the redemptive work of God is best grasped when it is set against the backdrop of the Old Testament stories of creation and fall.

Ultimately, the implications of the gospel are paramount because it is by means of receiving the gospel that sinners are transformed into worshippers and find their place within the larger story of God. Bartholomew and Goheen remind us that "The world of the Bible is our world, and its story of redemption is also our story. This story is waiting for an ending—in part because we ourselves have a role to play before it is all concluded."[40] What is our role? Simple. Tell the whole story and tell it well. After all, it is the greatest story ever told.

How to Tell the Story

If you have been reading this chapter hoping that I would provide some sort of practical outline for evangelism as storytelling, you may be disappointed. In order to refine our skills in storytelling, we need look no further than the Bible for guidance. Schnabel reminds us, "In mission and evangelism the search for a method that will guarantee success in our attempt to convince listeners of the truth of the gospel of Jesus Christ is misguided."[41] What I have attempted to do here is show that when we communicate the gospel with the general framework of the grand narrative—creation, fall, redemption, restoration—we have faithfully evangelized. Success is defined by faithful obedience, not outcomes. Even so, in the midst of writing this chapter I have had dozens of opportunities to tell the story and the one response that I have heard most is, "For the first time it makes sense to me why Jesus had to die."

In this chapter I have alluded the premise that fallen humanity is grappling with four simple, universal questions that are each addressed in the biblical narrative:

1. Where did we come from?
2. What went wrong?
3. What hope is there?
4. What does the future hold?

Everyone, regardless of worldview, is already attempting to answer these questions in some form. Understanding that, Christians need to approach people with a sense of gospel intentionality.[42] We are to tell the story of creation, the fall, redemption, and restoration. Piper reminds us, "God's role in

---

[40] Bartholomew and Goheen, *The Drama of Scripture*, 196–97.
[41] Schnabel, *Paul the Missionary*, 401.
[42] Chester and Timmis, *Total Church*, 63.

bringing about the new birth is decisive, and our role . . . is essential."[43] So through the art of evangelism as storytelling, we are simply addressing the fundamental questions of life with biblical answers, and trusting that God will act on his word and transform rebellious idolaters into humble worshippers.

There are countless subplots that can be brought in when we are sharing the gospel in order to emphasize the point. The New Testament evangelists chose different contextual stories depending upon the audience with which they were speaking. There is not a list of particular verses that you have to memorize in order to get started. With the four simple words that form the basis of this book—and the basis of the biblical grand narrative—any believer can retell the greatest story ever told and thereby answer the four questions that virtually everyone is asking. The only non-negotiable when it comes to telling the story is that every aspect must point to the bloody cross and resurrection of Jesus which stands as the climactic event of the entire mission of God.

CONCLUSION

The Bible is a story book. Though it is made up of hundreds of lesser stories, passages, and imperatives, there is one over-arching divine story that transcends all sixty-six books. This divine grand narrative is the story of God on a mission to redeem and restore creation so that authentic worship fills the earth. The story is good news; it is gospel truth. And yet, many fail to receive it as such. In this chapter I have argued that though the gospel contains propositional truth, it is best communicated in the form of the story of God. Fallen, finite humans need context in order to determine meaning. When we understand that we were created to worship God and lost that at the fall, the cross becomes not only the means to forgiveness of sins, but also the basis of restoration of worship. And when we look at the grand narrative through the interpretive lens of the cross of Christ, we see that it is the cross that not only makes sense of the story; it makes our part in the story possible.

As believers we have been commissioned by God to be master storytellers. In light of this understanding, evangelism should then focus less on disjointed lists of single scriptures, and more on the story that makes those verses make sense. This approach treats the whole canon of Scripture as God's sacred gospel story. And this approach allows the audience to find their place in the story through repentance and faith in Jesus, followed by learning to become a faithful storyteller. Anything less is a reductionist approach and will likely lead to decisions, but not to worshippers. Go tell God's amazing story to someone today and be a part of filling the earth with worship.

---

[43] Piper, *Finally Alive*, 166.

Chapter Seven

THE GOSPEL AND SOCIAL RESPONSIBILITY

Sean Cordell

INTRODUCTION

M any agree that helping the homeless, the hurting, the diseased, the broken, and the imprisoned are good and compassionate things to do. However, is it the responsibility of every Christian or every local church? Or is it only for those who are "called" to such a ministry? Another large issue is not only the Christian's social responsibility but how social responsibility intersects with the gospel. Is caring for the poor conflu-ent with the gospel? Is it antithetical to the gospel? Can a church be gos-pel-centered and still care for the poor? Much confusion and a multitude of answers have arisen in response to these questions: one thinks of the social gospel movement which departed from the gospel, or of reactionary Chris-tians who unnecessarily abandoned care for the poor in light of the danger of a social gospel, or of the present resurgence of gospel-centered churches who are passionate about the social implications of the gospel. This chapter seeks to point the way forward, arguing that the gospel must be proclaimed and that Christians must care for the poor.

In order to prove the necessary and intimate connection between the gos-pel and social responsibility without losing their distinctions, this chapter will define the gospel and define the poor, biblically, while discussing the relationship between the two. For a better grasp of why the gospel-changed life must be involved in ministry to the poor we will look at Jesus' earthly ministry and how he "proclaimed the good news to the poor" (Luke 4:18, paraphrased). Much of Christ's motivation will be better understood as we take a brief trek through the Old Testament's portrayal of the kingdom of God through the creation, fall, redemption, and restoration motif. Finally, even if we are convinced biblically that every Christian must follow Christ's example in pouring out mercy upon the poor, the question remains as to how followers of Christ can faithfully live this out. Our hope in this chapter is to provide solid answers for these questions that are shaped by biblical themes and biblical texts. The answers to these will affect how we live and minister as we spend our lives for the glory of God and the joy of all peoples.

THE GOSPEL

The gospel is the "power of God for salvation to everyone who believes" (Rom. 1:16). It has at its core what is of first importance, "Christ died for our sins . . . , was buried . . . , [and] was raised on the third day in accordance with the Scriptures" (1 Cor. 15:3–4). This good news demands a response. When Peter proclaimed that Jesus is the Christ, crucified by lawless men, yet raised by the glory of God, he called all hearers to respond in repentance and faith (Acts 2:38,41). Salvation is not granted to those who work for their salvation, but who humbly call upon Jesus as Lord and believe that God raised him from the dead (Rom. 4:5; 10:9). We must continually proclaim the gospel, for at least two reasons.

First, followers of Jesus should never "get over" this glorious truth that Jesus Christ by his amazing grace looked at sinners like us, deserving condemnation, and chose to deliver us from condemnation by laying down his sinless life and dying a sinner's death. Although he did not deserve the Father's wrath, he took our sin upon himself and stood in our place—the righteous for the unrighteous—so that we might not be estranged from God, for whom we were created to live and love. He shed his blood on our behalf and yet did not remain in the grave, but in a magnificent display of the power of God, the Father raised him from the dead and gave him glory in order that our faith and hope would be in him and not in ourselves. Christian Scripture, and the gospel it proclaims, is not a book to be studied and then placed on the shelf and never read again. Because Christ crucified is central to all that we believe and do, and because it is of the greatest value to us, the biblical gospel must be analyzed and applied, and it must become the filter through which we view all of life. Without an appropriate love for the gospel, which fosters a deep satisfaction in Christ, any ministry we endeavor will be centered on our goals, our ministry, and our fame rather than Christ's glory. Without Christ as our deepest satisfaction, we will also grow weary. George Mueller, a man known for his strong prayer life and his care for thousands of orphans in the late 1800s, writes:

> Other things may press upon you, the Lord's work may even have urgent claims upon your attention, but I deliberately repeat; it is of supreme and paramount importance that you should seek above all things to have your souls truly happy in God Himself! . . . The secret of all true effectual service

is joy in God, having experimental acquaintance and fellowship with God Himself.[1]

Second, we must proclaim the gospel because history has shown that where the gospel is merely assumed it will slowly be perverted and lost.[2] With the social gospel having such prominent sway in recent history, we must never dilute the gospel by equating justifying faith with the fruit of faith, simply meeting the needs of the hurting and hopeless. As the Lausanne covenant states, we don't want to confuse the issues: "Reconciliation with other people is not reconciliation with God, nor is social action evangelism, nor is political liberation salvation."[3]

WHO ARE THE POOR?

Although we want to avoid confusion by keeping the gospel at the center of our ministry, we must recognize that gospel-transformed believers cannot be indifferent to social needs, and in particular ministry to the poor. Jesus was poor. He had no place to lay his head (Matt. 8:20). The grace of our Lord Jesus is known in that "though he was rich, yet for your sake he became poor, so that you by his poverty might become rich" (2 Cor. 8:9). But how does this apply to the church's ministry to the spiritually and physically impoverished? In order to begin to understand the church's responsibility to minister to the poor we need to define "the poor" biblically and then explore the whole of the biblical message to see how the gospel and ministry to the poor intersect in those who are followers of Christ. In case there is concern that this focus is too narrow, let's look at how the Bible seems to define the poor.

Although Scripture sometimes speaks of the poor in a solely monetary manner,[4] the description "those with little to no money" is insufficient for a thoroughly biblical definition. The terminology used in the Old Testament (OT) for "poor" (*ani* and *dal*) broadly defines the poor as those who were "weak, miserable, helpless, and suffering."[5] This definition allows for both

[1] George Mueller, *A Narrative of Some of the Lord's Dealing with George Muller, written by Himself, Jehovah Magnified*. Addresses by George Muller Complete and Unabridged, 2 vols. (Muskegon, MI: Dust and Ashes, 2003), 2.730–31.

[2] D. A. Carson, *The Cross and Christian Ministry* (Grand Rapids, MI: Baker Books, 1993), 63.

[3] *The Lausanne Covenant* (Lausanne, Switzerland; 1974), paragraph 5.

[4] Some examples are: Proverbs 14:31: "Whoever oppresses a poor man insults his Maker, but he who is generous to the needy honors him" (*poor* is contrasted with *generous*); Proverbs 16:19: "It is better to be of a lowly spirit with the poor than to divide the spoil with the proud" (*lowly* is contrasted with *proud* and *poor* stands over against *dividing the spoil*); Mark 12:42: "And a *poor* widow came and put in two small copper coins, which make a penny" (emphasis added, where *poor* is connected to her small financial gift).

[5] Hans Kvalbein, "Poor/Poverty," in *The New Dictionary of Biblical Theology*, eds. T. Desmond Alexander, Brian Rosner, D. A. Carson, and Graeme Goldsworthy (Downer's Grove: IVP, 2000), 687. Of course, this is a complex issue that can't be too easily summed up with sweeping statements. For greater clarity refer to the entire article referenced above, 687–90.

physical and spiritual poverty. In the OT, physical poverty is broadened beyond simply financial need, with financial concerns often being secondary. The poor in the OT were those people who experienced poverty (1) from natural causes, including crop failure, famine, storms, sickness, death, and the death of husbands or parents; (2) because of their own laziness; or (3) because they were oppressed by the wealthy and powerful, finding themselves needy and destitute materially.[6] The message of the prophets, for example, confirms this broader conception of the poor. The poor individual is one who is "needy" (Amos 4:1) in part because of the injustices of others. Because they have been exploited, these victims have become materially impoverished or physically needy, manifested in imprisonment, hunger, and other forms of poorness (Amos 6:4–6). Likewise, the Psalms confirm a broader reading of the concept of poverty, affirming both physical and spiritual aspects of it. The term is usually so general as to not only include physical hunger, imprisonment, and sickness, but also poverty of spirit. Take Psalm 41:1 for example: "Blessed is the one who considers the poor! In the day of trouble the LORD delivers him." To attempt to force an exclusively physical (vs. spiritual) reading upon the word would be unfair to the psalmist's intent.

   The intimate connection between physical and spiritual poverty. In the New Testament (NT) the word *ptochos*, the Greek word most commonly used for "the poor," can also refer to both physical and spiritual poverty. It encompasses "those who receive charity and those who hear the gospel and inherit the kingdom of God."[7] The flexibility of the word points to an underlying reality in the biblical text that physical realities are meant to help us understand spiritual realities. This heaven and this earth are shadows but are still meant to give us a longing for the new heavens and the new earth. Physical hunger and thirsting are meant to help us understand the groaning of our hearts for something greater than ourselves, which is hungering and thirsting for God. This reality explains the different uses of poor in the Beatitudes as recorded by Matthew and Luke. Matthew 5:3–4 reveals that the "poor in spirit" will inherit the kingdom of heaven while Luke 6:20 tells us the poor will receive the kingdom. Luke is not saying that physical poverty is the litmus test for entrance into the kingdom. Jesus was addressing the disciples who in their obedience to Christ encountered suffering, whether by persecution from others, lack of material goods, or hunger. Jesus comforted the disciples with the assurance that the physical poverty they encountered for Christ revealed a spiritual poverty. Paul also uses physical poverty as a backdrop for highlighting humanity's spiritual need and God's amazing grace to save. God's glory is seen in that he chooses the weak, the low, the despised "even things that are not, to bring to nothing things that are, so that no human being might boast in the presence of God" (1 Cor. 1:28–29). Paul shows that it is just like God to work intentionally among the lowly—physically and spiritually—so that it is

---

   [6]   Christopher Wright, *Old Testament Ethics for the People of God* (Downer's Grove: IVP, 2004) 169–70.
   [7]   Ibid., 689.

clear to all that God is gracious and mighty to save. James 2:5 and Revelation 2:9 display the intimate interplay between physical and spiritual poverty and riches, where those poor in possessions or condition are "rich" in faith.

The poor are not merely the financially destitute. The New Testament conception of poverty regularly includes many of poverty's interrelated pains such as imprisonment, hunger, sickness, and weakness. Luke 4 is a prime example. Standing in the synagogue, Jesus unrolled the scroll of the prophet Isaiah and read Isaiah 61:1–2, "The Spirit of the Lord is upon me, because he has anointed me to proclaim good news to the poor. He has sent me to proclaim liberty to the captives and recovering of sight to the blind, to set at liberty those who are oppressed, to proclaim the year of the Lord's favor" (Luke 4:18–19). After reading this he sat down and said, "Today this Scripture has been fulfilled in your hearing" (4:21). Then following the people's initial amazement, he was driven out of town. The punctuation rendered here by the ESV reflects the intent of Isaiah 61 where the poor is not one category in a list, but the banner that summarizes the list that follows. Here Jesus' coming to proclaim good news (gospel) to the poor is described by setting captives free, giving sight to the blind, liberating the oppressed, and proclaiming the year of the Lord's favor. The "poor" then in this text would be better defined as those who are lowly, weak, or oppressed. This is further confirmed when Jesus traveled down to Capernaum already acknowledging that the Spirit of God rested upon him to proclaim good news to the poor. What did he do? He taught them on the Sabbath, astonishing them with his teaching (4:32), but he also healed a man with an unclean demon (4:35–36), rebuked fevers (4:39), healed sicknesses and diseases (4:40), and cast out more demons (4:41). Then while the people were pleading with him to stay he explained that he had to, "preach the good news of the kingdom of God" and now he must do that in other towns as well, "for I was sent for this purpose" (4:43). Jesus' purpose was to preach the gospel of the kingdom of God, which necessarily meant that he was to also care for the poor.

It is important to see who the poor are in this chapter. They are the lowly, the oppressed. Jesus had been fulfilling his purpose when he preached, but also as he healed, cast out demons, and rebuked fevers. For Jesus, all of these afflictions were "poverty." As we see in Luke's beatitudes, the poor are paralleled with the hungry, the weeping, and the persecuted. Jesus' burden is to preach the good news of the kingdom, which centers on the King, but which also compels care for the poor—the lowly, the oppressed, the hurting, and the afflicted. Therefore when Jesus said he must preach the good news to the poor (in Luke 4), he seemed to have this broader understanding of the poor in mind.[8] Christ's goal for connecting the gospel and the poor seems to be in

---

[8] The goal is not to say that every time one sees the word *poor* they should interpret it broadly. Context will be the ultimate indicator. However, if we are asking what King Jesus came to do, his expressed purpose was to proclaim the good news not just to the financially bad off, but to the lowly, the oppressed. Should we wonder if this should affect our churches' strategies?

part to provide a fleshy picture through physical poverty of the more serious spiritual poverty of the human heart.

Jesus' ministry to the poor extends to all followers of Christ. In Jesus' life his mission was to proclaim the good news of the kingdom and to show his Messianic nature through caring for the poor. Although Jesus' mission was unique to him in that he alone was the Messianic king who would be the Savior of the world, Jesus made it clear that those who are followers of Christ must preach the good news and meet the needs of the poor as well. To confirm this, we will look at Jesus' own words and then at the lives of some of his followers—Peter, Paul, and James.

At the end of Matthew 25, Jesus paints a sober picture of the end times when the Son of Man in his righteousness will be on his throne with all the nations gathered around him and "he will separate people one from another as a shepherd separates the sheep from the goats" (Matt. 25:32). After he separates the sheep on the right and the goats on the left, he will invite the sheep into his blessed presence *because* "I was hungry and you gave me food, I was thirsty and you gave me drink, I was a stranger and you welcomed me, I was naked and you clothed me, I was sick and you visited me, I was in prison and you came to me" (Matt. 25:35–36). Then the righteous will ask, in summary, "When did we do all this to you, Jesus?" and Jesus' response is, "Truly, I say to you, as you did it to one of the least of these my brothers, you did it to me" (Matt. 25:40). The grave part is what follows. Those who are on his left will be "cursed, into the eternal fire prepared for the devil and his angels" (Matt. 25:41). One might ask why. Jesus points to their lack of care for the poor—the hungry, thirsty, naked, sick, and imprisoned. He concludes with, "Truly, I say to you, as you did not do it to one of the least of these, you did not do it to me" (Matt. 25:45).

It is incredible to see how unbelievably serious Jesus is that his followers produce the fruit of love in their lives, specifically the fruit of loving the poor. Every example he gave at the end of Matthew 25 was of those whom Jesus would call poor. Jesus' followers must pursue the poor. Yet this text could also appear to blur the lines from what we have already said, namely that the gospel changes lives by faith alone through grace and produces the fruit of compassion toward the poor. Upon first glance this passage seems to be indicating that it was the *doing* that got the "sheep" into heaven and the *not doing* that kept the "goats" out of heaven. What is helpful here is to notice how those who were welcomed in for doing acts of mercy upon the poor were *unaware* that they were caring for Jesus. They asked, "Lord, when did we see you hungry and feed you?" This tips the reader off to the fact that the "sheep" were not seeking to earn their way to God through these acts of kindness, but that these acts were natural for the life transformed by the grace of Jesus. Jesus was simply welcoming them in not because these deeds earned their righteousness, but because these deeds were external objective evidence that the gospel had taken root in their hearts. D. A. Carson writes:

The reason [the righteous] are welcomed and invited to take their inheritance is that they have served the King's brothers . . . . [The unrighteous] are banished from the King's presence and sent to eternal fire [because] they have refused to show compassion to King Messiah through helping the least of his brothers . . . . [They] are admitted or excluded on the basis of how they treat Jesus.[9]

The gospel is of crucial concern at this juncture. Christians find their righteousness in Christ alone rather than in their external deeds of kindness. However we also must not miss the fact that Jesus' followers *will* be caring for the poor. To fail to intentionally show mercy to the poor could be a strong indicator that one has never received the saving mercy of Christ. As those who have received the mercy of forgiveness in Christ, the Christian is called to be a mercy giver. Grace is for the undeserving and mercy is for the miserable, those of lowly state.[10] Just as we are of lowly state spiritually and maybe physically, we should be ministers of mercy to those who are in a lowly, miserable state. In following our merciful master we too must be merciful.

As we look at Jesus' followers, they were concerned for the poor as they followed the pattern of their King. Galatians 2:9–10 informs us: "and when James and Cephas and John, who seemed to be pillars, perceived the grace that was given to me [Paul], they gave the right hand of fellowship to Barnabas and me, that we should go to the Gentiles and they to the circumcised. Only, they asked us to remember the poor, the very thing I was eager to do." Here the apostles who walked with Jesus and Paul and Barnabas, new church planting leaders sent to the Gentiles, were all eager to care for the poor. Second Corinthians 8–9 also reveals Paul's deep burden for the poor of Jerusalem church as he seeks to take up an offering for them from the other churches. First Timothy 5:10 reveals one of the criteria for those who were "really" widows; they would be those who are faithful, and faithfulness to Paul in part was "[caring] for the afflicted"; some versions render it "[those who] assisted those in distress" (see NASB). These are "the poor," and this is what the follower of Christ does. James, an apostle and half-brother of Jesus, insisted on care for the poor saying, "Religion that is pure and undefiled before God, the Father, is this: to visit orphans and widows in their affliction, and to keep oneself unstained from the world" (James 1:27). The orphan and the widow are the oppressed and lowly of society. These examples solidify that Jesus and the early church saw caring for the poor as vital for a life changed by Christ.

Summary of the poor in Scripture.

1. "Poor" to Jesus is more than financial neediness. In today's context it would include *contributors to* and *results of* economic poverty such as oppression by others, sickness, diseases such as AIDS, hunger,

---

[9] D. A. Carson, "Matthew," *Expositor's Bible Commentary*, vol 8, ed. Frank E. Gaebelein (Grand Rapids, MI: Zondervan Publishing House, 1984), 521–22.

[10] John Piper, *Future Grace* (Sisters, OR: Multnomah, 1995), 190.

imprisonment, homelessness, those with extended joblessness, etc. (Luke 4:16–21; 6:20–26; 1 Tim. 5:10).[11]

2. Physical and spiritual poverty are intimately connected. Physical poverty is a fleshy depiction of the intense spiritual neediness of the human heart (Matt. 5:3–12; 1 Cor. 1:26–29; James 2:5).

3. Jesus extends his mission of ministry to the poor to *every* follower of Jesus because:

   a. when we minister to the poor we are ministering to Jesus.
   b. ministering to the poor helps us see physical pictures that remind us of our spiritual condition.
   c. caring for the poor—"the least of these"—is a significant potential indicator of the presence of genuine of faith.
   (Matt. 25:31–46; 2 Cor. 8–9; Gal. 2:9–10; James 1:27; 2:1–5)

Creation, fall, redemption, restoration, and the kingdom. The question arises: Is there more that motivated Jesus to make ministry to the poor central to his ministry and therefore to the ministry of his followers? Is there another angle from which to argue for justice and mercy for the poor? To answer this, we now turn to a brief sketch of creation, fall, redemption, and restoration, as treated in the Old Testament. The goal here is to give a brief synopsis of how the King and his kingdom are deeply concerned about justice for the poor at every stage of the narrative.

Creation. When God created the heavens and earth, he created a kingdom where he is the king and people made in his image are his subjects, who are to rule the earth under his authority. The reader is tipped off to this in Genesis 1:26 when God commands man, who is made in his image, to exercise "dominion over" creation as we follow his authority over us. His kingship over his people is confirmed as we see his response to Israel's request for a king like the other nations had. God tells Samuel in 1 Samuel 8:7, "Obey the voice of the people in all that they say to you, for they have not rejected you, *but they have rejected me from being king over them*" (emphasis added). God is king over his image-bearers, and when we reject his authority we are rejecting him as king. Yet if we follow his authority as image-bearers, we will treat one another with justice and righteousness and kindness like our King treats us.

Fall. Israel's rebellion against God as their king in Samuel was rooted in the rebellion of their parents, Adam and Eve. In Genesis 3, we learn that Adam and Eve followed their own ways and their lustful eyes, and they sinned against God because of their prideful desire to be autonomous, to be their own king and lord. In the aftermath of their fall, all humanity finds themselves sinners by nature and by choice. Injustice enters God's just kingdom. Indeed, the entirety of the biblical canon expounds this theme and outlines

---

[11] Although many categories of "poor" exist, the Christians' responsibility is not to all categories equally. The thrust of Scripture is the simple yet clear directive to care for the poor as we follow the example of Jesus.

how God in his holiness and love punishes this sin, and yet in an amazing display of grace promises a coming kingdom where he will lovingly redeem his people from their sin. We see the first glimpses of his justice and mercy as king when he throws Adam and Eve out of the garden for their sin, a *just* exile, and yet in *mercy* he clothes them, covering their nakedness.

Redemption. The peril of the fall leaves a people who groan for the promised king to come and to bring with him the kingdom. The promise of that King began in Genesis 3:15, and throughout the OT the portrait of a just and merciful king and his glorious kingdom takes on more shape and more detail. The King who will bring about redemption for his people will be the Son of God (Ps. 2:7,12), the servant (Isa. 42:1), from the line of Judah (Gen. 49:10), from the stump of Jesse (Isa. 11:1). He will rule triumphantly (Isa. 2; 66), but he will be rejected (Zech. 12:10); he will suffer, being pierced (Zech. 12:10), betrayed (Isa. 53:3) and killed for our sins (Isa. 53:5), even forsaken by God (Ps. 22:1). However, this suffering servant King will rise from the dead triumphantly (Ps. 16:11) to rule God's people forever (2 Sam. 7:12–13,16; Dan. 7:13–14). All of these Old Testament prophecies were fulfilled in Jesus Christ the King, whose life-giving sacrifice purchased redemption on our behalf, to the praise of his glory.

Restoration. The King's coming was not only anticipated for his redemption of a people from their sins, but also for the consummation of his coming kingdom. When sin entered the world through Adam and Eve and God's kingdom was marred, God promised a glorious return when he would usher in a restored kingdom. As the OT unfolds this restored kingdom, certain characteristics begin to emerge. The kingdom has core characteristics, as well as a core within the core. This language assumes that characteristics exist outside the core characteristics, but for the scope of this chapter we will hone in on what seems to be most central to the coming kingdom. We are drawn back to the previous section on redemption that highlights the coming King. At the core of the core is the King and the message he brings. The Spirit-anointed Christ crucified for sinners to find forgiveness and peace with God for the glory of his name and the joy of his people is the core of the core. As this good news of the kingdom is spelled out in greater detail, the OT Prophets and the Writings mention the common themes of justice for the poor, oppressed, and lowly, and equity for the nations as part of the core of the coming kingdom.[12]

Perhaps we find a helpful analogy in the opening of a business. When you see a vacant building in a shopping center begin to get tables, chairs, kitchen equipment, food, and servers, and finally the manager hangs the sign that says, "Restaurant Now Open for Business," you know you are looking at a restaurant. There are signs that a restaurant is coming and then finally

---

[12] The core is determined first by its presence in key OT texts that serve as compositional sutures which highlight main themes of the OT, especially in the Psalms and the Prophets, which serve as commentaries on earlier OT themes such as Psalms 1–2, 22, 72, 145–150; Isaiah 1–2, 11, 42, 52–55, 60–66; and the Minor Prophets. The core is also chosen based upon the general frequency of these themes in the OT and then by its reiteration in the NT.

that the restaurant has opened. Likewise there are signs that the kingdom is inbreaking and there will be a time when it is fully realized. As the people of God thought about the coming kingdom they knew the kingdom was coming with the message of the King (the core of the core); further, they knew the kingdom was coming with justice for the poor and equity for the nations (the core). The centrality of "equity for the nations" is seen, for example in Isaiah 49:6 where it is "too light a thing" that the coming servant King must go only to the Jews, but he also must go as "a light for the nations, that my salvation may reach to the end of the earth."[13] That this is extended to Christ's church as Christ's priority is clarified in Matthew 24:14 and his Great Commission is given to his followers in Matthew 28:19–20. In these verses, the message and the power for the task is clarified. It is his kingly authority behind the *gospel of the kingdom* that fuels his followers to prioritize speaking the gospel to all the nations so that he would come again and consummate his kingdom.

The same motivation and power fuel the core characteristic of justice for the poor. The OT Prophets and the Writings show the extension of mercy and justice to the lowly and oppressed as an expression of our God's mercy and justice. One example is Isaiah 42.[14] Here we see God's passion for unjust living undone by the righteous action of his people. We also see his call for mercy to the needy as central to his coming kingdom. As discussed above, Jesus as Messiah (Matt. 12:17–21), including his ministry and message (Matt. 25; Luke 4), only serve to confirm his desire for his people to work toward these kingdom characteristics with their lives until he comes again to restore all things.

Paul saw his mission as one in which he proclaimed and did the work of the kingdom while helping the churches he started join him in this kingdom work. As one reads Luke–Acts it becomes clearer that the core of the core is the emphasis of the church's labor. In other words, proclaiming the gospel of repentance of sin and faith in Christ for the forgiveness of sins is our primary ministry to the poor because their greatest need is heart transformation rather than merely circumstantial transformation. However, the core of the coming kingdom (equity for the nations and justice for the poor) still accompanies the core of the core (the gospel of the kingdom proclaimed) as the necessary work of Christ's church. That is why we see in Revelation that John, who describes himself in Revelation 1:9 as a "partner in the tribulation and *the kingdom*" with Christ's church (emphasis added), writes of churches who are "poor" in

---

[13] Some other examples are: Genesis 12:1–3; 48:19; 49:10; Psalms 2:8–9; 9:18–20; 22:27; 72:11; 96:1–10; Isaiah 2:2–3; 11:9–11; 12:3; 19:16–25; 42:6–9,12; 51:4–5; 56:7; 60:9; 62:1–2; 66:18; Amos 9:11–12; Obadiah 19; Jonah; Micah 4:1–2; Habakkuk 2:4–5; Zechariah 2:10–11; 14:16.

[14] Some other examples of justice for the poor are also numerous. *For the widow and orphan*: Exodus 22:22; Isaiah 1:17; 9:17. *For those in financial difficulty*: Exodus 22:25; Leviticus 19:9–10; 25:35ff (the year of jubilee). *For the poor in general*: Leviticus 19:13–14; Psalms 9:18–20; 22:26; 72:2,4,12–14; 82:3–4; 140:12; 146:5–10; 147:3; Proverbs 17:5; 21:13; Isaiah 11:4; 29:18–19; 30:26; 41:17; 42:7; 53:7; 61:1–2,8; Hosea 14:3; Joel 2:26–27; Micah 4:3,10; Zechariah 7:8–10; Malachi 4:2.

status but "rich" toward God (Rev. 2:9) and those from all nations (Rev. 5, 7) who will comprise the multitudes that will gather around the throne of their king (Rev. 21:3–5; 22:2–3,17). We are to be about God's kingdom work until he comes to usher in the restoration of all things in the consummation of his kingdom in the new heavens and the new earth.[15]

So, in summary and adding application, the entire biblical message motivates Jesus and all Christians to care for the poor because:

1. *In creation*, God created all people in his image to follow him as king, and therefore we must not exclude people from our intentional love based upon their physical condition.
2. *In the fall*, God extended his justice and mercy to us and therefore as we image him forth, we should extend it to others.
3. *In redemption*, God promised to redeem his fallen people through the promised king who will establish a kingdom where justice to the poor is near to his heart.
4. *In restoration,* God will right all wrongs and empower his people to do his kingdom work of proclaiming good news to the poor, extending his mercy to the hurting, and fighting for his justice to prevail among the oppressed.
5. A gospel-centered follower of King Jesus cannot be indifferent to Christ's kingdom care for the poor.

How are we to care for the poor? As believers we must care for the poor. But what does that mean? In answering the "How?" question, we seek to show that there are biblical priorities and biblical categories in caring for the poor. We work toward, and pray for, a biblically informed approach that instructs the believer and encourages the church on how to faithfully live out our social responsibility, and an obedient church willing to fulfill its calling.

We will begin by stating three brief principles from Scripture to guide our care for the poor, and then proceed by expounding upon them:

- The church, in her care for the poor, begins with the poor who are believers. This principle acknowledges that ministry to the poor is to begin with the church but not to the neglect of the unbelieving poor (Acts 2; Gal. 2:10; 6:9–10; 1 Tim. 5:3,5).
- The missional church prioritizes the "guiltless poor" over the "guilty poor" (Jer. 2:34; Isa. 9:17).
- The missional church is composed of believers who are overflowing with God's love; they proclaim and apply the gospel clearly not only among believers but to the lost world that needs Jesus through what might be called the 60/40 trajectory of care.

---

[15]   To be clear, we are not trying to make his kingdom now in a post-millennial understanding where everything will get better and the kingdom will come in before the king returns. The king will bring in his kingdom. However, we are to be about the work of the king. We are fellow-workers for the kingdom, that is, participants in the kingdom by doing kingdom work.

The first principle is an often-overlooked biblical idea, namely that the church must care for the church. We see the early church's care for one another in Acts 2:42–47 as a priority for the believers and an evangelistic tool for converting the unbeliever. Acts 6:1–7 reveals the organization of servant leaders to organize care for the believing widows in their midst. In 1 Timothy 5 Paul commands Timothy to "honor," or take care of spiritually and financially, those who are "truly widows" (v. 3). These were widows who were characterized as women who have "set [their] hope on God" (v. 5). The logic Paul is conveying here seems to be that when the church doesn't care for the church, they bring reproach upon the church and therefore upon Christ (1 Tim. 5:7,14). Paul, in Galatians 6, reveals the priority of the church in doing good works when he says, "So then, as we have opportunity, let us do good to everyone, and *especially to those who are of the household of faith*" (v. 10, emphasis added). Therefore, if the church loves Christ, then the church must prioritize his bride.

The second principle gives priority to the "guiltless poor" over against the "guilty poor." In Jeremiah 2:34 the people of Israel had forgotten God and one indicator was that, "Also on your skirts is found the lifeblood of the *guiltless poor*" (emphasis added).[16] There seems to be a distinction made by the biblical author between the "guiltless poor" in Jeremiah 2:34 and the "guilty poor," so to speak, of Isaiah 9:17. The guiltless poor of Jeremiah 2:34 are those who are poor but guiltless because they are poor by "no fault of their own." Specifically in this instance, "guiltless" meant they were not found doing the injustice of "breaking in" to houses (v. 34b). Other examples of the guiltless poor are widows and orphans. They are poor by "no fault of their own." That is, they are poor because something happened to them beyond their control, such as the death of a spouse for the widow or abandonment for the orphan. Therefore Jeremiah's indictment of Israel was not only their neglect of such poor people, but also their intentional oppression of such people. God's anger toward those who intentionally oppress the poor is another example of God's desire for his people to be about justice for the poor.

However, these who are poor by no fault of their own are not beyond transgressing God's ways. Isaiah 9:17 reveals the fatherless and the widow who are "godless" and "evildoers." In this case, God is not fighting for their cause but against them as he withholds his compassion from them. God is eager to defend the cause of the "guiltless" poor, but he is not indifferent to godless living even if the people are physically poor. The focus of his care is on those who walk in his ways.

Therefore, we have God's passion to care for the poor shaped by biblically informed categories and God's priorities. A way to think of this as we attempt to faithfully live out care for the poor could be drawn up as follows:[17]

---

[16] I owe this point to Kent Capps.

[17] These quadrants are simply applications of biblical principles stated above. Categorizing specific real-life scenarios will be unclear at times, and therefore extending care to the poor must be accompanied by great wisdom and sensitivity to the Spirit.

CHAPTER 7, FIGURE I

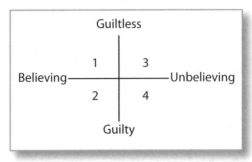

A paradigm in the church's care for the poor: believing guiltless (quadrant one); believing guilty (quadrant two); unbelieving guiltless (quadrant three); unbelieving guilty (quadrant four)

Below are four brief but true stories that help us understand each quadrant.[18]

Quadrant one: the believing guiltless. Nancy, a passionate follower of Christ, has a husband who beats her. She has stayed home to care for her kids, and as the husband abandons her, she has no present way to produce income and the kids are too young to work.[19] Betty, an infant orphan, was abandoned at birth, perhaps because her parents did not want her, could not adequately care for her, or were dying of disease.[20] The widow needs spiritual care but also financial assistance, while the orphan needs a God-fearing home. Some other examples of the guiltless believers are: believing widows, believing orphans, child orphans from believing parents, and believers who are oppressed by governments, social structures or individuals, which have led to their physical poverty.[21]

Quadrant two: the believing guilty. Bill and Susie made poor choices in their college years, mostly as an expression of their life apart from Christ. They now find themselves with over $100,000 of non-mortgage debt. Although they are now followers of Christ, much tension resides in their marriage because every month is a reminder of bills that are barely getting paid and debt that is not being reduced. They need to be reminded regularly of Christ's forgiveness and power of provision. They also need wise financial

---

[18]   These are individuals or couples who have attended or who are members of our church, Treasuring Christ Church, which ministers in the inner city of Raleigh, North Carolina. The names have been changed.

[19]   First Timothy 5 describes a common scenario in the early church where a woman in her sixties who has set her hope on Christ loses her husband and, having no living family, does not make enough money to pay her bills.

[20]   The orphan is not a believer by definition as we saw in Isaiah 9:17, but I lump infant/child orphans in this first category of care from James 1:27. I am defining orphan as one who has lost both parents due to death, abandonment, or other forms of neglect.

[21]   A potential scenario could be a believer who lost his or her job because of the bad economy and cannot get hired even at the local McDonalds in order to pay this month's rent.

counseling, budget accountability, ways to provide more income, insight into refinancing or consolidation, and regular and/or generous financial aid from the church. In a nutshell, guilty believers are those who find themselves in physical hardship because of sinful choices made, yet they have repented of them and they are followers of Christ by his amazing grace.[22]

Quadrant three: the unbelieving guiltless. Dashanda, a single mom, has been saving her money to buy the house she is presently renting, faithfully working several jobs to make ends meet and provide for her two teenage boys and her daughter (who is herself a single mom with two children). Unknown to her, the city had created the stipulation that the home she was renting could not be rented. The city had invested money to build these homes and, noticing a trend of crime associated with rental property as compared to single-family-owned homes, they decided to create such regulations. However, in order to purchase the home (because she is not allowed to rent it), the city also requires her to attend homeowners' classes, which would qualify her for city-sponsored grants and interest-free loans. Although she has gone to all the classes the city has asked her to attend, she still must work another year to save up enough money for a down payment to secure the house. A neighbor realized she was renting and reported her to the city. The city told her she had to buy the house or move within the month, meaning that unless she secures a place she will be homeless. She is an unbeliever but finds herself in need because information was withheld from her by her landlord and the city was not willing to work with her. She needs the good news of Jesus Christ to change her heart, but it could be the Christians' extension of mercy through pursuing the city for an extension, helping her find a place to move, helping her move, or more, that God uses to soften her heart to the gospel message. To help the guiltless unbeliever is not to say that the person did not sin at all or that his or her past sin hasn't contributed to the situation, but as a Christian goes to care for her, the guiltless unbeliever's life situation stands in contrast to the unbelieving guilty person, who is poor primarily because they are given to licentious, godless living. Some other examples of the guiltless unbeliever are widows and orphans who do not trust in Christ, as well as unbelievers who are oppressed by governments, social structures, or individuals.[23]

Quadrant four: the unbelieving guilty. Randy was a millionaire, but on his fortieth birthday he found that because of his cocaine addiction, he had snorted all of his money away and was sent to Wake County Jail. He was homeless, broke, and hurting. Through believers at the Raleigh Rescue Mission he heard the gospel and also received food, a bed, and rehabilitation

---

[22] Diseases such as AIDS can reside in believers who made bad choices while not walking with Christ and would reflect "physical hardship," i.e., poverty as described above.

[23] Other ways our church has sought to care for the unbelieving guiltless are through teaching ESL to international students who are struggling financially, providing meals for some who are hungry, caring for orphans in countries where we have international workers, and adopting or fostering children who are in their situation by no fault of their own.

when he was released from jail. When he came to our church he heard the gospel again, professed faith, and was baptized in our baptismal pool. He was able to hear the Word in our corporate worship, he was partnered with a mentor, and he began to come to our weekly community groups for ongoing spiritual care. With his needs of housing, transportation, work, and food, the church tried to connect him with options or help him some financially.[24]

The numbers in each quadrant represent biblical priorities, while the crosshairs communicate biblical categories. In light of the two principles outlined above, faithful care for the poor is not only for the unbelieving homeless drug addict, where most of our energies and resources are usually concentrated. As symbolized by the highest quadrant number, they are the lowest in terms of biblical priorities. We are not saying that we withhold mercy from those in quadrant four (the guilty unbeliever) totally, or even that mercy for them should be withheld until all the other types of poor are cared for. However, the quadrants of care are meant to communicate our need to focus our mercy efforts upon those who are believers and upon those who are more innocent recipients of poverty—the orphaned, oppressed, widowed, etc. This frees up the church to legitimately regard their care for their members' physical needs as biblical care for the poor (Matt. 25:40). It also reverses the horrid trend in churches where the unbelieving pagan is cared for while the church members are not sharing what they have with each other so that no one is in need (Acts 2:45).

Now the stage is set for the final principle, lest we be misunderstood. Every believer is meant to be clearly loving, applying and proclaiming the gospel not only among believers, but also to the lost world that needs Jesus: the 60/40 trajectory (emphasis) of care. Although we need to think in the biblical priorities of caring for the believer (community) and the innocent first, we cannot neglect intentionally caring for the lost (mission).[25] Community and mission must be simultaneous pursuits. A holy huddle filled with thin evangelists has weak roots. Biblically, followers of Christ are meant to be in love with truth, rooted in the local church where they are committed to living out the "one anothers" as a family, while at the same time being broken, passionate gospel-sharers with the lost world around them.

---

[24] Because he became a believer, you might think the church's help was really in quadrant two. So a few other examples are: (1) As a church we also feed breakfast to the poor who walk in off the streets on a Sunday morning. Most of them are unbelievers, but our light breakfast allows for continual gospel interaction through conversation and our Sunday corporate worship. (2) When we care for this category, which is often because of our downtown context, we try to help them the first time, but ongoing care is connected to their interest in spiritual things like church, further gospel conversation, or their desire for friendship with a believer. We also make it a rule not to hand out cash, but to care for them by providing services such as bus tickets, groceries, laundry, or driving them to a destination for housing, etc. For more guidelines go to our website www.tccraleigh.org and look under resources at "Guidelines in Caring for the Poor."

[25] These two summary terms come from Tim Chester and Steve Timmis, *Total Church: A Radical Reshaping around Gospel and Community* (Wheaton: Crossway, 2008), 69–84.

Therefore as we seek to care for the poor, I talk about it as the "60/40 trajectory of care." It could be illustrated like this:

CHAPTER 7, FIGURE 2

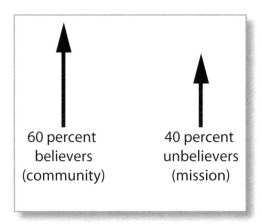

At Treasuring Christ Church, where I am one of the pastors, we aim to focus approximately 60 percent of our energies upon the church and 40 percent of our energies and resources upon the unbelieving world. These percentages are not meant to be exact, but to communicate a trajectory for our care. They are meant to communicate the priority of our care for the believing poor while keeping our mission to extend mercy to the unbelieving poor at our core, especially when ministries of mercy are one of the main means God uses to break down hard hearts to the gospel. Although this does not answer every mercy opportunity we will encounter, hopefully it makes us aware of the need around us, stirs our hearts to love the hurting, and helps inform us as we pursue biblical faithfulness in caring for the poor.[26]

CONCLUSION

The church must be about the gospel. Yet Jesus says a gospel-shaped life will be evidenced by its care for the poor—the weak, the lowly, the oppressed, and the hurting. Poverty is a complicated social phenomenon with many

---

[26] When caring for the poor few resources have been as helpful as Steve Corbett and Brian Fikkert, *When Helping Hurts: How to Alleviate Poverty Without Hurting the Poor . . . and Yourself* (Chicago: Moody Publishers, 2009). The book provides so many biblical insights and helpful paradigms in knowing when and how to provide relief, rehabilitation, and development in the four relationships that effect every poor person. "A helpful first step in thinking about working with the poor in any context is to discern whether the situation calls for relief, rehabilitation, or development. In fact the failure to distinguish among these situations is one of the most common reasons that poverty-alleviation efforts often do harm," 104.

different layers. There exist many expressions of poverty, many of which are visible, such as homelessness, hunger, unemployment, debt, bad credit, and poor education. There exist many contributing factors, such as exploitation by the rich, predatory lenders, gentrification, unjust landlords or employers, a low minimum wage compared to the cost of living, sickness, and the sins of generations of families. Yet other more internal or behind-closed-door realities involve idols such as sex, drugs, alcohol, or leisure; other realities involve secret attempts to escape physical and emotional abuse, drug addictions, gang affiliations, and reentering society from the prisons. In this fallen world, the complexities of poverty should be addressed primarily by the simplicity of the gospel of the kingdom. It alone has the power to change the heart of the unbelieving poor or the unbelieving oppressor as well as sustain the hope of the oppressed believer or the debt-ridden follower of Christ. This chapter is meant to emphasize Christ's call to love him dearly, speak his gospel message clearly, and care for the poor intentionally. So with joy-filled love for our Creator, a sober realization of our fallen world, a deep affection for our Redeemer, Jesus, and a longing for the consummation of his coming, the church must lay down its life in love, anticipating salvation in Christ for the spiritually poor and the restoration of all things, including the alleviation of the pains that contribute to the physically poor.

Chapter Eight

THE GOSPEL AND CULTURE

Bruce Riley Ashford

INTRODUCTION

Mission is necessarily accomplished at the intersection of gospel, church, and culture. While the evangelical church has given substantial theological treatments of gospel and church, it has not given equal theological treatment of the concept of culture.[1] This oversight is unfortunate, however. One's theology of culture is the difference between a gospel missionary and a cultural imperialist or cultural separatist. For this reason, the concept of culture is not only an academic matter, but also a practical one. In academic circles the questions raised center on how to define *culture* and how to analyze it, while in the church and on the mission field the questions often involve cross-cultural communication of the gospel, the embodiment of the church in culture, and the posture of Christians towards their surrounding culture.

---

[1] Evangelical missiologists have devoted much attention to human culture, as evidenced by scores of books on anthropology for missionaries, cross-cultural communication, and contextualization. More rare, however, are robust theologies of culture, although in recent years, an increasing number of evangelical books and articles give theologies of culture. For a sampling of recent evangelical theological treatments of culture, see Michael S. Horton, *Where in the World Is the Church?* (Phillipsburg: P&R, 2002); Albert M. Wolters, *Creation Regained*, 2nd ed. (Grand Rapids: Eerdmans, 2005); T. M. Moore, *Culture Matters* (Grand Rapids: Brazos, 2007); David Bruce Hegeman, *Plowing in Hope*, 2nd ed. (Mosco, ID: Canon, 2007); Andy Crouch, *Culture Making* (Downers Grove: IVP, 2008); and David VanDrunen, *Living in God's Two Kingdoms* (Wheaton, IL: Crossway, 2010). Reinhold Niebuhr's *Christ and Culture* (New York: Harper, 1951) is the classic treatment of Christianity and culture, but it is not particularly helpful for the type of constructive theological and missiological conversation for which this chapter aims.

This chapter provides a theological introduction to some of the important issues at the intersection of mission and culture. It will begin by giving
a basic definition of culture and then proceed to delineate a biblical theology of culture, constructed from within the Bible's narrative of creation, fall,
redemption, and restoration. Finally, this chapter provides a discussion of the
gospel *in* culture (contextualization) and *for* culture (cultural mandate).

CLARIFYING THE QUESTION

What is meant when one uses the English term *culture?* What is the common use of the word? A survey of the history of cultural anthropology reveals
that there is little consensus on the notion of culture or on how to analyze and
interpret various cultures. Over the years, various schools of anthropology
have arisen, including social Darwinism, cultural relativism, functionalism,
and symbolic anthropology. In the nineteenth century, social Darwinism ruled
the day, arguing that societies and cultures should be placed on a spectrum
from simple to complex. Some cultures were highly evolved, while others
were less evolved or perhaps were even in a state of arrested development.[2]
In response to the highly speculative and rationalist school of social Darwinism, Bronislaw Malinowski and the functionalists built a method that was
empirical and field-based. In gathering and analyzing field data, they sought
to identify the institutions that made up the skeleton of society and then give
a deep-level and detailed explanation of how those institutions function.
Malinowski defined culture as "the integral whole consisting of implements
and consumers' goods, of constitutional charters for the various social group-
ings, of human ideas and crafts, beliefs and customs. . . . We are confronted
by a vast apparatus, partly material, partly human, and partly spiritual, by
which man is able to cope with the concrete, specific problems that face
him."[3] Malinowski and the functionalists, therefore, provide an empirical and
field based model that has proven helpful for evangelical missiologists.

After the functionalists there have arisen a myriad of schools of thought
in the field of anthropology. Perhaps the most significant is symbolic anthropology and its progenitor Clifford Geertz, for whom culture is a system of
symbols.[4] For Geertz, the job of the anthropologist is to decipher the system
of symbols, to interpret the culture like a text. Reading a culture is like reading a complex work of fiction. The reader must seek out elements of the
socio-cultural context, understand those elements as well as or better than

---

[2]   For a concise introduction to the various schools of cultural anthropology, two particularly
helpful texts are: Abraham Rosman and Paula G. Rubel, *The Tapestry of Culture*, 8th ed. (New
York: McGraw Hill, 2004), 1–26; Paul G. Hiebert, *Cultural Anthropology*, 2nd ed. (Grand Rapids: Baker, 1983), 69–86.

[3]   Bronislaw Malinowski, *A Scientific Theory of Culture* (Chapel Hill: UNC, 1960), 36.

[4]   Geertz's symbolic anthropology is laid out in comprehensive fashion in Clifford Geertz,
The Interpretation of Cultures (New York: Basic, 1973).

the people do, and understand how these elements illuminate other elements within the same context.

While Malinowski and Geertz are towering figures in their field, their work in the field of cultural anthropology may not be applied to missiology *carte blanche*. Neither Malinowski nor Geertz allowed biblical theology to provide the starting point, trajectory, and parameters for their theories, and therefore both are unable to give a comprehensively accurate account of man's works or his world, his origin or destiny. For this reason, Paul Hiebert's work is helpful. Hiebert, an evangelical anthropologist and missiologist, has sought to combine the best insights from several schools of anthropology, including Malinowski's functionalism and Geertz's symbolic anthropology, and apply them to missiology. For Hiebert, culture is "the more or less integrated systems of ideas, feelings, and values and their associated patterns of behavior and products shared by a group of people who organize and regulate what they think, feel, and do."[5] This definition is perhaps the most oft-quoted and used conception of culture in evangelical missiology, and is as good as any to give us a handle on the concept, from the stance of the social sciences.

Hiebert's work provides a social science model that is informed by, and complements, the biblical doctrines of creation and man. These doctrines reveal man as one who produces culture, but at the same time is shaped by it. In other words, culture is both a work of human hands and a world in which humans live. This is Kevin Vanhoozer's point when he argues that culture is both a "work" and a "world" of meaning. He writes that culture "is a *work* because it is the result of what humans do freely, not as a result of what they do by nature," and that it is a world because "cultural texts create a meaningful environment in which humans dwell both physically and imaginatively."[6] The concept of culture, therefore, is inextricably bound up with the doctrine of man. Man produces culture and then, in turn, is shaped by the very culture he helped to produce. For this reason we must go to the Christian Scriptures in general, and to the doctrine of man in particular, to get a handle on the notion of culture. Christian theology alone reveals man's nature as an image-bearer of the Triune God, and therefore Christian theology alone can render intelligible man's works and his world. Christian theology, therefore, will give the starting point, trajectory, and parameters for our discussion of culture. To the Scriptures we now turn in search for a basic theological framework for understanding culture.

---

[5] Paul G. Hiebert, *Anthropological Insights for Missionaries* (Grand Rapids: Baker, 1985), 30. Hiebert makes clear that neither functionalism or symbolic anthropology can be imported wholesale. Both paradigms arose from within frameworks of thought not entirely consonant with the Christian faith.

[6] Kevin J. Vanhoozer, "What Is Everyday Theology? How and Why Christians Should Read Culture," in Kevin J. Vanhoozer, Charles A. Anderson, Michael J. Sleasman, eds., *Everyday Theology* (Grand Rapids: Baker, 2007), 26.

A THEOLOGY OF CULTURE

The unified biblical narrative, stretching from creation and fall through to redemption and restoration, enables us to understand this notion of culture, this "more or less integrated systems of ideas, feelings, and values and their associated patterns of behavior and products shared by a group of people who organize and regulate what they think, feel, and do,"[7] to which we referred earlier in the chapter. This narrative alone can foster a constructive missiological conversation about human culture. Each of the narrative's plot movements is significant; indeed, if we are to think well about gospel and culture, we must think about all of them at once when treating the subject.[8]

Creation. The Bible's opening narrative tells us about God's creation, including God's design for human culture. In the very first chapters, we are told that God created the heavens and the earth. He created out of nothing, he shaped what he created, and he called the work of his hands "good." At each step along the way, the narrative affirms the goodness of God's handiwork. Moreover, when God completes his creation by making humanity in his image and likeness, the narrative affirms that God's creation was "very good."

Humans are the culmination of God's good creation. They are different from God's other handiwork. Indeed, the first statement about humans is that God made them in the image and likeness of God, male and female alike. They are like God in many ways, including but not limited to their capacities for spirituality, morality, relationality, language, rationality, and creativity.[9] Man's likeness to God, Calvin argues, "extends to the whole excellence by which man's nature towers over all the kinds of living creatures."[10] Because of these capacities, God could place the man and woman in the garden to have dominion over God's good creation (Gen. 1:26–27) and to work it and keep it (Gen. 2:15).

After having created man, God commanded him to "work" the garden, and in so doing to participate with God in his ongoing work of creation and providence. Man is to work the garden, change it, and even enhance it. His work in the garden manifests itself not only in agriculture, but in all types of culture. He may "work the garden" not only by cultivating plant life, but also by cultivating the arts, the sciences, or the public square. When man obeys this command to responsibly cultivate the earth, he is pleasing God.

What, then, does the creation narrative contribute to a discussion of culture? First, human culture is part of the physical and material world, which is part of God's creation and therefore is not inherently bad. We must not allow

---

[7] See fn. 5.

[8] D. A. Carson makes a point similar to this in D. A. Carson, *Christ & Culture Revisited* (Grand Rapids: Eerdmans, 2008), 44–45.

[9] Wayne Grudem provides a helpful treatment of the *imago Dei*, along the lines of the position taken in this chapter. Wayne Grudem, *Systematic Theology* (Grand Rapids: Zondervan, 1994), 442ff.

[10] John Calvin, *Institutes of the Christian Religion 1*, ed. John T. McNeill (Philadelphia: Westminster, 1960), 188.

ourselves to fall into a form of neo-Gnosticism, treating "spiritual" things as good and "material" things as bad. Albert Wolters affirms this: "God does not make junk, and we dishonor the Creator if we take a negative view of the work of his hands when he himself takes such a positive view. In fact, so positive a view did he take of what he had created that he refused to scrap it when mankind spoiled it, but determined instead, at the cost of his Son's life, to make it new and good again. God does not make junk, and he does not junk what he has made."[11] Therefore, we may not assume that "spiritual" things (such as prayer and meditation) alone are inherently good, while "material" things (including the products of human culture) are inherently bad. To do so is to misdraw the line. The line that must be drawn is between God and his creation, not between two aspects (material vs. spiritual) of his creation.[12]

This distinction was Paul's point in Colossians 2:8 when he rebuked those who said, "Do not handle, do not taste, do not touch!" (Col. 2:21, NASB). Such a (metaphysically dualist) philosophy is hollow and deceptive. In like manner, John's first chapter makes clear that our Lord took on human flesh, which is part of God's good creation and therefore is not inherently bad. Even the fall could not make God's creation ontologically bad. Though God's creation is affected by the fall, and though humans sometimes wrongly love God's creation more than they love the Creator himself, his creation remains good precisely because it is his creation.[13] Christians may not take a metaphysically dualist view of the creation, with its attendant impulse toward cultural separation and withdrawal. To do so is to adopt a hollow and deceptive philosophy, to denigrate God's good creation, and implicitly to undermine the incarnation.

Second, the creation narrative reveals that God gave humans the capacity to create culture and then commanded them to use those capacities. God created humans in his image and likeness, thereby giving them capacities for spirituality, morality, relationality, language, rationality, and creativity: "We are able to produce works and worlds of meaning because we are created

---

[11] Albert M. Wolters, *Creation Regained*, 2nd ed. (Grand Rapids: Eerdmans, 2005), 48–49.

[12] This was Irenaeus' point in *Against Heresies*, when he used Romans 1 to defeat the "pernicious doctrines" of the Gnostics. Irenaeus, *Against Heresies*, 1.22.1. For further reflection on the goodness of creation in relation to dualism, Michael Wittmer provides a particularly helpful and accessible exploration of the ontological distinction between God and creation, and its implications for a theology of culture. Michael Wittmer, *Heaven Is a Place on Earth* (Grand Rapids: Zondervan, 2004), 37–49. Also recommended are James P. Boyce, *Abstract of Systematic Theology* (Cape Coral: Founders, 2006), 166–74; A. H. Strong, *Systematic Theology* (Philadelphia: Judson, 1907), 378–83; and David P. Nelson, "The Work of God: Creation and Providence," in *A Theology for the Church*, ed. Daniel L. Akin (Nashville: B&H, 2007), 242–67.

[13] Contemporary Christian dualists point to passages such as Colossians 3:2 which instruct us to set our minds on "the things above" rather than on "earthly things." But such passages do not speak against what we are arguing here. In Colossians, Paul begins by protecting the goodness of creation and only after doing so does he explain that there are earthly things that are "bad." The badness to which he is referring is moral, not ontological, badness. The most accessible discussion of this is found in Wittmer, *Heaven*, 63–65.

in the image of God."[14] However, God has not only given us the *capacity* to make culture. He has *commanded* us to use those capacities. Genesis 1:28 gives Adam and Eve their basic task which involved both producing ("work the garden") and reproducing ("multiply"). This command is often called the cultural mandate because it calls man and woman to bring their influence to bear in every dimension of society and culture. Creation is what God made, but culture is what humans make out of God's good creation. When man rules, fills, works, and keeps, he is shaping culture. Plantinga writes, "There's so much to do in the world—so much caretaking and earth keeping, so much filling and multiplying, so much culture to create."[15] God has given us responsible dominion over his creation, and this dominion includes culture shaping.[16]

Fall. God's creation of the world is the opening scene of the Scriptures and constitutes the first major plot movement of the overarching biblical narrative. However, immediately after this opening scene, Adam and Eve rebelled against God, seeking to set themselves up as autonomous. The effect of this sin for them, and for all of humanity, was disastrous. Humanity no longer lives in paradise, but instead lives in a world pervaded with sin and its effects. The fall "was not just an isolated act of disobedience but an event of catastrophic significance for creation as a whole."[17] Humanity's relationship with God was broken, as well as man's relationship with himself, with others, and with the rest of the created order.

In Romans 1, Paul describes the result of humanity's broken relationship with *God*, pointing out that humans now worship the creature rather than the Creator. The image of God in man is now distorted and defaced. However, not only is man alienated from God; he is alienated from *others*. Rather than loving his neighbors as himself, he lies, murders, rapes, and otherwise demeans his fellow image-bearers. Further, he is alienated from the *created order*, as his attempts to "work the garden" are full of frustration and pain. Finally, he is alienated even from *himself*, as life becomes meaningless because of his separation from God.

The implications of the fall for a discussion of human culture are massive. "Sin defiles and disfigures every inch of the creation," writes Wolters. "Since humankind's fall, the center of each culture is found in some form of communal idolatry that shapes all aspects of social and cultural life and organizes them in rebellions against God."[18] Spiritually, humans are idolaters, worship-

---

[14]   Vanhoozer, "What Is Everyday Theology?," 43.

[15]   Cornelius Plantinga Jr., *Engaging God's World* (Grand Rapids: Eerdmans, 2002), 29.

[16]   For further reflection upon the doctrine of creation in relation to the cultural mandate, one may consult the Wolters, Horton, and Crouch texts mentioned in the first footnote. Also recommended are David Bruce Hegeman, *Plowing in Hope: Toward a Biblical Theology of Culture* (Moscow, ID: Canon, 1999), 26, 41–47; Craig G. Bartholomew and Michael W. Goheen, *The Drama of Scripture* (Grand Rapids: Baker, 2004), 29–40; Craig G. Bartholomew and Michael W. Goheen, *Living at the Crossroads* (Grand Rapids: Baker, 2008), 31–45.

[17]   Wolters, *Creation Regained*, 53.

[18]   Bartholomew and Goheen, *The Drama of Scripture*, 49.

ping God's gifts instead of worshipping God himself. Rationally, they have difficulty discerning the truth and use their capacities to construct vain philosophies. Creatively, they use their imagination to create and worship idols rather than to worship the living God. Relationally, they use their power to exploit others and serve themselves. As a result, any and all human culture is distorted and defaced by sin. No dimension of culture is left untouched.

The fall and its consequences do not, however, make God's creation (or, by implication, human culture) inherently bad. Even though the world is corrupted by sin, it is still materially good. Recognizing this frees us from false asceticisms and gnosticisms that view the use and enjoyment of God's creation as wrong. For this reason, we must distinguish between the ontological and moral aspects of God's creation. As Wolters points out, God's creation remains *structurally* good, although since the fall it is *directionally* corrupt. Structure refers to the order of creation, while direction refers to the order of sin and redemption: "Anything in creation can be directed either toward or away from God," he writes. "This double direction applies not only to individual human beings but also to such cultural phenomena as technology, art, and scholarship, to such societal institutions as labor unions, schools, and corporations, and to such human functions as emotionality, sexuality, and rationality."[19] The directional results of the fall, for human culture, are revealed in such things as poor reasoning in the realm of science, kitsch in the realm of art, and human hatred in the realm of relationships. Anything in creation can be directed toward God or away from him. It is this direction that distinguishes between the good and the bad, rather than some distinction between spiritual and material.

In spite of the fall, things are not as bad as they could be. Without common grace and the Spirit's restraining work (2 Thess. 2:6–7), this world would be an utter horror: "He exerts that grand restraining influence without which there can be no such things as home, society, government, civilization, or individual enjoyment anywhere among all the millions of the sinning human race. He restrains both the sinful acts and the natural tendencies of the acts within some tolerable bounds."[20] One facet of the Spirit's restraining work is the common graces he bestows upon humanity, enabling his image-bearers to use their God-given capacities within the created order. Plantinga writes, "The Holy Spirit preserves much of the original goodness of creation and also inspires new forms of goodness—and not only in those people the Spirit has regenerated. . . . The Spirit also distributes 'common grace,' an array of God's gifts that preserves and enhances human life even when not regenerating it."[21] Because of God's grace through his Spirit after the fall, we may continue to produce culture, thereby utilizing our uniquely human capacities.

Redemption and restoration. The Bible's third plot movement occurs immediately after the fall. God gives not only a promise of death (Gen. 2:17),

---

[19] Wolters, *Creation Regained*, 59.
[20] C. R. Vaughn, *The Gifts of the Holy Spirit* (Carlisle, PA: Banner of Truth, 1994), 32–33.
[21] Plantinga, *Engaging God's World*, 58.

but also a promise of life (Gen. 3:15). He immediately declares that one day the offspring of the woman would destroy the serpent. Paul recognizes this promise as a prophecy of Jesus Christ (Gal. 3:16), God's Son who is "born of a woman" (Gal. 4:4, NASB). This declaration, therefore, is God's promise to send the Messiah to whom the entirety of Scripture ultimately testifies as it declares how God, in spite of seemingly insurmountable obstacles, would fulfill his promise to send this Savior.

God affirms that by the Savior's stripes man is healed, and upon the Savior's shoulders the sin of the world was borne (Isa. 52:13–53:12). Further, the redemption he provides reaches into every square inch of God's creation, including the non-human aspects of creation. In John's gospel, we read that "God so loved *the world*, that he gave his only Son, that whoever believes in him should not perish but have eternal life. For God did not send his Son into the world to condemn the world, but in order that *the world* might be saved through him" (John 3:16–17, emphasis added). Although some theologians have taken this inclusive language to imply some sort of pluralism or universalism, such a reading would contradict other biblical teaching (e.g., Acts 4:12). How then might we understand God's promise to save the world? In this case, the universality of the Bible's *world* language is rendered intelligible by three other biblical teachings.

First, Scripture makes clear that God will save for himself worshippers from among *every* tribe, tongue, people, and nation. In the glorious vision of Revelation 5, all of heaven breaks forth into song, proclaiming the Savior's worthiness to redeem. They sing, "You are worthy to take the scroll, and to open its seals; for You were slain, and have redeemed us to God by Your blood, *out of every tribe and tongue and people and nation*." (Rev. 5:9, NKJV, emphasis added). The inclusivity of God's salvation through Christ is found in his redemption of every type of person he created. He is no tribal deity, and his salvation is not limited to a few select peoples or nations. In elevated terms, the Scriptures proclaim that his Word is so profoundly true, his character so comprehensively good, his countenance so majestically beautiful, that he will find worshippers among every type of person on the face of the earth that he created.[22]

Second, Scripture makes clear that God's redemption extends beyond humanity to include a restored heavens and earth. At the beginning of the Bible, we learn that God created the heavens and the earth (Gen. 1:1) while at the end we see him giving us a "new heavens and a new earth" (Isa. 65:17; Rev. 21:1). The redemptive work of Christ extends through God's *people* to God's *cosmos*, so that in the end "creation itself will be set free from its bondage to corruption and obtain the freedom of the glory of the children of God"

---

[22] The best concise exposition of this aspect of eschatology is John Piper, *Let the Nations Be Glad*, 2nd ed., rev. and exp. (Grand Rapids: Baker, 2003), 155–200.

(Rom. 8:21). This world will be one "in which righteousness dwells" (2 Pet. 3:13), thus fulfilling God's good purposes for his world.[23]

Third, the salvation that God provides will restore man at all levels of his being. God will restore not only man's relationship with God, but also man's relationships with others, with the created order, and even with himself. During the present age, the process of sanctification, which reverses alienation and restores man's relationships, is incomplete and uneven. However, the day will come when our Lord returns and brings with him a new heavens and earth on which we will dwell in unbroken fellowship with him and the entire created order. In that day, there will be sin no more, tears no more, pain no more.[24]

Therefore, the final two plot movements tell the story of God redeeming both his image-bearers and his earth. Two cultural implications are important to notice. First, the doctrines of redemption and restoration are confluent with the doctrine of creation in affirming the goodness of God's creation. God values his creation, and in the end times he will not reject it. There really will be no such thing as the end of this world. God will renew the heavens and earth so that they give him glory. Further, he promises to give us glorified bodies in that day. While God could have promised man an eternity floating around in a bodiless state, in some sort of ethereal wonderland, instead he promises to give man a resurrected bodily existence in a restored universe that shines with the glory of God himself. This promise is yet more reason to view God's creation as good, and our cultural interaction with it as something that pleases God.

Second, the doctrine of restoration is confluent with the doctrine of creation in its affirmation of the cultural mandate. Because God (in the beginning) values his good creation and commands man to produce culture, and because he promises (in the end) to give us a glorious creation replete with its own culture, we ought to live culturally in a manner consistent with God's designs. "The difference between the Christian hope of resurrection and a mythological hope," writes Bonhoeffer, "is that the Christian hope sends a man back to his life on earth in a wholly new way."[25] This new way includes

---

[23]   Although theologians most often reference the passages in Isaiah, Romans, 2 Peter, and Revelation, John's gospel is also significant for treating the renewal of God's creation. Andreas Köstenberger argues that John's gospel can be seen as espousing a "new creation" theology that present's Jesus incarnation and mission in light of the renewal of creation. He writes, "This is most apparent in the introduction to the gospel, which casts the Word's coming into the world in terms reminiscent of creation, most notably by way of references to 'life' and 'light,' both of which constitute creation terminology. Also, John's presentation of Jesus' early ministry as encompassing a week in keeping with the week of creation is suggestive of a new creation." Andreas Köstenberger, *A Theology of John's Gospel and Letters* (BTNT; Grand Rapids: Zondervan, 2009), 337. For further reflection on the new earth and its implications, see Russell D. Moore, "Personal and Cosmic Eschatology," in Akin, *A Theology for the Church*, 912–16; Grudem, *Systematic Theology*, 1158–67.

[24]   Moore, "Personal and Cosmic Eschatology," 912–16.

[25]   Dietrich Bonhoeffer, *Letters and Papers from Prison*, ed. Eberhard Bethge, trans. Reginald Fuller and others, rev. ed. (New York: The Macmillan Co., 1967), 176.

glorifying God from within our cultural contexts, providing a sign of the already-and-not-yet kingdom, of what the world will be like one day when all of creation and culture praises him. As we interact within various dimensions of culture—the arts, the sciences, education, public square, etc.—we are called to do so by bringing the gospel to bear upon those dimensions.[26]

In our evangelism and church planting, we must recognize that the gospel is always proclaimed, the church is always planted, and the Christian life is always lived within a cultural context (through human language, oratory, music, categories of thought, etc.). Instead of chafing against this reality, we may delight in our charge to make the gospel at home in those cultures, and to allow the gospel to critique them and bring them under the scrutiny of God's revelation. "We await the return of Jesus Christ," writes D. A. Carson, "the arrival of the new heaven and the new earth, the dawning of the resurrection, the glory of perfection, the beauty of holiness. Until that day, we are a people in tension. On the one hand, we belong to the broader culture in which we find ourselves; on the other, we belong to the culture of the consummated kingdom of God, which has dawned upon us."[27] God restores his creation instead of trashing it and expects us to minister within our cultural context rather than attempting to extract ourselves from it.

THE GOSPEL IN CULTURE (CONTEXTUALIZATION)

We now turn to a discussion of how to proclaim and embody the gospel *in the midst of human cultures*. This process, often referred to as "contextualization," is one of the most hotly debated in the theological world in general, and in evangelical missiology in particular.[28] As Hiebert points out, "On the one hand, the gospel belongs to no culture. It is God's revelation of himself and his acts to all people. On the other hand, it must always be understood and expressed within human cultural forms."[29] The task of this brief section will be to point out that Scripture provides us examples of contextualization, that contextualization is inevitable, and that in order to contextualize well, one must proclaim and embody the gospel in ways that are faithful, meaningful, and dialogical.

---

[26] Howard Peskett gives a helpful treatment of Revelation 21 and 22, pointing out the embodied nature of our future existence in a new heavens and new earth, and some of the implications for the church's mission today. See Howard Peskett and Vinoth Ramachandra, *The Message of Mission: The Glory of Christ in All Time and Space* (Downers Grove: InterVarsity, 2003), 261–75.

[27] Carson, *Christ and Culture Revisited*, 64.

[28] The word "contextualization" first appeared in 1972 in *Ministry in Context*, a publication of the Theological Education Fund. Dean Gilliland points out that their concern was that "both the approach and content of theological reflection tend to move within the framework of Western questions and cultural presuppositions, failing to vigorously address the gospel of Jesus Christ to the particular situation." This text described contextualization as "the capacity to respond meaningfully to the gospel within the framework of one's own situation." Dean Gilliland, "Contextualization," in *Evangelical Dictionary of World Missions*, ed. A. Scott Moreau (Grand Rapids: Baker, 2000), 225.

[29] Hiebert, *Anthropological Insights*, 30.

New Testament models of contextualization. The New Testament provides abundant examples of theology conceptualized and communicated contextually. The four gospel writers shaped their material for engaging particular communities of readers. Paul shaped his sermons and speeches according to each particular context. An examination of his sermons in Acts 13 (to a Jewish Diaspora), Acts 14 (to a crowd of rural animists), Acts 17 (to the cultural elite of the Areopagus), and his testimonies in Acts 22 (to a mob of Jewish patriots) and Acts 26 (to the elite of Syria–Palestine) reveal Paul's deft ability to communicate the gospel faithfully, meaningfully, and dialogically in a variety of settings.

In Acts 17, for example, Paul preaches to the cultural elite on Mars Hill. In so doing, he was first and foremost *faithful* to God's revelation. He spoke of God's creation of the world, God's sovereignty and providence over his world, and finally God's judgment through Christ Jesus who was resurrected from the dead. Second, Paul spoke in a manner that was *meaningful* to the socio-cultural and situational context. He referenced the altar to the unknown god, quoted the pagan intellectuals Aratus and Epimenides the Cretan (v. 28), and referenced multiple Stoic and Epicurean convictions.[30] As Eckhard Schnabel has pointed out, Paul's "points of contact" included his description of God (vv. 22–23,24–28), critique of manmade temples (v. 24), critique of sacrifices (v. 25), humanity's search for God (vv. 27–28), and critique of idol images (v. 29).[31] But finally, Paul also communicated in a *dialogical* manner. Although he began with points of contact, he did not end there. Over and again, Paul corrected pagan idolatry by showing how the Scriptures subvert and overthrow pagan idolatry as manifested in their literature, philosophy, and theology. Schnabel references nine clear points at which Paul contradicted the pagans in his Mars Hill Sermon.[32] Although Paul began by using some categories familiar to the Athenians and answering some questions they likely would have raised, he followed through by also introducing them to biblical categories and answering questions that they had not raised.

The inevitability of contextualization. The call to contextualize the gospel is not limited to dramatic scenarios such as the one portrayed in Acts 17. Just as the four Gospel writers shaped their books for engaging particular communities of readers, and just as each of Paul's sermons and speeches are fashioned according to a particular context, so our gospel communication is always accomplished within a context: the *gospel is always expressed in cultural forms* and cannot be otherwise. "Disciples do not follow the gospel in a vacuum but wend their Christian way through particular times and places, each with its own problems and possibilities."[33] Indeed, "American Christians have a tendency to think of contextualization as something missionaries and overseas Christians do 'over there,' and many serious Christians

---

[30] F. F. Bruce, *Paul: Apostle of the Heart Set Free* (Grand Rapids: Eerdmans, 1996), 242.
[31] Eckhard Schnabel, *Paul the Missionary* (Downers Grove: IVP, 2008), 171.
[32] Ibid., 174–83.
[33] Vanhoozer, "What Is Everyday Theology?"16.

in the Western world worry about how far non-Western churches go in their contextualization efforts. However, in reality, every Christian alive today is actively involved in contextualization. Every American Christian worships in a contextualized church."[34] Christianity is and always has been believed and practiced contextually.

Indeed, every church contextualizes by the type of building and décor it chooses and the style of music that is played. Every preacher does the same by choosing, for example, a form of rhetoric, a way of relating to others, and a manner of clothing.

> The question is not whether or not we are going to do it. The question facing every believer and every church is whether or not they will contextualize well. Anyone who fails to realize that they are doing it, and who fails to think it through carefully and Biblically, simply guarantees that they will probably contextualize poorly. Syncretism can happen as easily in Indiana or Iowa as it can in Indonesia![35]

The question is not whether we will contextualize; the question is whether we do it appropriately or not. In order to proclaim the gospel and plant churches in an appropriately contextual manner, we must proclaim and plant in three ways: faithfully, meaningfully, and dialogically.

Faithfully. Biblical fidelity is imperative. We must pay careful attention to our beliefs and practices, ensuring that we express and embody the gospel in cultural forms that are *faithful to the Scriptures*. In being faithful to the Scriptures, we seek to interpret the Scriptures accurately before proclaiming them within a cultural context. Although some scholars view texts as vast oceans of indeterminate symbols that lack transcendent grounding, and while we acknowledge that the reader does come to a text through finite and fallible interpretive frameworks, we nonetheless argue that faithful interpretation is possible.

The triune God enables faithful communication, and indeed is the paradigm of all message sending and receiving. The Trinitarian God's communicative action provides a general hermeneutic for the faithful reader. The triune God is Father (the One who speaks), Son (the Word), and Spirit (the one who illumines and guides and teaches); God the Father speaks through his Son, and we as humans are enabled to hear and understand that communication by his Spirit. Vanhoozer writes, "The Trinity thus serves the role of what Kant calls a 'transcendental condition': a necessary condition for the possibility of something humans experience but cannot otherwise explain, namely, the experience of meaningful communication."[36] The Trinity is a demonstration, contra linguistic antirealists, that accomplished communication is possible.

---

[34] Central Asia mission leader, "Biblical Foundations and Guidelines for Contextualization (Pt. 1)," http://betweenthetimes.com/2008/08/28/guest-blog-by-central-asia-rl-biblical-foundations -and-guidelines-for-contextualization-pt-1/.

[35] Ibid.

[36] Kevin J. Vanhoozer, *Is There a Meaning in This Text?* (Grand Rapids: Zondervan, 1998), 456. Vanhoozer gives a comprehensive and persuasive argument for a Trinitarian hermeneutic.

Faithful interpretation is driven by the quest to discern the author's intent. H. L. Hix puts it well: "Any theory of interpretation that misunderstands what an author is cannot hope to understand what a text is and how it conveys . . . meaning."[37] We discern the meaning of a biblical passage by reading it in light of its intentional context; in other words, we read it against the backdrop of that which best enables us to answer the question of what the author is doing. We read a passage in John's Gospel, for example, by reading it in light of John's entire book, which provides the intentional context for the human author. Moreover, we read the same passage in light of the entire canon of Scripture, which provides the intentional context for the Divine Author. Vanhoozer writes, "If we are reading the Bible as the Word of God, therefore, I suggest that the context that yields this maximal sense is the canon, taken as a unified communicative act."[38] In order to interpret a biblical passage faithfully, therefore, we must strive to understand both its immediate and broader intentional contexts.

Meaningfully. Moreover, we must proclaim and embody the gospel in a way that is *meaningful for the socio-cultural context.* James McClendon writes, "If hearers were (minimally) to understand the gospel, if there was to be uptake, the preacher must understand the culture addressed."[39] Indeed, we want the hearer to understand the words we speak and the actions we perform in the way that we intend, and we want them to be able to respond in a way that is meaningful in context. This type of proclamation takes hard work; learning a culture is more complex than learning a language because language is only one component of culture. Pastors and professors must work hard to teach their audiences not only how to read the Bible, but also how to read the culture.[40]

Ultimately, as we note in the next section, cultural insiders will take the lead in determining how to communicate the gospel in their sociocultural matrix. This communication is premised upon the inherent "translatability" of the Christian Scriptures. Because of the Bible's inherent translatability, Lamin Sanneh speaks of contextualization as "vernacular translation" and Christianity as a "vernacular translation movement."[41] Unlike Islam, which affirms Arabic as the only suitable language for Allah's words, Christianity is

He builds upon ordinary language theory and provides a theological treatment of related philosophical issues such as realism and rationality. For reflection on how the doctrines of God and Revelation undergird the process of cross-cultural communication and interpretation, see David J. Hesselgrave, *Paradigms in Conflict* (Grand Rapids: Kregel, 2005), 243–77. For a comprehensive Christian exposition of cross-cultural communication, see David J. Hesselgrave, *Communicating Christ Cross-Culturally*, 2nd ed. (Grand Rapids: Zondervan, 1991).

[37] H. L. Hix, *Morte D'Author* (Philadelphia: Temple University, 1990), 12.

[38] Vanhoozer, *Is There a Meaning?* 265.

[39] James Wm. McClendon Jr., *Witness,* vol. 1 of *Systematic Theology,* ed. James Wm. McClendon Jr. (Nashville: Abingdon, 2000), 40.

[40] For further reflection on reading cultures, see Vanhoozer, Anderson, and Sleasman, *Everyday Theology*; for a discussion on how to read the worldviews underlying culture, see Hesselgrave, *Communicating Christ Cross-Culturally,* 193–285.

[41] Lamin Sanneh, *Translating the Message* (Maryknoll: Orbis, 2005).

a vernacular translation movement, growing and expanding as the Scriptures are translated into the speech of common people. Sanneh, Andrew Walls, Kwame Bediako, and others have demonstrated that no one sociocultural or linguistic matrix has a corner on the universal or exclusive norm for Christian faith or theology. The Christian Scriptures may be proclaimed and embodied meaningfully from within any socio-cultural and linguistic context.[42]

Dialogically. Finally, we must also allow the gospel to critique the culture in which it is embodied and proclaimed. There is an ever-present danger that Christian preachers, missionaries, and communities will equate the gospel with a cultural context, the consequence of which is devastating. In an attempt to communicate the gospel meaningfully within a culture, and in an attempt to affirm whatever in a culture can be affirmed, Christians may lose sight of the effects of depravity on that same culture. Therefore, we must remember that the gospel stands in judgment of all cultures, calling them to conform themselves to the image of Christ. The gospel does not condemn all of a culture, but it is always and at the same time both affirming and rejecting. If the gospel we preach does not have a prophetic edge, then we are not fully preaching the gospel.

In seeking to proclaim the gospel in a way that is meaningful, we listen to the questions that a culture asks, acknowledge the categories within which it thinks, and learn the language that it speaks. But at the same time, we recognize that without the gospel the host culture does not know all of the right questions to ask, does not have the all of the right categories within which to think, and does not possess a fully adequate vocabulary. As Plantinga puts it, one must engage in the "very common human enterprise of diagnosis, prescription, and prognosis, but to do so from inside a Christian view of the world, a view that has been constructed from Scripture and that centers on Jesus Christ the Savior."[43] Some theologians have called this process "dialogical" contextualization. David Clark writes, "Using a dialogical method implies we notice the danger in simply asking Scripture to answer the culture's concerns. A dialogical approach requires that the Bible not only answer our concerns but also transform those concerns."[44] In taking a dialogical approach the Christian who seeks to evangelize, plant churches, disciple, or pastor within a particular context will find himself in a continued dialogue with that cultural context.

Take, for example, a church planter.[45] Those seekers with whom he converses raise questions from within their particular cultural and sub-cultural contexts. The church planter offers initial responses from the Scriptures. As these seekers come to faith in Christ, begin to obey, and keep their hearts open to God, they also allow the Scriptures to critique the cultural viewpoint from

---

[42]   Andrew Walls, *The Missionary Movement in Christian History* (Maryknoll: Orbis, 1996), 3–54; Kwame Bediako, *Christianity in Africa* (Maryknoll: Orbis, 1995).

[43]   Plantinga, *Engaging God's World*, 15.

[44]   David K. Clark, *To Know and Love God* (Wheaton: Crossway, 2003), 115.

[45]   This example is adapted from the seven-step model in ibid., 114.

which they raised their questions. Through Bible study and prayer, they begin to form a (contextual) theology.[46] If they are able, they discuss their theology with believers from other contexts (whether by reading historical theologians and writers, or by conversing with contemporaries who find themselves in a different cultural or sub-cultural context). Again and again, they return to the Scriptures, evaluating their emerging theological framework and praying that God will guide them into a proper interpretation, synthesis, and application of the Scriptures for their particular culture.

One notices here that both "insider" and "outsider" critiques are helpful. In the process of contextualization, participants from within a culture need to take the lead. They have both explicit and implicit (tacit) knowledge of their culture that the cultural outsider will never match.[47] However, the cultural outsider also has the advantage of being able to see that same culture from a different vantage point. This is why Clark argues that "questions framed in the terms of non-Western cultures can help illuminate blind spots" in Western theology.[48] Christian Scripture provides a particular set of categories, poses a particular set of questions, and provides particular answers to those questions. These categories, questions, and answers should challenge the conceptual framework of all cultures. For this reason, we endeavor to read the church fathers, the reformers and others who preached and embodied the gospel in eras different from our own, and to read and converse with Asian, African, and Latin American Christians who proclaim and embody the gospel in socio-cultural contexts different from our own.

Conclusion. The upshot of all of this is that we need to work hard to exegete both Scripture and culture. "In order to be competent proclaimers and performers of the gospel," Vanhoozer writes, "Christians must learn to read the Bible and culture alike. Christians cannot afford to continue sleepwalking their way through contemporary culture, letting their lives, and especially their imaginations, become conformed to culturally devised myths, each of

---

[46] Some "contextual" theologies are not faithful to the biblical teaching once for all delivered to the saints. The method I am proposing, however, seeks to uphold the full authority of Scripture by unleashing Scripture to speak faithfully, meaningfully, and dialogically to each individual culture. Although I have applied this model to international church planting, it is just as easily applied to work here in the United States. In fact, this type of contextualization is no different than the one employed (either well or badly) by pastors in, for example, the rural South of the United States.

[47] Tacit knowledge differs from formal knowledge in that it is not codified and not easily shared. A person who learns to ride a bicycle, for example, has both formal and tacit knowledge of how to do so. His formal knowledge would include "one must pedal" and "one must balance." His tacit knowledge, however, is the learned experience of how to balance, pedal, and steer. This knowledge is not easily communicated but nonetheless very important. Cultural insiders have tacit knowledge of their culture that a cultural outsider (including a bicultural person) might never gain. Michael Polanyi brought attention to tacit knowledge within the fields of science and philosophy, but the concept is helpful also for missiology. Michael Polanyi, *Personal Knowledge* (Chicago: University of Chicago, 1958).

[48] Clark, *To Know and Love God*, 118.

which promises more than it can deliver."[49] The Christian who ignores cultural context does so to his own detriment and to the detriment of those to whom he ministers.[50]

THE GOSPEL FOR THE CULTURE

Finally, we turn to the Christian task of applying God's Word to God's world, of bringing Christian theology and practice to bear on all of the dimensions of human society and culture. As this chapter argued earlier, the doctrine of creation undergirds this discussion. Because God is the Creator and King over all that exists, Christians seek actively to demonstrate his kingship in every dimension of human culture and across the fabric of human existence. If we do not "embody our faith in the shapes of everyday life,"[51] we limit our witness. Therefore, we endeavor to proclaim and embody the gospel, and allow it to guide our thinking and acting, in every station in society and culture.

Vocatio*: Mission and stations of life.* One significant way Christians apply God's Word to God's world is through honoring him in the various and manifold situations in which we find ourselves. We make manifest the implications of our faith in every station of life: family, church, workplace, and community. Martin Luther spoke of this in terms of *vocatio* (calling). For him, these stations of life are not peripheral to faithful living, but central.[52]

Luther's contention was that wherever we find ourselves, in whatever station of life, this life situation (if we are being obedient) is the one to which God has called us. This can be seen readily when God calls us to a workplace. God instituted work before the fall; God takes pleasure in the work of his image-bearers. Their work is not merely for financial gain. It is also God's way of providing for his world. When God wants to feed a hungry child, usually he does not do so by sending manna from heaven. Instead, he does so through the farmer who grows the food, the trucker who transports it, the carpenter who constructs the grocery store, and the grocery clerk who shelves it. All four of these workers (farmer, trucker, carpenter, clerk) can labor either with great significance or no significance, either with an eye toward loving God and their neighbor or with no thought toward such things. Christians in the workplace share life with and work alongside of unbelievers, and their obedience to Christ in that arena is of no small significance.

---

[49] Vanhoozer, "What Is Everyday Theology?" 35.

[50] For further reading on the dangers stemming from missionaries who contextualize poorly, see David J. Hesselgrave, "Syncretism: Mission and Missionary Induced?" in *Contextualization and Syncretism: Navigating Cultural Currents*, EMS Series #13 (Pasadena, CA: William Carey, 2006), 71–98.

[51] Vanhoozer, "What Is Everyday Theology?" 16.

[52] For the best concise popular exposition of Luther's doctrine of vocatio, see Gene E. Veith, *God at Work: Your Christian Vocation in All of Life* (Wheaton: Crossway, 2002). For a robust academic defense of the doctrine of vocation, see Douglas J. Schuurman, *Vocation: Discerning Our Callings in Life* (Grand Rapids: Eerdmans, 2004).

The same can be said for the Christian's other callings, such as his calling to a family, a church, and a community. In fact, as Gene Veith argues, these callings are "comprehensive and day-by-day, involving almost every facet of our lives, the whole texture of relationships, responsibilities, and focuses of attention that take up nearly every moment of our lives."[53] The Christian who takes seriously his callings determines not to limit his faith to the four walls of a church building but to apply it to all of life. He views himself as *sent* by God into these various arenas, and his calling becomes part of his mission.

Possessio*: Mission and dimensions of culture.* Another significant way to apply God's Word to his world is by thinking and acting "Christianly" in the various dimensions of human society and culture, including the arts, the sciences, and the public square. In so doing, the Christian allows Christ to take possession of non-Christian societies and cultures. J. H. Bavinck referred to this process as *possessio*.[54] If God is the Creator of man, the one who gives man the ability to create human culture, then he also has the right to be glorified in those same dimensions. No realm of creation or culture may be excluded. This is Abraham Kuyper's point when he writes, "The Son [of God] is not to be excluded from anything. You cannot point to any natural realm or star or comet or even descend into the depth of the earth, but it is related to Christ, not in some unimportant tangential way, but directly."[55] If all things are created by Christ, and indeed subsist in him, then the ministry of the Word to the world includes the application of the Word to all areas of life. "Faith seeking understanding" applies not only to the study of Scripture, but also to the study of creation and human culture.

It is incumbent upon believers, first of all, to learn to think "Christianly" in all of their cultural endeavors. Human cultures are underlain by worldviews which are in turn connected to various religions and philosophies. To the extent that the culture's underlying worldview-religion-philosophy amalgamation is dissonant with a Christian theistic worldview, it is distorted, fragmented, and adverse to the gospel. Human sinfulness inevitably issues forth in cultural disobedience, resulting in a degradation of the cultural activity for which God created humans. The battle raging between competing worldviews, religions, and philosophies is often fought in the arts, the sciences, education, the political arena, and other dimensions of human society and culture. Therefore, faithful Christians seek to be a redemptive influence in those same dimensions, and such influence involves critical engagement with

---

[53] Veith, *God at Work*, 133.

[54] J. H. Bavinck used this term to argue that the gospel "takes possession" of any non-Christian framework for understanding life, redirecting and stripping it of its idolatry. J. H. Bavinck, *An Introduction to the Science of Mission* (Grand Rapids: Baker, 1960), 155–90.

[55] Abraham Kuyper, *You Can Do Greater Things Than Christ*, trans. Jan H. Boer (Jos, Nigeria: Institute of Church and Society, 1991), 74. This is the translation of a section from the first volume of Kuyper's *Pro Rege*, of Het Koningschap van Christus (Kampen: J. H. Kok, 1911).

culture rather than passive consumption, on the one hand, or cultural withdrawal, on the other.[56]

This critical engagement issues forth in two practices: the church must
learn both to *read* and to *write* culture.[57] We must learn to *read* the culture, to
understand our socio-cultural context and its attendant works of philosophy,
art, science, and popular culture. But we must also learn to *write* culture, to
create and construct works of culture within those same arenas.[58] The church
should encourage her younger members to take their studies and vocations
seriously, and her more established members to take their professions seriously, realizing that such things are a calling from God and hold forth potential for his glory.[59] The founders of Harvard College understood this. In a
pamphlet published in 1643, they set forth their mission statement: "Let every
student be plainly instructed, and earnestly pressed, to consider well [that]
the maine end of his life and studies is *to know God and Jesus Christ which is
eternal life*, John 17:3, and therefore to lay *Christ* in the bottome, as the only
foundation of all sound knowledge and learning."[60] The whole world is the
sphere of God's sovereignty and, therefore, the whole world is the sphere of
the church's activity to glorify him. In the Christian life, no room exists for
cultural indifference.

---

[56] Sociologist James Davison Hunter has argued convincingly that cultures change from the
"top" down, meaning that cultural change is often forged by the elites in the arts, sciences,
education, etc. Hunter writes, "In short, when networks of elites in overlapping fields of culture
and overlapping spheres of social life come together with their varied resources and act in common purpose, cultures do change and do profoundly. Persistence over time is essential; little of
significance happens in three to five years. But when cultural and symbolic capital overlap with
social capital and economic capital, and in time, political capital, and these various resources are
directed toward shared ends, the world, indeed, changes." James Davison Hunter, *To Change the
World* (Oxford: Oxford University, 2010), 43. While a sound biblical theology of culture gives
reason for Christians to do faithful and excellent work in the arts, sciences, business, education,
and the public square, Hunter's sociological argument suggests that gospel influence on a culture
may very well come through those who, because of their faithfulness and excellence, rise to the
top of their fields.

[57] Vanhoozer, "What Is Everyday Theology?" 18.

[58] For further reading, see Andy Crouch, *Culture Making*. Crouch gives a helpful biblical
theology of culture making, a theology which issues forth in a recognition of God's grace in
allowing us to make culture out of his good creation: "The way to genuine cultural creativity
starts with the recognition that we woke up this morning in our right mind, with the use and activity of our limbs—and that every other creative capacity we have has likewise arrived as a gift we
did not earn and to which we were not entitled. And once we are awake and thankful, our most
important cultural contribution will very likely come from doing whatever keeps us precisely in
the center of delight and surprise." Crouch, *Culture Making*, 252.

[59] For an introductory exposition of a Christian's role in culture (including philosophy, the
arts, the sciences, work, and leisure), see Horton, *Where in the World Is the Church?* For an
exposition of various culture-shapers throughout church history, see T. M. Moore, *Culture Matters*. For a theological treatment of work and leisure as part of the cultural mandate, see Leland
Ryken, *Redeeming the Time: A Christian Approach to Work & Leisure* (Grand Rapids: Baker,
1995).

[60] "New England's First Fruits," quoted in Perry Miller and Thomas H. Johnson, *The Puritans* (New York: American Book, 1938), 702.

CONCLUSION

God created the world in which we minister, and God gave us the capacities to minister therein. God's world is good and—although it has been corrupted—we may use any and all aspects of God's world to bring Him glory. Further, God created man and gave him the capacity to create culture. God himself inspired the Scriptures which are written in the midst of human culture, and he calls us to proclaim the gospel in the midst of such culture.

God claims sovereignty over all of his creation, and he directs his church's mission to extend across all of creation. He is the Lord over every tribe, tongue, people, and nation—over every type of person who has ever lived across the span of history and the face of the globe. And he is the Lord over every facet of human life—over the artistic, the scientific, the philosophical, the economic, and the sociopolitical. "The earth is the LORD's and the fullness thereof, the world and those who dwell therein" (Ps. 24:1). May we take the opportunity God has given us to proclaim the gospel across the fabric of human existence and in every dimension of human culture, and do so in a way that upholds his gospel, builds his church, and advances his kingdom.

Chapter Nine

THE GOSPEL AND LIFESTYLE

Alan and Katherine Carter

INTRODUCTION

When God spoke the world into existence, he declared that it was good. And one day he will again make all things right and good. In the meantime, we are redeemed sinners, living in a sinful and fallen world. This is the gospel message: in spite of mankind's rebellion, God, through Jesus Christ, has completed and is in the process of completing his plan of redemption and restoration. He put this very plan into motion long before the beginning of time, and he calls us to join him as agents of redemption and restoration.

As we join him, however, we must face human rebellion and its devastating consequences. Sin's effects clearly manifest themselves in the created order and in God's image-bearers, from earthquakes, famines, genetic defects, and disease, to selfishness, hatred, bitterness, and abuse. Sin threatens to prevent us from loving and seeking the good of our fellow image-bearers. Sin complicates our role as stewards of the created world and its resources.

The good news is that the very same power that raised Christ from the dead daily transforms believers into the very image of Christ. The Holy Spirit enables us to faithfully use all that we are and all that we have been given to live out our unique role in God's redemptive and restorative plan. Genuine spiritual rebirth results in a genuinely transformed lifestyle. Thus those who have truly been brought from death to life will rebel against the patterns of this sinful world (Rom. 12:2; 2 Cor. 10:1–5) and live missionally for the glory of God.[1]

MISSIONAL LIFESTYLE AND THE SURROUNDING CULTURE

By its very nature, a missional lifestyle is one that is distinct from the surrounding culture. As we seek first his kingdom and his righteousness, God creates within us a very singular desire: his glory in all things and before all people. Thus, an authentic Christian lifestyle is one that clearly reflects this single desire. It is not a life simply altered to replace morally abhorrent actions with good, moral deeds. The Holy Spirit transforms our inner man, creating new thought patterns, desires, and worldview. This inner reality then manifests itself outwardly even in the most mundane and "insignificant" details of our lives.

In so living, we are faced with the stark contrast between Christ's commands and the mandates of our own culture. Believers often feel torn between the two worlds, and the temptation to compromise can be overwhelming. As a result, it is all too easy to respond to the pressure in an extreme manner, either by uncritical assimilation (blending in completely) or withdrawal from the culture.[2]

Uncritical assimilation. Christians face the temptation of assimilating or living a life that reflects the worldly values of the surrounding culture. Some believers claim to live a "Christian" lifestyle, but have in reality only added a few church-related activities and subtracted some moral vices. Their distinction from the world is surface, while their time, talents, and treasures are used in much the same ways as those of a "morally good" pagan. Such a lifestyle may stem from a fundamental misunderstanding of the gospel and the church's mission in the world. It may reflect a lack of concern for that mission. It may even result from an overemphasis on cultural relevance, which can lead to biblical infidelity. Whatever the reasons may be, a life that reflects the world more than the Savior is useless to bring about God's mission. Salt cannot create a thirst for living water if it is not salty (Matt. 5:13).

Withdrawal. Christians must also fight the opposite tendency to withdraw from the surrounding community and the culture at large, as isolated individuals, families, or micro-communities. Withdrawn believers do not live

---

[1] For the sake of clarity, this chapter will refer to a lifestyle aligned with the mission of God as a "missional lifestyle." The 1980 Lausanne document "An Evangelical Commitment to Simple Life-Style" described such a lifestyle as "simple," insofar as it is simple for the purpose of "contribut[ing] more generously to relief and evangelism." The term "simple lifestyle," however, has gained such recent popularity in society at large that its meaning could be deemed somewhat ambiguous. For this reason, we have chosen to use the term "missional lifestyle"—in the sense of a lifestyle marked by, but not limited to, good stewardship and simplicity for the sake of living on mission with God (http://www.lausanne.org/all-documents/lop-20.html).

[2] For a thorough treatment of the subject, see H. Richard Niebuhr, *Christ and Culture* (New York: Harper & Row, 1951).

well as agents of redemption and change in their community, nor do they effectively take the gospel to the ends of the world. Instead, these believers or groups of believers meet their needs and spend their time almost completely within the church community. They may make forays into the secular world for work and other necessities. Cloistered believers may even try to attract outsiders to church programs and events, but the lost often find it difficult to truly understand the life-transforming gospel from a Sunday sermon alone. While these sheltered Christians maintain their distinctive "saltiness," their lost neighbors and co-workers have little opportunity to "taste" and respond to the good news.[3]

Active engagement as community. The biblical lifestyle model advocates neither assimilation nor withdrawal. Instead, the body of Christ, as a distinct community of faith, lives out the gospel and actively engages the surrounding culture. Individual believers love and serve each other and the lost as part of the larger body of Christ. In this model, the lost have opportunity to witness the transforming power of the gospel before they ever enter a church building. Those who do not yet believe can still experience the overflow of Christ's love in action within the body, rather than be treated as targets or forgotten completely. They witness believers practicing the "one-anothers"[4] and see tangible effects of body life lived out within their own community. The church body calls those outside to join the family of God through repentance and faith, but their discipleship does not involve unnecessarily extracting new believers from their present life and relationships. This allows new believers to live out the gospel within their own community and circle of influence, and it enables the gospel to flow along natural relationship lines.

This pattern of Christian living emanates from a biblical understanding of the church as a body or a family and not merely a building or a schedule of programs. Through the power of the Holy Spirit, this love and service transforms next-door neighbors and extends to neighbors across the globe.

MISSIONAL LIFESTYLE AND STEWARDSHIP

Biblical stewardship governs a truly missional lifestyle. This principle is rooted in creation and God's original command to Adam and Eve that they be stewards of the created world (Gen. 1). The language of stewardship continues throughout the New Testament to describe the responsibility of believers

---

[3] Withdrawal can also take the form of believers waging a "culture war" against the culture at large. Some Christians engage culture mainly by warring against the media and pop culture in relation to politics, morals, and ethics. While they do engage the culture, it is possible for them to fall into the trap of communicating primarily in the form of debate or activism. This can curtail real relationships with the lost and distort the gospel message.

[4] Here we use "one-anothers" to describe the many New Testament commands concerning how believers must relate within the body of Christ, i.e., love one another, serve one another, forgive one another.

to use that with which God has entrusted to them for his own glory and the furtherance of his kingdom.[5]

The word normally translated "steward" in Scripture literally means a household manager. A steward was a servant or slave entrusted with the responsibility of managing the finances and everyday affairs of a wealthy person's household.[6] God has blessed each individual believer and each community of believers with a particular combination of resources over which we are to be stewards or managers. For the sake of simplicity, we will refer to these resources as time, talents, and treasures. These resources include but are not limited to: [time] actual minutes and days, work hours and free time, seasons of life; [talents] natural abilities and strengths, training and experience, spiritual gifts; [treasures] financial assets, material possessions, physical health and energy, spiritual heritage, the gospel itself, educational opportunities, sphere of influence, and those resources at our disposal based on our location, citizenship, or position in society. All of these resources are from God and for God, because "from him and through him and to him are all things" (Rom. 11:36).

In one sense, we can describe lifestyle as the way we manage or steward the resources at our disposal. A missional lifestyle is one in which a believer's time, talents, and treasures are well stewarded and therefore bring the greatest good to God and his kingdom.

This concept of stewardship is rooted in all four movements of the biblical narrative: creation, fall, redemption, and restoration.

We must look back to creation and the fall. God created and owns all things. He created mankind to be stewards of this present earth. Thus, man's stewardship of his own time, talents, and treasures is rooted in the dominion that God gave man over his world before the fall. Man's dominion over God's world is not absolute, because it belongs to God. God has entrusted it to man to care for in a way that brings God glory. In the same way, God has entrusted man with time, talents, and treasures for the purpose of bringing glory to his name. The fall made the task of stewardship more difficult. Selfishness and pride give birth to feelings of entitlement and lust for more. Man so easily believes he is lord over his own life and resources. However, the fall did not change God's plan or humanity's responsibility to obey him.

We must face our present responsibility. God's glory is ultimate and his redemptive plan is clear. Until Jesus returns, God has entrusted believers with the responsibility to streamline all available resources towards the success of his mission here on earth. One might argue that God, in his omnipotence, could do this work without us. Almighty God has no need or lack. He could have chosen differently. However, we must focus on what God *has*

---

[5] A few passages concerning stewardship and wise management of that which God has given include: 1 Cor. 4:1; Eph. 5:15–16; Col. 1:24–28; and 2 Tim. 1:8–14.

[6] J. Goetzmann, "House, Build, Manage, Steward," in Colin Brown, ed., *The New International Dictionary of New Testament Theology,* vol. 2 (Grand Rapids: Zondervan, 1971), 254.

sovereignly chosen to do. He has chosen to entrust his resources to our stewardship for the purpose of carrying out his plan.

We must gain eternal perspective by looking forward to the new heavens and the new earth. A true understanding of lives in the perspective of eternity should significantly alter our stewardship decisions. Randy Alcorn writes, "I'm convinced that the greatest deterrent to giving is this: the illusion that earth is our home."[7] If we could truly grasp the beauty of Christ and the nature of our eternal home, we would not be so easily satisfied with paper mansions. We would pour our treasures into that which has eternal value, and we would do everything in our power to ensure that our neighbors had eternal homes as well.

Jesus commands us to lay up our treasure in heaven, not on earth. A man can choose either to live for "accumulating valuable things on earth" or for "accumulating valuable things in heaven."[8] He can either serve God or become a slave to what the world treasures (Matt. 6:19–34; 1 Tim. 3:2; 6:9). Based on the New Testament use of the word *treasure*, it appears that our heavenly treasure relates directly to the restoration of our relationship with God and with our fellow man.[9] As we join God in his work of restoring mankind's relationship with himself, through Christ, we in some way add to the enjoyment we will experience when our own relationship with God is restored perfectly and completely for eternity.

Luke 19:11–27 relates Jesus' parable about a wise steward who invested well the money entrusted to him and was praised when his master returned. In this parable, Jesus connects wise stewardship with a proper understanding of his return. When Christ returns, he will call us to account for what he has entrusted to us. Therefore we cannot trust in the world's treasure. Instead, we must labor tirelessly at his business until he comes again. Scripture also warns that the day will come when believers will have to give account of how they have lived their life on earth (Rom. 5:9–11; 1 Cor. 3:5–15; 2 Cor. 5:9). The more we delight in God and seek after his glory in this lifetime, the greater our joy will be throughout eternity.

In the following chart, note the radical difference between the two ways of understanding the use of time, talents, and treasures:

---

[7]   Randy Alcorn, *The Treasure Principle* (Colorado Springs: Multnomah, 2005), 44.

[8]   John Piper, "Don't Be Anxious, Lay Up Treasure in Heaven (Part 1)," sermon (March 2, 2003) available at www.DesiringGod.org.

[9]   J. Eichler and C. Brown, "Possessions, Treasure, Mammon, Wealth, Money," in Brown, *The New International Dictionary of New Testament Theology*, 832.

Worldly Model: Personal or Joint Account	Biblical Model: Corporate Account
Contents: The account includes the sum total of my personal time, talents, and treasures.	*Contents:* The account includes the sum total of our time, talents, and treasures (in the context of the body of Christ)
Beneficiary: I use my resources to benefit myself and those people and causes I see as worthy.	*Beneficiary:* I use my resources for God's glory as he works out his mission in the world. This benefits not only me and those I care for, but ultimately all the people of the earth
Decision-Making Authority: I seek advice from others or allow them influence, but ultimately the decision is mine. Sole accountability is to governmental authorities, decisions, and actions bounded by human laws alone.	**Decision-Making Authority:** God is the owner of the account and I am the manager/steward. I submit to God's word, as the Holy Spirit illuminates and leads, in the context of the body of Christ. Decisions accord with God's mission.
Decision-Making Influences: <ul><li>Personal beliefs and desires (both positive and negative; include desires of the sin nature: greed, selfishness, pride, and personal appetites)</li><li>External circumstances</li><li>Societal influence</li><li>*And in the case of believers:* church, Bible, other Christians</li></ul>	**Decision-Making Influences:** <ul><li>God's Word illumined by his Spirit</li><li>Wisdom from within the body of Christ</li><li>My unique strengths, talents, spiritual gifts, life experience, etc.</li><li>Scripture commands us to make these decisions based on:<ul><li>unselfishness/self-denial (1 Cor. 15:1–6)</li><li>generosity and kindness</li><li>humility of mind, regarding others as more important (Phil. 2:3)</li><li>self-control (Gal. 5:22)</li><li>sober-mindedness</li><li>love</li><li>fear of God and joy of pleasing him (Rom. 5:9–11; 2 Cor. 5:9)</li><li>desire for eternal reward</li></ul></li></ul>
Typical uses: <ul><li>Personal well-being and future security—"Take care of yourself."</li><li>food/shelter/clothing</li><li>physical wellness (health, rest, etc.)</li><li>education and self-improvement</li><li>financial investments and savings</li><li>The well-being and future security of others I deem worthy—"Take care of those you love."</li><li>family and friends</li><li>church, charity, and other "worthy causes"</li><li>My pleasure, comfort, and convenience—"Treat yourself."</li></ul>	**Typical Uses:** God's mission as it is accomplished and carried out by the body of Christ <ul><li>meeting basic needs: yours and those entrusted into your care</li><li>carrying out God's mission on earth, including: disciple-making (both at home and to the ends of the earth), service, helping the needy, etc.</li></ul>

Missional Lifestyle and Stewardship of the Gospel

The New Testament writers use stewardship language most commonly and explicitly to describe our responsibility concerning the gospel message. Though evangelism and missions are addressed separately in this volume, we must briefly discuss them here, because the gospel itself is the foremost treasure we are called upon to steward.

In Ephesians 3:2, Paul speaks of the stewardship of the gospel which was entrusted to him by God, so that through the church, God's plan of salvation for the nations might be made known. Several other passages address the stewardship of "the gospel," "God's grace," and the "mysteries of Christ" (1 Cor. 4:1; 9:16–17; Col. 1:24–28; 1 Pet. 4:10). The greatest treasure we are privileged to steward is the gospel itself—the mystery of God's grace and mercy in Christ Jesus. We steward the gospel well by proclaiming it to all of mankind. And we steward all other resources well by using them to further the task of spreading the gospel.

Let us not take this stewardship of the gospel lightly. Most believers born in the West have hundreds—even thousands—of opportunities to read or listen to the gospel message in their lifetime. Laws protect our freedom to choose our own religion, and few believers experience real persecution. In contrast, 65.2 percent of the world's population (more than four billion people) have little or no access to the gospel[10] and much of this segment of the global population risks significant persecution if they publicly profess their faith in Jesus. The Western church, both individual believers and corporate church bodies, cannot ignore this enormous global imbalance in gospel access. In order for our generation to steward the gospel well, we must respond to this desperate state of affairs with an unprecedented increase in prayer, sacrificial giving, and sending workers to bring the good news to the billions who have not yet heard.

Marks of a Well-Stewarded Life

A life well stewarded for the sake of God and his mission will inevitably bear distinguishing marks. We have chosen to limit our discussion of this enormous topic to some of the marks that most distinguish a missional lifestyle from a typical Western lifestyle. While these marks are natural outworkings of sanctification, we must also choose to pursue them as we work out our salvation with fear and trembling (Phil. 2:12).

Satisfaction. A believer who finds his satisfaction in God rests as contentedly as a newborn in his mother's arms. In Genesis, God promised Abraham that he himself will be Abraham's reward, and Abraham chose to find his satisfaction in God and his promises. We are heirs to the promises of Abraham. Not only has God promised us an eternity in his very presence; he has also

---

[10] IMB Global Research GSEC (April 2010), www.imb.org/globalresearch/downloads.asp.

chosen to care for our present needs and fill our lives with all manner of good things. When we choose to be satisfied with God's provision, including the type and amount of resources he has chosen for us to manage, God enables us to live as godly stewards of those resources.

Western believers live in a culture enslaved to the masters of *more* and *better*. We work and slave for the next promotion or possession only to discover that it does not quite satisfy. Advertising capitalizes on this by stirring up discontent with our possessions, our appearance, or our station in life. Instead of gaining satisfaction, though, we enslave ourselves to the unending pursuit of *more*.

Just as in Luke's parable of the three stewards, we have each been entrusted with varying types and amounts of resources. This parable underscores the fact that Christian contentment does not provide an excuse for apathy, complacency, or laziness. Conversely, Christian contentment enables us to thankfully receive what God has entrusted to us and joyfully use it to further his kingdom. Likewise, Paul challenges Timothy to receive what God has given with joy and humble thanksgiving (1 Tim. 4:4) and to be content in times of plenty or of want (1 Tim. 6:17). A missional lifestyle is one of satisfaction in what God has provided, be it much or little. Therefore we must also reject an extreme ascetic view of material possessions as evil. Christian contentment rests on the belief that everything we have is a gracious gift from God and that it is *enough*. Satisfaction and contentment break our bondage to the endless pursuit of more, freeing us *from* anxiety and freeing us *to* bring glory to our Redeemer.

Slowness. A well-stewarded life often will reflect a particular type of slowness. This mark of stewardship is less tangible and thus difficult to describe. By slowness we do not mean laziness or inefficiency. We use this word in the sense of an inner quiet and stillness that produces a lifestyle of effective, not frantic service. Within the Western church, busyness itself has almost become a mark of spirituality and overcrowded schedules a proof of holiness. Christians wind up exhausted, with nothing left to give, wondering why there is no overflow of living water to offer to the spiritually thirsty around them.

A lifestyle of "slowness" involves investing the time necessary for those things that cannot be rushed (character development, maturity). The New Testament qualifications for church leadership (1 Tim. 3:1–7; Titus 1:5–9) focus more on holiness and character than on specific actions and abilities, though some *are* included. Certainly God desires church leaders to work diligently in ministry. However, the implication is that inner godliness (being the right kind of person) will necessarily manifest itself outwardly in actions (doing the right things).[11] Inner godliness results in the outward expression. We will never create technology capable of speeding up sanctification or expediting character development.

In order to live a missional lifestyle, we must be willing to *slow down enough to allow God to do his work in us*. Jesus calls his disciples to abide in

---

[11] For further reading on church leadership in relation to character, see John Frame, *Studying Theology as a Servant of Jesus* (booklet published by Reformed Theological Seminary).

him (John 15). In Luke 10, Jesus calls Martha to sit rather than to serve. Though he does not condemn Martha for working hard to help others, he condemns the worry and anxiety driving her busyness. Mary chose what is better—sitting still at the feet of her Lord. Good stewardship sometimes means slowing down enough to regularly *sit in his presence—to worship, to listen, and to learn.*

A conspicuous absence of silence and solitude marks our contemporary culture. Jesus himself lived a very public life, surrounded by people. Scripture gives no indication that he sought or valued much personal privacy. However, all four Gospel writers note Jesus' habit of getting away for time alone with his Father (Matt. 14:13,23; Mark 1:35; Luke 6:12; John 6:15; 8:1). Though Jesus knew his time on earth to teach and heal was very short, he regularly stopped everything and pursued silence and solitude. He recognized the great value in simply being with the Father. Likewise, good stewards must humbly seek out *silence and solitude* in order to hear God's voice.

Good stewards also recognize the value in physically *slowing down to rest.* Charles Spurgeon said this about rest: "In the long run, we shall do more by sometimes doing less. On, on, on forever, without recreation may suit spirits emancipated from this 'heavy clay,' but while we are in this tabernacle, we must every now and then cry halt, and serve the Lord by holy inaction and consecrated leisure."[12] In his book *Humility*, C. J. Mahaney contends that our need for sleep and rest is a God-given reminder of our dependence on him. "There is only One who 'will neither slumber nor sleep' (Psalm 121:4), and I am not that One."[13] Let us not be too proud to rest for the purpose of serving God more effectively.

Good stewardship also demands that we *slow down enough to be available.* In Luke 10, Jesus tells the story of a man who shared generously of his own time and personal resources to help a stranger in need. He made himself available for God to use him. We must not allow ourselves to become so busy that we are unavailable to God. As Richard Swenson puts it, "[God's] asking us to walk the second mile, to carry others' burdens, to witness to the Truth at any opportunity, and to teach our children when we sit, walk, lie, and stand all presuppose we have margin and that we make it available for His purposes. Obedience to these commands is often not schedulable."[14]

We recognize that different seasons of life and different energy levels will call for vastly different levels of activity or ministry involvement. Certainly Paul warns against idleness and often labored night and day for the sake of the gospel (2 Thess. 2:6–13). However, as stewards we must recognize the absolute necessity of abiding, of sitting in his presence, listening, and resting—not selfishly but in humble recognition of our weakness and dependence on God.

Simplicity. In recent years, simplicity has become a popular ideal in American culture at large. Materialism and excess have given birth to a longing for

---

[12] John Piper, *When I Don't Desire God* (Wheaton: Crossway, 2004), quoted from Gilbert Thomas, *William Cowper and the Eighteenth Century* (London: Ivor Nicholson & Watson, 1935), 202.

[13] C. J. Mahaney, *Humility* (Colorado Springs: Multnomah, 2005), 84.

[14] Richard Swenson, *Margin* (Colorado Springs: NavPress, 2004), 76.

simplicity, as evidenced by the presently lucrative business of professional orga-nizing and life coaching, as well as the overnight success of brands like Real Simple. Simplicity itself is a worthy goal, but as believers, we do not seek it for its own sake. Instead, we choose to simplify our lifestyles in order to be better stewards of our time, talents, and treasures. In so doing, we free up our resources in order to carry out God's redemptive and restorative work in the world.

"Seek ye first the kingdom of God, and his righteousness; and all these things shall be added unto you" (Matt. 6:33, KJV). True simplicity starts at the center. If our greatest desire is God's glory and the outworking of his mission on earth, we will focus our time, talents, and treasures accordingly. We can trust him to provide for our needs. This principle frees us to direct our resources *away* from those things with no eternal value and *toward* those that will last.

In Hebrews 12:1, Paul encourages us to "lay aside every weight and the sin that so easily ensnares us" (HCSB). In 2 Timothy 2:4 he challenges us not to entangle ourselves in the affairs of everyday life. In order to properly steward our resources, we must systematically simplify our lives of clutter and excess. We must prayerfully consider every area of life, from time use to finances, getting rid of anything that does not fit our single purpose. While some of these "hindrances" may be actual sins, many could be more aptly described as weights or traps. They may not be inherently wrong, but they hinder us from our main goal. A simplified lifestyle will likely not look the same for each person, though, and we must scrupulously avoid the tendency to judge others' lifestyles instead of examining our own.

While we need godly simplicity in many areas of our life, let us address a few of the most significant:

Simplicity: material wealth and possessions. In the gospels, Jesus repeat-edly addresses how we view and manage our money and possessions.[15] Perhaps this is because the way we manage our finances quite accurately indicates our spiritual state. Where our treasure is, there our heart will be also (Matt. 6:21). Temporal treasures can twist a man's heart so that he ultimately neglects the eternal. Thus, the Bible repeatedly warns God's people to flee the enticement of wealth. Jesus taught that it is all too easy for wealth to entice people into wasting their time on earth, replacing the Creator with what he has created. Jesus shocked his listeners by teaching that it almost impossible for rich people to enter the kingdom of heaven. Those who do follow Jesus must flee the love of money and possessions. The Bible does not condemn people for possessing wealth, but it does warn that they will be held account-able to God for how they steward their riches on earth.[16]

The issue of financial stewardship is quite pertinent to contemporary Western believers. Richard Foster observes, "Jesus speaks to the question of economics more than any other single social issue. If, in a comparatively simple society, our Lord lays such strong emphasis upon the spiritual dangers of wealth, how

---

[15] Alcorn, *The Treasure Principle*, 8.

[16] For further reading on money idolatry, see Tim Keller, *Counterfeit Gods* (New York: Dut-ton, 2009), 48–71.

much more should we who live in a highly affluent culture take seriously the economic question."[17] The use of material resources is also directly connected to the kingdom of God. In Craig Blomberg's *Neither Poverty nor Riches*, he writes, "A major component of the material dimension [of salvation] is transformation in the way God's people utilize 'mammon'—material possessions. To the extent that the kingdom has been inaugurated from the cross of Christ onward, Christians individually and corporately are called to model the transformation, however imperfectly, as a foretaste of the perfect redemption that must ultimately await the age to come."[18] The redeemed community's view and use of money should point to the coming kingdom.

Most Western evangelicals live in the midst of unprecedented abundance, insulated from an adequate understanding of global poverty. This makes it difficult for us to gain a realistic perspective about what a Christ-honoring, simple lifestyle looks like. In the most current study on comparative global wealth, researchers took into consideration annual income, as well as other assets like homes, property, and vehicles. Based on this research, if you view American wealth in a global perspective, average middle class Americans would be considered wealthier than 90 percent of the world population.[19] Even lower-class Americans might still be counted among the wealthiest 50 percent of people in the world. We must let this sink in. Though we may consider ourselves poor by American standards, we are actually among the world's richest people. Many evangelical Christians simply do not understand the comparative wealth and luxury of their lives in relation to the overwhelming majority of the world. As a result, they do not feel compelled to respond to scriptural commands addressed to the wealthy. We must recognize our relative wealth, for it is the first step in moving toward a simpler lifestyle and accepting the responsibilities God places on those who have been blessed with much. We as individuals may be powerless to change the relative financial inequalities in the world, but we can do something about our own relative wealth and affluence.[20]

To say that Christians should seek to live more simply is not to say that possessing wealth is sinful. However, it is a sin to misappropriate what has been entrusted to us. It is a sin to hoard or spend on our own comforts those things that have been given to us for the purpose of furthering God's work of redemption and restoration in the world. John Piper writes, "The issue is not how much a person makes. Big industry and big salaries are a fact of our times, and they are not necessarily evil. The evil is being deceived into thinking a $100,000 salary must be accompanied by a $100,000 lifestyle."[21] God calls those blessed with material wealth to live out responsible stewardship instead of entitled ownership.

[17]   Richard Foster, *Celebration of Discipline* (New York: HarperSanFrancisco, 1998), 83.
[18]   Craig L. Blomberg, *Neither Poverty nor Riches: A Biblical Theology of Possessions* (Downers Grove: IVP 1999), 246–47.
[19]   World Institute for Development Economics Research of the United Nations University, www.wider.unu.edu.
[20]   Lausanne Occasional Paper 20.
[21]   John Piper, *Desiring God* (Sisters, OR: Multnomah,1996), 172.

When we do simplify possessions and free up financial resources to pour into God's work of redemption and restoration, he blesses us with a peace far beyond that of financial security. Dietrich Bonhoeffer wrote, "Earthly possessions dazzle our eyes and delude us into thinking that they can provide security and freedom from anxiety. Yet all the time they are the very source of all anxiety . . . . The fetters which bind us to our possessions prove to be cares themselves."[22] Many helpful resources have been designed to help with the practical aspect of simplifying our finances and possessions. Two of the most helpful are the Lausanne Occasional Paper on Simple Lifestyle (LOP) and Richard Foster's writing on "outward expressions of simplicity." Based upon those sources and others, we offer these principles:

- Re-examine income and expenditure in order to manage on less. This is not in order to save more for a "rainy day," but in order to give away more.
- Renounce waste and oppose extravagance in personal living, clothing and housing, travel and church buildings.
- Accept the distinction between necessities and luxuries, so as not to despise the gifts God has given us (1 Tim. 4:4–5) nor the obligation to be responsible for our own family (1 Tim. 5:8).
- Reject anything that produces a personal addiction and anything that breeds the oppression of others.[23]
- Value usefulness above status.[24]
- Cultivate the habit of generously giving our money and possessions away.

Regarding simplicity and lifestyle decisions, we should prayerfully examine our own lives, inspire and incite one another to do likewise, and guard vigilantly against sitting in judgment over one another. We should also corporately seek the perspective of third-world believers. The LOP concludes, "One difficulty is that what may seem to Christians in developed countries a dramatically voluntary reduction in life-style may appear to believers in less developed countries a pathetically small step. So those of us who belong to the West need the help of our Third World brothers and sisters in evaluating our standards of spending."[25]

The way a believer manages his resources directly affects his ability to share the gospel effectively.[26] The 1980 LOP makes the connection explicitly: "So the call to a responsible life-style must not be divorced from the call to responsible witness . . . . It is impossible with integrity to proclaim Christ's salvation if he has evidently not saved us from greed, or his lordship if we are not good stewards of our possessions, or his love if we close our hearts

---

[22] Dietrich Bonhoeffer, *The Cost of Discipleship* (NY: Simon & Schuster, 1959), 178.
[23] Foster, *Celebration of Discipline*, 90–95.
[24] Ibid.
[25] Lausanne Occasional Paper 20.
[26] Consider the strong wording of 1 John 3:16–20 and James 2:14–17.

against the needy. When Christians care for each other and for the deprived, Jesus Christ becomes more visibly attractive."[27] Again, we live missionally and steward wisely for the purpose of spreading the gospel.

Simplicity: time and energy. Each of us is given a finite amount of time and energy to manage, and one day each of us will be called into account for its use. Instead of calling believers to increase their commitment to Christian activities, there are times when stewardship calls for the opposite: imploring them to *simplify* their schedules and commitments in order to make themselves more available to God missionally.[28] It is entirely possible to fill our lives so full with so many "good" activities that we find ourselves with no significant time or energy for actually sharing the gospel with the lost.

In recent years, American society has reached new heights of activity and commitment overload. According to a 2002 report by the National Institute for Occupational Safety and Health, the average work year for "prime age working couples" has increased by nearly 700 hours in the past 20 years.[29] The over-scheduling of children has even become a recent topic of academic research and media attention. We must individually and corporately examine what exactly we are pouring our time and energy into. We must ask hard questions. What do our lives communicate to the world about who or what is truly valuable? Does the world even have an awareness of our lives? It is so easy for us to affirm God's mission in theory but not in practice.

Simplifying our lifestyle in terms of time and energy use makes us more available for God's purposes. We must not merely replace secular busyness with sanctified busyness. Good stewardship of time involves both planning activities of eternal significance *and* leaving space for those things that cannot be planned. Much of what is eternally significant cannot be scheduled into thirty-minute time slots.

Discipleship demands time as well, for it cannot be reduced to weekly Bible studies and accountability groups. The Bible describes discipleship more in terms of a transfer of life, of a more mature believer sharing his life with a younger believer so that he matures and grows in faith.[30] Structured teaching is important to the disciple-making process, but young believers should also have access to the lives of more mature believers. Paul instructs his disciples to emulate him as he emulates God. People can only emulate what they are given the opportunity to see.

Biblical hospitality is another important way to steward the resources God has given us (Lev. 25:35–43; Acts 3:43–47; Rom. 12:9–13). God commands all believers to practice hospitality. However, the biblical concept of hospitality goes far beyond scheduled times of "entertaining guests." Henri Nouwen

---

[27] Lausanne Occasional Paper 20.

[28] Consider again Hebrews 12 and 2 Timothy 2:4.

[29] Swenson, *Margin*, 115.

[30] Consider 1 Corinthians 11:1 and 1 Thessalonians 2:8, as well as the overall example that Jesus, Paul, and the apostles set in their own disciple-making.

describes hospitality in terms of bringing others into our lives.[31] Rather than limiting itself to singular events, biblical hospitality is a lifestyle. God calls believers to offer up their homes and possessions to be used by him whenever a need arises. Across the world, Muslims and others from many different cultures commonly practice this type of hospitality to a degree that most Western Christians could not imagine. Perhaps we should open up our schedules so that we may open up our homes.

One helpful practice to this end is that of writing a simple family statement of purpose. This statement should line up with God's mission in the world, taking into account the family's unique blend of time, talents, and treasures. The family can compare their actual use of time and energy with their stated purpose. This will allow prayerful evaluation and simplification of activities and commitments, with the opportunity for regular reevaluation.

Simplicity: creation and natural resources. Good stewardship of creation demands that we make thoughtful and prayerful decisions concerning God's created world, including our use of natural resources. Evangelicals have tended to lag far behind when it comes to environmental responsibility and stewardship of natural resources. Many evangelicals fear that demonstrating environmental concern constitutes a type of idolatry in which creation is worshipped above the Creator. While some environmentalists indeed idolize the created world, we should not allow their wrong theology to prevent us from living out our responsibility of stewardship. We should steward these resources well because we value God above all and take seriously the stewardship God has entrusted to us. A missional lifestyle reflects God's work of redemption and restoration in the world. For example, stewardship of natural resources results in an ability to share more of these resources with those in need. In so doing, we show love and honor to those created in God's image.

Americans are by far the largest consumers of world energy resources. While the U. S. constitutes less than 6 percent of the world's population, it consumes about 33 percent of the world's energy. As recently as the last decade, air conditioners in the United States alone use the same amount of energy as does the entire country of China."[32] Regardless of their individual political affiliation, Christians must recognize that unexamined consumption of natural resources by Western Christians cannot proclaim God's love and mercy to the watching world.

The Lausanne committee calls believers to simplify their lifestyle so as to use resources more efficiently: "[Biblical teaching in Genesis and in Matt. 6:25–32] implies man's trusteeship, and the requirement not to waste what God provides carries with it an obligation to use resources efficiently . . . . As Christians we may wish to define the satisfaction of needs rather than wants as the objective of economic life, but the goal of efficiency in meeting those needs will again be incumbent upon us."[33] Resources abound in the areas of

---

[31] Henri Nouwen, *Wounded Healer* (New York: Doubleday, 1979).
[32] Foster, *Celebration of Discipline*, 92.
[33] Lausanne Occasional Paper 20.

lifestyle simplification and efficient use of natural resources. We must simply use them.

Selflessness, sacrifice, and suffering. We will now address three related marks of a missional lifestyle: selflessness, sacrifice, and suffering. These will be treated in more detail in a separate chapter, so we will narrow our focus to a few specifics as they relate to lifestyle and stewardship of time, talents, and treasures.

Jesus Christ emptied himself of his glory and made himself poor for our sake. As Philippians 2:1–11 attests, God calls us to follow Christ's example of self-sacrifice for the sake of others and ultimately for God's glory. The New Testament also provides other examples of those who followed Christ's example to the furtherance of God's mission on earth (Acts 4:32–37; 2 Cor. 8:1–5; 1 Thess. 2:6–9).

God calls all believers to give generously. However, we should seriously consider whether or not he desires us to make significant sacrifices in terms of lifestyle. Christ called some of his disciples to voluntary poverty (Matt. 10:1–15; 19:6–22; Luke 10:1–16). This does not mean Jesus considered poverty to be meritorious in and of itself. In fact, Scripture teaches that believers should serve and give in order to alleviate poverty (2 Cor. 8:1–15; 1 John 3:16–20). Voluntary poverty by believers is something quite different, and in certain cases it can be used to advance God's mission on earth. Those writing the Lausanne Paper agree: "We believe that Jesus still calls some people (perhaps even us) to follow him in a life-style of total, voluntary poverty. He calls all his followers to an inner freedom from the seduction of riches (for it is impossible to serve God and money) and to sacrificial generosity ("to be rich in good works, to be generous and ready to share"—Timothy 6:18)."[34]

Though God may not call each believer to a lifestyle of poverty, he calls each believer to live a life of selflessness, sacrifice, and generosity. According to Scripture, those whose lives are characterized by poor stewardship, love of money, and greed cannot be children of God, for the love of money is essentially idolatry (Prov. 11:28; Isa. 2:7–8; Matt. 6:19–34; 19:6–22). Generosity should mark the lives of individual believers and of churches. Again the Lausanne Paper addresses this issue: "This principle of generous and sacrificial sharing [Acts 4:34], expressed in holding ourselves and our goods available for people in need, is an indispensable characteristic of every Spirit-filled church . . . . In the same spirit, we must seek ways to transact the church's corporate business together with minimum expenditure on travel, food and accommodation."[35] Imagine the potential increase in missions giving if individuals and churches examined their budgets in this light.

Let us not rationalize hoarding and comfortable living as if they were essential to provide the energy and peace of mind we need in order to minister. Good stewardship of abundant resources may greatly advance God's kingdom, but spending all of our resources on personal security, comfort, and

---

[34] Ibid.
[35] Ibid.

pleasure tends to have the opposite result. History attests to this fact. Times of great need and suffering among Christians often results in rapid church growth and spiritual revival, while church prosperity and success tends to yield little growth. John Piper writes in *Let the Nations Be Glad*, "The lesson is that comfort and ease and affluence and prosperity and safety and freedom often cause a tremendous inertia in the church. The very things that we think would produce personnel and energy and creative investment of time and money for the missionary cause, instead produce the exact opposite: weakness, apathy, lethargy, self-centeredness, preoccupation with security . . . . Statistics show that the richer we are, the smaller the percentage of our income we give to the church and its mission."[36] In conclusion, "Persecution can have harmful effects on the church. But prosperity, it seems, is even more devastating to the mission God calls us to . . . . [W]e should be very wary of prosperity and excessive ease and comfort and affluence."[37]

CONCLUSION

God has redeemed us by the blood of Jesus Christ and made us stewards of a treasure valuable beyond comprehension—God's glorious grace made manifest in the gospel. He has made known to us the mystery of his salvation, and he calls his church to make known this mystery to the ends of the earth. We must flee the temptation to bury such wealth under the rubble of a safe, comfortable, and unexamined lifestyle. Rather, our Lord summons us to diligently invest this gospel treasure in the lives of the lost, from our neighborhood to the ends of the earth.

May we as God's church, both corporately and individually, examine our lifestyle with all earnestness. May we purge our lives of that which does not help advance God's mission on earth. May we faithfully steward that which has been entrusted to us. "Only let your manner of life be worthy of the gospel of Christ" (Phil. 1:27).

---

[36] John Piper, *Let the Nations Be Glad* (Grand Rapids, MI: Baker Books, 1993), 97.
[37] Ibid., 98.

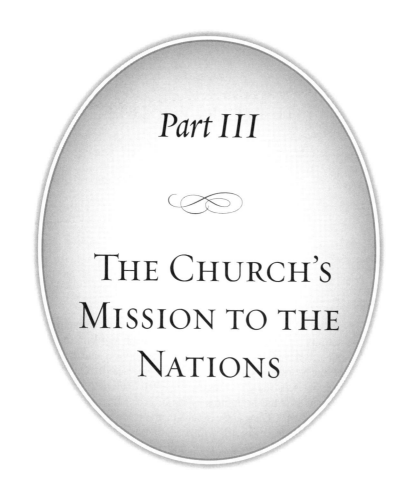

Part III

THE CHURCH'S MISSION TO THE NATIONS

Chapter Ten

THE HEBREW BIBLE
AND THE NATIONS

Tracy J. McKenzie

INTRODUCTION

When Jesus declared that the gospel should be preached to all nations, his message should not have been startling to his audience, as it was based upon the Law, the Prophets, and the Writings. In his two-volume work, the physician-author Luke uses the Old Testament Scriptures as the basis for the gospel being preached to all nations. Indeed, he shows us that Jesus saw the Scriptures as the basis for his mission. In Luke 24:43–44, Luke writes, "Then [Jesus] said to them, "These are my words that I spoke to you while I was still with you, that everything written about me in the *Law of Moses and the Prophets and the Psalms* must be fulfilled" (emphasis added). Then he opened their minds to understand the Scriptures and said to them, "Thus it is written, that the Christ should suffer and on the third day rise from the dead, and that repentance and forgiveness of sins should be proclaimed in his name *to all nations*, beginning from Jerusalem" (vv. 46–47, emphasis added). Jesus drew from the Old Testament not only what was written concerning himself but also that there should be a proclamation of this message *to all nations*. For Jesus and thus also Luke, God's mission concerning himself and the nations was written in Israel's Scriptures.

Upon the heels of this statement Luke recounts the last few moments that Jesus spent with his disciples on earth. While they were waiting on the Holy Spirit, the disciples asked, "Are you at this time restoring the kingdom to Israel?" (Acts 1:6, author's own translation). As if he were waiting for this particular question, Jesus indicated that it was not for them to know the timetable of the father but rather they were to preach the gospel beginning with Jerusalem and *"to the end of the earth!"* (v. 8, emphasis added). After this statement, he disappeared into the clouds. This statement raises a question: Was the notion that the gospel should be preached to all nations a novel idea of which the disciples were unaware? In other words, did this come from Jesus' divine knowledge of God's plan? Did it come because he wanted this new movement to be a worldwide movement? Or is Luke drawing our attention to a progression from the Scriptures of Israel to its outworking in his day?

Although it is not commonly recognized, the disciples ask a very perceptive question. Typically derided for their supposed nationalistic, earthly agenda,[1] the disciples are following the biblical storyline from the Law into the Prophets and through the Psalms. To begin with, at the end of the book of the Law, Moses speaks of a covenant in addition to the covenant of law that was given at Sinai (Deut. 29:1). Moreover, he warns of impending calamity for Israel in the last days (Deut. 31:29). It is in between these two important comments where he also speaks of a *restoration of fortunes* in which God will gather them from the peoples and circumcise their hearts. This internal circumcision will bring obedience to the law and enable them to remain in the land (Deut. 30:6). One might wonder how the nations fit into this picture presented at the end of the Pentateuch. We will return to this question below.

On the heels of the Law is the Prophets. The author of the book of Jeremiah, for example, seems to pick up on the notion of an internal heart change as well as a new covenant. He makes this clear within a collection of salvation oracles from Jeremiah 30–33. In these oracles, the author also speaks of "the latter days" (Jer. 30:24) when the Lord will accomplish his purposes, "restore the fortunes" of Israel and Judah (Jer. 30:3,18; 31:23; 32:37,44; 33:7,11,26), cut a new covenant with them (Jer. 31:21), and compel them with an internal heart change (Jer. 31:31–34).[2] In these days, Jeremiah prophesies of an ingathering, an assembling of God's people from all the nations where he has driven them because of their idolatry. Interestingly enough, it is not only Israel and Judah who experience a "restoration." Other Gentile nations such as Moab, the sons of Ammon, and Elam also have a restoration in the last days although not as fully articulated as Judah and Israel.[3] Other prophetic books likewise echo these themes at key eschatological, messianic moments.[4] In other words, the restoration the disciples were expecting seems to extend to Gentiles as well as the people of Israel.

---

[1] George Eldon Ladd, *A Theology of the New Testament*, rev. ed. (Grand Rapids: Eerdmans, 1993), 352, 368–69.

[2] For the association between Deut. 30:1–3; Jer. 30–33; and Ezek. 36:26, see J. G. McConville, "1 Kings VIII 46–53 and the Deuteronomic Hope," *Vetus Testamentum* 42 (Jan. 1992): 77.

[3] Jer. 48:47; 49:6; 49:39.

[4] Is. 27:13; 49:5–6; 52:8–10; 56:7–8; Ezek. 39:25 (along with Egypt in 29:14 and Sodom and Samaria in 16:53); Hos. 6:11; Joel 4:1; Amos 9:14; Mic. 5:1–2; Nah. 2:2; Zeph. 2:7; 3:20; Zech. 10:6–10.

After the Prophets are the Writings, which begin with the Psalms. The Psalms also speak of a *restoration of fortunes*. Psalm 14 looks forward to the time when God would restore the fortunes of his people so that Jacob and Israel could be glad. Psalms 85 and 126 likewise echo this theme and associate it with a time of salvation and great rejoicing. Moreover, other books within the third section of the Hebrew Bible also contain a restoration of fortune and although much study remains to be done on the precise understanding arising from these occurrences, at least some association with that which is found in the Torah and Prophets is appropriate (Job 42:10; Lam. 5:21).[5]

This brings us back to the book of Acts, with which we opened our discussion. Luke's treatment of the restoration in relation to its execution among the nations raises two questions. First, in what places along the biblical storyline can one see God's missional purposes among the nations? Second, are there sound exegetical arguments in which the reader of Scripture perceives intentionality within the structure of a biblical book through which the author makes clear God's purpose to gather individuals from all the nations? In the remainder of the essay, we will deal with these questions from the framework of the Hebrew Bible: the Law, the Prophets, and the Writings.

THE LAW: GENESIS–DEUTERONOMY

The purpose of the Law extends beyond mere legal or historical reportage. Most people who read the Old Testament do so with the expectation of finding God's historical dealings with Israel. That is, they expect to find history when they open up the first few books of the Bible. To be certain, that is what they find, for the authors of Scripture use historical narratives to communicate their message. Interestingly enough, however, historical narratives are not the only type of medium they use. They also use poetry, legal code, discourse, genealogies, and other literary material. From the manner in which they put these and other genres to use in their books, we can discern that they are not merely telling us what happened. They are also communicating a message with their depictions of what happened. In other words, the purpose of the Pentateuch (Genesis, Exodus, Leviticus, Numbers, and Deuteronomy) is not only to tell us what happened in the early period of Israel's history. We must find out its primary purpose by discerning the structure of the book itself.

When one reads through the Pentateuch, they find that the author uses past events to tell us about a future day. As strange as it might sound to modernistic readers of the Pentateuch, by noting the way texts interface with one another and are arranged in the Pentateuch, the reader can discern that the Pentateuch is about the last days![6] The Pentateuch is not merely recounting

---

[5]   Ernst Ludwig Dietrich, שוב שבות *Die Endzeitliche Wiederherstellungbei den Propheten*, BZAW 40 (Germany: Alfred Töpelmann), 25–28, 33–37.

[6]   By "modernistic readers of the Pentateuch," I mean readers who for generations have been trained to get inside the head of author, audience, and characters inside the narrative in order to divine the meaning of the text. None of these options are possible. Instead we must arrive at

past events. It is a recounting of past events in order to communicate a message about the future. One scholar traces the phrase "the last days" and other messianic themes that consistently appear together throughout the Pentateuch and asserts that there is a "fully developed messianic eschatology" in the Pentateuch.[7] Another scholar, Otto Procksch writes, "Already in Genesis 1:1 the concept of the 'the last days' fills the mind of the reader."[8] If this is true, it should not surprise us that the Pentateuch reveals God's plan for Israel and the nations through his anointed king in the last days. This section will explore the Pentateuch and God's mission to the nations in two ways. First, it will note God's concern for the nations as seen along the storyline and in the characters of the Pentateuch. Second, it will note God's concern for the nations within the structure of the Pentateuch itself.

A common reference to God's concern for the nations in the Pentateuch is God's covenant to Abraham. Throughout the book of Genesis, the author records God's varied promises to Abraham, Sarah, their children, and grandchildren. The first of these references can be found shortly after the introduction of Abraham in Genesis 12:3. God promised Abraham that he would make him into a great nation, that he would bless him, that he would make his name great, and that in Abraham all the families of the earth would be blessed.[9] From this simple poem, one begins to discern that God had much more in mind than blessing one race of people through this Patriarch. As the reader follows the storyline of Abraham and his promised "seed," this theme of blessing all nations occurs repeatedly. In Genesis 13:15–16 and 15:1–18, God affirms his covenant with Abraham although the promise concerning the nations is absent. Then in 17:1–8,16, and 22:17–18, God's plan for the nations returns with its association with God's covenant to Abraham. The covenant is then reaffirmed through Isaac and Rebekah (Gen. 24:60; 26:3–4) and Abraham's grandson, Jacob (Gen. 28:13–15). This covenant is central to the book of Genesis and becomes the foundation of God's actions throughout the remainder of the Pentateuch and into the conquest and monarchy.[10]

The Pentateuch did not begin, however, with Abraham. As the focus of the Pentateuch narrows to Israel, the nation, it is important to consider what was chronicled in Scripture prior to the narratives concerning Abraham. Genesis 1–11 depicts God's concern for humanity from a universal perspective. It is

---

meaning by discerning how the text has been written and shaped by an author in order to communicate a message.

[7] John Sailhamer, "Hosea 11:1 and Matthew 2:15," *WTJ* 63 (2001): 87–96.

[8] Otto Procksch, *Die Genesis uebersetzt und erklaert* (Leipzig: Deichertsche Veragsbuchhandlung, 1913), 425, quoted in Sailhamer, *Genesis Unbound* (Sisters, OR: Multnomah, 1996), 43.

[9] The phrase at the end of 12:3, "All the families of the earth" is to be understood from the perspective of all humanity because of its association with the same familial term associated with the disbursement of Noah's children (and therefore, everyone who was alive) after the flood in Gen. 10:32.

[10] Exod. 2:24; 32:13; Lev. 26:42; Num. 32:11; Deut. 1:8; 34:4; Josh. 24:2; 1 Kgs. 18:36; 2 Kgs. 13:23.

from this universal perspective that Scripture begins. Later biblical authors often return to the early chapters of Genesis as an edenic portrayal of God's blessing in the last days.[11] It is here in Genesis 1 that God first blessed Adam and Eve. Before Israel became the center of the biblical narrative, God blessed mankind, created them in his image, spoke to them (unlike the rest of creation), and gave them a stewardship in his creation. It is prior to any mention of the nation of Israel that God first provides the institution of marriage that will one day result in the promised seed of woman. It is here with Adam, Eve, Cain, Noah, Lamech, the men of Babel, and all remaining mankind, where God must graciously deal with man's fallen state in a manner that compromises neither his justice nor his mercy. Gerhard von Rad puts it well,

> The whole primeval history, [Gen 1–11] therefore, seems to break off in shrill dissonance, and the question we formulated above now arises even more urgently: Is God's relationship to the nations now finally broken; is God's gracious forbearance now exhausted; has God rejected the nations in wrath forever? That is the burdensome question which no thoughtful reader of chapter 11 can avoid; indeed, one can say that our narrator intended by means of the whole plan of his primeval history to raise precisely this question and to pose it in all its severity. Only then is the reader properly prepared to take up the strangely new thing that now follows the comfortless story about the building of the tower: the election and blessing of Abraham.[12]

Von Rad is saying that the universal man has miserably failed and apparently has been left under God's wrath. Von Rad continues describing the intersection between the failure of the Tower of Babel and the gracious election of Abraham. Most readers assume the author is merely reporting what happened, and thus their focus immediately turns to Israel. These readers miss the question posed by the author before the subject of Israel actually commences. The question is, "Will God forever be wrathful against the nations?" In missing the question, they must also miss the answer given in Abraham's election.

In other words, the narrative of Abraham, his seed, the blessing to the nations, and the entire story of Israel is an answer to the dilemma of the universal sin of all mankind and God's wrath found in the first eleven chapters of Genesis. Von Rad answers his own question, "The question about God's salvation for all nations remains open and unanswerable in *primeval* history. But our narrator *does* give an answer, namely, at the point where sacred history begins. Here in the promise that is given concerning Abraham something is again said about God's saving will and indeed about a salvation extending far beyond the limits of the covenant people to "all the families of the earth."[13] Abraham and his seed, the eventual messiah, are the answer to the sin and rebellion found in "all the families of the earth." While there is no question that subsequent to Genesis 12, Israel is a focal point of the Hebrew Bible, it

[11] For example, Hos. 2:16–23 and Ezek. 36:8–15.
[12] Gerhard von Rad, *Genesis* (Philadelphia: Westminster Press, 1972), 153.
[13] Ibid., 154.

is noteworthy that the author does not turn to the patriarchal narratives without purpose. His purpose for turning the reader's attention to the patriarchal narratives is revealed in the way Abraham's seed will bring blessing to "all the families of the earth." Seen from this perspective, the author's attention is primarily on the future, not on the past. Moreover, God's gracious and loving care for all humanity is declared from the outset of the Bible.[14]

The structure of the Pentateuch itself demonstrates additional evidence for God's mission to the nations. By "structure" I mean an intentional arrangement through which a reader can discern an author's argument. One manner in which scholars are finding structure within larger units of text is through the repetition of language, themes, and stylistic choices.[15] I have already pointed out above one such study that traces the phrase "the last days" and other recurring terminology and style to a messianic theme within the Pentateuch.[16] Elsewhere I have demonstrated recurring language and stylistic uses associated with a theme of Israel's idolatry within the Pentateuch itself. The importance of this theme is not in the statement that Israel committed idolatry.[17] Rather, the importance lies in the consistent distribution of this portrayal throughout the Pentateuch and its result in the final passage associated with this motif. It is to this theme and its result that we now turn.

The following texts contain related allusions to the idolatrous practices of Israel: the Ten Commandments, the narratives of the golden calf, the covenant renewal after the golden calf, the laws of the sacrifice of Leviticus 17, the laws of the holiness code of Leviticus 26, the incident of Baal Peor, and repeated allusions to these incidents in Deuteronomy. Consistently through these texts, Israel is depicted as making the Lord jealous through her devotion to other gods and provoking him to jealousy by idolatry.[18] The final text in this distribution of passages deals with the result of Israel's idolatry. Moses says in the poem of Deuteronomy 32:16, "They made him jealous with strange things, with abominations, they provoked him to anger" (author's own translation). After several other comments about idolatry and Israel's provocation, the Lord says in Deuteronomy 32:21, "They, they made me jealous with 'not-a-god;' they provoked me to anger with their vanities. I, I will make them jealous with 'not-a-people;' with a senseless nation, I will provoke them to anger" (author's own translation). The poem uses the same two verbs in each verse. Furthermore, in Deuteronomy 32:21, each pair of verbs is used with Israel as the subject of the first line of the verse and God as the subject of the second line. In other words, Israel is making God jealous and provoking him

---

[14] Other narratives along the storyline of the Pentateuch describe important roles for non-Israelites: Melchizedek, Esau, and the foreigners who apparently entered into covenant with God (Deut. 29:11–13).

[15] For a technical treatment of this subject, see McKenzie, *Idolatry in the Pentateuch* (Eugene, OR: Wipf & Stock, 2010).

[16] John H. Sailhamer, *The Pentateuch as Narrative* (Grand Rapids: Zondervan, 1992), 34–39.

[17] McKenzie, *Idolatry*.

[18] These passages are: Exod. 20:3–6; 32:1–35; 34:14–17; Lev. 17:1–7; 26:1–46; Num. 25:1–13; Deut. 4:3–28; 5:7–9; 9:7–21; 31:16–30; and 32:16–22.

to anger with their devotion to other things. God's response is similar in that he will make them jealous and provoke them to anger with another people!

The question can be developed further: How will God make them jealous and provoke them to anger? Traditionally, Old Testament scholars have considered the way in which he will make them angry is through a military defeat. It is understandable how one arrives at this comprehension since Deuteronomy 28 indicates devastation will occur and, indeed, a military destruction did eventually follow both for the northern and southern kingdoms. The reason, however, that this understanding cannot be the appropriate connotation for this prophecy is that a military defeat would not make Israel jealous in the same way that Israel had made God jealous through devotion to other gods. A provocation through military destruction might defeat them; it might make them miserable; it might even make them angry presuming God had abandoned them. But it would not provoke them to jealousy in the same manner in which God had been provoked to jealousy by his special people embracing false gods.

The appropriate understanding given in Deuteronomy 32:16–21 is that God would embrace a people who were without sense in view of God's historical blessing and giving of the law (Deut. 32:1–15). He would embrace a people who did not have knowledge of the patriarchs, did not have knowledge of his holy law, and did not have knowledge of his salvific deliverance from Egypt. This other nation is none other than the non-Jewish nation known as the Gentiles.[19] Deuteronomy 32 reveals the author's important message of the role of the nations in God's future plans. In the last days, God would turn from Israel and embrace a nation in order to provoke Israel to jealousy.

In addition, the role of Deuteronomy 32 and its proximity to the messianic-eschatological discussion in which Moses spoke of a covenant other than the covenant of law given at Sinai and the evil which would befall Israel in the last days (Deut. 29:1 and 31:29) demonstrates how the inclusion of the Gentiles in God's salvation program also falls within the same structural context of the Pentateuch. This structural context is the climactic final chapters of Deuteronomy in which the author of the Pentateuch clearly uses the narratives and legal code of the past to speak about the future (Deut. 1:5; 31:29); for our purposes in this chapter, it is a future in which God will embrace the Gentiles in order to provoke Israel to jealousy in the last days.

THE PROPHETS: JOSHUA–THE TWELVE

Similar to studies in the Pentateuch, scholars are also discerning an eschatological emphasis in the Prophets. One such scholar, Otto Plöger, describes the literary clash between two different camps in post-exilic Israel. On the one hand, there are those who desire an immediate nationalistic agenda. On the

---

[19]   The Hebrew word for nation in Deuteronomy 32:21 is the singular noun also commonly translated as Gentile(s).

other hand, there are also those who write with an agenda that goes beyond the borders of Israel and extends God's kingdom to a universal agenda.[20]

Another well-known scholar, Joseph Blenkinsopp, has also written about the eschatological influence reverberating in the Prophets. In a section of his essay entitled "Eschatology and Canon Formation," Blenkinsopp writes,

> One of the most striking features shared by the book of Isaiah and several of the Twelve is that they conclude by presenting a scenario of the future and final condition of Israel, in some instances coinciding with the consummation of history and the transformation of the cosmos. This complex scenario sometimes stays more or less within the bounds of historical plausibility, including such prospects as return from the Diaspora and a mission to foreign peoples, but more often than not it describes a "singularity" involving a universal meteorological catastrophe, warfare on a cosmic scale, new heaven and new earth, a final judgment by fire, and similar motifs.[21]

Blenkinsopp is attempting to show how an eschatological shaping has influenced the canon, in particular, that section of the Hebrew Bible that is referred to as the Prophets. This eschatological shaping includes a mission to Gentile nations. Later in the essay he considers in more detail the book of Isaiah. He writes, "Chapter 66, and therefore the book as a whole, ends with three oracular pronouncements (*ne'um YHWH*) (vv. 17–21,22–23) that speak of the ingathering in Jerusalem at the end-time, *a mission to the Gentiles preceding the final theophany*, and the creation of the new heavens and a new earth."[22] From the perspective of that eschatological influence, he indicates that one often finds a mission to non-Jewish peoples.

These studies demonstrate an association between Israel in the last days and a mission to the Gentiles. The association and integration of eschatology and missiology will have enormous impact on our understanding of eschatology and God's mission to the nations and our current role in the program. This gives new impetus to the notion of missions. In other words, God's agenda, which was written about in the Scriptures, has always concerned Israel and the nations in the last days.

This section will further explore *The Prophets* and God's mission to the nations in two ways. First, it will note God's concern for the nations as seen along the storyline and in the characters of the Prophets. Second, it will note God's concern for the nations within the structure of a particular prophetic book.

God's plans and purposes for the nations receive more attention in the prophetic section of the Hebrew Bible than in any other section of the *TaNaK*.[23]

[20]   Otto Plöger, *Theocracy and Eschatology*, trans. S. Rudman (Oxford: Blackwell, 1968).

[21]   Joseph Blenkinsopp, "The Formation of the Hebrew Bible Canon: Isaiah as a Test Case," in *The Canon Debate*, ed. Lee M. McDonald and James A. Sanders (Peabody, MA: Hendrickson, 2002), 65.

[22]   Ibid., 66, emphasis added.

[23]   The *TaNaK* is an acronymous moniker indicating the threefold section of the Hebrew Bible: The Torah is the Law, the *Nevi'im* is the Prophets, and the *Ketuvim* is the Writings.

In this section of the Hebrew Bible, one can more consistently discern a role for the nations, in particular, in that eschatological period so often referred to in the Prophets. The nations become both an object of God's mercy and an object of his judgment. For this reason, we will not attempt to exhaust all occasions of God's mission to the nations but will limit our discussion to a few examples found within the prophetic books.

Similar to the Pentateuch, Gentile characters occasionally play significant roles along the storyline of the prophetic corpus. One only has to read a few chapters into the Prophets when Rahab the harlot enters the scene. Not only is Rahab a Gentile, but she is also a woman and even more shockingly a harlot. And yet, through Rahab's confession of faith and her demonstration of that faith through her actions, she and her family are preserved and "she has lived in the midst of Israel to this day, for she hid the messengers whom Joshua sent to spy out Jericho" (Josh. 6:25, NASB). Rahab's fear of God and trust in his mercy saves her and earns her a respected place within the Old Testament in spite of her Gentile heritage.

Another prophetic book infamous for its treatment of the non-Jewish personages is the book of Jonah. Positioned within the Book of the Twelve, the book of Jonah advances a certain plot line within the Twelve.[24] Our concern here is simply to show the numerous encounters that Jonah had with Gentiles in the short narrative. In Jonah 1, Jonah encountered the sailors who at first "each cried out to his god" (Jonah 1:5). After hearing Jonah's testimony and seeing the wind-whipped sea, the sailors feared greatly and finally cried out to the Lord. The author does not depict them as crying out to the more generic Hebrew term for God, *Elohim*, to whom they cried out earlier in the narrative. Rather, after hearing Jonah's confession, they use his personal name, *Yahweh*. The Lord then calms the sea, and the narrator reports that the sailors feared the Lord greatly, sacrificed sacrifices, and vowed vows.

The significance of Gentiles in the book of Jonah does not stop there, however. The people of Nineveh also play a role within the book. Long-time enemy of Israel, Nineveh was a wicked city and God had told Jonah to go and cry out against them. Despite his attempts to flee from God's assignment for him, Jonah acquiesced and delivered a five word (in Hebrew) "evangelistic" message to the inhabitants of Nineveh. "Yet forty days, and Nineveh shall be overthrown!" (Jonah 3:4). The people of Nineveh, from the king to the lowest servant, promptly believed in God and turned from their wicked ways donning sackcloth and ashes, the typical garb for repentance and mourning. Jonah was disappointed in the entire episode of God's mercy and grace shown to this Gentile city. This leads to the final chapter where Jonah showed concern for a simple plant when it died. The book ends with God asking the rhetorical question, "Should I not have compassion on Nineveh . . . ?" (Jonah 4:11, NASB). The answer seems obvious enough: God will have compassion on whomever he will have compassion. This even includes those Gentiles who

---

[24] See the article by Michael Shepherd in *Zeitschrift für die alttestamentliche Wissenschaft* 121, no. 2, 2009.

were Israel's enemies as well as one among Israel's most pious of positions, the prophet Jonah.[25] This section has noted God's concern for the nations as seen along the storyline and in the characters of the Prophets.

Next, we must consider God's concern for the nations within the structure of a particular prophetic book. Here, as in the Pentateuch, we are looking for evidence of intentionality that is discernible through the structure of a book. How has the author communicated in such a way as to put prominence upon the nations and their role within a particular book? We find this scenario in the introduction to the Book of the Twelve, Hosea 1–3. The book of Jonah has already provided indications of an emphasis upon a Gentile people within the Book of the Twelve. Other indications of a universal focus include passages such as Amos 9:11–12 and Joel 2:28–32.[26] However, a central consideration to the structure of any book is its introduction. Among those scholars who consider the Twelve as one book rather than a collection of twelve individual books, Hosea 1–3 provides a significant introductory frame to the overall book.[27]

Hosea 1–3 sets the eschatological and missiological agenda for the entire Book of the Twelve. It does so in part by exhibiting many texts that allude to important passages within the Pentateuch. For example, one is able to ascertain the interplay between Hosea 1:9 and Exodus 3:14 through the negation of "I am." The Lord reveals the name by which he desires to be known forever when he says in Exodus 3:14, "God said to Moses, 'I AM WHO I AM'; and He said, 'Thus you shall say to the sons of Israel, "I AM has sent me to you"'" (NASB). Although standard English versions translate Hosea 1:9 using the term "God," it is absent from the Hebrew text and could appropriately be translated as "For you are not my people and I am not 'I am' to you." This illustrates a keen awareness of Exodus 3:14 and indicates the author's tendency to allude to previous Scripture in order to communicate a message.

Moreover, Hosea 1:10 says, "Yet the number of the sons of Israel will be like the sand of the sea, which cannot be measured or numbered" (NASB). This alludes to Genesis 22:17 through the phrase, "sand which is on the seashore" and the notion of immeasurable offspring. Likewise, the collocations of agricultural terms in Hosea 2:8, "grain, new wine, and oil" (NKJV) allude to the same collocations of terms in Deuteronomy 7, 11, 12, 14, 18, 28, and 33. Likewise, Hosea 3:5 alludes to the structurally important phrase "in the last days" (NASB) occurring in Genesis 49:1, Numbers 24:14, and Deuteronomy

---

[25] See also Johannes Verkuyl, "The Biblical Foundation for the Worldwide Mission Mandate" in *Perspectives on the World Christian Movement*, 3rd ed., Ralph D Winter and Steven C. Hawthorne, eds. (Pasadena: William Carey Library, 1999), 30–33.

[26] For example, see the Septuagint translation of Amos 9:11–12 and the way Luke quotes it in Acts 15:15–18.

[27] Although no consensus exists over whether it is one book or twelve books, it is not uncommon for it to be considered as one book. For one example, see James Nolgaski, *Literary Precursors*, BZAW vol. 217 (Berlin: Walter de Gruyter, 1993). For Hosea 1–3 as an introduction to the Twelve, see Craig Bowman "Reading the Twelve as One: Hosea 1–3 as an Introduction to the Book of the Twelve (the Minor Prophets)," *Stone-Campbell Journal* 9 (Spring 2006): 41–59.

31:29. It says, "Afterward the sons of Israel will return and seek the LORD their God and David their king; and they will come trembling to the LORD and to His goodness in the last days" (NASB). Once again, this demonstrates the author's awareness of a significant messianic phrase from the Pentateuch and signals an intentional usage in a congruous way. Finally, the book of Hosea opens with a very clear condemnation of Israel's idolatry. For anyone reading through the canon, the condemnation of idolatry has been a significant theme since its outset, and by now the reader can easily discern the significance of the motif.

The next allusion signals the important connection to Deuteronomy 32:16–21, a passage that underscores the inclusion of the Gentiles in God's eschatological program. In conjunction with the above linguistic connections to key pentateuchal texts, it appears that the name "Lo-ammi" in Hosea 1:9 (NASB) and the phrase "not My people" in Hosea 1:10 and 2:23 (NASB) is also associated with Deuteronomy 32:21. Hosea 1:9 reads, "Call his name Lo Ammi for you are not my people and I am not 'I am' to you" (author's own translation). The personal name of God was once a reassuring memorial in the ears of Israel but now, in some sense, has not only been forfeited but has become a negative reminder of God's rejection.

The shock of the rejection is quickly assuaged by the following clause in Hosea 1:10, which recounts the familiar covenantal blessing mentioned above that God made to Abraham, Isaac, and Jacob: "The number of the sons of Israel will be like the sand of the sea, which cannot be measured or numbered" (NASB). Although only explicitly mentioned in this formula twice in the Pentateuch (Gen. 22:17; 32:13), this promise of abundant offspring in its many similar turns of phrase throughout the Pentateuch becomes a hallmark of God's blessing through the Abrahamic covenant. Although God has rejected the house of Israel, God's covenant with Abraham still remains in force.

The next clause in Hosea 1:10 exposes the allusion to Deuteronomy 32:21. It reads that "in the place where it is said to them, 'You are not My people,' it will be said to them, 'You are the sons of the living God'" (NASB). It should come as no surprise that God would bless those outside the nation of Israel. The covenant regarding the numerous offspring often included the statement that in Abraham "all the *nations* of the earth shall be blessed" (Gen. 22:17–18, NASB). What is remarkable about Hosea 1:10 is not necessarily the perception that the nations could be included in the familial blessings of the Abrahamic covenant but rather that this understanding is associated with Deuteronomy 32:21. As was stated above, Deuteronomy 32:21 reads, "They, they made me jealous with 'not a god;' they provoked me to anger with their vanities. I, I will make them jealous with 'not a people;' with a senseless nation, I will provoke them to anger" (author's own translation). In the Hebrew text, the words "Lo-ammi" in Hosea 1:9 and "not My people" in Hosea 1:10 and 2:23 share the same syntactical arrangement and virtually the same verbal content as do Moses' words in Deuteronomy 32:21, "not a people." In view of the many allusions already observed between Hosea 1–3 and key pentateuchal texts, it is no surprise that the author has utilized the meaning of Deuteronomy 32:16–21 in order to rebuke Israel for its consistent idolatry and reveal God's aged plan for the inclusion of the Gentiles.

Thus, Hosea 1–3 alludes to the inclusion of the Gentiles in God's salvation program in conjunction with his chastisement of Israel because of idolatry. Since this is the case in the introduction to the Book of the Twelve, the reader is now prepared to discern God's role for the nations, his plan in the last days, the administration of the Abrahamic covenant, and the coming Davidic king throughout the Book of the Twelve.

THE WRITINGS: PSALMS–CHRONICLES

The Writings pose a unique challenge to an understanding of God's mission to the nations. This third section of *TaNaK* does not have the frequent number of explicit references to the role of the nations either through a positive depiction of Gentile characters or during an eschatological ingathering of God's people as in the Law and the Prophets. The Writings include a mixture of genre: apocalyptic texts, laments, psalms, narratives, interpretive history, love poems, and wisdom literature. These texts often convey a notion of judgment, the righteous in contrast to the wicked, suffering, and the importance of proper fear of the Lord. It is in the Psalter that these themes first appear within the Writings, and it is probably here in which God's mission to the nations is most prominent within the section.

The role of the nations has often been heralded from the Psalms, in particular from Psalm 67.[28] It is within this psalm that many of the themes of the Psalter and the rest of the Hebrew Bible reverberate. The psalmist asks that God's grace and blessing be given in order that God's salvation could be known among all the nations. He asks that the peoples and the nations praise God because his judgment will be upright and give guidance to the nations and his blessings will result in the ends of the earth fearing him. The overall framework of the Psalter itself conveys a similar emphasis of grace, blessing, salvation, peoples, nations, praise, judgment, and fear. The following discussion presents this framework.

Psalms 1 and 2 open with judgment upon the wicked while the righteous are blessed and obviously have a reverential delight in the law of God. The nations and the peoples stand against the Lord and his Anointed One while he speaks against them, proclaiming the coming judgment through his anointed King, giving the nations and the ends of the earth as an inheritance. These very kings and people are then commanded to be wise and discerning, to serve the Lord in fear, to rejoice in trembling, to pay homage to the son because in a while his anger will be kindled. Psalm 2 concludes in the same manner as Psalm 1 opens: "Blessed is the man . . . ." However, this occasion

---

[28] Walter C. Kaiser Jr., *Mission in the Old Testament: Israel as a Light to the Nations* (Grand Rapids: Baker, 2000), 30–33.

calls for blessings upon anyone who takes refuge in the Son who will soon come in judgment.

The nations in these introductory Psalms are not unlike the nations in the prophetic books. They appear to be made up of individuals, some of whom will experience judgment and some who will humbly submit themselves to this King. The King, who in yet a little while will come in judgment, is also prepared to bless his people when their posture before him is appropriate. In this connection, it is significant to discern in what manner each "book" of the Psalter and its five-chapter conclusion comes to an end.

The Psalter is divided into five books (1–41, 42–72, 73–89, 90–106, 107–150). Each book concludes with a version of the doxological line, "Blessed be the LORD . . . forever . . . amen" (Ps. 41:13; 72:18–19; 89:52; 106:48). Moreover, the Psalter concludes with a doxological climax that resounds with praise toward God. Beginning in Psalm 145:1, the psalmist indicates that he will bless the name of the Lord forever. Psalm 145:2 continues stating that he would bless the Lord all days and would praise his name forever. The psalm continues with nearly every clause from Psalm 145:1–13 using a distinct term to indicate that God's creation will extol his greatness in some manner. Psalm 145:14–20 develops the notion that God is merciful to those who humble themselves before him but will judge the wicked. The psalm ends in the same manner as it begins—blessing! This "blessing" theme echoes the conclusion of each of the psalter's books. This time, however, it is not the psalmist who blesses the Lord but "all flesh will bless his holy name forever" (Ps. 145:21, NASB). The crescendo of praise is only beginning.

Each of the next psalms, 146–149, opens with a command to praise and concludes with a command to praise. What is instructive for our purposes in this chapter is not only *what* one is supposed to do but *who* is supposed to do it. Although Zion and Israel are constantly encouraged to praise the Lord, it is all of his creation that will also praise the Lord: "Kings of the earth and all peoples; princes and all judges of the earth . . . let them praise the name of the LORD" (Ps. 148:11,13, NASB). Furthermore, judgment against the nations is as sure as it was in Psalm 2, but this does not seem to negate the praise the Lord receives from the humble and afflicted of his people and creation. Psalm 150, a final apex of praise, uses at least two imperatives in every verse calling God's people to praise him in all places and with all sorts of instrumentation. As if to leave no doubt concerning the subject of who is to praise, the Psalter concludes with the injunction for everything that has breath to praise the Lord.

From this perspective, there is little doubt that the psalmist wants no one left out of this chorus of praise. Israel and any among the nations who take refuge in the Lord are to be included in this participation of attributing to Yahweh the glory and praise that is due him.

CONCLUSION

We have seen that the nations have been a subject of biblical authors from the very beginning of the Bible. Not only is it a subject that one stumbles upon as the biblical story unfolds, but the nations are also at the very heart of the structure through which biblical authors communicate a message. Whether it is the universal perspective in the Bible's opening chapters, an aspect of the central covenant to Abraham, a result associated with Israel's idolatry, participation in the lineage of Messiah, or a comprehensive chorus of praise, the concern for all humanity has never been far from the heartbeat of Scripture. Moreover, the biblical witness testifies that the nations come into focus in the last days when God's Messiah King comes into focus. That time has come. In the gospels Jesus said the kingdom of heaven is at hand. He then sent his disciples instructing them to report the same thing. Before his ascension and upon the advent of the Spirit, he told his disciples to go to the very ends of the earth witnessing to him.[29] Why? Because the day of which the prophets had spoken had arrived.

---

[29] Matt. 4:17; 10:7; and Acts 1:4–9.

Chapter Eleven

THE NEW TESTAMENT
AND THE NATIONS

Keith Whitfield

INTRODUCTION

The story of the Bible is the story of God's mission. Christopher
Wright puts it well when he writes that the plot of the whole biblical
narrative is "the story of God's mission through God's people in their
engagement with God's world for the sake of God's whole creation."[1] Mission then, in biblical terms, is God's plan. While it no doubt includes God's
people, it arises from the plan and initiation of God. Richard Bauckham, in
his book *Bible and Mission*, captures one of the main themes of this story
with the rubric "from the one to the many." He writes,

> The Bible is a kind of project aimed at the kingdom of God, that is, towards
> the achievement of God's purposes of good in the whole of God's creation.
> This is a universal direction that takes the particular with the utmost serious-
> ness. Christian communities or individuals are always setting off from the
> particular as both the Bible and our own situation defines it and following
> the biblical direction towards the universal that is to be found not apart from
> but within other particulars. This is mission.[2]

---

[1]   Christopher J. H. Wright, *The Mission of God: Unlocking the Bible's Grand Narrative*
(Downers Grove: IVP, 2006), 51. See also ibid., 23.
[2]   Richard Bauckham, *Bible and Mission: Christian Witness in a Postmodern World* (Grand
Rapids: Baker Academic, 2003), 11.

Bauckham's rubric offers a missional hermeneutic for understanding the narrative of Scripture.[3] It is a missional hermeneutic because it supplies a map for reading the revelation of God, his acts, and his purposes in missional terms. In this chapter, we use Bauckham's rubric to demonstrate the *missional structure* and *missional movement* in the New Testament with respect to the gospel being *for*, and going *to*, the nations. In addition to this rubric, we will follow the fourfold plotline of creation, fall, redemption, and restoration. The purpose for following this plotline is to locate the New Testament story of mission to the nations within the whole of the biblical narrative. What we hope to demonstrate is that God always pursues his mission by choosing a specific person or group of people to accomplish his mission to fill the whole earth with his worshippers. The design and structure for this plan is discerned in creation. The fall of humanity introduces opposition to God's plan. Humanity resists God's plan in their sin and rebellion. God recovers his intentions for creation in the plan of salvation. Finally, God's plan is established in the new earth.

CREATION

God's mission is explicitly directed by the creation mandate to "be fruitful and multiply and fill the earth" (Gen. 1:28), and it is anticipated by the very nature of creation itself. Humanity, created in the image of God with the capacity to know and love God and with the faculties to reflect God's creative works, is instructed by God to "subdue [the earth] and have dominion over the fish of the sea and over the birds of the heavens and over every living thing that moves on the earth" (Gen. 1:28). The creation mandate points humanity to a new horizon, which would involve population growth, fruitfulness in productivity, and new territories to subdue and occupy. The execution of the creation mandate across this vast and diverse world would produce diverse cultures. The food sources, materials to build, and the ingenuity needed to survive would vary from place to place. Societies and cultures would have to form. After all, Moses had to make plans to organize one nation in order to lead it (Exod. 18). How much more would civilizations be needed if the whole world is populated? G. K. Beale says, "[Adam and Eve] were to extend the geographical boundaries of the garden until Eden covered the whole earth. They were on the primeval hillock of hospitable Eden, outside of which lay the inhospitable land. They were to extend the smaller livable area of the garden by transforming the outer chaotic region into a habitable territory."[4]

---

[3]   Christopher Wright offers a very useful discussion on the nature of a missional hermeneutic. He says, "A missional hermeneutic, then, is not content simply to call for obedience to the Great Commission . . . , nor even to reflect on the missional implications of the Great Commandment. For behind both it will find the Great Communication—the revelation of the identity of God, of God's actions in the world and God's saving purpose for all creation." Wright, *The Mission of God*, 60.

[4]   G. K. Beale, *The Temple and the Church's Mission: A Biblical Theology of the Dwelling Place of God* (Downers Grove: IVP, 2004), 82.

Thus, we find within the structure and movement of creation the "from the one to the many" framework. There is one God. There is one earth. There is one mandate. There is one first family. But the natural unfolding of the creation mandate in the diversely created world would have ultimately resulted in the formation of groups of people with a common identity and unique from other groups of people.

FALL

The flow of God's plans in creation "from the one to the many" is, however, complicated by the fall of humanity. The cultural mandate in creation was challenged before any steps were taken toward being fruitful, multiplying, and filling the whole earth. When Adam and Eve sinned, they were removed from the garden, which was to be the pattern for the rest of the world. Rather than taking this pattern into the whole world, they became separated from their God and his garden. As a result of the sin, God cursed the earth outside the garden with "thorns and thistles" (Gen. 3:18), so that Adam would have to work hard to garden. Extending the garden to the rest of the world is frustrated by the daily job of tending, maintaining, and managing in order for one's family to eat (Gen. 3:17). The presence of sin also led to disharmony in human relationships. The call to be fruitful and multiply is rejected by Cain, who in his anger killed his brother (Gen. 4:8).

The presence of sin and the corrupting consequence of sin filled the earth. Ultimately, this did not come as a result of the plans of sinful humanity, but of the will and judgment of God. We are told in Genesis 6 that the Lord looked upon the earth and saw the universal and pervasive effects of sin. God then determined to "start over" with one man and his family. After the flood, the corrupting influence of sin did not decline. It continued to grow in the hearts of humanity. Corrupt humanity had no interest in filling the whole earth. In Genesis 11, the whole earth had one language, and as the people traveled from the west, at a certain spot they settled and decided to build a tower so that they might not be scattered throughout the earth (Gen. 11:4). Contrary to the creation mandate, they did not view being dispersed as a blessing.

The plans of sinful humanity, however, did not prevent the formation of diverse cultures. In judgment, God confused their language and scattered them across the whole earth. This was not merely an act of God's judgment. God worked in this event to thwart the sinful intention of the human heart and providentially advanced his purpose for creation. With the scattering of sinful humanity, however, the blessings and difficulties with ethnicity began. "The dividing wall of hostility" between the Jews and Greeks addressed in the New Testament indicates the enduring effects of God's merciful judgment on the hubris of humanity in these early pages of the biblical narrative (Eph. 2:14). Jesus' teaching in the parable of the good Samaritan reminds us that God had, indeed has, a different plan for humanity (Luke 10:25–37).

REDEMPTION

Old Testament context. Before we look at the gospel for the nations in the New Testament, we want to give a brief overview of the Old Testament context. The best way to discern the scope of God's mission embodied in Jesus and his disciples is to locate it in the Old Testament. What one perceives from reading the Old Testament is the anticipation that God would bless all the people groups of the world and that these groups would come and worship the true God.

God's plan to bless the whole earth is recovered in the calling of Abraham and in the formation of Israel as a nation. After the fall of humanity, the focus of the biblical story had been on the universal effects of sin on humanity, but in Genesis 12, God initiates his plan again through one man, Abraham. In this one man, God renews his vision for creation and reestablishes his mandate for humanity. In Genesis 1, God blesses his creation because it is good and it functions according to his purpose for it. But, here in Genesis 12, God promises Abraham that he will bless him by making him a great nation, and through him God will bless "all the families of the earth" (Gen. 12:1–3). *From the one* man, Abraham, God intends *to bless the many* people of the earth. W. J. Dumbrell says, "Genesis 12:1–3 is the rejoinder to the consequences of the fall and aims of the restoration of God for the World to which Gen. 1–2 directed our attention. What is being offered in these few verses is a theological blueprint for the redemptive history of the world."[5]

The great nation that God promised to give Abraham was Israel. During the time of Israel's enslavement in Egypt, God's promise to Abraham appeared to be "on the ropes." But, God remembered his promise to Israel and called them from slavery in a sequence of dramatic events that underscored that "there is a God in Israel," who desires to be known and rules supreme over all the gods of the nations. God then led his people to the foot of Mount Sinai. There, he rehearsed before them how he brought them to himself. He called them to obey him as a treasured people. He declared that the whole earth is his, and Israel will for him be a "kingdom of priests and a holy nation" before the nations of the earth (Exod. 19:3–6). When God called Israel to Sinai, he called them to serve him as a people, but also to be "a display-people, a showcase to the world how being in covenant with Yahweh changes a people."[6] The rest of Israel's history is a story of Israel's unfaithfulness to God's call. God, however, was faithful to his plan to bless the nations of the earth. God judges Israel for their unfaithfulness and sends them into exile. While under his judgment, God called his people to be a people for his mission in the foreign land (Jer. 29:4–9; Esth. 8–17). God also promised to

---

[5]   Quoted by Michael Goheen in an unpublished paper given at 2006 AAR/SBL meeting. William Dumbrell, *Creation and Covenant* (Nashville: Nelson Publishers, 1984), 66.

[6]   Quoted by Michael Goheen in an unpublished paper given at 2006 AAR/SBL meeting. John I. Durham, *Exodus*, World Biblical Commentary, vol. 3 (Waco, TX: Word Books, 1987), 263.

Israel that he would send a righteous King to them, who would lead them to be a righteous people (Isa. 62:1–5; Jer. 31:31–40) and who would be King for all the nations (Ps. 2:7–9; Isa. 55:3–5; Dan. 7:13–14).

The nations and the New Testament gospels. The opening page of the New Testament introduces the man Jesus of Nazareth as the King for the nations. Matthew's Gospel begins with the genealogy of Jesus Christ, proclaiming that he is the Messiah, the long-awaited king of Israel, who is the son of David. Therefore, a "new one" is at the center of God's mission. He is presented also as the son of Abraham, to whom the divine promises were given and with whom God's plan of redemption began to unfold. Jesus came to establish the eternal kingdom promised to David and to receive all the blessings promised to Abraham. So, in the beginning pages of the New Testament, the establishment of a kingdom for the nations is anticipated through Jesus. Matthew, in starting his gospel this way, prepares his readers for the commission that Jesus gives his disciples in Matthew 28, to "go . . . and make disciples of all nations" (Matt. 28:19).

After Jesus' birth, he was presented in the temple, following all the Jewish customs. His parents gave an offering. He was circumcised, which united him to the covenant community of Israel. The eagerly awaiting, pious temple servants Anna and Simeon confessed that in Jesus, they had seen salvation for the people of God. They also realized that this salvation was not just for the people of God, but for all the nations as well (Luke 2:32,38).

Jesus began his mission when he went out to John the Baptist, whose ministry was to prepare Israel for the coming Messiah by calling them to repentance. Jesus did not need repentance for himself, but he was baptized to identify with the nation of Israel. As he came out of the waters of baptism, the Spirit of God descended upon him, and words were spoken from heaven. The Father said, "You are my beloved Son" (Mark 1:11), announcing that Jesus is Israel's king and the kingdom has come (cf. Ps. 2:7). Although baptism for the church is now a dramatic sign of a new beginning in the life of an individual, depicting death to sin and a new life (cf. Rom. 6), Jesus' baptism does not depict that type of new beginning. Rather, it depicts a new beginning for the kingdom of God and restoration of the world.

Following Mark's account of Jesus' baptism, Jesus fasted for forty days and faced temptation in the wilderness. Mark's short account of Jesus' baptism and temptation makes clear that in being identified as God's Son and receiving the empowerment of the Spirit, Jesus is able to establish God's kingdom. Coming victorious out of the wilderness temptation, Jesus declared, "The kingdom of God is at hand" (Mark 1:15). Shortly after the beginning of his ministry, Jesus made a similar announcement in the synagogue in Nazareth. He took the scroll and proclaimed that the words of Isaiah 61 are fulfilled in him (Luke 4:18–19; cf. Isa. 61:1–2). This is no small announcement in the mission of God. Craig Bartholomew and Michael Goheen capture its importance, commenting: "This is not the sort of announcement that would be tucked away in the religion section of *Time* or *Macleans*: this is front-page stuff! *'God is now acting in love and power through Jesus and by his Spirit to restore all of creation and all of human life to again live under the benevolent reign of God himself.'"*[7]

Jesus' ministry of bringing the kingdom of God to this world continues to prove Bauckham's rubric, "from the one to the many." Jesus brought the kingdom of the gospel "to the Jew first and also to the Greek" (Rom. 1:16). The *one* man, Jesus, brings the kingdom of God to the *one* nation, Israel, and then to *all* the nations of the earth. This pattern is discerned in each of the four Gospels. Although Matthew begins and ends his gospel on the universal implication of Jesus' life and ministry, when Jesus first sent out his disciples on their kingdom mission, he told them, "Go nowhere among the Gentiles and enter no town of the Samaritans, but go rather to the lost sheep of the house of Israel" (Matt. 10:5–6; cf. Matt. 15:21–28). This same pattern is present in Mark's gospel (Mark 7:27). Luke begins and ends his gospel in a similar way as Matthew (Luke 1:32–33,49; 2:30–32; 3:6; 24:47), but as is in Matthew and Mark, Israel gets first priority in Luke's Gospel (Luke 1:16,68; 24:47b).

The gospel of the kingdom is "to the Jews first" in John's Gospel as well. John's Gospel begins with the universal claims of salvation. Jesus is portrayed as the "light of men," "which enlightens everyone" (John 1:3–5,9; cf. 3:17–21; 8:12; 9:5) and as the one who came to take "away the sin of the world" (John 1:29). One of the main themes in this Gospel, however, is that "He came to his own, and his own people did not receive him" (John 1:11). This theme continues throughout this Gospel, as Jesus was confronted by the Jewish religious leaders (John 5:18; 8:32–36; 9:13–41) and, ultimately, rejected by them to the point of death (John 18:3,39–40; 19:7,15–16). Though Jesus came first to the Jews, he did minister to Gentiles in his earthly ministry, and some came to faith in him, fulfilling "to all who did receive him, who believed in his name, he gave the right to become children of God" (John 1:12–13). The main mission to the Gentiles, however, was still to come (John 12:20–23; 16:8–10). Jesus said, "I, when I am lifted up from the earth, will draw all people to myself" (John 12:32). John's emphasis on Jesus being the light of the world, the necessity of faith for salvation, and the rejection of the Jews all serve to establish that salvation in the kingdom of God is universally offered to all people. "For God so loved the world, that he gave his only Son, that whoever believes in him should not perish but have eternal life" (John 3:16).

Though in the Gospels national Israel is given a certain kingdom priority, Gentiles express faith in the Messiah and receive grace. The kings who came from the east to celebrate Jesus' birth rejoiced with exceeding joy and worshipped the newborn King (Matt. 2:10–12). The Syrophoenician woman willingly took the crumbs from the master's table (Mark 7:28). Luke tells the faith story of the Gerasene demoniac (Luke 8:26–39), and in John's Gospel,

---

[7] Craig G. Bartholomew and Michael W. Goheen, *The Drama of Scripture: Finding Our Place in the Biblical Story* (Grand Rapids: Baker, 2004), 135.

the Samaritan woman gained faith and received salvation (John 4:1–45). Not only do we see the firstfruits of the mission to the nations in the Gospels, but Jesus also predicts in his teaching that there will be a mission to the nations, following Israel's rejection of the Messiah. One of those teachings is the parable of the vineyard, where the tenants abused the servants sent by the master and ultimately killed the master's son. This parable portrays Israel's rejection of the prophets and, finally, their rejection of the Messiah (Mark 12:1–11). According to Luke, Jerusalem will be "trampled underfoot by the Gentiles, until the times of the Gentiles are fulfilled" (Luke 21:24). When Jesus teaches, in John's gospel, that he is the good shepherd he states that his salvation is for more people than just the nation of Israel (John 10:16).

In his life, death, and resurrection, Jesus accomplished God's promises to the nation of Israel and the nations of the earth. He embodied Israel's mission in his life, and he fulfilled the Old Testament promises. He accomplished salvation for the world in his death. He gathered a people to continue God's mission to bless the people of the earth through Abraham (Gen. 12:1–3). After the resurrection, Jesus sent his disciples to preach repentance and forgiveness in his name to all the nations (John 20:21–23; cf. Matt. 28:18–20; Luke 24:44–49; John 17:18).

The nations and the Acts of the Apostles. The disciples' commission is repeated in Acts. Their witness is supposed to be worldwide, and follows the biblical rubric "from the one to the many." Jesus tells the disciples to go to Jerusalem and all of Judea and Samaria, and the end of the earth (Acts 1:8). The dividing lines between Jews and Gentiles, though, are ultimately removed in Acts. The story of Acts is the narrative of how God's purpose and plan is realized in the formation of the church, a predominately Gentile body. The gospel is proclaimed across ethnic lines: to the Jew, the Gentile, and the Samaritan. The gospel is also proclaimed across social and economic lines: people with physical impairments, pagan worshippers, a prominent merchant woman, a jailer and his family, the Greek philosophers in Athens, government officials, and kings. This continues a similar theme from Luke's Gospel, where he makes clear that Jesus undermined manmade divisions between ethnic groups (Jew and Gentile), social structures (men and women, rich and poor), and moral categories (righteous and sinner). Thus, the gospel of the kingdom for the nations that was hinted at in the Gospels is realized in Acts. The gospel of the kingdom comes to all people (Acts 2–15), and Jews grow increasingly antagonistic and many ultimately reject this gospel that Jesus is the Christ (Acts 16–28).

The Acts narrative begins with two important events for the nations in the New Testament. One frames the mission of the church toward the nations of the earth (Acts 1:8). The other forms the church and empowers the church's mission for the nations of the earth (Acts 2:1–11). Acts 1:8, the first event, is Jesus' response to his disciples' questions concerning when the kingdom of Israel will be restored (Acts 1:6). His answer is not so much a refocusing of their attention on the mission from eschatological speculation or a refocusing of their aspiration from nationalistic hopes in Israel's kingdom. Rather, Jesus' reply establishes the means by which the kingdom of Israel will be established, and he redefines the nature of his kingdom. He says, "You will receive power when the Holy Spirit has come upon you, and you will be my witnesses in Jerusalem and in all Judea and Samaria, and to the end of the earth" (Acts 1:8). In other words, Jesus locates the future of Israel in God's redemptive plan for the whole earth.

Paul's recorded words at the end of Acts echo what Jesus said to the disciples. He views the nature of his ministry to the Gentiles as being *for* the future of Israel. At the end of Acts, Luke quotes Paul, who is imprisoned in Rome for preaching that Jesus is the Christ (Acts 21:17–28). Paul says, "it is because of *the hope of Israel* that I am wearing this chain" (Acts 28:20, emphasis added). Paul claimed that he was not against the Jews. His mission was indeed Jewish, and it was to proclaim to the whole world that Jesus is the hope of Israel. The Jews had rejected the mission God gave to them (Acts 22:1–16). God gave Paul the universal mission to the Gentiles (Acts 22:21). Jews rejected this message. He warned them that they were falling into the nationalistic pattern of disbelief, so the message would go to the Gentiles who would listen (Acts 28:17–28). The one mission of God which began with one people (Israel) is carried to completion as the gospel of Jesus Christ is proclaimed to all the nations of the earth; Paul says that is *the hope of Israel*. Similar to what Jesus said to the disciples in Acts 1:8, the kingdom of Israel is restored with the gospel of the kingdom.

Before observing the next event that significantly shaped the mission to the nations, consider the phrase "the end of the earth" in Acts 1:8. This phrase does not point to specific geographic locations. Rather, it captures the universal scope of God's mission to redeem a people from every nation. In Acts, Luke carefully records how the gospel broke out from Jerusalem (Acts 2), to Samaria (Acts 8:4–25), to the Ethiopian traveler (Acts 8:26–40), to Caesarea and the Gentile Cornelius and his family (Acts 10–11), to Antioch (Acts 11:19–30), throughout Cyprus and Asia Minor (Acts 13:4–14:21), to Europe through the evangelization of some in Greece (Acts 16:6–18:17), and then on to Rome (Acts 27:1–28:16). Paul's journey to Rome at the end of Acts does not represent "the ends of earth," but rather represents the trajectory of God's mission and what it looks like to pursue it. Thus, the challenge of God's mission to reach "the end of the earth" extends beyond the pages of Luke's second volume. As Jesus himself said, "And this gospel of the kingdom will be proclaimed throughout the whole world as a testimony to all nations, and then the end will come" (Matt. 24:14).

The second event that significantly shaped the mission to the nations is Pentecost, where the church was formed and was empowered for its mission. The disciples were gathered together after Jesus had ascended to the right hand of God the Father, and from heaven came a sound like a great wind. The disciples were filled with the promised Holy Spirit, and they began to speak in tongues (Acts 2:1–4). At this sound a great crowd gathered, which consisted of many Jews from all over the Roman Empire. The people were amazed that these men from Galilee could speak their native languages. Peter stood up to proclaim that these men were not drunk as assumed, but what they had seen and heard was the fulfillment of Joel's prophecy concerning the Spirit (Acts 2:15–21). This event was a witness to the identity of Jesus of Nazareth. Peter declared, "Let all the house of Israel therefore know for certain that God has made him both Lord and Christ" (Acts 2:36), and three thousand responded, "What must we do [to be saved]?" (Acts 2:37, HCSB) The church was formed by scattered Jews, who were presumably "united" when the tongues spoken in their own language got their attention. "This multilingual witness," William Larkin concluded, "coheres with the universal offer of salvation in the church's message and its consequent worldwide mission. It also highlights the church's multicultural character."[8]

In addition to these events, three other key markers in Acts shape our understanding of the nations in the New Testament. The first marker is the calling of Paul to take the gospel of Jesus to the Gentiles. Paul's calling inaugurated the church's first mission specifically for the Gentiles, and his calling also inspired the persecuted church (Acts 9:15). After Paul's conversion, the church in Judea, Galilee, and Samaria "had peace and was being built up . . . . [I]t multiplied" (Acts 9:31). Second, Peter's vision distinguished the practice of Jewish culture, which prevented Jewish and Gentile Christians from fellowship, from the Christian message, which unites all Christians in fellowship with God and one another (Acts 10:9–11:18). In a vision, God told Peter not to call anything unclean that he has made clean (Acts 10:14–15, 28). The point of this vision was driven home to Peter when Cornelius fell down at this feet (Acts 10:25–26). Peter said to him, "God shows no partiality, but in every nation anyone who fears him and does what is right is acceptable to him" (Acts 10:34–35). While Peter was talking with Cornelius and his family, they received the Spirit and were baptized (Acts 10:44–48). Peter reported what happened to Cornelius and his family to the church in Jerusalem, and they glorified God, saying, "to the Gentiles also God has granted repentance that leads to life" (Acts 11:18).

Third, the Jerusalem council in Acts 15 settled that "there is no other name under heaven given among men by which we must be saved" (Acts 4:12). The council dealt with the question as to whether the Gentile Christians must be circumcised. Peter, at the meeting, referred back to his encounter with Cornelius, and argued that God made no distinction between Jews and Gentiles, "having cleansed [both] their hearts by faith" (Acts 15:9). Further, he said, "we believe that we will be saved through the grace of the Lord Jesus, just as they will" (Acts 15:11). These words of Peter agree with what Paul wrote in his letter to the church at Rome. He reasoned, "Is God the God of Jews only? Is he not the God of Gentiles also? Yes, of Gentiles also, since

---

[8]   William J. Larkin Jr., *Acts,* The IVP New Testament Commentary Series (Downers Grove: IVP, 1995), 51.

God is one—who will justify the circumcised by faith and the uncircumcised through faith" (Rom. 3:29–30).

The nations and the New Testament Epistles. The tension found in the Gospels regarding the gospel of the kingdom going first to the Jew and then to the Gentile is mostly absent in the New Testament epistles. Paul says in Galatians, "For as many of you as were baptized into Christ have put on Christ. There is neither Jew nor Greek." (Gal. 3:27–28). Similarly, in Ephesians, he says, "Gentiles . . . remember that you were at that time separated from Christ, alienated from the commonwealth of Israel and strangers . . . . But now in Christ Jesus . . . by the blood of Christ . . . he himself is our peace, who has made us both one and has broken down in his flesh the dividing wall of hostility . . . that he might create in himself one new man in place of the two" (Eph. 2:11–15).

Paul does say in Romans that the gospel was to the Jews first and then to the Gentiles (Rom. 1:16; cf. 15:8–13), but he says this to explain the trajectory of the gospel mission and more particularly his own mission, as he practiced preaching in the synagogues first whenever he entered a new town. In Romans 9–11, Paul makes it clear that a different time in the history of salvation has come, where the Gentiles have been chosen to take a prominent place in God's plan. The Gentiles are elected unto salvation for the sake of God's mission.[9] It is evident in God's election of people that God chooses to use particular persons and groups of people to accomplish his universal purposes.[10] In the New Testament, the focus of God's election is the church, a new humanity in Christ, made up of Gentiles and Jews, but mostly Gentiles. Observing the missional significance of divine election fits well with the rubric "from the one to the many" that we are working under in this chapter. Implicit in election is the choosing of one to become a part of God's mission.

This is the first time this chapter has treated divine election as a missional theme in the biblical narrative. But the New Testament Epistles are not the first place in the biblical story where God chooses a people or nations to be a

---

[9]   The idea of election carries all kinds of theological connotations. We are not interested in getting into most of those discussions here. One theological connotation that almost everyone misses is the missional purpose for divine election. We first saw this connection in Newbigin's writings. See Lesslie Newbigin, *The Gospel in a Pluralist Society* (Grand Rapids: Eerdmans, 1989), 80–88. He writes, "it is the universality of God's saving love which is the ground of his choosing and calling a community to be the messengers of his truth and bearers of his love for all peoples" (85). He explains: "The logic of election is all of one piece with the logic of the gospel. God's purpose of salvation is not that we should be taken out of history and related to him in some way which bypasses the specificities and particularities of history. His purpose is that in and through history there should be brought into being that which is symbolized in the vision with which the Bible ends—the Holy City into which all the glory of the nation will finally be gathered. But—and of course this is the crux of the matter—that consummation can only lie on the other side of death and resurrection. It is the calling of the Church to bear through history to its end the secret of the lordship of the crucified" (87).

[10]   Christopher Wright offers an extended exposition of how God uses particular persons, people, and events to accomplish his universal/ultimate goal. See Wright, *The Mission of God*, 222–88.

part of his mission. God chose Abraham to be a blessing to the nations (Gen. 12:1–3). Through Abraham, Israel was commissioned to be God's people among the nations (Deut. 7; cf. Num. 23:8–10). God chose Paul on the road to Damascus to take the gospel to the Gentiles (Acts 9). God chose for himself in the New Testament a people, the church, to proclaim his glorious grace (1 Pet. 2:9–10; cf. Eph. 1:4–6). The church is a new humanity in Christ Jesus, and the church is a body of people chosen by God to fulfill his mission. Paul said to the Corinthians,

> For consider your calling . . . not many of you were wise according to worldly standards, not many were powerful, not many were of noble birth. But God chose what is foolish in the world to shame the wise; God chose what is weak in the world to shame the strong; God chose what is low and despised in the world, even things that are not, to bring to nothing things that are, so that no human being might boast in the presence of God. And because of him you are in Christ Jesus, who became to us wisdom from God, righteousness and sanctification and redemption, so that, as it is written, "Let the one who boasts, boast in the Lord." (1 Cor. 1:26–31)[11]

The church's boasting in the Lord is supposed to be visible, living as those who embody the gospel of Christ and the life in the kingdom of God.[12] Paul implores the church in Rome, based on God's mercy and grace, to be transformed (Rom. 12:1–2), and he instructs them in a number of specific ways how they are to do this. The church is to humble itself (12:3), to love with sincere affection (12:9–10), to reject evil (12:9), to be fervent in spirit (12:11), etc. He instructs them in a more general way to "give thought to do what is honorable in the sight of all" (Rom. 12:17). Likewise, the church in Philippi is challenged to live their lives in a way that is worthy of the gospel, so that they may be "without blemish" and "shine as lights in the world" (Phil. 2:15). With a similar message, Peter addresses the "elect exiles" who are scattered across the eastern side of the Roman Empire. He reminds them that they have a God, who has "great mercy" and caused them "to be born again to a living hope," and he formed them into a people for his own possession (1 Pet. 1:3). God made them a people (who were once not a people), so that they might proclaim the greatness of God. He instructs them to proclaim God's greatness in the very way they live among the Gentiles, so that the Gentiles might see their godly way of life and "glorify God on the day of visitation" (1 Pet. 2:12).

Paul's words in Ephesians complement Peter's counsel to the church. Ephesians 3:10 says that "now" the church is the vehicle by which God will make known his abundant wisdom in salvation. The mystery of God's will for salvation is made known through the church, "the fullness of him who fills all in all" (Eph. 1:23; cf. 3:9–10). Peter O'Brien says, "A new multi-racial

---

[11] My reading of this text was influenced by Richard Bauckham. See Bauckham, *Bible and Mission*, 49–54.

[12] Bartholomew and Goheen, *The Drama of Scripture*, 194.

community was 'taking concrete shape before people's eyes' and in it the wisdom of God was being displayed. The resulting new humanity of Jews and Gentiles as fellow members of the body of Christ was 'to serve throughout the universe as an object-lesson of the wisdom of God'. . . . Paul's phrase means nothing other than that the *church itself* is the manifestation of the hidden secret."[13] This mystery is not only manifested by the moral example of the church. The church is also directed to be verbal witnesses of the gospel by putting on the shoes of readiness, the "gospel of peace" (Eph. 6:15), and by "being prepared to make a defense to anyone who asks you for a reason for the hope that is in you" (1 Pet. 3:15).

RESTORATION

It is common for people to draw a distinction between the missional scheme of the Old Testament and the missional scheme of the New Testament. The Old Testament is described as a centripetal model, where the nations of the earth come to Israel. The New Testament is described as centrifugal, where the disciples of Jesus are to go out to the nations. As Christopher Wright observes, "There is an obvious level of truth in this broad assertion, but it is not entirely adequate." He goes on to argue, "[I]n the New Testament . . . while it is certainly true that the centrifugal commission of Jesus to go to the nations is a radical new departure, consistent with the dawning of the new age of salvation, the purpose of that *going out* is so that the nations might be *gathered into* God's kingdom, in fulfillment of the scriptural vision."[14] This "ingathering" of the nations is so that they would become worshippers of the one true, living God (1 Thess. 1:10). Paul casts his ministry to the Gentiles in liturgical terms. In Romans 15:16, he expresses the desire to accomplish his "priestly service . . . so that the offering of the Gentiles may be acceptable."[15]

One day every knee will bow and every tongue will confess that Jesus is Lord (Phil. 2:10–11). But, Jesus did not die just so that "every knee would bow" to him. The "One" came to give his life for "many" (Mark 10:45). He died that "repentance and forgiveness of sins should be proclaimed in his name to all nations" (Luke 24:47) and that he might ransom a people for God (Rev. 5:9). Philippians 2 tells us that Jesus' glory is not diminished in any way by those who reject him, but there is a more glorious praise that Jesus sought in laying down his life. He is the Good Shepherd, who has sheep not of Israel, and who brings them in to the sheepfold (John 10:16; cf. 11:49–52).

---

[13] P. T. O'Brien, *Gospel and Mission in the Writings of Paul: An Exegetical and Theological Analysis* (Grand Rapids: Baker, 1995), 18–19.

[14] This interpretation of Ephesians 6:15 is contested. We have been persuaded by the work of Robert L. Plummer that it refers to calling of the church to be gospel witnesses. See Robert L. Plummer, *Paul's Understanding of the Church's Mission: Did the Apostle Paul Expect the Early Christian Communities to Evangelize?* (Waynesboro, GA: Paternoster, 2006), 77–80.

[15] Wright, *The Mission of God*, 523.

The ingathering of the nations is not a gathering to Jerusalem, but it is an ingathering to the Shepherd himself (cf. 1 Pet. 2:25). The final restoration of the earth will be signified when all things are united in Christ (Eph. 1:9–10; cf. Rev. 14:6). Some will be united as his people and for his praise and glory (Eph. 1:22–23; Rev. 7:9ff), while others will be made a footstool for his feet (Heb. 10:13).

John in his vision sees and hears that Jesus indeed accomplishes his mission. The song of the heavenly host proclaims that Jesus ransomed a people from every nation for God (Rev. 5:9–10; cf. 15:3–4). The heavenly hosts also are joined by "every creature in heaven and on earth and under the earth and in the sea" to worship Jesus for saving a people for God (Rev. 5:13). We see the great crowd of the redeemed in Revelation 7:9–12. John describes them in an unforgettable picture: a crowd that cannot be counted, which consists of people from every nation. They cry out in a loud voice, declaring, "Salvation belongs to our God who sits on the throne, and to the Lamb!" (Rev. 7:10). At the end of John's revelation, the nations gather into the New Jerusalem. The nations walk by the light of God's glory, and the kings of the nations bring into the city the glory of the nations (Rev. 21:22–26).

Chapter Twelve

MISSION AND UNREACHED PEOPLE GROUPS

Philip O. Hopkins

INTRODUCTION

One of the greatest joys in heaven will be watching believers from every tribe, tongue, and nation worship before the throne of God (Rev. 7:9). The promise that all peoples, even the smallest and most remote, will be represented before God's throne serves as a motivator to go to the ends of the earth and proclaim the gospel in areas rife with anti-Christian sentiment, disease, and turmoil. Unbelievers will not call on Christ until they believe, and they will not believe unless they hear, and they will not hear unless someone shares with them the beauty of the good news (Rom. 10:14). Salvation comes only through the atonement of Christ and only through faith consciously focused on Christ.

God's assurance that he will save people from all tribes, tongues, peoples, and nations is (or ought to be) near and dear to every Christian's heart. It is for this reason that evangelicals often speak of working with "unreached people groups." It is the task of this chapter to answer questions surrounding the notion of mission to unreached people groups. What is a people group? Who is considered unreached? Is the concept biblically grounded and missiologically fruitful? Is the task almost complete? These questions and ones similar to them will be answered in this chapter.

WHAT IS AN UNREACHED PEOPLE GROUP?

The English phrase "people group" does not have an exact corollary in Scripture. While there are many similar concepts in Scripture, including "tribes," "peoples," "nations," and "families" seen in passages such as Genesis 12:1–3 and Revelation 5:9 and 7:9, Scripture does not clearly differentiate them. John Piper suggests that if the term were to have an exact biblical definition, then Christians at some point could state that missions is complete, and they would perhaps stop sharing the gospel.[1] To define the term missiologically and to provide a medium for understanding, the Lausanne Committee, along with the Evangelical Fellowship of Mission Agencies, standardized the terminology. They identified a people group as a "significantly large sociological grouping of individuals who perceive themselves to have a common affinity for one another because of their shared language, religion, ethnicity, residence, occupation, class or caste, situation, etc. or combinations of these. From the viewpoint of evangelization this is the largest possible group within which the gospel can spread as a viable, indigenous church planting movement without encountering barriers of understanding or acceptance."[2]

Similarly, the English term "unreached" does not have an exact corollary in Scripture, but it does resonate with several biblical concepts. For example, Paul writes of his desire to go where Christ has not been named (Rom. 15:20), an indication of his longing to witness to people groups that have not heard and received the gospel. The terminology of unreached people groups arises from missiologists who seek to determine which peoples are the least evangelized, and therefore they have classified people groups as unreached when less than 2 percent of their population is evangelical Christian.[3] The Joshua Project experts admit that the percentages are "somewhat arbitrary" and add that for people groups to be unreached they also must be less than 5 percent Christian and should have no "indigenous community of believing Christians with adequate numbers and resources" for evangelism."[4]

In combining the above-mentioned definitions of "people group" and "unreached," we acknowledge that the contemporary understanding of an "unreached people group" is the largest possible ethnolinguistic community where less than 2 percent of its population is evangelical Christian and the

---

[1]   John Piper, *Let the Nations Be Glad! The Supremacy of God in Missions*, 2nd ed. (Grand Rapids: Baker 2003), 188.

[2]   Ralph Winter, "Frontier Mission Perspectives," 65; in Alan Johnson, "Major Concepts of the Frontier Mission Movement," *International Journal of Frontier Missions* 18, no. 2 (Summer 2001), 91. See also: Joshua Project, "What Is a People Group?," http://www.joshuaproject.net /what-is-a-people-group.php, site editor, Joshua Project, accessed 6 March 2009.

[3]   Joshua Project, "Definitions," http://www.joshuaproject.net/definitions.php#unreached, site editor, Joshua Project, accessed 6 March 2009; International Mission Board, "Unreached People Groups," http://centralasia.imb.org/explore/upg.html, site editor, International Mission Board, accessed 6 March 2009.

[4]   Joshua Project, "Definitions." For an incisive and thought-provoking assessment of the Joshua project and its attendant "reached" and "unreached" categories, see M. David Sills, *Reaching and Teaching: A Call to Great Commission Obedience* (Chicago: Moody, 2010), 105–28.

local Christians do not have the people and means to evangelize their own population. We must also acknowledge that the 2 percent criterion is an extra-biblical and contemporary understanding. So, while we must undoubtedly take the gospel to those who have not heard and followed, we must resist the temptation to take a logical leap and deem those people groups that are more than 2 percent as "reached" and therefore the work complete. Debate exists regarding the actual number of people groups; therefore, there are questions as to the exact number of unreached peoples. At the very least, there are 1,200 people groups that have no missionaries or indigenous church.[5]

REACHING UNREACHED PEOPLE GROUPS: OLD AND NEW TESTAMENT

Introduction to the unreached and redemptive history. Mission to unreached people groups began soon after creation.[6] In his act of creation, God gave us a good world. There was no sin, and everything honored and glorified its maker. Man, who reflected God's glory by being made in his image, worshipped God and walked with him daily. However, in the biblical story of the fall, we learn that man chose to dishonor his creator by eating of the tree of knowledge of good and evil. His failure to submit to God's authority ruined this perfect relationship, corrupted man and his posterity, and resulted in a state where man sought to glorify himself rather than to glorify God. Immediately after the fall, God promised to provide a redeemer (Gen. 3:15) who would save man from his sin and unite man's worship with God's glory. This is evident in both testaments. In the Old Testament, redemptive history focuses on Israel's responsibility to glorify God and bless the nations, while in the New Testament, redemptive history centers on the church's responsibility to proclaim God's glory to the nations.

The unreached in redemptive history: The Old Testament. Israel's role in redemptive history begins with God's promise to bless Abram's posterity (Gen. 12:1–3). Genesis 12:1–3 is perhaps the most significant Great Commission passage in the Old Testament (see also Gen. 18:18; 22:18; 26:4;

---

[5] Piper, *Let the Nations Be Glad!*, 188, states the one common trait that distinguishes tribes, tongues, nations, languages, families, etc., is language, though the biblical understanding of language is unclear. This is one reason why experts disagree in numbering people groups. Further, some terms are almost indistinguishable from one another. Patrick Johnstone, "Unreached Peoples: How Many Are There?" *International Journal of Frontier Missions* 13, no. 2 (April 1996), 60, estimates that there are around 12,000 people groups. Of those, 3,000 have no "viable" church and 1,200 have no missionaries or indigenous church. Johnstone acknowledges that he differs from Winter, who states there are 24,000 people groups, 17,000 of them unreached, but states that the numbers of David Barrett and Global Mapping Project's Bob Waymire come relatively close to his.

[6] The following section is adapted from Philip O. Hopkins, "Missions to the Glory of God: An Analysis of the Missionary Theology of John Piper" (Ph.D. diss., Southeastern Baptist Theological Seminary, 2005), 44–47; 101–8. For documentation of Piper's beliefs, please see the dissertation.

28:14). It states that God promises to bless *all* the families of the earth. The phrase "all the families," in Genesis 12:1–3, designates a group smaller than a tribe, and similar to a clan. As God began to fulfill his promise, he moved Abraham's descendants into Egypt where they were eventually enslaved. In freeing them, God hardened Pharaoh's heart and used plagues to show his power and reveal his glory to the whole world—at that point a mostly unreached world.

God gave Israel the Promised Land to glorify her Lord and to share his glory with the nations. This declaration is especially seen in Psalms and Isaiah. These books explain that God commands his glory be proclaimed to all peoples. Psalm 96:3–4 charges that God's glory must be spoken to the nations to magnify his greatness. Isaiah 12:4 states, "Make known [God's] deeds among the peoples, proclaim that his name is exalted." Psalm 117:1 (LXX) calls all the *panta ta ethné* (the same phrase used in Matt. 28:18–20) to praise God. The reason for the nations' praise is God's love toward Israel because through Israel God would send the Savior, Jesus Christ. God also promises that all people groups will worship him. Isaiah 52:15 maintains all peoples will hear the gospel, and kings will be in awe that the one who suffered on the cross is now exalted before God. A few chapters later, Isaiah 55:5 makes clear that God's call of salvation will be heard and received. Psalm 86:9 guarantees God will convert the nations to worship and glorify his name. Further, the psalmist prays with certainty that salvation will reach all people groups. Psalm 72 states that all nations will serve God and be a blessing to him. Psalm 67 expresses confidence that all nations will receive salvation and explains that God blesses his people to bless the nations. The psalmist himself expresses desire to participate in making God's name recognized among all people groups. Psalm 18:49 states that he praises God among the nations. Psalm 87:9 and 108:3 states that he sings praises of God's name among the nations. God's purpose for all the people groups is that he be known, praised, enjoyed, and feared. God desires that the nations know that he alone is God; he is righteous, sovereign, powerful, and gracious to those who believe in him.

Israel's failure to honor God results in exile, but even here there are some (e.g., Daniel, Esther, Nehemiah, and Ezra) who acted as witnesses to the unreached peoples in the Babylonian and Median/Persian empires. God, however, promised Israel restoration for the sake of his name. A new king, a redeemer, would lead her to worship him alone.

The unreached in redemptive history: New Testament. The new king arrived with the incarnation of Jesus Christ. He is the God-man, the Savior, whose life, ministry, death, and resurrection were bent on glorifying God. Christ demonstrated God's righteousness and showed the world the infinite value of the Father's glory by appeasing the Father's wrath in taking the punishment of sin for all those who believe. Now, those who place their faith in Christ are forgiven, free from sin, able to glorify God in Christ, and will worship and enjoy him forever. They, as models of Christ, must share their understanding of God's glory with others and go to all people groups.

The goal to reach the nations with the gospel is seen throughout the New Testament. John 17:20 states that God uses the preaching of the word to bring people groups to himself. Great Commission passages such as Luke 24:45–47 indicate that Christ's command to reach the people groups is found in the Old Testament. Acts 1:8 suggests the task of missions is for Christians to proclaim the gospel to the whole world, even to those who were yet unreached with the news of the Messiah. Matthew 28:18–20, perhaps the most popular Great Commission passage, commands that all people groups be discipled. John Piper sees Jesus' command to make disciples of "all the nations" (*panta ta ethné*) as a reference to all people groups, rather than to individuals or geopolitical entities. He explains that the singular *ethnos* always refers to a people group or nation, and, while the plural *ethné* (and its variants) may mean Gentile individuals, it usually refers to a people group. Additionally, of the nearly one hundred times the Greek Old Testament uses the term (or its variants), almost every time it designates people groups other than Israel. When Paul examines Genesis 17:4–5 (the promise that Abraham will be a father of a "multitude of nations"), Paul sees nations as people groups not related to Israel. Piper's interpretation of *panta ta ethné* is especially helpful. It is summarized in the following ten statements.

1. The term *ethnos* in the New Testament never depicts Gentile individuals.
2. Usually, the term *ethné* can mean either Gentile individuals or people groups in the New Testament.
3. Only once in the New Testament does *panta ta ethné* mean Gentile individuals; nine times it means people groups, and eight times the meaning is unclear.
4. Almost every time the Greek Old Testament uses *panta ta ethné* it means nations outside Israel.
5. The promise God gave Abraham in Genesis 12:1–3 (and other places) is cited in the New Testament and gives the mission of the church a people-group focus.
6. The Old Testament shows how God's glory is manifested to all people groups.
7. Paul relates his understanding of missions back to the Old Testament promises concerning people groups.
8. The apostle John sees the goal of missions as gathering the elect from all people groups.
9. Based on the Old Testament, Luke 24:46–47 demonstrates that *panta ta ethné* indicates people groups.
10. Mark 11:17 explains that Christ may think about people groups when thinking about God's purpose for the world.[7]

Romans 4:11–17 explains God justified Abraham by faith before circumcision, which further demonstrates people from all people groups who place

---

[7] Piper, *Let the Nations Be Glad!* 160, 187.

their faith in Christ are heirs of Abraham and included in his blessing (Gen. 12:1–3). Paul's understanding of the Great Commission's focus on people groups is also seen in Romans 15 where Paul quotes Old Testament passages that relate to peoples: Psalm 18:49 (Rom. 15:9); Deuteronomy 32:43 (Rom. 15:10); Psalm 117:1 (Rom. 15:11); and Isaiah 11:10 (Rom. 15:12). Later, in Romans 15:18–24, Paul emphasizes the need for frontier missions. He states that he has completely proclaimed the gospel from Jerusalem to Illyricum, but realizes evangelism is still needed in areas where missions is complete. His desire is to reach unreached peoples by evangelizing them and discipling and teaching them. Revelation 5:9 and John 11:52 state that Christ purchased from every tribe, language, people, and nation those who will be his children. Other passages in Revelation depict the goal of missions as reaching all people groups for Christ (Rev. 7:9–10; 14:6–7; 15:4; 21:3). Revelation 21:3 is especially important because it states there will be *peoples* (not people) in heaven, indicating a diversity and multiplicity of ethnic groups. At the second coming of Christ, God will perfect his children and history will end. In short, God's glory will be manifested fully and people from all people groups, even those in the hardest places where Christ is not named or is severely misrepresented, will worship him before the throne.

REACHING UNREACHED PEOPLE GROUPS: FROM THE NEW TESTAMENT UNTIL NOW

The unreached before the modern missions movement: the early church. Missions to the unreached did not stop with the apostles and then restart with William Carey. Admittedly, missionaries were few in number, but they did go forth to preach the gospel. Pre-Constantinian Christianity grew because believers were caring for the lost around them and involving themselves in evangelistic endeavors to the perimeters of Christendom. Stephen Neill quotes ancient church historian Eusebius of Caesarea (c. 260–340) regarding the importance early Christians placed on reaching the unreached: "leaving their homes, they set out to fulfill [*sic*] the work of an evangelist, making it their ambition to preach the word of the faith to those who as yet had heard nothing of it . . . . They were content to lay the foundations of faith among these foreign peoples: they then appointed other pastors, and committed to them the responsibility for building up those whom they had merely brought to faith. They then passed on to other countries and nations with the grace and help of God."[8]

As Christianity became an accepted religion in the Roman Empire, Patrick's missionary efforts to unreached Ireland in the fifth century serves as an example for those who suffer hardship. Taken by Irish marauders as a child

---

[8]   Eusebius, *Hist. eccl.* III.37.2–3; in Stephen Neill, *A History of Christian Missions*, rev. (London: Penguin, 1990), 35. See also Alan Kreider, "Beyond Bosch: The Early Church and the Christendom Shift," *International Bulletin of Missionary Research* 29, no. 2 (April 2005), 62–67.

from his home in Britain, Patrick returned to share Christ with the people who enslaved him. Twelve times he faced life-threatening situations, including a two-week captivity and a kidnapping. Because of his efforts, he saw God spark spiritual awakening in Ireland. Ruth A. Tucker estimates that Patrick started close to two hundred churches and baptized one hundred thousand.[9]

Roman Catholic and Orthodox. Roman Catholics have a long history of missions. In the Middle Ages, Boniface (c. 680–754) stands as the greatest.[10] His desire was to see the good news proclaimed to peoples lacking a Christian witness, which led him to focus on Germany and, in his later years when Germany became Christianized, the Frisians in Holland.[11] Roman Catholics also developed religious orders that promoted missions, especially the Franciscan, Dominican, Jesuit, and Augustinian. Two well-known Catholic missionaries (Francis Xavier and Matteo Ricci) arose from them in the sixteenth century and went to Japan and China, respectively, when few Christians were in those areas. With Spain and Portugal expanding their empires around this time, Roman Catholics also were witnessing in the Philippines, Indochina, India, the Americas, and Africa.[12]

The Orthodox were doing missions in unreached areas as well. They translated the Scriptures into the vernacular and devised alphabets for illiterate cultures in unreached areas.[13] In fact, the first work translated into Armenian after monk Mesrop Mashtots created its alphabet in the fifth century (Armenians were the first people group as a whole to adopt Christianity in AD 301 and see their tradition stemming from the Orthodox faith) was the Greek Bible.[14] The Orthodox also spent much time in Russia, Siberia, and China beginning in the early 1700s.[15]

Admittedly, neither Roman Catholic nor Orthodox groups shared the gospel with the unreached in the same manner as Protestants. In fact, their methodology sometimes is questionable at best. Nevertheless, both groups brought their traditions to those who never heard.

Protestants before the Enlightenment Era. The Protestants did not expand geographically as the Catholics did during the Reformation; nonetheless, the widely held belief that Protestants were not interested in the

---

[9]   Ruth A. Tucker, *From Jerusalem to Irian Jaya: A Biographical History of Christian Missions* (Grand Rapids: Zondervan, 1983), 39–40.

[10]   Neill, *A History of Christian Missions,* 64.

[11]   J. Herbert Kane, *A Concise History of the Christian World Mission: A Panoramic View of Missions from Pentecost to the Present* (Grand Rapids, Baker, 1982), 42.

[12]   Ibid., 57.

[13]   James Stamoolis, "Eastern Orthodox Mission Theology," *International Bulletin of Missionary Research* 8, no. 2 (April 1984), 61.

[14]   http://www.armeniaemb.org, site editor, Armenian Embassy in Washington, DC; in "Language and Literature," http://www.hyeetch.nareg.com.au/armenians/ language_p1.html, site editor, Armenians on the Internet, December 27, 2002, accessed 10 March 2009. Cf. Neill, *A History of Christian Missions,* 47–48.

[15]   Neill, *A History of Christian Missions,* 181–84, 370.

unreached or "non-Christian peoples" during this time is only partially true.[16] Protestants were not nearly as organized as Catholics until Carey, but the Anabaptists were interested in missions as were Reformers such as William Tyndale and John Calvin.[17] Tyndale, the first translator of the Bible into English, wrote of his love for the Turks, who were expanding Islam into southern Europe, and his need to win them to Christ.[18] Calvin sent his followers to Brazil to, among other things, evangelize the locals.[19] Differing from Roman Catholic missions, and in large part because of the Reformation, Protestants generally placed a higher priority on Scripture and getting it into the hands of the people,[20] even though, until the time of Carey, they lacked the infrastructure needed for large-scale missions activities.

Protestants during the Enlightenment Era. During the Enlightenment, it seems, missions to the unreached began further to develop. If Carey is considered the father of modern missions, the Moravians and Puritans could be considered the grandparents. Missions historian Kenneth Scott Latourette implies that the Moravians were the first Protestant denomination to focus on missions.[21] Arthur F. Glasser considers Count Nikolas Ludwig von Zinzendorf, the founder of the Moravian movement, the "Father of Modern Biblical Missions" instead of Carey.[22] The Moravians sent people to the West Indies and Greenland in the early 1700s, made an impact on Carey's work,[23] and sent missionaries to other places including the Samoyedes, Lapps, Iran,

---

[16]   Kenneth S. Latourette, *A History of the Expansion of Christianity*, vol. 3, *Three Centuries of Advance, A.D. 1500-A.D. 1800* (New York: Cambridge University Press, 1939), 25–26; in Donald Dean Smeeton, "William Tyndale's Suggestions for a Protestant Missiology," *Missiology: An International Review* 14, no. 2 (April 1986), 174, gives several reasons for the lack of involvement in missions among Protestants during the Reformation period: (1) a focus on developing their own theology; (2) denial of the requirement to share Christ; (3) involvement in religious wars; (4) lack of political encouragement among Protestant governments; (5) lack of an official clergy; and (6) little contact with unreached peoples. See also: Neill, *A History of Christian Missions*, 187–204.

[17]   For further reading on Anabaptist missions, see Robert Friedmann, *The Theology of Anabaptism* (Scottdale, PA: Herald Press, 1973).

[18]   William Tyndale, *Doctrinal Treatises and Portions of the Holy Scripture (1848)*, 338; in Smeeton, "William Tyndale's Suggestions for a Protestant Missiology," 178.

[19]   Amy Glassner Gordon, "The First Protestant Missionary Effort: Why Did It Fail?," *International Bulletin for Missionary Research* 8, no. 1 (Jan. 1984) 12–14.

[20]   Roger S. Greenway, "The Bicentennial of Modern Missions, Part VII—The Bible and Missions: William Carey's Pervasive Principle Serampore Covenant, Article IX," *Missions Monthly* 99, no. B:6 (Aug. 1993), 4–6; in The Network for Strategic Missions, http://www.strategicnetwork .org/index.php?loc=kb&view=v&id=17780 &fti=carey&, 1, site editor, The Network for Strategic Missions, accessed 9 March 2009.

[21]   Latourette, *A History of the Expansion of Christianity*, 47.

[22]   Arthur F. Glasser, "A Tribute to the 'Father of Modern Biblical Missions,'" *Missions Monthly* 99, no. C:7 (Oct. 1994), 8–10; in The Network for Strategic Missions, http://www.strategicnetwork .org/index.php?loc=kb&view=v&id=17850&fwo=moravians&, 1, accessed 7 March 2009.

[23]   David A. Schattschneider, "William Carey, Modern Missions, and the Moravian Influence," *International Bulletin of Missionary Research* 22, no. 1 (Jan. 1998), 9; "This Month in Moravian History," http://www.moravianchurcharchives.org/thismonth/08%20jan%20greenland.pdf, site editor, Moravian Archives, January 2008, accessed 6 March 2009.

China, Ceylon, East Indies, Istanbul, Wallachia, the Caucasus region, Egypt, Surinam, and South Africa. German missiologist Gustav Warneck stated that the Moravians did more for missions than "the whole of Protestantism in two centuries."[24]

The Puritans focused on the unreached as well. One reason they came to New England was to evangelize the Native Americans.[25] David Brainerd and Jonathan Edwards were especially helpful. While Brainerd's missiological methods may not want to be emulated, Brainerd did become a missionary to the American Indians (as did Jonathan Edwards). His diaries, published by Edwards, served to motivate many who went to the unreached, including Carey; Thomas Coke (1747–1814), founder of Methodist missions; and Henry Martyn (1781–1812), Anglican missionary to India and Iran.[26] The impact Brainerd and Edwards had on the modern missions movement should not be underestimated. Writer J. A. DeJong states, "If the two major forces behind the nineteenth-century Anglo-American missions could be isolated, a convincing case could be constructed for their being the theology of Jonathan Edwards and the example of David Brainerd."[27]

The unreached and the modern missions movement. From the time of Carey until now, reaching the unreached with the gospel has played a prominent role within the Protestant tradition. To help distinguish the different types of efforts, Ralph Winter proposed that the Protestant modern missions movement be divided into three eras with two transition periods: Era One: Coastlands, 1792–1910 (Carey as the figurehead); Transition One: 1865–1910; Era Two: Inland, 1865–1980 (Hudson Taylor as the representative); Transition Two: 1934–1980; and Era Three: Hidden Peoples, 1934–1980 (Cameron Townsend and Donald McGavran as the spokespeople).[28] The forming of each period centers on reaching the unreached with the gospel in a new and different manner.

The first era of modern missions: coastlands. It was not until Carey that Protestant missions gained steam and mission agencies began to grow rapidly.[29] Carey believed that the Great Commission was not just intended for the

---

[24] Thomas Soerens, "Zinzendorf's Zeal for Missions," *Missions Monthly* 99, no. D:4 (April 1995), 11–12, 31; in The Network for Strategic Missions, http://www.strategicnetwork.org/index.php?loc=kb&view=v&id=17685&fwo=moravians&, 1, site editor, The Network for Strategic Missions, accessed 7 March 2009.

[25] John B. Carpenter, "New England Puritans: Grandparents of Modern Protestant Missions," *Missiology: An International Review* 30, no. 4 (Oct. 2002), 519.

[26] Ibid., 526–27.

[27] J. A. DeJong, *As the Waters Cover the Sea: Millennial Expectations in the Rise of Anglo-American Missions, 1640–1810* (Kampen, the Netherlands: J. H. Kok N.V., 1970); in Carpenter, "New England Puritans," 526.

[28] Ralph Winter, "The Concept of a Third Era in Missions," *EMQ* 17, no. 2 (April 1981), 72. See also: Ralph Winter, "3 Men, 3 Eras: The Flow of Missions," *Mission Frontiers* 3, no. 2 (Feb. 1981), 1, 4–7; and Ralph Winter, "Four Men, Three Eras," *Mission Frontiers* 19 (Nov. 1997), 11–12, 18.

[29] Kane, *A Concise History of the Christian World Mission*, 86, states because of Carey's effort the mission societies that started include: the London Missionary Society, Scottish and

apostles, but for Christians of his time. Latourette notes that Carey "seems
to have been the first Anglo-Saxon Protestant either in America or in Great
Britain to propose that Christians take concrete steps to bring their Gospel
to all the human race."[30] Carey also stressed: (1) the need for the Bible to be
translated into the language of the people and that local churches must be
self-governing;[31] (2) widespread preaching of the gospel; (3) establishment
of the local church as soon as possible; (4) studying the background of the
people one is trying to reach; and (5) training indigenous leaders.[32]

Others beside Carey symbolized first era missions. Martyn, Adoniram
Judson (Burma), Alexander Duff (India), Robert Moffat (southern Africa),
and David Livingston (Africa) all spent much of their lives trying to reach
the unreached. God used the first era missionaries' dedication to bring many
into the kingdom, but it came at a cost. Winter notes that in the sixty years
of first era missions to Africa, for example, the majority of missionaries died
within two years. He expresses the mentality of those who went out when
he states: "The gruesome statistics of almost inevitable sickness and death
that haunted, yet did not daunt, the decades of truly valiant missionaries who
went out after 1790 in virtually a suicidal stream cannot be matched by any
other era or by any other cause."[33] As a result, the Bible was translated into
numerous languages and the missionaries inspired others to share Christ in
areas far from home.

The second era of modern missions: inlands. By the beginning of the
early 1900s every Protestant country had sent out missionaries.[34] Many of
the missionaries centered on the coastlands (especially of Asia and Africa).
As they were being evangelized, James Hudson Taylor, the founder of China
Inland Mission, spearheaded an effort to go into the inlands and reach the
unengaged. Taylor moved from the active mission centers to inland China
where there were eleven unreached provinces.[35] Taylor required his people to
adopt a "faith mission" strategy that allowed no one to solicit funds personally.[36] He also stressed a form of contextualization that emphasized dressing

---

Glasgow Missionary Society, Church Missionary Society, British and Foreign Bible Society,
American Board of Commissioners for Foreign Missions, American Baptist Missionary Union,
and the American Bible Society.

[30] Kenneth S. Latourette, *A History of the Expansion of Christianity: The Great Century,*
68; in Google Books, http://books.google.com/books?id=g0cOAAAAQAAJ, site editor, Google
Books, accessed 9 March 2009.

[31] Dick L. Van Halsema, "Von Zinzendorf and Carey," *Missions Monthly* 97, no. 3 (March
1990), 11–12; in The Network for Strategic Missions, http://www.strategic network.org/index.
php?loc=kb&view=v&id=17451&fwo=great%20commission&fti=carey&, 1–2, site editor, The
Network for Strategic Missions, accessed 9 March 2009.

[32] Neill, *A History of Christian Missions,* 224.

[33] Winter, "Four Men, Three Eras," 2.

[34] Kane, *A Concise History of the Christian World Mission,* 93.

[35] J. Herbet Kane, "My Pilgrimage in Mission," *International Bulletin of Missionary
Research* 11, no. 3 (July 1987), 130.

[36] Dick L. Van Halsema, "J. Hudson Taylor," *Missions Monthly* 97, no 4 (May 1990), 16–18;
in The Network for Strategic Missions, http://www.strategicnetwork.org/ index.php?loc=kb&v

and living like the locals. Because of Taylor's influence over forty new mission agencies formed that focused on engaging the unreached in the inlands of Asia and Africa.[37]

There were many missionaries in this period that began to have some type of focus on the unreached. Two of the notable names are Lottie Moon and Robert P. Wilder. Moon, now famed for the Lottie Moon Christmas Offering (a time of missions giving around Christmas to the Southern Baptist mission sending agency, the International Mission Board), spent many years reaching the unreached in China.[38] Wilder, the founder of the Student Volunteer Missions Movement, coined the phrase, "The evangelization of the world in this generation.[39]

The third era of modern missions: people groups. Similar to the transition from the first era to the second era of modern missions (coastlands focus to inland focus), another transition occurred from the second era to the third (and present) era of modern missions. People groups were now the focal point instead of inland areas. While missionaries in the first two periods were reaching the unreached, it was not until the third era when a heart for people groups began. As Winter notes, Cameron Townsend went to Guatemala in the second era of missions and began to recognize that many of the country's tribes spoke their own tongue and could not understand the national language, Spanish. This resulted in him starting Wycliffe Bible Translators, an organization that centered on reaching "hidden" (or unreached) peoples. Donald McGavran, considered the founder of the church growth movement, discovered something very similar in India and labeled the groups homogenous units, which are now called "people groups."[40]

The idea of people groups led experts (see footnote 5) to develop a means to calculate the exact number of peoples in the world. The Joshua Project's findings indicate there are unreached people groups in many areas, even in traditional Christianized places such as South America.[41] Most of the unreached people groups, however, are located in the 10/40 Window (10° N latitude to 40° N latitude), home to many of the world's largest religions including Hinduism, Buddhism, and Islam.[42] There are many barriers to the gospel in the 10/40 Window. Missiologist Nik Ripken enumerates some of these barriers.

---

iew=v&id=17463&fwo=, 1, site editor, The Network for Strategic Missions, accessed 9 March 2009.

[37] Alan Johnson, "Analyzing the Frontier Mission Movement and Unreached People Group Thinking. Part One: The Frontier Mission Movement's Understanding of the Modern Mission Era," *International Journal of Frontier Missions* 18, no 2 (Summer 2001), 82.

[38] Tucker, *From Jerusalem to Irian Jaya*, 237.

[39] Kane, *A Concise History of the Christian World Mission*, 103.

[40] Winter, "3 Men, 3 Eras: The Flow of Missions," 1, 4–7. See also: Winter, "Four Men, Three Eras," 11–12, 18.

[41] "Progress of the Gospel by People Group," http://www.joshuaproject.net/ global-progress-scale.php, site editor, Joshua Project, accessed 11 March 2009.

[42] "The Turko-Persian World," http://centralasia.imb.org/explore/map.html, site editor, International Mission Board, accessed 10 March 2009, states that the largest unreached affinity group (percentage wise) is the Turko-Persian World, with .016% of Turkic and Persian peoples

1. A Harvest Mentality: The New Testament mandates that Christians tell the good news, not convert, but often those who see more conversions receive more money. In unreached areas, the fruit is less.
2. We Know One Way to "Do Church": The vast majority of the unreached are not literate or semi-literate. The idea of meeting in a building for church and "doing church" Western style adds to the necessary supracultural truths of Scripture.
3. Security: Funds are generated when information is provided, but if information cannot be given because nationals could die, then how are funds raised?
4. Persecution: Abuse and death are normal for those who convert from unreached people groups. Dietrich Bonhoeffer's famous quote, "When God calls man, he bids him to come and die," rings true for those in unreached areas.
5. Ignorance and Prejudice toward Christianity: Many think Christianity means doing drugs, committing adultery, and eating unclean foods. In some parts of the world Christianity is equated with the Crusades or is related to a particular (often Western) culture.
6. Climate: Many of the unreached live in hot and uncomfortable places. Where the temperatures are high, there are fewer missionaries.
7. It's Expensive: There needs to be more than just one way to reach the unreached. Missionaries should live modestly; tent makers are needed; national [even near-culture] Christians all must be involved.
8. High Personnel Maintenance: After the missionary leaves home, he usually lives in relative isolation from the Christian environment and spiritual warfare takes on a new meaning. The church at home, if not intentional, forgets about him; "out of sight, out of mind" mentality.[43]

It is because of these barriers that it sometimes takes many years of missions work and sacrifice for a people group to experience spiritual awakening.[44] Further, understanding these difficulties will help believers develop effective means to reach the remaining unreached peoples for Christ. When discussing these barriers to mission, and our human attempts to overcome those barriers, ultimately we must keep two truths in tension. First, we must remember the central truth of chapter 3, that God has chosen humans to accomplish his mission. The responsibility for proclaiming the gospel to the nations is ours. But second, we must remember the central truth of chapter 2; that God himself is the ultimate agent of mission, and that it is he alone who brings conversion to the heart of the unbeliever.

Christian, about one Christian for every 6,800 people and one church made up of Muslim background believers for every 364,000 people.

[43]   Nik Ripken, "Why are the Unreached, Unreached?" *EMQ* 32, no. 3 (July 1996), 284–88.

[44]   Sociologist Rodney Stark is one of the most recent to point this out. See Rodney Stark, *The Rise of Christianity* (San Francisco: HarperCollins, 1997), 3–27.

CONCLUSION

Missions to the unreached is not a new phenomenon; it started in the Old Testament; continued with various degrees of emphasis through the New Testament, early church, Middle Ages, Reformation, and Enlightenment; and grew tremendously with renewed urgency in the modern missions movement. Today, much attention is given on winning the remaining unreached people groups to Christ. Many are leaving the comforts of home and dedicating their lives to see God's name glorified among those who have never heard. When will the task be complete and how will it be completed? These are questions for theologians, missiologists, missionaries, and indeed for all faithful Christians to contemplate, but the answers belong only to the Lord. Our primary focus, therefore, is obedience to the task rather than asking questions that only God can answer. At the end of history, when God's promise is fulfilled and people from all people groups are worshipping before his throne, missions will be no more. Unreached people groups will be no more. What a great joy it will be to honor and glorify the Lord and experience his presence with peoples from every tribe, tongue, and nation.

Chapter Thirteen

MISSION AND DISCIPLESHIP

M. David Sills

INTRODUCTION

"When was Jesus' conversion?"
"Was it before or after the resurrection?"
"Which woman was it who converted him?"

Such questions cannot be answered as stated for they reveal a serious misunderstanding of basic truth, which must be corrected first. Sadly, these are actual questions that pastors in traditional mission fields have asked me. Even more disconcerting is the reality that they are only representative of a long list I have received. It would be understandable to hear such eager inquiries from new believers in areas where the gospel had just arrived, but some of these men pastor two or more churches and are the only Christian leaders that former missionaries left behind. How did we get to this point, and what is the path to healthier churches with sound leadership?

THE SITUATION

Part of the problem may be that we have had too few doing too much. Those whom God has called as missionaries know that they are laboring in a world where everyone will perish apart from hearing the gospel and being born again. Realizing that there is a lot more to be done than they can do, the temptation is to streamline the task to make it manageable. Little by little, well-intentioned but overwhelmed missionaries have reduced the task of missions to proclaiming the gospel message to everyone who has never heard it. Of course, that is an essential aspect of the Great Commission, but it is not all. Jesus did not commission us to go and get decisions from all men, and he certainly did not command us to preach the gospel and leave before they understood and truly received it.

In the Great Commission, Jesus said to go and make disciples of all nations, baptizing them and teaching them to observe everything that he has commanded (Matt. 28:18–20). He was not referring to geopolitical entities such as Indonesia, Italy, and India, but rather to the people groups—the ethnicities of the world. This is clearer in the original language where Jesus said to make disciples of *panta ta ethne* (*panta*= all, *ta* = the, *ethne*= ethnic groups). In order to reach these ethnic groups, we must learn their languages and cultures, their worldviews and traditional religions. Only then will we be able to reach them and teach them in ways that they can understand.

PHILOSOPHIES AND MISSION

Unfortunately, many faithful missionaries have sacrificially served through the years without this perspective. Like most of us, they intuitively believed that although the world's peoples speak different languages, they are basically the same as we are. It was logical to assume that missionaries simply needed to learn the language and translate their old sermons with no adjustment for worldview differences. They built red brick church buildings in areas where every other structure is made of mud and thatch. They furnished their churches with pews, an upright piano, a pulpit, choir loft, and a little sign on the wall reporting how many were in Sunday school and brought their Bible. They started Sunday school at 9:45 and worship service at 11:00, used the same order of service, the same hymns with the same melodies, and the same preaching style they used at home. Sadly, these churches and the gospel they preach seem foreign to the people in the regions they serve.

Other missionaries, realizing that this would be simply importing that which is important to the missionary and would not speak to the heart of the nationals, took a minimalist approach. This presented itself in situations where a missionary would pull into the village and preach through an interpreter, then see a national—or perhaps many nationals, raise a hand during the invitation of the missionary. What the missionary did not realize was that rather than indicating a spiritual transformation, the raised hand indicated a cultural response out of deference to the visitor's request or curiosity to see what would happen next. Although the nationals did not fully understand the message, the missionary assumed they were sincere converts.

THE MOTIVATION OF THE MISSIONARY CALL

When godly men and women become aware of the command to take the gospel to the world, a holy burden fills their hearts. Moreover, the knowledge of the eternal separation that awaits a lost and dying world haunts the hearts of God's people. The Lord combined this burden and knowledge in the hearts of many faithful men and women as he gave them a call to missions. Ralph Winter said, "God cannot lead you based on information you do not have"[1] and often when disciples see the needs, understand the Bible, and hear God's call, they are ready to go. But, what is it that he has called them to go and do?

One of the most important things that missionaries should do is keep their Bibles open. When we set them aside to consider the latest marketing and management strategies, we can very easily slip into the pit of pragmatism and "whatever works" mentalities. The goal of missionaries should be to reach and teach the nations. This will entail many activities, all fulfilled by God-called missionaries in diverse, Spirit-led ministry expressions according to the gifts he has given them. In an effort to reach the lost and dying as quickly as possible, some missionaries have embraced a streamlined missiological strategy that seeks to proclaim the gospel, form the new groups into churches, and then move on. The motivation is understandable given the great need of so many lost souls and so few workers, but the result of this philosophy is devastating.

The challenges. One of the greatest challenges that missions faces today is the tragic reality that a third of the world's population has never heard the gospel message, and of the two-thirds that has heard, most have not heard it in a way that makes sense to them. The one-third of the world's population that has never heard represents about one-half of the people groups in the world. Thousands of people groups are still waiting to hear the gospel, and each has its own language, worldview, and traditional religion.

Taking into account the dialect differences, the roughly 7,000 languages in the world grow to nearly 12,000 languages and dialects, and there are Bibles for only 411 languages.[2] These linguistic challenges of the missionary task are only the tip of the iceberg. Diverse worldviews, world religions, cultural differences, and gospel-hostile governments complicate these challenges. Effective missionary strategies must consider these challenges and not gloss over traditional religions and practices, assuming they will disappear when people pray the sinner's prayer.

In Nigeria, where animism and traditional religions have existed in force for centuries, I encountered pastoral teams who were sacrificing cows in black magic juju ceremonies in order to have bigger crowds on the weekends, more influence over their people, and tears in the invitation time. Throughout Latin America, missionaries face a unique blend of Catholicism and the traditional animism of the indigenous people that is characterized by superstition, biblical illiteracy, and doctrinal ignorance. In Ecuador, I have taught on the basic gospel message to groups of pastors and had pastors pray to receive Christ, saying that they had never heard that message before. In Peru, the majority

---

[1] Ralph D. Winter, "Are You Finding Your Way Into God's Highest Call for You?" *Mission Frontiers* (January/February 2007): 5.

[2] "Summary by Area" in M. Paul Lewis, ed., *Ethnologue*, 16th ed. (Dallas, TX: SIL International, 2009). Online version: http://www.ethnologue.com.

of the evangelical churches lack a pastor, and the majority of Latin America's evangelical pastors lack theological and pastoral training.

Many would argue that there is no need to spend time, lives, and money in these areas since the gospel is at least known while there are areas of the world that have never heard. The perennial debate of search versus harvest theology centers on this dilemma; *should missionaries reach those who have never heard or stay to disciple and teach those who have?*

Reached or unreached. Missiology is an expanding and developing field of study, and its taxonomy has grown rapidly as well. For instance, the term cross-cultural once meant everything related to cultures and missions. Yet, in recent years missiologists realized that they needed a term to refer more precisely to that which is true in all cultures, and therefore cross-cultural, as well as another term to refer to the interaction *between* cultures. Increasingly, the term *cross-cultural* refers to something such as women's rights or family relationships that we find in all cultures. *Intercultural* refers to one culture interacting with another in distinct cultural expressions, as in missions. In like manner, as missiologists discussed the various levels of "reachedness" among people groups of the world, they realized that they needed commonly accepted terms to refer to these levels. They called people groups with Christians in their population, ready access to Christian literature and resources *reached*, and those with virtually nothing *unreached*. Yet, the challenge remained to identify the criterion by which a people group would be considered "unreached."

Some missiologists sought to apply the marketing philosophy that maintains that if 20 percent of a population adopts a new idea, they can influence the rest of the population without outside help, and are thus "reached."[3] Others thought 20 percent was too high, believing that a smaller percentage of evangelicals could finish the work and free the missionaries to move on. Additionally, it would be difficult to defend leaving a group before it was "reached," and it could take decades before reaching the 20 percent threshold. Ultimately, after a period of discussion, the lower percentage of less than 2 percent of evangelicals in a people group was decided upon as the criterion for it to be considered "unreached." Please note that those who adopted this arbitrary percentage never intended it to determine the placement of missionaries or resources, nor did they intend those groups that were more than 2 percent evangelical to be considered "reached"; rather it was simply to identify the groups that were less reached. Unfortunately, the arbitrary 2 percent figure is employed in exactly this way in the deployment and reassignment of missionaries, and the significance of the definition and determination has drifted into missiological lore as an accepted fact on par with the laws of physics. Often, it is just as missionaries have learned the culture, language, survived culture shock, developed relationships with the nationals, and become effective in evangelizing, preaching, teaching,

---

[3] Space will not allow a comprehensive explanation of how the "reached" and "unreached" concepts came to be, but a thorough historical recounting is given in my book, *Reaching and Teaching* (Chicago: Moody Publishers, 2010).

and discipling that they are reassigned to another people group because their current one is drifting toward the 2-percent mark.

Search versus harvest. Much confusion abounds when devising strategies to engage the reached or unreached due to a failure to understand search and harvest theologies. Search theology believes that the highest priority is to reach those who have never heard. Those driven by a search mentality, believing that the missionary task is best defined by preaching to those who have never heard, often believe that those who are not pressing the charge into new areas are hindrances to completing the task. Indeed, the rallying cry, "No one deserves to hear the gospel twice until everyone has heard it once," represents the search mentality.

Harvest theology emphasizes the need to bring in the harvest where God is stirring hearts and saving souls, seeking to be good stewards, and protecting the harvest with sound teaching and deep discipleship. The well-known phrase from Henry Blackaby's *Experiencing God*, "Find where God is working and join him there," represents the thinking of harvest theology. Those who possess a harvest mentality and judge those who want to reach the "unreached" exclusively or who refuse to stay and teach fail to understand that God calls both kinds of missionaries. We must not fall prey to a harsh judgmental attitude that categorizes missionaries going to pioneer areas, or those who feel called to evangelize, disciple, and teach in harvest areas, as inferior or irresponsible. The biblical balance is both search and harvest, as God calls and the Holy Spirit guides.

An open Bible finds both of these ideas not only well represented, but presents them as inseparable. When we divide them, we inevitably place them in a list of tasks and prioritize one over the other. Yet, not only is this dichotomy unwarranted biblically, the fact is we will never finish the first until we incorporate the second, precisely because they are inseparable. When we teach those we have reached, they will be able to then reach others, truly completing our work with those we have reached. The Great Commission that Jesus gave his church includes reaching *and* teaching.

When missionaries discuss how "reached" a country should be before they pull out to go elsewhere, they are asking the wrong question. The question we ask should not be "What percentage has heard the gospel?" as if attaining an arbitrary percentage releases us from our task. The questions should be, "Have we done everything here that God called us here to do?" and "Is God leading us somewhere else?" The task of reaching the unreached is necessary and biblical, but it is simply the first step in our obedience to Christ's Great Commission among the peoples where we serve. Jesus did not send us to "Go therefore and get decisions from all men" but rather to "make disciples of all nations."

If an arbitrary percentage of evangelicals in a country were sufficient for missionaries to leave, one country in Africa would have been the "reached" country poster child. Rwanda once counted over 90 percent of its population as baptized Christians, and in the wake of this success, many missionaries left. Yet, in 1994, between 800,000 and a million of them were hacked to death in less than 100 days as one tribe brutally murdered nearly one-fifth of this "Christian" country's population by wielding machetes against another tribe in one of the world's worst genocides. Nominal Christianity is a bankrupt religion; it may have the Bible, crosses on the tops of meeting houses, and even the name of Christian, but its adherents are not saved.[4]

Certainly, missionaries care about the lost who have never heard, and they should always seek to reach them. However, those who *have* heard may not have understood, or been taught, how to live out the gospel in daily life. When that happens, they naturally continue what they have always known and add Jesus to it. Adding Jesus to Islam, Hinduism, or Wicca is not Christianity. A guideline for missions needs to be, "Jesus plus anything equals heresy."

Finding the balance should never be easy, and we must pray for our missions leaders as they seek divine direction. Reaching the nations and teaching them all that Christ commanded are both biblical and essential elements in the missionary task. We should never dichotomize the two and pit them against each other; they are two sides of the same coin.

Syncretism. When peoples embrace the forms of Christianity without understanding their meaning, the result is not salvation; neither is it the desired end of the missionary task. One indigenous man explained to me that his people had accepted Christianity for less than honorable reasons and that for them it was like "changing our shirt; nothing changed on the inside." Tragically, missionaries assumed that their work was completed, leaving without asking too many hard questions. Syncretism, the blending of two religions, is what happens without critical contextualization coupled with thorough discipleship—the result is a third religion altogether that saves no one.

Much of what appears to be biblical Christianity around the world is not; it is the old with a cross on top. The lines around the gospel and the biblical definitions of Christian, church, and pastor have been blurred.

The prosperity gospel with its health and wealth teaching is another danger that is growing exponentially in the traditional mission fields of the Global South.[5] Missionaries have worked for years and established churches in these areas of the world, and one would think that we should be through there by now. However, self-promoting health-and-wealth church leaders preach their prosperity-gospel schemes to undiscipled and untaught congregations as the answer to the world's poverty and diseases. So dangerous is this burgeoning threat that John Piper issued a third edition of *Let the Nations Be Glad!* that begins with an open letter to the leaders of this heresy.[6]

---

[4] James F. Engel, "Beyond the Numbers Game," *Christianity Today* (August 7, 2000), 54.

[5] For a further exploration of the missiological issues related to the Southern Church or societal issues in the Global South, see Philip Jenkins, *The Next Christendom: The Coming of Global Christianity* (Oxford: Oxford University Press, 2002). For an examination of the rise of Pentecostalism within these mission fields see Harvey Cox, "Christianity Reborn," *The Economist*, December 23, 2006, 49.

[6] John Piper. *Let the Nations Be Glad*, 3rd ed. (Grand Rapids, Baker Academic, 2010), 21–32.

Orality. One of the waves crashing onto the contemporary missions beach is the understanding of the world of orality. Over 70 percent of the world's peoples are primary oral learners who think in ways that the literate West does not. These peoples cannot or do not read, but instead process information through stories, songs, proverbs, riddles, and drama. Unfortunately, we have naturally developed over 90 percent of our resources for evangelism, discipleship, and leadership training for highly literate Western peoples, and only 10 percent for this majority of the world.[7]

The challenges of discipleship and teaching among oral cultures discourage some missionaries from even trying, believing that the missionaries must be the ones to preach and administer since they cannot teach the nationals to do so through traditional means. Throughout history missionaries have repeatedly insisted that oral peoples be taught to read and write as part of their discipleship. After all, how can they grow as Christians without the ability to read the Word for themselves?

While primary oral learners would gain little from a traditional classroom or book study, other effective methods for discipleship and teaching abound. Chronological Bible storying, telling Bible stories from creation to the cross, creates a biblical worldview for people with no biblical background or understanding. Telling these stories and assisting hearers to apply the meaning to their lives guides them to understand that there is a Creator who hates sin and will judge sin, but who loves his people so much that he sent his Son to die for them. Not only is this an effective way to communicate biblical truth to oral peoples; they are also able to remember and retell these stories, applying their lessons to the lives of their hearers. First and foremost, it is in this way that 2 Timothy 2:2 is possible among them.

In addition to storying, missionaries have effectively used a model of repetition based on information and review. This interactive model requires the teacher and students to dialogue so that the hearers are able to retain the information and repeat it in similar fashion.[8] Another method that has been useful for centuries is the use of catechism. In Tom J. Nettles' edited collection of Baptist catechisms, he includes one developed by E. T. Winkler for the instruction of oral culture slaves in the South.[9] While serving among the Highland Quichua people in Andean Ecuador, we utilized the children's catechism that we had used to teach our own children with great success.

Oral cultures are certainly able to learn how to read, but countless missionaries have found that even when they attain a literacy level that would allow them to enter the highly literate world, the culture prefers the old ways

---

[7]   Durk Meijer, "How Shall They Hear," presentation at International Orality Network Meeting, February 2008.

[8]   Daniel Sheard, *An Orality Primer for Missionaries*, 2007 (available at dssheard@wanadoo.fr).

[9]   E. T. Winkler's 1857, *Notes and Questions for the Oral Instruction of Colored People*, in Thomas J. Nettles, *Teaching Truth, Training Hearts: The Study of Catechisms in Baptist Life* (Merrick, NY: Calvary Press Baptist Heritage Series, 1998).

and considers reading and writing a passing novelty.[10] While oral cultures may understand the general idea of a missionary's three-point sermon, it is much more likely that they will not. Or, it may be that they will arrive at a totally foreign conclusion to the message, and they will certainly not be able to repeat the message to others. Missionaries have found that the use of stories and parables are much more effective if oral cultures are to understand, remember, and retell the gospel truth that they share. Since scholars believe that Jesus' hearers were roughly 90 percent oral culture people, it is no wonder that he often told stories to communicate his message rather than employing linear logical steps or deductive points.

Insider movements. Another challenge of missions today is a phenomenon known as insider movements. Some missionaries seek to promote these movements as a missiological strategy, while others at least believe that they can occur and wonder what to do with them. Rebecca Lewis defines insider movements as

> Any movement to faith in Christ where a) the gospel flows through pre-existing communities and social networks, and where b) believing families, as valid expressions of the Body of Christ, remain inside their socioreligious communities, retaining their identity as members of that community while living under the Lordship of Jesus Christ and the authority of the Bible.[11]

The typical expression is in the Muslim or Hindu contexts, where new believers remain in their former religions culturally, socially, legally, and in virtually every other way imaginable in order to avoid the extraction of new Christians from existing networks. While this chapter is not the place to debate the legitimacy of such efforts, if they are allowed as possible, then the dangerously slippery slope to syncretism is guaranteed since people remain in their "socioreligious communities" after coming to Christ. The use of insider strategies requires that missionaries be ever vigilant to recognize and counter syncretism. Most Hindu, and virtually all Muslim, cultural contexts can be described as a rope of three strands of culture, religion, and civil law. Questioning whether a person acted in some way because of cultural expectations, religious reasons, or the law would be met with confusion. The truth is that these strands are wound so tightly together that they are almost indistinguishable—in such settings, the religion *is* the law is the culture. When someone comes to Christ and is encouraged to remain in their social setting as before, dangers abound without a guide.

The guide that these and all new believers need is deep discipleship and biblical teaching. Some have argued that this is unnecessary and missionaries required to remain to do this would rob another from the ranks of evangelists

---

[10] Herbert Klem, *Oral Communication of the Scripture* (Pasadena, CA: William Carey Library, 1981), ix–xvii.

[11] Rebecca Lewis, "Promoting Movements to Christ within Natural Communities. Insider Movements: The Conversation Continues," *International Journal of Frontier Missiology* 24:2 (Summer 2007), 75.

to the unreached peoples. Indeed, some say that all these new groups need is the Holy Spirit and a Bible. However, Jesus' promise that the Holy Spirit would lead us into all truth must be understood in light of all of God's Word which commands us to teach and disciple those who come behind us (John 16:12–15). Many misguided preachers have the Holy Spirit and a Bible, but they only see in it what they expect to find or want to see.

People movements and awakenings. There was an awakening in the Ecuadorian Andes among the Highland Quichua people in the 1970s and 1980s. Sadly, this movement of the Holy Spirit has waned, and very little of the fruit remains. While many claim to be evangelicals, genuine New Testament Christianity is more rare than the numbers suggest.[12] Because my family and I worked among the Quichuas after the turbulent Awakening had settled into a calm, if not stagnant pond, I was intrigued to read D. A. Carson's thoughts on the aftermath of the Welsh revival. He and his wife had been traveling in Wales and stopped at a little Calvinist Methodist church, which had since embraced liberalism. They met an older lady who came to the Lord during that revival of 1904–05. She recounted the glories of the miraculous conversions of the Welsh miners and how their ponies were unresponsive to orders given since the previously frequent expletives were deleted. And yet, Carson reported that her only spiritual nourishment in the present day was from a radio program out of Morocco since her church had declined into liberalism. Carson lamented that so little fruit had been preserved from that turn-of-the-century revival. Pertinent to the role of missionaries and discipleship is the lesson he drew from that experience,

> Wider reading, and some humbling personal exposure to what God has done in various corners of the world during the past half century, have conspired to forge an unshakable resolution within me. Should the Lord in his mercy ever pour out large-scale revival on any part of the world where I have influence, I shall devote all my energy to teaching the Word, to training a new generation of godly pastors, to channeling all of this God-given fervor toward doctrinal maturity, multiplication of Christian leaders, evangelistic zeal, maturity in Christ, genuine Christian "fellowship." And all of this I should have learned already from Acts 2:42; 6:2; 1 Timothy 4:13–16; and 2 Timothy 3:14–4:5.[13]

God poured out his Spirit on the Highland Quichuas, in a wonderful awakening that certainly left many true believers, but many more are carnal

---

[12] Over the years, I have seen various statistics reported of the number of Quichuas who are Evangelical, often contradicting one another and varying greatly. One such statistic, reported by the Ecuadorian newspaper, *El Comercio*, in May 2001 stated that as many as 62 percent of Quichuas claim to be Evangelical, which number the Evangelicals among them in the millions. Yet, no missionary working among them believes the number of believers to approach anywhere near that figure.

[13] D. A. Carson, "What to Do If Revival Comes," *Modern Reformation* 12:1 (January–February 2003): 52.

nominal Christians. Today the spiritual need among them is clear in the dearth of genuine discipled and trained leadership—and rampant syncretism.

The realities described in the preceding paragraphs describe a few of the challenges to biblical Christianity in the world today. Traditional mission fields that many consider reached and no longer needing missionaries are increasingly abandoned by missionaries heading to lesser-reached areas. The syncretism that results from the unintentional blending of Christianity with traditional religions, the challenge of literates reaching nonliterate oral cultures, and the dangers inherent in insider movement methodologies are dynamics that contemporary missionaries struggle with daily. Guided by the Holy Spirit, church planters can find the way through these challenges and see healthy New Testament churches. However, the way is *through* not *around.* The difficulty of the time-consuming task of deep discipleship and training is worth the effort required to plant sound churches with biblically qualified leaders.

DISCIPLING THE NATIONS

Christ has called us to make disciples and to teach them all that he has commanded us. In order to be found obedient to this task, we must focus on the head, heart, and hands of those being discipled. The head emphasizes what the mentor should teach. While degrees in theological education are not necessary for every believer, there are basic truths that they must understand. Such essentials as the fundamental Christian doctrines, an overview of the Bible, how to study and interpret the Bible, and how to share their faith should be developed and practiced in the life of every believer.

The heart is often overlooked in discipleship programs and traditional classroom models. Focusing intently on the body of information to be learned, many simply assume that the heart and character of the disciple will automatically grow in Christlikeness. However, pride, arrogance, worldly allegiance, lust, anger, envy, and other sinful character issues are best "discipled" out of the new believer or aspiring leader. Rather than seeing discipleship as pure instruction, the goal and challenge is developing a heart for God as well as a mind for Truth.

The hands refer to the practical, daily life and ministry of the disciple. Such essential Christian practices as sharing your faith, helping the weak, providing for the needy, rescuing those in danger, and feeding the hungry must be cultivated. Identifying one's personal gifts and employing them in service to God is not automatic. Mentors, guides, and disciplers should seek to shepherd new believers down right paths for the service God has prepared for them (Eph. 2:10). Just as we must recognize the need for skilled hands for Kingdom tasks, so must we disciple those new believers to understand these realities.

Missionaries should disciple those they win to Jesus. This is not an optional work for those with more free time. Evangelizing without follow-up and discipleship is tantamount to having babies and leaving them on the sidewalk outside the hospital when we go home. There is a responsibility for parents to raise their children in the fear and admonition of the Lord, and a similar responsibility falls on missionaries. We best do this by modeling it in how we intentionally teach them, nurture their walk with the Lord, and mentor them in a life of ministry commitment.

TEACHING TEACHERS, TRAINING TRAINERS

The task of training nationals inevitably raises the issue of teachers. Some missionaries are eager to move on and prefer not to stay around to teach. Others do not believe they are gifted to teach. Citing the absence of such a gift raises the issue of missionary qualification, because teaching is an essential component of the Great Commission. Even those who believe that teaching is not their gift should at the very least seek to invite and enable others to come behind them to do so. Leaving the people undiscipled and untaught with no hope or remedy is biblically indefensible.

Perhaps, the missionary feels he should not teach because the nationals are better equipped linguistically and culturally to do so. The nationals certainly have better language skills, understanding of the culture, and deeper insights into the worldview, which will better enable them to avoid syncretism. Yet, the missionary is better equipped in theological and biblical preparation. This is what he must bring to the table, along with the goal to make the nationals the teachers as soon as possible. The missionary's goal must be to teach teachers, train trainers, and disciple disciplers. When this is done, the nationals will then be prepared to take on the task of not only reaching and teaching those within their own people group, but we will see them become a missionary force themselves.

Biblical basis. In addition to the biblical references considered thus far, throughout the Bible there is clear guidance for the responsibility of those who know more to teach those who are newer to the faith. Many passages address the responsibility of parents to teach their children to know the Lord and his law. We owe those for whom we are responsible the care and consideration of right knowledge of God, whether they are our physical or spiritual children. Certainly, those whom we find in darkness and lead to the light must not be left at the gate as we drive away. Read and consider the following passages that exhort us to teach those who come behind us: Genesis 18:19; Deuteronomy 4:9–10; 6:1–6; 11:19; 32:46; Psalm 78:4–6.

Teaching the ways of God to those whom we may influence is not a neutral option for consideration, but a command of God. Hosea 4:6 says:

> My people are destroyed for lack of knowledge; because you have rejected knowledge, I reject you from being a priest to me. And since you have forgotten the law of your God, I also will forget your children.

Hosea indicates that not only do the people perish for this lack of knowledge, but that he will judge the priests who fail in their duty to teach the knowledge of God and his Word. The people of the world who have just heard the gospel do not have the benefit of study Bibles and commentaries; so let me share some of what they could learn about this passage if they did. The Reformation Study Bible states, "Knowledge of God was inseparable from the law of God."[14] How can our hearers on the missions fields truly know him if we do not disciple them and teach them his Word?

Moreover, the people were not the only ones in danger. This passage is teaching that those who knew but did not teach the knowledge of God were guilty of gross sin and invoking God's wrath. The NASB Study Bible states, "Hosea warned the priests not to lodge charges against the people for bringing God's judgment down on the nation, for they themselves were guilty, and the people could also bring charges against them—as Hosea proceeded to do."[15] The HCSB Study Bible states, "The common people are identified as guilty, but especially guilty were the priests who were responsible for teaching the people. Leaders of God's people who shirk or violate that responsibility invite special judgment."[16] The ESV Study Bible continues this warning, "The priests had the responsibility of teaching the people God's laws, but they had failed miserably, and as a result, the people lacked knowledge of God and his ways . . . . But he puts the blame squarely on the priests."[17] Although our hearers on the mission fields do not have these study Bibles, a cursory reading of our own reveals our responsibility to teach them, and God's displeasure when we neglect this task. Not only do we have study Bibles; we have faithful commentaries from reliable men that we may read as well.

Matthew Poole wrote to explain Hosea's caution in this passage, "For the lack of knowledge of God, his law, his menaces, his providences, and government of the world. Had they known his holy nature, his jealousy for his own glory, his hatred of sin and his power to punish it, had they known their God, they would either have forborne to sin, or repented of what sins they had committed, and so prevented his wrath."[18] A contemporary commentator, Derek Kidner, wrote,

> What is even more striking than the poor showing of these men is the glory of the task entrusted to them: no less than to be the nation's spiritual educators. Unlike most religions, where priests were close guardians of the cultic mysteries while the people's part was more or less mechanical, the faith of the Old Testament was a revelation addressed to every mind and conscience, "making wise the simple." . . . Now we see it as not only profound but

---

[14]   *The Reformation Study Bible* (Phillipsburg, NJ: Ligonier Ministries, 2005), 1242.

[15]   *The Zondervan New American Standard Study Bible* (Grand Rapids: Zondervan, 1995), 1257.

[16]   *The Holman Christian Standard Study Bible* (Nashville: Holman Bible Publishers, 2010), 1461.

[17]   *The English Standard Version Study Bible* (Wheaton, IL: Crossway Bibles, 2008), 1627.

[18]   Matthew Poole, *A Commentary on the Holy Bible, Volume II: Psalms—Malachi* (Peabody, MA: Hendrickson Publishers, 1985), 859.

critical: a matter of life and death. . . . There is wrath as well as logic here, for the stumbling itself was no accident.[19]

Perhaps my favorite devotional commentator, Matthew Henry, wrote,

> The people strove with the priests that should have taught them the knowledge of God; justly they were destroyed for lack of knowledge. Note, those that rebel against the light can expect no other than to perish in the dark. Or is it a charge upon the priests, who should have been teaching the people knowledge (Eccles. 12:9), or they did not, or did it in such a manner that it was as if they had not done it at all, so there was no knowledge of God in the land; and because there was no vision, or none to any purpose, the people perished (Prov. 29:18). Note, *ignorance is so far from being the mother of devotion that it is the mother of destruction; lack of knowledge is ruining to any person or people.* (Emphasis added)[20]

If teaching the people right knowledge of God and his Word was imperative for God's people who had his law, prophets, traditions, and the advantage of a biblical worldview, how much more necessary is such instruction among people who have lived in pagan lands all of their lives? If God's own people needed instruction, think of those raised in the darkened worldview of false religious worldviews, or in animism, who have never known a Christian, and have no copy of God's Word in their own language? God sends them missionaries, but it is not merely to preach and leave.

I once was teaching some pastors and leaders in a Highland Quichua community in Ecuador on the importance of hearing the gospel and being born again. The eldest among them listened patiently and then asked to speak. He said that his people had lived for generations on the mountain where he and his family still lived. He said that his parents never heard this gospel message, that the only church they ever knew was the Catholic Church in the neighboring community. He went on to share that even that church did not have a priest, but one would come once a year or so to conduct a mass in Latin. He said that his parents did not even understand Spanish, much less Latin, and so even if they had heard one of the masses, they would not have heard the gospel. Then he asked, "What about my parents, where did they go when they died?" As respectfully and humbly as I could, I answered that according to what God has revealed in his Word, they did not go to heaven. He was silent for a moment, considering my response, and I was silent amassing my arguments to defend exclusivism—unnecessarily. When he spoke, he simply said, "I think those priests will have a lot to answer for."

I felt so vindicated and justified, at least until I drove back to my home in the city that evening. As I drove, I thought of all the times that I have preached without thinking whether my hearers really understood, and all the times that I have blasted my hearers with "turn or burn" evangelism with no

[19]   Derek Kidner, *The Message of Hosea* (Downers Grove: InterVarsity Press, 1981), 49.

[20]   Matthew Henry, *Commentary on the Whole Bible, Vol. 4-Isaiah–Malachi* (McLean, VA: McDonald Publishing Company), 1141.

care to follow-up or focus on discipling. I know that I have a lot to answer for as well.

CONCLUSION

In Matthew 28:18–20, the Great Commission is perfectly clear about the task of missions: "And Jesus came and said to them, 'All authority in heaven and on earth has been given to me. Go therefore and make disciples of all nations, baptizing them in the name of the Father and of the Son and of the Holy Spirit, teaching them to observe all that I have commanded you. And behold, I am with you always, to the end of the age.'" Jesus said to go to the nations, win them and baptize them, make disciples of them, and teach them everything he commanded us. No part of that is optional. There is not an easier Great Commission for the hard places, hard hearts, or hard heads.

As we go to the nations, we will see the Holy Spirit draw and convert people through our preaching, and we will form them into New Testament churches with biblically qualified pastors and elders. Such a task requires knowing the languages, cultures, and worldviews well enough to know when a raised hand in the invitation does not necessarily mean conversion. We should be eager to reach the nations as if their souls depended on our speed, but never minimize what we have been commanded to do in order to attain greater speed.

The challenges of discipling the nations are many: 12,000 languages and dialects, 70 percent of those to whom we go are oral culture peoples, syncretism from inadequate contextualization in prior years, and a gospel-hostile world. Additionally, we often find it difficult to concentrate amidst the cacophony of voices around us seeking to separate the reached people groups from the unreached and the search perspectives from the harvest perspectives; further, we find it difficult because we find ourselves laboring with a mentality that is different from many peers. The people movements of awakenings when the Holy Spirit pours himself out on a people, as well as possibly dubious ones of the insider movements, can be overwhelming. How do you discern the spiritual condition of so many people and disciple them adequately? The challenges are indeed real, but not insurmountable. God knew that these challenges to deep discipleship and teaching would be around when he gave us the command to do so anyway.

Let us never forget the words of Hosea to God's priests and teachers. Teaching is not optional. As missionaries, we must be discipling and teaching right knowledge of God and his Word. It is pleasing to the Lord of the Harvest when we labor according to his commands, and that certainly includes his command to make disciples.

Chapter Fourteen

MISSION AND CHURCH PLANTING

J. D. Payne

INTRODUCTION

Like most children, I grew up riding bicycles. In fact, I went through several over the years. While I have ridden bicycles that were both too small and too large for me, without brakes, with loose seats and handlebars, and with flat tires, I have never ridden a bicycle without a sprocket chain—except when coasting down a hill (and hoping the bike was one that had working front brakes).

This amazing invention, the sprocket chain, is the primary means by which the bicycle is propelled forward. As a child, I remember on several occasions when the chain on my bicycle would become too loose and would pop out of place, leaving me stranded until I managed to slip it back into place on the front and rear sprockets. A bicycle is more than the sprocket chain, but the chain is a very significant part of the overall machine, without which there is no forward motion.

In this chapter, I will discuss the significance of church planting to the mission of God. Like the fact that the bicycle is more than the sprocket chain, the mission of God involves more than church planting. However, just as the chain is the significant means by which the bicycle moves forward, the advancement of the kingdom is significantly dependent on the multiplication of churches across people groups and population segments, across villages, towns, and cities.

In the first section of this chapter, I discuss the theological framework for church planting and the four essentials for all church planting endeavors to carry out the mission of God. In the second section, I provide a definition and description of church planting. It is important from the outset that you know exactly what I am talking about when I refer to this ministry. Finally, I conclude with a description of the relationship of church planting to the mission of God.

In relation to the creation-fall-redemption-restoration theme that has been shown throughout this book, church planting is particularly related to redemption and restoration. As missionaries preach the gospel of redemption to others and gather those new believers into churches, those redeemed communities of faith in turn continue to disseminate the message of redemption and restoration across the world, carrying out the mission of God, until that final day of restoration occurs.

AT THE CROSSROADS OF ECCLESIOLOGY AND MISSIOLOGY

Stuart Murray was correct when he noted that church planting "can legitimately be subsumed under the theological disciplines of either missiology or ecclesiology."[1] I prefer to say that church planting can be found where missiology and ecclesiology converge (see fig. 14.1). Missiology is the study of the science and art of missions. This discipline is vast and also covers many areas that do not directly relate to church planting. Ecclesiology is the study of the doctrine of the church. Within this doctrine, there are many aspects of church life that do not specifically relate to church planting.[2]

FIGURE 14.1. CHURCH PLANTING: A THEOLOGICAL FRAMEWORK

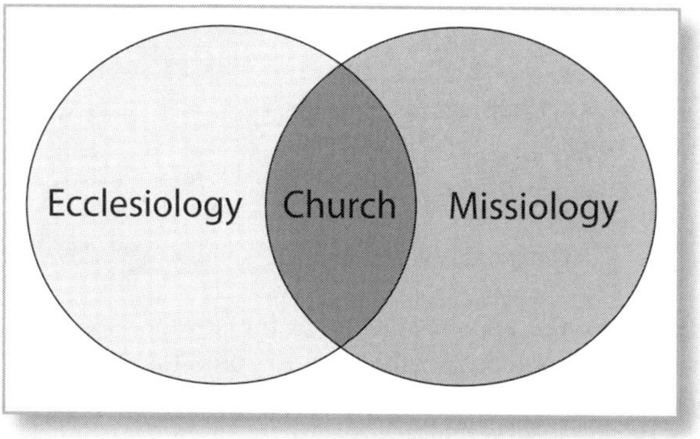

Regardless of the context, all church planting efforts have common characteristics. While Acts 13–14 provides us with a bird's-eye glimpse into such missionary practices, in his first letter to the church at Thessalonica, Paul

---

[1]   Stuart Murray, *Church Planting: Laying Foundations* (UK: Paternoster Press, 1998), 30.

[2]   Charles Brock, *Indigenous Church Planting: A Practical Journey* (Neosho, MO: Church Growth International, 1994), 30.

provides us with a closer perspective, referencing how the church was specifically planted in that city.

> For we know, brothers loved by God, that he has chosen you, because our
> gospel came to you not only in word, but also in power and in the Holy
> Spirit and with full conviction. You know what kind of men we proved to
> be among you for your sake. And you became imitators of us and of the
> Lord, for you received the word in much affliction, with the joy of the Holy
> Spirit, so that you became an example to all the believers in Macedonia and
> in Achaia. For not only has the word of the Lord sounded forth from you in
> Macedonia and Achaia, but your faith in God has gone forth everywhere,
> so that we need not say anything. For they themselves report concerning us
> the kind of reception we had among you, and how you turned to God from
> idols to serve the living and true God, and to wait for his Son from heaven,
> whom he raised from the dead, Jesus who delivers us from the wrath to
> come. (1 Thess. 1:4–10)

In his book *Indigenous Church Planting: A Practical Journey,* Charles
Brock observes that this passage in 1 Thessalonians contains the four essentials for all church planting.

FIGURE 14.2. THE ESSENTIALS FOR CHURCH PLANTING

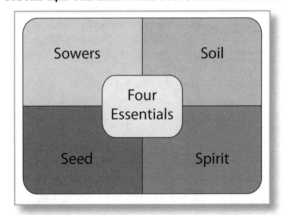

In this passage, the apostle notes that the sowers, seed, Spirit, and soil
were the necessary components that had to come together prior to the birth
of the church in order for the church to be birthed. Someone had to preach
the gospel to those without Christ in order for them to believe (Rom. 10:14).
And in conjunction with such evangelistic efforts, the Holy Spirit worked to
bring about regeneration and the birth of churches (John 3:5–6; 1 Cor. 12:3;
1 Thess. 1:5–6). A proper recognition of these four essentials is critical for
missionaries engaged in church planting.

WHAT IS CHURCH PLANTING?

Biblical church planting is evangelism that results in new churches. One should note that the word *biblical* is emphasized in this sentence. Such is necessary because there are many ways to plant churches, but not all of those methods are rooted in a solid biblical foundation and reflect a wise missiology that takes into consideration the mission of God to reach the nations of this world.

Within this basic definition, there is a wealth of material related to the mission of God. A few years ago I wrote a more detailed explanation of biblical church planting which included the following:

> Biblical church planting follows the way modeled by Jesus and imitated by the Apostolic Church for global disciple making. It is a methodology and strategy for bringing in the harvest, raising up leaders from the harvest, and sending leaders to work in the harvest fields. It is evangelism resulting in congregationalizing. Under the leadership and work of the Holy Spirit, biblical church planting seeks to translate the gospel and the irreducible ecclesiological minimum into any given social context, with the expectation that new communities of believers in turn will continue the process in their contexts and throughout the world.[3]

I will use the rest of this section to explain this description.

Church planting is biblical. Biblical church planting is not about transferring church members from one church to another church. It is not about cloning other "successful" church models into my context. It is not about projecting my culturally preferred way of "doing" church onto a group of new believers, because I "know" best. It is not about starting a new worship service with cool music, great preaching, and meeting in a dark room with a great vibe. Biblical church planting has nothing to do with building a building, stealing another pastor's sheep, or starting a church simply because my desired "brand" of church is not present in a particular community.

Rather, biblical church planting follows after the way of Jesus and the apostolic church. An examination of the New Testament reveals that those first church planters began by reaching people from the harvest fields. The biblical starting point for church planting is with unbelievers, *not* Kingdom citizens (Acts 13–14). As the gospel is taken into the highways and hedges of this world, the marketplaces, and the public squares, people will come out of the kingdom of darkness and into the kingdom of light, will gather together as local kingdom communities, and will journey together in learning what it means to know "Jesus Christ and him crucified" (1 Cor. 2:2) as they obey all that he commanded (Matt. 28:20). They in turn will continue to carry out the mission of God in their contexts and throughout the world.

---

[3]   J. D. Payne, "The Great Commission and Church Planting," in Thom S. Rainer and Chuck Lawless, eds., *The Challenge of the Great Commission* (Louisville, KY: Pinnacle Publishers, 2005) 107–8.

Church planting is a method. Church planting is a method of seeing the mission of God actualized among people. It is a "how-to," a means of making disciples. On several occasions the apostle Paul told newly planted churches to imitate him as he imitated Christ (1 Cor. 11:1; Phil. 3:17; 1 Thess. 1:7; 2 Thess. 3:7,9). Church planters recognize that an incarnational approach to church planting is critical. People reproduce what is modeled before them. Kingdom citizens involved in church planting activities understand that wise stewardship in such missional activities requires that church planting methods need to be highly reproducible, so that the new churches can quickly get involved in the mission of God through church planting. It is important that the church planters recognize that what they do among the people, even prior to their conversions, will serve as a model to them for future activities. If the model is too difficult to reproduce, then frustration and an inferiority complex are likely to arise. For example, if the church planting team models elaborate prayers, using polysyllabic Old English words, then the new churches will come to believe that is the "correct" way to pray. If the team uses an overly complicated or niche method for preaching and teaching the Scriptures that only the seminary-trained can reproduce, then few men will quickly rise to the need to preach the gospel. The method of church planting must be kept simple if we desire to see kingdom citizens reproducing what they have seen, heard, and experienced.

Church planters operating from a foundation of the mission of God have the world on their hearts. Such missionaries are not content with planting a single church. The mission of God requires that church planters operate from methods that are highly reproducible by the new believers themselves. If the church planters are laboring with methods that can only be used by those with years of education, advanced missiological training, charismatic personalities, and large sums of money, then the likelihood of any of those newly planted churches multiplying is significantly limited. The use of such methods reveals that the church planters have not allowed the mission of God to deeply influence their apostolic labors.

The irony of experiencing the mission of God through church planting is that while church planting is a very difficult ministry, church planting involves a few basic activities: evangelizing, gathering new believers together as a local church, teaching them to love and obey Jesus, and to love each other as well as those outside of the church. Knowing that the ministry of church planting is difficult enough as it is, church planters should do nothing to unnecessarily make such ministry more challenging. From Kansas City to Karachi and from Montreal to Mumbai, there are four billion people on the planet who do not know Jesus personally. In light of this fact, church planters concerned with the mission of God will make certain they *keep it simple*.

Church planters concerned with the mission of God cry out with the apostle Paul for prayer that the Word of the Lord will spread rapidly and with honor (2 Thess. 3:1). They labor as good stewards to make certain that the people to which they are called are challenged "to walk in a manner worthy of the Lord, fully pleasing to him, bearing fruit in every good work and increasing in the knowledge of God" (Col. 1:10), as they plant churches in their circles of influence. Let us remember that church planting can be rapid *and* result in healthy churches, for Paul himself clearly did not want one without the other. The apostle who desired the rapid multiplication of disciples, leaders, and churches was the same man who proclaimed the whole counsel of God (Acts 20:27).

Church planting is a strategy. Church planting is a strategy for carrying out the mission of God in the world. It is a plan for kingdom expansion, involving the conversion of men and women and the transformation of society. Many church planters, particularly those laboring in North American contexts, suffer from vision myopia. Ask most church planters what the end vision of their strategy is, and they will generally describe a church that is well organized and planting other churches. However, church planters who have been drinking deeply from the well of the mission of God recognize that the gospel has implications not only for individuals, but also for every dimension of society and culture. They see the gospel spreading rapidly and with honor (2 Thess. 3:2), resulting in the multiplication of disciples, leaders, and churches across their people groups, population segments, cities, and villages. They have a vision to see gospel transformation occur, resulting in those kingdom citizens living according to a kingdom ethic in their homes, schools, businesses, marketplaces, and throughout the world. Such church planters begin with the end in mind and recognize that such a scenario will result in societal and cultural transformation.

Church planters concerned with the mission of God look at a crowd of unbelievers comprising their mission field and do not see a church they can pastor, but they see multiple churches, multiple pastors, and hundreds of kingdom citizens. They do not simply see new believers gathered together once or twice a week for a good time of worship and fellowship, but rather an army of new kingdom citizens who will live according to the kingdom ethic and begin to transform their homes, schools, work places, towns, villages, cities, and the world for the glory of God. Church planting teams consumed with the mission of God understand themselves to be church-multiplying and pastor-multiplying machines. For such apostolic bands carry with them the gospel and the kingdom ethic to make disciples, teaching them to obey all that Christ commanded. It is in the going forth of such teams with this good news that the mission of God plays out in the world. Church planters have been on the front lines of kingdom expansion since the first century. They were the primary means by which the mission of God was carried out in church history, and they will continue to be until the coming of the kingdom.

Church planting is Spirit guided. The Spirit carries out the mission of God. J. B. Lawrence was correct when he wrote, "Human instruments, apart from the Holy Spirit, cannot change dead hearts, obstinate wills, evil imaginations, perverted understandings, and biased judgments."[4] Apart from the

---

[4] J. B. Lawrence, *The Holy Spirit in Missions* (Atlanta, GA: Home Mission Board, 1966), 64.

work of the Holy Spirit, all church planting labors are in vain. Consider the
following. Without the Holy Spirit:

- church planters would not be called by God (Acts 13:2)
- church planters would not be empowered for witness (Acts 1:8)
- church planters would not be guided to persons of peace (Acts 8:29;
  16:6–7)
- church planters would not have divine boldness for witness (Acts 4:13, 31)
- church planters would not have the wisdom of God to know how to
  speak clearly (John 16:13; Acts 4:13; 1 Cor. 2:13)
- the conviction of sin, righteousness, and judgment would not be upon
  people (John 16:8)
- no one would be born again (John 3:5–8; 1 Cor. 12:3)
- churches would not be birthed (1 Thess. 1:5–6)
- elders would not be appointed to oversee churches (Acts 20:28)[5]

As noted in the description of church planting found at the beginning of
this chapter, it is important to recognize that the Spirit is the one who provides the leadership and does the work to advance the kingdom.

Church planting is focused on the gospel and basic ecclesiology. Church
planting begins with the gospel and the New Testament understanding of a
local church. While teams cannot be culturally neutral, church planters must
work diligently to communicate the biblical gospel and nature and function
of the local church to the people. There is no room for paternalism, bigotry,
or ethnocentrism in the mission of God.

Missionaries laboring in Kentucky or Kazakhstan to plant churches are
not working to start a new business with rules and policies, a corporation
with a tax-exempt number, or a government sanctioned religious group, but
rather are laboring to start a family whose bond is stronger than blood (Matt.
12:46–50). They are not planting a social club, but rather a community (Acts
2:42) to transform communities in the Hunan Province, throughout Alberta,
and across California. Their labors to advance the kingdom are castrated if
they have worked to begin a weekly service with a few people serving, rather
than a fellowship of kingdom citizens who are sold out to Almighty God,
intending every waking moment as a living sacrifice (Rom. 12:1) and being
priests who declare his praises (1 Pet. 2:9) from San Diego to São Paulo.

Though bought with a great price, the church is a very simple thing. Jesus
intended for it to be this way. The church is able to exist among the middle
class, highly educated, Americans living in the twenty-first century, just as
much as it was able to exist among the poor, uneducated, people of Jerusalem
in the first century. The church is able to be alive and vibrant and healthy
among the Sherpa of Nepal, Bedouins of the Sahara, and Quebecois of Can-
ada. The church can exist among the scholarly, the ignorant, the free, and the
slave. If the health, power, zeal, and vitality of any local church is rooted in

---

[5]   J. D. Payne, *Discovering Church Planting: An Introduction to the Whats, Whys, and Hows
of Global Church Planting* (Colorado Springs, CO: Paternoster, 2009), 60.

anything other than the One who promised to build his church (Matt. 16:18), then that church is built on unstable ground. If a church ceases to exist or function as a missional community when the money disappears, the structures collapse, and the meeting place burns to the ground, then that church was not rooted in the God of mission.

Biblical teaching regarding the nature and functions of the local church must guide all church planting work regardless of context. The Bible teaches that the church is a bride (Eph. 5:22–33; Rev. 21:9), body (1 Cor. 12:20), family (Matt. 12:48–49), priests (1 Pet. 2:9), sheep (John 10:1–18), temple (1 Cor. 3:16), building (Eph. 2:19–21), branches (John 15:5), salt (Matt. 5:13), light (Matt. 5:14), and community (Acts 2:34; 4:34), but never teaches that it is an inanimate object such as a building, a worship service, or a time (e.g., "What time is church?"). In light of the biblical descriptions, therefore, church planters are well served to use these basic biblical descriptions of the church when planting a contextualized church among the people to whom they are called.

This basic ecclesiology provides an irreducible ecclesiological minimum necessary for a local church to exist among any people, in any place, at any time in history. A failure by missionaries to plant something less than the irreducible ecclesiological minimum is a failure to plant a New Testament church. If the church planter sets his heart on something other than a basic ecclesiology, he might very well hinder the rapid dissemination of the gospel and the multiplication of disciples, leaders, and churches throughout the people's social networks. For example, if he believes that the people must worship to a certain style of music that is difficult for the people to play themselves, kingdom expansion may be hindered. If the newly reached people believe they must have a salaried pastor in order to be a legitimate church because they observe other churches in their community using such methods, kingdom expansion will be hindered when they do not have the financial resources.

Church planting is to be contextual. Church planters approach a people group or population segment with wisdom and discernment. They desire to communicate effectively the gospel of the kingdom to unbelievers and then help the newly planted churches begin with a healthy DNA as a newly birthed kingdom community. In light of this desire, church planting methods must be contextualized among the people. Within proper biblical parameters, the church planting team strives to plant churches that are self-supporting, self-propagating, self-governing, self-expressing, self-identifying, self-teaching, and self-theologizing from the time of their birth.

While there is no one commonly accepted definition of the word *contextualization,*[6] Dean Gilliland notes that it is more helpful to talk about the "goal of contextualization." This goal, "is to enable, insofar as it is humanly possible, an understanding of what it means that Jesus Christ, the Word, is

---

[6] David J. Hesselgrave and Edward Rommen, *Contextualization: Meanings, Methods, and Models* (Pasadena, CA: William Carey Library, 1989, 2000), 35.

authentically experienced in each and every human situation."[7] Church planters must labor to effectively communicate the gospel to the people in a way
they can hear and understand and apply to their lives. Following conversion
and baptism of the new believers, the cultural "flavor" of the church develops
out of the context of those new believers. Rather than the church planters
bringing heavy elements of their preferred cultural expressions to the people
and teaching them that they must become like an American, Canadian, British, or other nationality of church, church planters attempt to use methods
that connect with the people and allow the culture of the church to develop
from the people.

When missiologists describe the church as manifesting the aforemen-
tioned "selfs," the correct understanding is that these characteristics are
Christ-sustained abilities. Self-supporting refers to the fact that the church
has all of the resources she needs to support her ministries. Self-propagating
notes that the church is fully capable of carrying out her evangelistic and
missionary ministries. Under the church's leadership and in accordance with
the Scriptures and the guiding Holy Spirit, the church is able to govern all of
her affairs. There is to be no outside authority over the church providing gov-
ernance. Self-expressing refers to the reality that within biblical parameters
the church is free to express herself in worship style and methods that are
reflective of the church's culture. Self-identifying reminds church planters
that a local church must understand herself to be a New Testament church, as
opposed to conceiving of herself as a Bible study, mission, preaching point,
campus, or site of another congregation. Self-teaching describes the church
that with her gifts and leaders she is able to teach herself the truths of the
Scriptures. Finally, self-theologizing is not the freedom for the church to
believe whatever she desires. Rather, this aspect of a local church builds from
a biblical theology; she is able to develop her own systematic theology and
correctly apply the truths of the Bible to herself and cultural realities.

But how can a newly planted church be all of this from the very beginning? The answer to this question is in the biblical DNA that has been instilled
in the new believers from the beginning. While a newborn baby does not bio-
logically and socially function as a twenty-year-old, the child nevertheless
is as fully human as the adult. In the beginning, a new church will be able
to manifest such characteristics in minute manners, but over time will show
forth such characteristics in more complex detail. More mature believers and
churches will come alongside to nurture the church from infancy to adult-
hood. Since the church is kingdom citizens growing through a sanctification
process, naturally the church will grow and develop through the influence of
discipleship from those more mature.

---

[7]   Dean Gilliland, "Contextualization," in *Evangelical Dictionary of World Missions,* A.
Scott Moreau, ed. (Grand Rapids, MI: Baker and UK: Paternoster Press, 2000), 225.

How Does Church Planting Relate to the Mission of God?

While church planting is not the same as the mission of God, it is a significant means by which the Lord has chosen to extend His rule and reign over the hearts of His people. Church planting is intimately connected to the mission of God. Church planters are concerned about the glorification of the Lord of the harvest as his kingdom is extended throughout the world.

Figure 14.3. Relation of Church Planting to the Mission of God

As the Holy Spirit empowers and guides church planters (Acts 16:6–10), he is also sovereignly working in the hearts of non-kingdom citizens. As with the Ethiopian (Acts 8:26–39), Cornelius (Acts 10), and Lydia (Acts 16:11–15), the Spirit continues to prepare hearts across the globe to receive the gospel message. The work of redemption and restoration is a part of the Spirit's activity in the world, while working through his messengers.

As kingdom citizens, church planters live according to the kingdom ethic. This way of life informs them as to how they are to live in relation to God, other kingdom citizens, and those outside of the kingdom. As Christ's followers they are to love God (Matt. 22:37), love their brothers and sisters (1 John 3:14), and love non-kingdom citizens, which involves sharing the good news with them (Matt. 28:19–20). As church planters venture into the mission fields, they go with God's authority as his ambassadors (2 Cor. 5:20) and understand that his Spirit has gone before them working through general and special revelation (Ps. 19:1; Rom. 1:20; 2 Tim. 3:16; Heb. 1:2). The strategy of church planting among any people group, population segment, subculture, etc., and the methods that serve to bring the strategy to completion work to reach people from the harvest field and see them return to the harvest fields to expand the kingdom.

Church planting is at the center of God's purposes in redeeming the lost and broadcasting his glory across every dimension of human society and culture. God's mission is furthered, his kingdom expanded, and his church multiplied as missionaries go preaching repentance and faith (Acts 20:21). For as people come out of the kingdom of darkness (Col. 1:13) and into the kingdom of light, the kingdom expands and the King is glorified. Such new believers are not to be left on their own to wander as "lone rangers for Jesus," but rather, the kingdom ethic notes that as the kingdom expands, kingdom citizens are to form intentionally local kingdom communities—local churches—whereby they are to live out the kingdom ethic. For as kingdom citizens live according to the kingdom ethic, lives are healed, families are mended, organizations are changed, societies are transformed, and God is glorified. These local expressions of the body of Christ are also limited reflections of life in the kingdom to come after the restoration of all things.

CONCLUSION

Church planting is one of the significant means that the Lord has ordained for the outworking of his mission in the world. While the church is nowhere told to plant churches, she has been commanded to make disciples from the harvest fields. Therefore, church planters do not ultimately long for a church planting movement, but rather a disciple-making movement. For the New Testament way reveals that as disciples are made and baptized, they are gathered together to be kingdom citizens, living according to a kingdom ethic in local kingdom communities known as churches. And it is through the multiplication of disciples, leaders, and churches that the mission of God continues until the day when all things are restored.

Chapter Fifteen

MISSION AND SUFFERING
Zane Pratt

INTRODUCTION

We come from a culture of entitlement. Westerners in general, and Americans in particular, are raised to believe that their rights are inviolable and that life owes them something. Our perceived entitlements go beyond the basic freedoms of religion and speech and assembly. The American Declaration of Independence, after all, says that everyone has an inalienable right to the pursuit of happiness, and that easily gets translated in people's minds into a right to happiness itself. In Western culture, comfort, convenience, and safety have become the normal experience of life for the vast majority of people. In such an environment, it is no surprise that these things have come to be regarded as non-negotiable entitlements as well. Furthermore, in a materialistic culture adverse to the concept of transcendence, values such as comfort, convenience, and safety seem to be ultimate for most people; those values trump everything else. Anything that threatens or disturbs the experience of these things is seen as automatically bad.

This kind of thinking has penetrated the Christian church. Western evangelicals sing about loving Jesus more than anyone or anything else, but often their commitment remains within the context of culturally determined expectations. As Westerners they, like others, unconsciously regard safety and comfort as their most important values, so they construct their understanding of the life of discipleship within those parameters. The supremacy of these concerns seems so self-evident that it does not even occur to anyone to examine them. They simply do not conceive of the possibility that God would require anything of them that was uncomfortable or unsafe, beyond perhaps the mild discomfort of sharing the gospel with somebody who gets offended in the process. When a man-centered gospel is preached, this tendency becomes even more pronounced. When people hear that the goal of salvation is to meet their needs or their desire for fulfillment (or even to give them an undefined "abundant life" such as "your best life now"), it makes no sense at all to think that following Jesus might involve pain or loss. Yet even in churches where a biblical God-centeredness is maintained, this unconscious aversion to suffering still holds true. Suffering as a normal part of life and as a normal component of following Christ simply is not on the mental agenda of most Western Christians. When believers undertake a path of obedience to Christ that entails discomfort, they are regarded as unusual heroes of the faith. When that path of obedience puts them at serious physical risk, they are often labeled fanatics and regarded as potentially unhinged. Even in the advance of the Great Commission, many churches and Christians in the West unconsciously value safety more than obedience, and they assume that God would never ask his followers to risk their lives for the sake of his work. Suffering is seen as unnatural, abnormal, and bad.

In this, as in so many things, Western cultural experience is out of step with most of the world throughout most of history. The majority of the human race has had no choice but to endure suffering as a common life occurrence. Without the massive protective shields that the West enjoys (technology, medicine, global food distribution systems, internal peace, and the rule of law), most of the human race has lived with the threat of disease, famine, natural disasters, and human violence as a normal condition. Even in the West, although suffering is corralled and hidden away, it can never be genuinely eliminated. Crime still happens. Natural disasters still sweep entire communities away, and economic crises wipe out years of savings overnight. We may have the best medical care in the world, but people still get sick, and everyone eventually dies—sometimes slowly and painfully. The difference is that people in the West are offended at suffering, as though their rights had somehow been violated by its mere existence. The rest of the world knows that suffering is simply a part of life.

It is particularly strange that Western Christians have such a diminished view of suffering. Suffering is a major theme of the Bible. The fact that Western Christians do not notice it (or unconsciously assume that it does not apply to them) is a classic example of cultural assumptions coloring the interpretation of Scripture. Whether they notice it or not, however, the Bible talks a lot about suffering, and it is a sound principle of biblical interpretation to pay particular attention to things that feature prominently in God's Word. Western evangelicalism desperately needs to recapture a biblical theology of suffering. Without it, we will make an idol out of our security and comfort, and we will marginalize our usefulness in the service of the Great Commission.

The Bible talks about suffering in several categories. Suffering exists everywhere and for everyone simply because this is a fallen world. Suffering sometimes happens as a consequence of wrongdoing, although the Bible cautions us against making snap judgments in such cases. Suffering is particularly promised to those who follow Jesus in a world that is in rebellion against him. Even more intensely, suffering is linked to the work of the advance of the gospel. Far from regarding suffering as altogether bad, the Bible points out benefits and blessings that flow from suffering. Finally, the Bible gives clear instruction on how believers are to respond when suffering comes their way in the wise providence of God.

SUFFERING IN A FALLEN WORLD

We live in a messed up world. The cause of this mess is our rebellion against God. When he created the world, he saw that everything was good, and it all stayed good until the human race disbelieved and disobeyed him. Adam and Eve's fall into sin introduced some form of suffering into every area of life. Immediately, their marriage relationship was marred as Adam sought to blame Eve for his own sin, and their oldest son subsequently murdered his younger brother. The first family was also the first dysfunctional family! The next few chapters of Genesis show the rapid downward spiral of human depravity, until Genesis 6:5 gives this sad indictment: "The LORD saw that the wickedness of man was great in the earth, and that every intention of the thoughts of his heart was only evil continually." As a result of human rebellion, human relationships are messed up, and everything from broken friendships and broken marriages to murder and oppression are the result. Everyone who lives in this fallen world is subject to suffering simply because of this innate propensity of fallen people to hurt each other.

The fall affected more than just human relationships, however. It disrupted the entire created order. Already in Genesis 3, God told Eve that her pain in childbearing would greatly increase, and he told Adam that his survival would depend on painful labor. Paul explained in Romans 8 that the entire creation was "subjected to futility," in "bondage to corruption," and "groaning together in the pains of childbirth" (Rom. 8:18–22). As a result of our rebellion, this world became a place of natural disasters, and our lives are now characterized by sickness and death. Earthquakes, hurricanes, tornados, droughts, floods, famines, landslides, cancer, heart disease, and the like all flow from the fact that this is a fallen world. These things strike the people of God and those who defy God alike. God never promises in his Word that his people will be exempt from any of these painful characteristics of a fallen world. In this world messed up by human sin, bad stuff happens to everyone.

Given the severity of sin, it is amazing that things are not worse. In the operations of common grace, God still provides blessings to the just and the unjust alike, and his Spirit restrains evil so that things do not get as bad as they could be. In his providential care, God also protects his people many times from disasters that could have happened. Every believer has testimony of ways that God has shielded them from potential harm, and most likely in heaven we will discover countless other times that God has protected us when we did not even realize it. However, he never promises that he will always protect us, and he is under no obligation to do so. Suffering happens simply because this is a fallen world. Some people experience less of it because of where they live, and part of this difference may be attributable to the impact of the Word of God on cultures over time. Everyone, however, is subject to the possibility of natural disasters or crime, everyone can get cancer or heart disease, and ultimately everyone dies. These forms of suffering come simply because the world is fallen, and they do not discriminate between believers and unbelievers.

SUFFERING FOR DOING WRONG

Suffering sometimes comes as a result of doing wrong. Some things are simply the natural consequences of disregarding God's directions. Alcoholism, drug abuse, and gluttony take their own natural toll on the human body. When someone commits a crime and gets caught, his or her subsequent punishment comes as a legal consequence of the wrongdoing. It is also true that in certain places in Scripture (such as the curses pronounced in Deut. 28), suffering and disaster are directly linked by God to disobedience to his commands. However, Scripture cautions us against making too quick a connection between a person's sin and his suffering. The book of Job, in particular, shatters this linkage. Job's friends were convinced that his troubles were somehow the result of some sin he had committed. Job protested otherwise, and in the end, God said that Job, and not his friends, had spoken correctly about this issue. Jesus rebuked the notion that a man who was born blind was being punished for some sin of his own or his parents (John 9:1–3), and when asked about two groups of people who died, one as a result of political oppression and the other as a result of a tower falling on them, he insisted that they were no worse sinners than others who had escaped those disasters. The safest thing that can be said is that wrongdoing does often have its own natural consequences, and God may use suffering as a wakeup call to people who are going the wrong way, but that it is seldom wise to assume that anyone who suffers is doing so because of a particular sin they have committed.

SUFFERING AS A CHRISTIAN

At this point, the thrust of Scripture runs directly counter to the cultural expectations of unreflective Western evangelicalism. The New Testament both assumes and states that suffering is a normal, expected part of what it means to follow Christ. Given what the Bible says about the fallen condition of the world, this should come as no surprise. In Jesus, God became a man and lived among us, and the world responded by murdering him. Far from seeking God, fallen humanity hates God and is trying to get away from him. Anyone who reminds rebellious sinners about the true God, or who exposes their self-righteousness for the sham that it is, incurs the same hatred that fell on Jesus. He made the connection clear: "Remember the word that I said to you: 'A servant is not greater than his master.' If they persecuted me, they will also persecute you" (John 15:20). They certainly persecuted him, so the conclusion should be obvious. In a world turned upside down by sin, it really is true that no good deed goes unpunished. Paul spelled it out when he said, "Indeed, all who desire to live a godly life in Christ Jesus will be persecuted" (2 Tim. 3:12). Under the inspiration of the Holy Spirit, he did not say "might be;" he said "will be." Suffering for the sake of Christ is even seen as a gift: "For it has been granted to you that for the sake of Christ you should not only believe in him but also suffer for his sake" (Phil. 1:29). The word here translated "granted" is from the *charis* word group in Greek, and could well be rendered "gifted." We are told that the apostles rejoiced that they were counted worthy of suffering for the name of Jesus (Acts 5:40–41). The churches in Jerusalem (Acts 8:1), Galatia (Gal. 3:4), Philippi (Phil. 1:29), Thessalonica (1 Thess. 2:14), and Asia Minor (1 Pet. 4:12) all experienced suffering, as did the recipients of the letter to the Hebrews (Heb. 10:32). Paul went through horrible suffering (2 Cor. 11:23–29), as did the other apostles (Acts 5–8). In Christian Scripture, the call to follow Christ is a call to abandon the safety, security, and comfort of this world in order to embrace the cross. This is not the picture of some extraordinary super-faith. This is the biblical picture of the normal life of the normal Christian.[1]

THE FELLOWSHIP OF CHRIST'S SUFFERINGS

Many of the references to suffering in the New Testament refer specifically to the suffering of Jesus. There is a strong sense in which these sufferings are unique to him. Only Jesus could suffer and die for the sins of the world. Only he, perfect God and perfect man, could suffer in our place to pay the penalty we deserved to pay. In that sense, Jesus suffered so that believers would not have to. Because he endured the wrath of God against our rebellion, those who trust in him will never have to face that wrath. No believer has ever suffered to make up for anyone's wrongdoing in the sight of God. The atoning death of Jesus is absolutely sufficient to pay for all the sins of everyone in every place and time who will ever trust in him. Nothing can be added to it.

However, Scripture tells us that those who trust in Christ are now themselves "in Christ." Through the indwelling Holy Spirit, believers now possess an intimate union with Jesus. Many incredible blessings flow to the people of God through this union with their Savior. This same union also unites them to his ongoing suffering in the world, not in the work of atonement but in the experience of the world's opposition to his holiness and love. Part of what it means to be "in Christ" is to share in the fellowship of his sufferings. Paul links knowing Christ and the power of his resurrection with sharing in his sufferings, as though they were a package deal (Phil. 3:10). He tells the Corinthians, "As we share abundantly in Christ's sufferings, so through Christ we

[1] For further reading on suffering in light of God's reign, see John Piper and Justin Taylor, eds., *Suffering and the Sovereignty of God* (Wheaton: Crossway, 2006).

share abundantly in comfort too" (2 Cor. 1:5). Peter echoes this same theme, saying, "Rejoice insofar as you share Christ's sufferings, that you may also rejoice and be glad when his glory is revealed" (1 Pet. 4:13). In Romans 8:17, Paul goes so far as to say that believers are "heirs of God and fellow heirs with Christ, provided we suffer with him in order that we may also be glorified with him." Suffering with Christ is so intimately connected with ultimate enjoyment of his glory that the two things cannot be separated. Unless Paul contradicts what he says elsewhere, this cannot mean that those sufferings are somehow salvific, but it does seem to demonstrate that suffering with Christ is such a normal part of being in Christ that Paul cannot conceive of one without the other.

In Colossians 1:24, Paul says, "Now I rejoice in my sufferings for your sake, and in my flesh I am filling up what is lacking in Christ's afflictions for the sake of his body, that is, the church." It is startling for us to hear Paul talking about anything being lacking in the afflictions of Christ until we realize that the word he uses here is never used of the atoning suffering of Jesus. Paul is not saying that he is contributing to the saving work of Christ in dying for our sins. Rather, this affliction of Christ is his experience, in union with his body on earth, of their affliction as his people in a hostile world. Apparently there is a full measure of such affliction that will be experienced by God's people before the end of the age, and Paul sees his own suffering as contributing to that measure. Such is the closeness of Christ's union with his people that their sufferings are his sufferings and his sufferings are theirs.

Does this mean that comfortable, affluent Christians in the West should go out and try to provoke persecution or intentionally afflict themselves with ascetic practices? No. Asceticism is useless as an instrument in sanctification (Col. 2:23), and believers are not commanded to seek out persecution. However, their condition should alarm them. It is dangerous and abnormal. They need particularly to beware the seductions of respectability and prosperity. They need to beware the subtle idolatry of making Jesus a means to the end of their own enjoyment of this life. They need to beware the worldliness of setting their hearts on things below and valuing possessions and health and security more than the glory of Christ. They need to examine themselves honestly and often to see if the desire to maintain their lifestyle has induced them to compromise their obedience in any way. They need to cultivate the mindset of readiness to lose anything and everything at a moment's notice for the sake of the surpassing value of Christ. Affluence and safety are dangerous conditions in which to be a disciple of Jesus, and those who live in them need to exercise special diligence. The normal condition of a follower of Christ is to share in the fellowship of his sufferings, and those who do not always need to ask themselves why they are not.

SUFFERING AND THE ADVANCE OF THE GOSPEL

Advancing the gospel is a hazardous enterprise. Those who take the light of Christ into the darkness of a rebellious world seem to experience an intensified level of suffering. This was certainly Paul's experience. At the very beginning of his Christian life, when Ananias was sent to Paul in Damascus to restore his sight, God linked a description of his missionary calling with these words: "For I will show him how much he must suffer for the sake of my name" (Acts 9:16). Paul understood that link, and he expressed it to Timothy at the end of his life when he described the gospel and said of it, "For which I was appointed a preacher and apostle and teacher, which is why I suffer as I do" (2 Tim. 1:11–12). Lest anyone think that this connection between suffering and the service of the gospel was unique to the apostles, Paul applied it to Timothy as well: "Share in suffering as a good soldier of Christ Jesus" (2 Tim. 2:3). Indeed, so close was this connection that Paul actually uses "share in suffering for the Gospel" where the context clearly indicates that he is talking about sharing in the work of the Gospel (2 Tim. 1:6–9).

This pattern has continued down to the present. Those who take the gospel where it has never before been heard have always been the particular targets of opposition and suffering. David Garrison, in *Church Planting Movements*, lists missionary suffering as one of the leading characteristics in most places where God has moved in extraordinary ways.[2] This should come as no surprise. The world, the devil, and our own flesh are all opposed to the work of God. Those who take the gospel where Christ is not yet known must do so with their eyes wide open to what may lie ahead. Furthermore, the church in the West must embrace the truth that the gospel is worth any price God may ask us to pay, and abandon its instinctive aversion to discomfort or danger. The Great Commission will not be fulfilled without suffering.[3] If one part of the body of Christ demonstrates that it is not willing to pay that kind of price, God will pass over them and use those whose values are more in line with his.

BIBLICAL WORLDVIEW AND SUFFERING

So far, this discussion has been pretty somber. Does all of this mean that biblical Christianity is some sort of grim asceticism? By no means! As C. S. Lewis put it, God is a hedonist at heart.[4] There are eternal pleasures at his right hand (Ps. 16:11). The Christian life is a matter of "joy that is inexpressible and filled with glory" (1 Pet. 1:8). Even in speaking of the suffering of Jesus, we are told that he endured the cross "for the joy that was set before

---

[2]   David Garrison, *Church Planting Movements* (Midlothian, VA: WIGTake Resources, 2004), 235–38.

[3]   For further reading on suffering and gospel advance, see John Piper, *Let the Nations Be Glad: The Supremacy of God in Missions*, 3rd ed. (Grand Rapids: Baker, 2010), 93–131; and J. Dudley Woodberry, ed. *From Seed to Fruit* (Pasadena: William Carey, 2008), especially chapter 24.

[4]   C. S. Lewis, *Screwtape Letters* (San Francisco: HarperCollins, 2001), 118.

him" (Heb. 12:2). Biblical Christianity does not value suffering for its own sake. It is simply a matter of a transformed value system. For the sake of real treasure, the believer is willing to let go of lesser things like possessions, temporal comfort and security, or even this life. The point is not what you lose. The point is the surpassing value of what you gain.

Paul summarized this perspective in his letter to the Philippians. In the context of talking about the possibility that he might be executed for his faith, Paul says, "For to me to live is Christ, and to die is gain" (Phil. 1:21). His greatest treasure in this life was to know Christ. The benefit gained in death was to be with Christ, which he regards as far better than anything this life can provide (Phil. 1:23). Either way, Christ is everything. He is the treasure hidden in the field worth selling everything to obtain (Matt. 13:44). He is himself the most precious thing that has ever existed on this earth. He is true life, true joy, true peace, and true satisfaction. In him the believer has forgiveness of sin, new birth, reconciliation with God, adoption into God's family, the gift of the Holy Spirit, progressive transformation into the image of Christ, and the guarantee of eternal life in the infinite joy and glory of God's presence. This is real treasure, and it is treasure that cannot be lost. All the things that the world values—possessions, comfort, health, and even life itself—are things that everyone will eventually lose. What rational person holds on as long as they can to things they must eventually lose, at the expense of things of far greater value that they can never lose? Seen from the perspective of God's truth, the truly sane person is the one who endures whatever temporal losses go along with genuine, eternal treasure. Once believers grasp the incredible value of Christ and his gospel, and the comparatively small and passing value of the good things of this life, they can see with the same eyes as Paul, who after all that he went through could write, "For this light momentary affliction is preparing for us an eternal weight of glory beyond all comparison, as we look not to the things that are seen but to the things that are unseen. For the things that are seen are transient, but the things that are unseen are eternal" (2 Cor. 4:17–18).

The problem, of course, is that what we can see is immediate and seductive, while what we cannot see can only be grasped by faith. Those who have a lot of good things that they can see here and now often have the hardest time grasping the superior value of what they cannot yet see. Most people, of course, would prefer to have their cake and eat it, too. They would rather enjoy the good things of this life *and* the better things of the life to come. In his wisdom, however, God knows that we cannot serve two masters (Matt. 6:24). He does not call on his children to renounce all possessions or pleasures, and he certainly does not command them to seek suffering for its own sake. Everything he created is good, including possessions and pleasures rightly used. He does, however, call on his children to look at things rationally. He calls on them to value that which is infinitely and eternally valuable over that which is small and temporary. He calls on them to invest what they have in this life in the things of the next. He calls on them to recognize that they are not their own, but that they live only by his grace and only for his glory. Once that perspective is attained, the call to endure suffering for the sake of the gospel ceases to be grim news and becomes a reasonable part of our joyful calling in Christ.

Christians who have grasped the worldview mind-set of the Bible embrace suffering for Christ because he is intrinsically worth it. In him they have found the greatest treasure in the world, and in comparison to him all the attractions and comforts of the world seem like tinsel-covered dung. With Paul, they can honestly say, "Indeed, I count everything as loss because of the surpassing worth of knowing Christ Jesus my Lord. For his sake I have suffered the loss of all things and count them as rubbish, in order that I may gain Christ" (Phil. 3:8). The stuff of this world just is not worth it, and Jesus is.

BENEFITS OF SUFFERING

Suffering for Jesus is worthwhile because he is so much greater than anything lost in the process. In addition, there are certain benefits that accrue to the believer through suffering. One of those benefits is that suffering tests and demonstrates whether faith is real or not. Jesus, in his parable of the four soils, speaks of those who give a superficial reception to the gospel, but who put down no roots in it. When persecution or trouble comes, they quickly fall away, showing that their faith was never real to begin with (Matt. 13:20–21). On the other hand, speaking to believers who had endured through suffering, Peter wrote, "You have been grieved by various trials, so that the tested genuineness of your faith—more precious than gold that perishes though it is tested by fire—may be found to result in praise and glory and honor at the revelation of Jesus Christ" (1 Pet. 1:6–7).

Another benefit of suffering is that it is an ally in the fight against sin. Later in his first letter, Peter writes, "Since therefore Christ suffered in the flesh, arm yourselves with the same way of thinking, for whoever has suffered in the flesh has ceased from sin" (1 Pet. 4:1). Suffering is not to be sought out, like the medieval ascetics, in the hopes that intentional self-punishment can do away with sin. However, when it comes, it is often used by God to make Christ more attractive and the world less attractive, and thus to help in the fight for holiness.

Suffering helps to shape the character of the believer in the image of Jesus. In a famous passage, Paul wrote, "We rejoice in our sufferings, knowing that suffering produces endurance, and endurance produces character, and character produces hope" (Rom. 5:3–4). As rigorous training shapes the body of an athlete and makes it fit for sports, so suffering shapes the character of a Christian and makes it fit for service.

Finally, suffering provides an opportunity for the believer to experience God's power. Paul grasped this when he said, "For the sake of Christ, then, I am content with weaknesses, insults, hardships, persecutions, and calamities. For when I am weak, then I am strong" (2 Cor. 12:10). God's strength is vastly greater than ours, but we are most likely to experience it when we come to the end of our own resources and rely on him alone.

RESPONDING TO SUFFERING

How should a Christian respond when suffering comes along? First, we should not be surprised. "Beloved, do not be surprised at the fiery trial when it comes upon you to test you, as though something strange were happening to you" (1 Pet. 4:12). Western culture may instill the expectation that life should be easy, but the Bible clearly indicates otherwise, especially for Christians. We should not be caught off guard or thrown off balance by suffering. God has told us to expect it.

Second, we are to patiently endure whatever suffering comes our way, without compromising our integrity in Christ. The New Testament sounds this theme over and over again. To give just a couple of examples, Paul tells Timothy, "As for you, always be sober-minded, endure suffering, do the work of an evangelist, fulfill your ministry" (2 Tim. 4:5). Peter says, "For this is a gracious thing, when, mindful of God, one endures sorrows while suffering unjustly" (1 Pet. 2:19). Our fleshly temptation is to make whatever compromises are necessary to make the suffering go away. God calls us to endure patiently.

Third, we are to love those who persecute us and pray for their welfare (Matt. 5:43–47). We are to take no revenge on those who wrong us (Rom. 12:14,17,19–21). Both our flesh and the world around us urge us to assert ourselves, but we are to respond to the human instruments of our suffering like Jesus, who loved the very people who killed him.

Fourth, we are to trust God in the midst of our suffering and respond by proactively doing good. "Let those who suffer according to God's will entrust their souls to a faithful Creator while doing good" (1 Pet. 4:19). The outcome of our suffering is in God's hands, and we can entrust that outcome to him. He may deliver us by bringing us home to be with him, but he will never leave us nor forsake us. Nothing can snatch us out of his hands or separate us from his love. Our job, then, is to repay evil with good. We are to leave the consequences to God and be proactive in doing the work of his kingdom in the face of whatever comes our way. We need to beware of the very real temptation to go into survival mode, and instead remain active in advancing his glory.

We are to use our experiences of suffering to comfort others who suffer. Paul discusses this at some length in the first chapter of his second letter to the Corinthians. Far from making us bitter or hardened, suffering should make us tenderhearted toward others in their afflictions.

We are to fix our eyes on Jesus (Heb. 12:1–3). This may be the most crucial response of all. Our flesh will always recoil from suffering. The world will always tell us we are crazy for getting ourselves into it in the first place. Only by maintaining a biblical perspective on the surpassing value of Jesus will we be able to endure patiently, while blessing our persecutors, comforting others who suffer, and actively continuing in the work of God's kingdom. This requires concentration in prayer and in the study of God's Word. This also requires the encouragement and challenge of others in the body of Christ, unless we find ourselves involuntarily cut off from other believers. Only in Christ can suffering be not only endured but redeemed into something that glorifies God and does us good.

Finally, we are even commanded to rejoice. Peter tells us, "Rejoice insofar as you share Christ's sufferings" (1 Pet. 4:13). This seems insane to the world, but it was the spontaneous reaction of the apostles, who rejoiced that they had been counted worthy to suffer for his sake (Acts 5:41). Joy like this can only come in the power of the Holy Spirit, from minds that have fully grasped the surpassing value of Christ, in lives that have their eyes fixed habitually on Christ. Only in him can joy in the midst of suffering make sense.

CONCLUSION

An essay like this is hard to write. If I have given the impression that I have already attained to all that I commend here to others, it is a very misleading impression indeed. Compared to my brothers and sisters in the persecuted church, I have hardly suffered at all. I still find the prospect of suffering and persecution intimidating. From reading the Word of God, and from talking to brothers who have endured much for the sake of the kingdom, I have learned one thing, however. God gives grace when it is needed. "Let us then with confidence draw near to the throne of grace, that we may receive mercy and find grace to help in time of need" (Heb. 4:16). He does not necessarily give it ahead of time. He does not give me the grace now that I might need to face something that may or may not happen in the future. However, at the moment of need, he is always faithful. In that confidence, we need to repudiate the fears of our flesh and the lies of the world, and endure suffering as good soldiers of Jesus Christ.

Chapter Sixteen

MISSION TO MUSLIMS

Theodore A. Curry

INTRODUCTION

This book presupposes that the Bible's redemptive narrative provides the clue to understanding its overarching message. It communicates its depiction of reality in the one form that is commonly understood across all cultures regardless of time or place—story. Story is so fundamental to the Bible that most of its major teachings, both doctrinally and ethically, are developed within the context of stories. Indeed, if one is to properly comprehend the Bible's teaching on the triune nature of God, the incarnation, the atonement, the church, eschatology, or ethics, these must be understood within the context of their organic relationship to the story narrated in the Bible and its redemptive theme. That story is ultimate, and it is the one story that envelops every aspect of cosmic history and human existence on earth.[1]

As Christians, we recognize that God has called us to live within that story, in conscious relation to it. God is fulfilling his promise to Abraham in Genesis that through his seed, peoples from every tribe and nation on earth will be blessed and redeemed.[2] This promise is being fulfilled among Muslim peoples, as unprecedented numbers of Muslims have embraced Christ in the

---

[1]   In addition to the opening chapter of this text, the most recent work to explore this theme in depth is Christopher J. H. Wright, *The Mission of God: Unlocking the Bible's Grand Narrative* (Downers Grove: IVP Academic, 2006). The expressions "grand biblical narrative" and "metanarrative" are used interchangeably throughout this essay to refer to the overarching story the Bible tells of the cosmos encapsulated by the four plot moves: creation, fall, redemption, and restoration.

[2]   See Gen. 3:15; 12:3; 18:18; 22:18; 26:4; 28:14; 2 Sam. 7:12–13; Matt. 1:1; Gal. 3:8,14,16, 19,29; Rev. 5:9; 7:9.

past century. The gospel is being proclaimed among Muslim peoples across the globe, including North Africa, the Middle East, Central Asia, South Asia, and the Pacific Rim. In light of this gospel advance, the present chapter will explore how the Bible's redemptive narrative relates to mission among Muslims. In so doing, the goal is to better equip Christians to proclaim the story of God's redeeming plan for all people through Jesus and invite Muslims to participate.[3]

THE STORY OF CHRISTIAN-MUSLIM ENCOUNTER IN HISTORICAL PERSPECTIVE

The early period. When Muslim armies spread out of Arabia in the seventh century and began conquering areas formerly controlled by the Byzantine and Persian Empires, Christians were subjugated under the rule of a system and faith that challenged the very foundations of their beliefs. Their responses soon took definitive form as they learned more about the message proclaimed by their Muslim occupiers. Writing in Greek during the early Islamic period, John of Damascus (d. 749) adopted a strongly polemical approach to Islam, deriding Muhammad as an Arian and the Qur'an as a ridiculous composition of superstitions.[4] The early Syriac Fathers generally followed course, producing treatises that challenged the burgeoning prophetology shaped by Muslim scholars during this time.[5] They also urged their followers to resist the temptation to convert under increasing social and religious pressure. Christian theologians writing in Arabic in the early Islamic period, like Theodore Abu Qurra (d. 830), sought to frame the presentation of the gospel in terms familiar to Muslims, even going so far as to adopt certain qur'anic phrases and concepts. In the West, Francis of Assisi (d. 1226) and later Ramon Lull (d. 1315/16) advocated peaceful means of bringing the gospel to Muslims when many were urging Crusades against them. Lull authored treatises in Latin and Arabic wherein he rooted his defense of the faith in the eternal love God experiences in the Trinity.[6] Thus, from the beginning Christians developed a range of approaches to Islam. Some were more conciliatory while others were highly contentious. Of central concern in all of these early approaches, whether in Greek, Syriac, Arabic, or Latin, was a theological response to the Qur'an's critique of the Trinity and incarnation.[7]

---

[3] Unless noted otherwise, what is written here is equally applicable to all major sects of Islam including Sunnis and Shiites.

[4] For more see Daniel J. Sahas, *John of Damascus on Islam: The "Heresy of the Ishmaelites"* (Leiden: Brill, 1972).

[5] On the Islamic view of the biblical prophets, see Robert Tottoli, *Biblical Prophets in the Qur'ān and Muslim Literature,* trans. Michael Robertson (Richmond, Surrey, UK: Curzon, 2002).

[6] For more see J. Scott Bridger, "Raymond Lull: Medieval Theologian, Philosopher, and Missionary to Muslims," *St. Francis Magazine* 5:1 (2009): 1–25.

[7] For a discussion of the various genres and strategies employed by Christians in defense of the gospel during the early Islamic period, see Sidney H. Griffith, *The Church in the Shadow*

Tawḥīd, belief in the monadic unity of God, was perceived as the fundamental difference between Christianity and Islam. Soon both Christian and Muslim theologians formulated apologetic strategies in response to the other's faith that centered on the doctrine of God's unity and the defense or denial of the incarnation.

Contemporary approaches. The general contours of the responses developed by Christians and Muslims during this early period continue to dominate Christian–Muslim interaction today. It is rare to find a book on Christianity and Islam without some mention of the difference in their conceptions of God's unity. But there are two problems with missional approaches to Muslims that begin by focusing on Christian doctrines like the Trinity, Incarnation, or Jesus as the eternal, pre-existent "Word of God." First, they tend to isolate and abstract these doctrines from the narrative context within which they are progressively revealed throughout Scripture. Second, they fail to appreciate the "juridical" (and ethical) lenses through which Muslims evaluate Christianity and indeed all of life. If Christians are to properly evaluate Islam and communicate biblical truth to the Muslim mind, they must take their cue from the Bible's narrative structure. Doing so will enable them to better understand points of contact with, and divergence from, the Muslim worldview. Furthermore, this will ensure that the communicative strategy adopted for sharing the gospel with Muslims remains relevant. God's purpose in bringing Muslims to faith in Christ is to display his glory and magnificence through them. He is calling them out in order that they might faithfully embody the message of the gospel of the kingdom in their particular time and place until he ushers in the fullness of his kingdom.

THE METANARRATIVE OF ISLAM

Islam claims to be the final revelation of God to all of humanity. This belief is rooted in an understanding of revelation and prophecy peculiar to Islam. At the heart of that view is belief in the miraculous nature of the Qur'an, a book viewed as so miraculous that it is rendered inherently untranslatable by many.[8] Contrary to the Bible, which Christians believe is inherently translatable since it is a message God intends all people to hear in their own language, some Muslims actually boast about the difficulty in understanding the Arabic of the Qur'an.[9] This view has the practical consequence of

---

of the Mosque: Christians and Muslims in the World of Islam (Princeton, NJ: Princeton, 2008), especially pages 75–105.

[8] This sentiment is echoed in Falzur Rahman, *Major Themes of the Qur'an* (Chicago: Bibliotheca Islamica, 1980), 105.

[9] The inherent "translatableness" of the gospel message is a theme taken frequently in the works of Lamin Sanneh, a convert from Islam to Christianity. He sees this as one of the fundamental differences between the two faiths. See Lamin Sanneh, *Translating the Message: The Missionary Impact on Culture* (Maryknoll, NY: Orbis, 1989).

silencing anyone who might make an argument about the Qur'an by appealing to the Muslim's superior knowledge of Arabic.

Muslims claim that Islam is the final revelation from God, necessary because the Jews and Christians had corrupted previous revelations. Sura 3:3 notes, "He has sent down unto you [Muhammad] the book [i.e., the Qur'an] in truth, confirming that which was sent down beforehand in the Torah and Gospel."[10] As this verse makes clear, the Qur'an's self-understanding is that it is a continuation of the revelation present in the Torah and the Gospel (i.e., the New Testament).[11] It also assumes the primary mode for the reception of divine revelation is dictation, something which slants the Muslim evaluation of the Bible. Therefore, in order to understand Islam's self-description as the "final" revelation, it is important to understand how Islam conceives of all the "prior revelations" given to humanity by the prophets.

Creation, fall, and the primordial law. Islam's self-appointment as a monotheistic religion in the Abrahamic tradition means that there is a resemblance in many of the beliefs both traditions affirm. One of those is that God created the heavens and the earth *ex nihilo* in six days. Another is that God created humanity from the dust of the earth (or clay, *ṣalṣāl*; according to the Qur'an). Both depict Adam and Eve eating from a tree in the Garden and subsequently being punished. However, upon closer examination of the details surrounding the fall of humanity the differences are severe. Part of that narrative is found in Sura 20:115–24:

> In the beginning we made a covenant with Adam, but he forgot and we found in him no constancy. Then we said to the angels, "Prostrate yourselves before Adam," and they all prostrated themselves except the Devil for he refused. So we said to Adam, "O Adam! Indeed, this is an enemy to you and your wife. Do not let him expel you from the Garden causing you to toil. You need not go hungry or go naked, nor should you thirst or be exposed to the sun." But Satan whispered to him saying, "O Adam, shall I lead you to the Tree of Eternity and a Kingdom that never decays?" So they both ate from the tree and their misdeeds were shown to them. Then they sewed together leaves for themselves from the Garden. So it was that Adam rebelled against his Lord and was tempted. Then his Lord turned to him and relented, giving him guidance. Then he said to them both: "Go down together in enmity both of you [from the Garden]. However, surely guidance comes to you from me, and whoever follows my guidance will not be led astray nor experience strife. But whoever turns away from remembrance of me shall have a precarious existence, and we shall raise him up blind on the Day of Resurrection.

In his analysis of the two metanarratives of the Bible and Islam, Miller draws four conclusions from these passages that help one understand their differences.[12] First, the language used to describe Adam's sin in the Qur'an's

---

[10] All translations from the Qur'an are the author's.

[11] See the discussion below on the qur'anic view of the various parts of the Bible.

[12] Duane Alexander Miller, "Narrative and Metanarrative in Christianity and Islam," *St. Francis Magazine* (June 2010). I am thankful to Mr. Miller for allowing me to read his article prior to publication.

rendition of the story is weaker than that found in the Bible. Second, the results of Adam's sin are quite different from those found in Genesis 3:16–19. Third, while there is a focus on Adam, the whole narrative is prefaced by a discussion of the devil's sin in refusing to prostrate before Adam. Miller notes that this makes the fall, as narrated in the Qur'an, appear as a contest between God and Satan. Finally, the notion of "guidance" (*hudā*) comes to dominate the entire Islamic metanarrative.

The net result is that Islam offers a very different interpretation of the creation narrative compared to that found in the Bible. This leads to a very different estimation regarding the condition of human nature after the fall and a very different solution to humanity's problem. In Islam, humanity's "fall" is attributed to ignorance (*jahl*) and self-deception or moral laxity (*ghurūr*).[13] God punishes humanity by casting them out of the Garden, which is seemingly situated somewhere beyond the earth. But there is no indication that anything radical has happened to human nature or creation. He sends them to earth where they are told that if they follow God's guidance (*hudā*) and remember him, they will be preserved.

In the Bible, human sin has disastrous consequences. It ruptures the harmony that existed between humans, creation, and God. Death, destruction, and decay are all introduced into the natural order as a result of human rebellion. What was created good has now been marred by sin. Human illness, death, and natural disasters are all traceable to the fall and its consequences. But in the midst of God's pronouncement of judgment, he also gives humanity the promise of redemption. However, it will come at a price as Genesis 3:15 suggests. Already in the Garden humans were introduced to the notion that a bloody sacrifice is needed to cover their shame. God provided this for Adam and Eve when he replaced the leaves they used to cover their nakedness with skins ostensibly taken from animals God himself sacrificed (Gen. 3:21).

Christianity and Islam envision two very different solutions to human rebellion. Christianity presupposes something radical has taken place in the created order and necessitates a radical intervention by God himself in order for humanity's relationship with him to be restored. Islam assumes that humanity's relationship with God remains basically intact and that no major rupture has taken place. All that one needs is to follow God's guidance. These contrasting solutions, "redemption" in the Bible and "guidance" in Islam, are at the heart of the differing conceptions of revelation and the role of prophets found in the two traditions. For Muslims, guidance forms the essence of the primordial law given to humanity in order to rightly guide them on the straight path. Some even interpret the Muslim testimony, the *shahāda*, "there is no God but Allah," as "there is no legislator but the Legislator."[14] Thus, much like the theme of redemption in the Bible, guidance through divine law forms the lens one needs to evaluate Islam in the proper light.

---

[13] On ignorance see Q 3:154; 48:26. On self-deception see Q 8:49; 31:33; 35:5; 67:20.

[14] Gai Eaton, *Islam and the Destiny of Man* (Albany, NY: George Allen & Unwin, 1985), 164.

Prophecy and revelation. According to Islam, God has used messengers throughout history to convey his laws to humankind whether they are mentioned in the Qur'an or not (Q 4:164–66; 40:78). Conceiving of divine revelation as the conveyance of laws to prophets assumes something about the capacity of humanity to receive and understand those laws. The Qur'an teaches that when God created humanity he imparted to them the innate ability (*fiṭra*) to know and obey the laws given by his prophets. Thus, Islam has no doctrine on human depravity or incapacity to follow Allah's law.

Adam was the first prophet in Islam who, according to Muslim tradition, received laws that God wanted him to follow. He was no different in that respect from the many other prophets throughout history. Indeed, some Muslims believe there have been over 124,000 prophets throughout human history.[15] Over time, however, Muslim theologians came to distinguish between those who were given a distinct message (*risāla*) apart from a book containing a revealed law (*sharī'a*). Moses, Jesus, and Muhammad are given the title of messengers (*rasūl* pl. *rusul*) since they all brought books (*kutub*)—the Torah, the Gospel, and Qur'an.[16] Those who simply acted as bearers of good news and forewarners of judgment without being given any type of divinely inspired book are called prophets (*nabī* pl. *anbiya'*) (Q 6:48).

Two characteristics are important to keep in mind regarding the Islamic conception of prophecy and divine revelation. First, Muslims believe that the prophets' basic message has been constant since the beginning. "All Messengers have preached essentially the same message, that there is one, unique God to Whom alone service and worship are due."[17] That basic message from time immemorial has been belief in the monadic unity of God (*tawhīd*) and submission (*islām*) to his will. Additionally, these laws were marked by a distinct ethical agenda that was given to humanity in order "to implement an ethically-based social order." Muhammad was the last of these messengers, and his message above all "has to be accepted by man and implemented."[18]

Second, Muslims believe the message of the Qur'an is essentially ahistorical. "The Koran is not concerned to demonstrate a historical succession of apostles and prophets but rather to highlight the unity of revelation transcending history, regardless of when and how it was proclaimed. No distinctions are made among the apostles and prophets and their revelations: All believe in God, his angels, his scriptures and his apostles (Q 3:84)."[19] This belief

---

[15] Crone cites al-Tabari as a source for this belief. See Patricia Crone, *God's Rule: Government and Islam: Six Centuries of Medieval Islamic Political Thought* (New York: Columbia University, 2004), 10.

[16] See Q 4:163. David is attributed with having received the Zabur (i.e., the Psalms). The Qur'an frequently refers to the Bible by the tripartite division of Torah, Zabur, and Injil (i.e., the Pentateuch, Psalms, and New Testament). These make up the substance of the "prior revelations."

[17] Rahman, *Themes*, 83.

[18] Ibid.

[19] Abdoldjavad Falaturi, "Experience of Time and History in Islam," in *We Believe in One God: The Experience of God in Christianity and Islam*, ed. Annemarie Schimmel and Abdoldjavad Falaturi (New York: Seabury, 1979), 66.

manifests itself in Islam's appropriation and reinterpretation of the narratives of several biblical figures. Of particular interest in this regard is Abraham. Unlike in Genesis 12, where God chooses to reveal himself to Abraham, the Qur'an posits that Abraham arrived at his belief in *tawhīd* on his own (Q 2:260; 6:76). It is for this reason that he is considered a prophet *par excellence* in Islam and the "original monotheist" (*hanīf*). Yet what is immediately apparent to someone familiar with the story of the Bible is that the Qur'an lacks the narrative details surrounding God's promise to Abraham in Genesis 12:3. No mention is made of Abraham's role in being the source of blessing to all tribes and peoples. Instead, the Qur'an offers its revelation as a "proof" (*bayyina*) to Jews and Christians regarding the original message of *tawhīd* (Q 98:1–5). As a consequence, the qur'anic reinterpretation of the biblical narratives is a mere torso, lacking the redemptive context and narrative details that enables one to properly understand the significance of biblical figures like Abraham, Moses, and Jesus. But this serves a very important function in later Islamic tradition and theology as Rahman notes: "This . . . unshakable assurance (*bayyina*) is such that on its basis the religious personalities of the Old Testament are dissociated from Jewish and Christian communities and claimed for Islam—just as, all prophets have been Muslims: 'Or, do you say that Abraham, Ishmael, Isaac, Jacob, and the [prophets of the] Tribes were Jews or Christian? Do *you* know better, or God?' (2:140)."[20] The Qur'an's explicit goal is to detach these biblical figures from their narrative context within the Bible. And this detachment serves to subvert the biblical narrative and its message of redemption. These two characteristics define how Muslims evaluate the Bible and its progressively revealed story of redemption. They also explain why Muslims developed the doctrine of the Bible's corruption and the sufficiency and finality of the Qur'an.[21]

The story of Shari'a Law. Islamic law is viewed as an all-encompassing way of regulating every aspect of human society and life, including familial relations, education, economics, and politics. As Nasr notes, "Divine Law

---

[20] Rahman, *Themes*, 101. Italics in the original.
[21] The Qur'an itself makes no accusation toward the Bible of textual corruption (*tahrīf lafzī*). Rather it accuses Jews and Christians of interpretive corruption (*tahrīf ma'nawī*). Nevertheless, the belief that Jews and Christians intentionally altered the very words of their sacred texts became a standard part of the Islamic narrative by the eleventh century. The reasons for this varied, but the bottom line appears to be the wide-scale rejection of Muhammad as a prophet by Jews and Christians. Muhammad's prophethood became the standard by which all other religions were evaluated. And since the Bible tells a very different story about the nature of the world, the purpose of God's sending of messengers, and the content of their message, Islam slowly developed an alternative narrative that sought to subvert the biblical narrative through the accusation of corruption. This distinct Islamic narrative was shaped over the course of at least two centuries and was constructed in a "sectarian milieu" (i.e., Muslim interaction with Jews and Christians). See John E. Wansbrough, *The Sectarian Milieu: Content and Composition of Islamic Salvation History* (Oxford: Oxford University, 1978). For more on the development of the Islamic doctrine of the Bible's corruption and an attempt by one modern Muslim scholar to rectify the unsustainable Muslim position toward the Bible, see Saeed Abdallah, "The Charge of Distortion of Jewish and Christian Scriptures," *The Muslim World* 92 (2002): 419–36.

embraces every aspect of life and removes the distinction between sacred and profane or religious and secular. Since God is the creator of all things, there is no legitimate domain of life to which his Will or his Laws do not apply."[22] In the Muslim view, humanity's problem is a lack of divine guidance, and this can easily be rectified through the imposition of a divine code of laws. Adam was given a set of laws, as were Moses and Jesus. The final version of these laws was given to Muhammad, who through his life and sayings exemplified how it is that man can live in obedience to this divine code.

The *sunna* refers to the "right practice" or "sacred custom" of Muhammad and is composed of various reports (*akhbār*), sayings (*ḥadīth* pl. *aḥādīth*), and traditions regarding what he said and did.[23] Technically, the *ḥadīth* is the documentation of Muhammad's *sunna*, i.e., his practice.[24] It forms the first and most authoritative commentary on the Qur'an. The *sunna* includes a myriad of traditions and customs covering every conceivable arena of life, reporting Muhammad's ritual, economic dealings, manner of greeting people, and even such details as how he cleaned his orifices (*istinja' wa istibra'*).[25]

The *sharī'a*, as it is usually conceived today, did not begin to take definitive shape until well after the death of Muhammad when his sayings were collected and recorded. Muslims refer to the two most famous collections of *ḥadīth* as the two "sound ones" or *ṣaḥīḥs* by Bukhari (d. 870) and Muslim (d. 875). Sunnis eventually came to recognize six canonical collections of *ḥadīth*, all of which were selected from a multitude of sayings by these ninth-century scholars.[26] Once they were recognized as canonical, they were "elevated to the rank of decisive sources for ascertaining the Prophet's *sunna*."[27]

Parallel with the movement to record the purported sayings of Muhammad was another movement. Muslim jurists called *fuqahā'* (sing. *faqīh*) sought to develop a unified methodology that would govern how the various statutes of Islamic law were ascertained and applied. Al-Shafi'i (d. 820) set the principles that led to the codification of the sacred law followed by the four main Sunni schools of Islamic law recognized today.[28] His primary principle was that "nothing can override the authority of the Prophet, even if

---

[22] Seyyed Hossein Nasr, *The Heart of Islam: Enduring Values for Humanity* (New York: HarperCollins, 2004), 119.

[23] For a survey of the positions of critical scholarship over the past 150 years toward the traditional Muslim narrative regarding the reliability of the various "sound" chains of *ḥadīth* transmitters (*isnād*), see Fred M. Donner, *Narratives of Islamic Origins: The Beginnings of Islamic Historical Writing* (Princeton: Darwin, 1998), 1–31.

[24] Ignaz Goldziher, *Introduction to Islamic Theology and Law* (Princeton: Princeton University, 1981), 39.

[25] See http://www.islamicshariah.co.uk/Tahara/11.Istinja.htm.

[26] These scholars developed an intricate system of determining true or "sound" sayings from fabricated ones. In addition to Bukhari and Muslim, there are the collections by Abu Dawud (d. 888), al-Nasa'i (d. 915), al-Tirmidhi (d. 892), and Ibn Maja (d. 886).

[27] Goldziher, *Introduction to Islamic Theology and Law*, 39.

[28] While a number of different schools (*madhhab* pl. *madhāhib*) have existed throughout Islamic history, only four have survived in the Sunni world today (Hanafi, Maliki, Shafi'i, and

it be attested only by an isolated tradition, and that every well-authenticated tradition going back to the Prophet has precedence over the opinions of his Companions, their Successors, and later authorities."[29] Al-Shafi'i's position necessitated having a codified set of *ḥadīth* that could be attributable to Muhammad, and it highlights the fact that this was not yet the case during his lifetime in the ninth century.[30]

Muslims believe that Islamic law, when properly interpreted and applied, will enable all of humanity to live in harmony with God's will. They believe that the whole of what is known as Islam today, including the Qur'an and *sharī'a*, was delivered to humanity in pristine form during Muhammad's lifetime and codified shortly thereafter. Muhammad and the early Islamic community, which existed in Medina from roughly 622 to 632, provide the model for how subsequent societies are to operate.[31]

At the heart of the Islamic philosophy of law is the absence of any differentiation between natural law, ethical statues, or the basic customs and traditions promulgated by the early Muslim community and exemplified in the life of Muhammad.[32] Natural law refers to certain truths about God, the world, and basic moral principles which are accessible to all people in all times and places. And it is something clearly taught in Scripture (cf. Rom.

Hanbali). They are named after their founders: Abu Hanifa (d. 767), Malik ibn Anas (d. 795), al-Shafi'i (d. 820), and Ahmad ibn Hanbal (d. 855).

[29] Joseph Schacht, *The Origins of Muhammadan Jurisprudence* (Oxford: Clarendon, 1953), 11–20.

[30] For a more recent and comprehensive treatment of Islamic law, see Michael Cook, *Commanding Right and Forbidding Wrong in Islamic Thought* (Cambridge: Cambridge University, 2000), particularly pages 561–84 where he discusses the origins and foreign influences on Islamic law. Al-Shafi'i identified four sources and methods for ascertaining Islamic law: the Qur'an, the *sunna*, the consensus of faithful Muslims (*ijmā'*), and analogy (*qiyās*). Other schools of law included "independent reasoning" (*ijtihād*) from multiple sources. This was particularly the case before the time of al-Shafi'i. But most Sunnis believe the "door to *ijtihād*" closed at some point during the tenth century. It was (and is) believed that every conceivable circumstance had been addressed by that time, and it was thus possible to treat new cases based on the precedents established in the now codified body of divine Islamic law. Given this set of circumstances it is no wonder that today many Muslims argue that the "door of *ijtihād*'" should be reopened to enable Muslims to deal with the ever-changing circumstances of life in the modern world (e.g., whether it is permissible to divorce one's wife via a SMS message sent to her cell phone). However, more conservative elements find this discussion unsettling since it suggests the *sharī'a* is deficient in meeting the modern Muslim community's needs. On the status of *ijtihād* in the Shiite world, see Nasr, *Heart*, 123–24.

[31] For an examination of how this rather utopian view has shaped the Muslim perspective on history, see Tarek Fatah, *Chasing a Mirage: The Tragic Illusion of an Islamic State* (Mississauga, ON: J. Wiley & Sons, 2008).

[32] There are actually five categories for judging various ethical decisions and ritual practices: they can be ruled obligatory (*wajib*), recommended (*mustaḥabb*), indifferent (*mubāḥ*), disapproved (*makrūh*), or forbidden (*ḥarām*). If there is precedent in the *sunna* that Muhammad performed a particular action, then this usually makes it an obligatory part of every Muslim's ritual observance. Part of the reason for the absence of a differentiation between natural law and divine law is the absence of a doctrine of depravity. In its place, Muslims have a doctrine of divine guidance. No special revelation is needed for humanity to be saved; humans only need guidance.

1:19–20; 2:15). But Muslims make no distinction between these "laws" and those found in the "divine" shari'a. For example, Muhammad cleansed his bodily orifices in a specific way, as mentioned. He also frequently used a wooden toothbrush (*miswāk*) before prayer. As a result, these acts have not been codified as a part of Muhammad's *sunna*, making it meritorious for Muslims to emulate. In the Muslim mind all of these components make up the *sharī'a* and are just as much a part of the fabric of the cosmos as are the laws of gravity. As Qutb explains, "Each word of God, whether it is an injunction or a prohibition, a promise or an admonition, a rule or guidance, is a part of the universal law and is as accurate and true as any of the laws known as the 'laws of nature'—the divinely-ordained laws for the universe, which we find to be operative every moment according to what God has prescribed for them from the dawn of creation."[33]

Christians have traditionally distinguished between natural law, divine law (i.e., special revelation needed for salvation), and what are understood to be local traditions, customs, or the canon laws of the church. The latter developed over the course of several centuries and are subject to change with time and circumstance. Christians have also never sought to emulate Jesus in every detail of his life (e.g., remaining celibate, wearing a seamless garment, or riding on a donkey through Galilee). It is clear that these were particular to the time and culture of Jesus in first-century Palestine. Also Paul's command to "kiss the brethren" in 1 Thessalonians 5:26 has rarely been taken as a command to be followed literally by every Christian in all times and places and that if one does not do this it is sin. In biblical ethics, the history of Israel, the life and ministry of Jesus, and the early church provide *paradigms* that are relevant to all believers regardless of time or place. Most important however is the overarching redemptive narrative within which these paradigms are revealed.[34]

Divine law, salvation, and eternity in Islam. Muslims today view the *sharī'a* as the sole means mandated by God for pleasing him and attaining what Christians would term "salvation" (i.e., an eternity spent with God). Law epitomizes religion in the Muslim mind for it alone provides the divine *hudā* or guidance that humanity needs to properly structure their societies in ways that honor God. This explains why Muslims view the world through "juridical" lenses. It also helps explain why Christians can face a myriad of ethical questions when they first meet Muslims, like whether they eat pork or drink alcohol. Law-keeping is sacrosanct in Islam, and it is the sole basis on which God judges human actions and determines their eternal destiny.

---

[33] Seyyid Qutb, *Milestones,* trans. unknown (Damascus: Dar al-Ilm, 1964), 88–89.
[34] For a treatment of this approach to biblical ethics, see Christopher J. H. Wright, *Old Testament Ethics for the People of God* (Downers Grove: IVP, 2004), particularly 62–74 where he discusses Israel as God's paradigm for ethical behavior.

While the Qur'an does not explicitly speak of redemption in the biblical sense of the word,[35] some scholars have demonstrated that Islamic theology and tradition developed an alternative narrative of redemption, in contrast with the Christian Scriptures.[36] In Islam, God's goal is for all of creation to surrender to him, and his program for achieving this goal is to provide divine guidance to his messengers. "The proclamation of this goal and the means for attaining it make up the content of every revelation; what is proclaimed as revealed may not be accomplished gradually or in steps—surrender to God (Islam) is not something which can be gradually realized only in the course of time, through generations and races, and in response to several generations." Consequently, "It is . . . impossible on the basis of the goal and means to construct a history of salvation which is gradually realized either in a Christian or non-Christian sense, neither Muhammad nor the Muslims thought of such a possibility. For the Koran recognizes no original sin and no corresponding redemption, so that the Koran presents no salvation history comparable to the Christian tradition."[37] This perspective provides insight into why Muslims have such a hard time accepting that God has progressively revealed his will and unfolded his plan of redemption over the course of several centuries.

The Qur'an has a number of different names for heaven, calling it a garden (*janna*), paradise (*firdaws*), and Eden (*'adn*). It also describes the nature of heaven in great detail, mentioning celestial virgins,[38] pearls, rubies, milk, wine, and abundant streams. Not surprisingly, entry into heaven is conceived of in legal terms. On the Day of Judgment (*yawm al–dīn*) God will give each person a "book" or an "account" (*ḥisāb*) wherein all his actions are inscribed. These are then weighed on a scale (*mizān*). If one's good deeds outweigh one's bad, God will give him his "book" in his right hand, but if his bad deeds outweigh his good, he will receive it in his left hand. Some Muslim theologians came to reject this quantitative approach to judging the merit of one's deeds. Instead, they interpreted the qur'anic verses that mentioned balancing and weighing one's deeds metaphorically, focusing on the quality of one's life and not his individual deeds. Still others argued that punishment in hell will be a temporary experience for Muslims who committed great sins (*kabā'ir*). For these, Muhammad will intercede for them, cutting short their time there. In some traditions Jews, Christians, and others are each destined for a different level of hell, though the Qur'an seems to suggest they will

---

[35] See Hava Lazarus-Yafeh, "Is There a Concept of Redemption in Islam?," in *Types of Redemption,* ed. R. Zwi Werblowsky (Leiden: Brill, 1970).

[36] This is the focus of Wansbrough's *Sectarian Milieu.*

[37] Falaturi, "Time and History," 65.

[38] Recently, Luxenberg has argued that the verses that mention these celestial virgins (Q 44:54; 52:20) have been misinterpreted and that Muhammad was probably referring to the "white, crystal clear grapes" of heaven commonly known in the Syriac Christian tradition. See Christoph Luxenberg, *The Syro-Aramaic Reading of the Koran: A Contribution to the Decoding of the Language of the Koran* (Berlin: Verlag Hans Schiler, 2007), 247–65.

be in paradise.[39] All Muslims agree however that one's destiny is related to one's deeds and God's mercy (*raḥmat allah*). Ultimately, there is no solid basis other than God's will that determines one's eternal destiny.[40] One other aspect of Islamic eschatology is important to discuss—the role of Jesus.

The return of Jesus in Muslim eschatology. Jesus plays a key role in the buildup to the day of judgment in many works of Muslim apocalyptic. But because of the Muslim denial of the crucifixion, his second coming is for very different reasons than those spelled out in Scripture. Reynolds notes that from the earliest period classical interpreters of the Qur'an, including Muqatil b. Sulayman (d. ca. 767), al-Tabari (d. 923), al-Zamkhashari (d. 1144), and Ibn Kathir (d. 1373), have been essentially unanimous in their affirmation Jesus was not crucified on the basis of Q 4:157.[41] "The great majority of classical exegetical traditions explain . . . that someone other than Jesus was transformed to look like him and then died in his place, while Jesus was taken up to heaven alive, body and soul."[42] The interpretation of Q 4:157 in this manner necessitated interpreting Q 3:55 as referring to Jesus' post-parousia death. Sura 3:55 states:

> Thus God said: O Jesus! I am putting you to death and causing you to ascend unto me, and I am cleansing you of those who disbelieve. I am placing those who follow you above those who disbelieve until the Day of Resurrection. Then you all will return to me, and I shall judge between all of you regarding what you differed.[43]

Though some scholars, both Christian[44] and Muslim,[45] have recently argued on theological and philological grounds that the Qur'an does not, in fact, deny the crucifixion, it is important to understand why most classical interpreters would do so. At the heart of this denial is the idea that such a ghastly death is not befitting a prophet of God. If Jesus were truly a prophet of God, so it is reasoned, he would not have suffered such a degrading death at the hands of his enemies. Such a defeat would be tantamount to a miscarriage of God's sovereign power in protecting his chosen one and delivering his law to humanity. Hence, it is not possible that Jesus would suffer like this.

---

[39] Louis Gardet, "Ḥisāb," in *Encyclopedia of Islam*, 2nd ed., ed. P. Bearman et al. (Leiden: Brill), 465. For more on the afterlife in Islam see Robert Tottoli, "Afterlife," in *Encyclopedia of Islam*, 3rd ed., ed. G. Krämer et al. (Leiden: Brill).

[40] In his evaluation of Muslim eschatology, Rahman holds to something akin to the Christian view regarding the restoration of the current created order. See Rahman, *Themes*, 111.

[41] This is the primary verse Muslims use to deny Jesus' crucifixion.

[42] Gabriel Said Reynolds, "The Muslim Jesus: Dead or Alive?" *Bulletin of SOAS* 72:2 (2009): 240. Reynolds goes into great detail examining the various explanations and alternative narratives these interpreters offer to explain what happened during Jesus' crucifixion.

[43] Interestingly Q 3:54 states that God "schemed" or "deceived" people regarding Jesus. It boasts that God is the best or "Greatest of the Deceivers."

[44] See the article by Reynolds, "Muslim Jesus."

[45] See Mahmoud Ayoub, "Towards an Islamic Christology, II: the Death of Jesus, Reality or Delusion?: A Study of the Death of Jesus in Muslim Tafsīr Literature," *The Muslim World* 70 (1980): 104.

Therefore, it makes sense that God would spare Jesus and then send him back to the earth as a portent prior to the great and final day of judgment.

But the denial of Jesus' crucifixion created an apparently unforeseen set of problems for subsequent generations of Muslims. Due to the sparse details regarding Jesus' rescue from death at the hands of the Jews (per the classical interpretations of Q 4:157–59 and Q 3:55) and one verse that possibly connects Jesus to the end times (Q 43:61), Muslim tradition filled in the gaps regarding Jesus' destiny. If he was not crucified then he is still alive which posed a potential challenge to the supremacy of Muhammad as the final prophet. For this reason a number of traditions developed that described Jesus' return and sought to allay the apparent ambiguity found in the afore-mentioned qur'anic verses. Initially, many of these traditions were triumphalistic, depicting Jesus as a savior who comes back to rescue the Muslims from the dreaded anti-Christ (al-dajjāl). Over time, however, Jesus' role as savior of the Muslims began to wane. There is a clear development in certain traditions whereby Jesus comes to play a smaller role in the end-times scenario. Many of those traditions have Jesus fighting Christians upon his return to earth in order to punish them for turning him into a god.[46]

Conclusion. Islam claims to be the final revelation to humankind, and it bases this assumption on a high level of continuity with the previous revelation. But upon closer examination, the presumed continuity is lacking in both form and substance. The style, content, and purpose of the Islamic notion of revelation is completely out of step with that of the Abrahamic tradition (i.e., the Bible). The Islamic metanarrative is based upon a subversive revision of the Bible's creation-fall-redemption-restoration story and posits law as the essence of all revelation. In the qur'anic version, Adam and Eve's sin is not the cause of the corruption that pervades creation. Abraham was chosen but not to be the father of all those who, by faith in his seed, Jesus, would be redeemed by God. And Jesus, though he is returning again, was not crucified in order to atone for humanity's sin. Therefore, his return is not to wrap up God's plan of redemption and usher in the long-awaited kingdom foretold by the prophets. So how can Christians communicate the Bible's message to Muslims in a way that appreciates their "juridical lenses," but makes clear that the true story of the cosmos is only found in the Bible? Several observations are pertinent in this regard.

Mission to Muslims: A Biblical Approach

Narrative control. Probably the most apparent conclusion one can draw from this treatment of Islam's story is that any presentation of the gospel message to Muslims must begin by laying out a framework for the proper interpretation of the Bible's comprehensive narrative:

---

[46] See G. C. Anwati, "'Īsā," in *Encyclopedia of Islam*, 2nd ed., ed. P. Bearman et al. (Leiden: Brill), 81. The most comprehensive treatment of Islamic apocalyptic traditions to date is the work by David Cook, *Studies in Muslim Apocalyptic* (Princeton, NJ: Darwin, 2002).

creation-fall-redemption-restoration. In isolation, the stories of Adam and Eve, Noah, Abraham, Moses, and Jesus do not make sense when abstracted from their narrative context. It is that context which provides the redemptive lenses one needs in order to properly read and understand the Bible. If Muslims are to understand the great doctrines of the Trinity, incarnation, and atonement, they must be presented in a manner that displays their organic relationship to the grand story God is telling about the world. Without this redemptive context, the message of salvation by the Son of God will not be understood. Ultimately, the Bible must be allowed to exert its narrative control over how the story of the prophets is told. And the only way to do this is to share the whole story with Muslims. This will ensure they are continually exposed to the overarching redemptive metanarrative which envelops each of the Bible's smaller narratives. Continued exposure like this acts as a sort of metanarrative replacement therapy, revising and correcting that which has been garnered from the Qur'an and Islamic tradition. Without this continued exposure, Muslims will struggle to properly evaluate Christian doctrine and will fail to understand why the good news of the gospel is God's news for humanity.

Ethics, morality, and law in Christian mission. Muslims believe Islam touches every facet of life, and they frequently criticize Christians (or at least Western Christians) for dichotomizing and compartmentalizing life into sacred and secular categories. In their view, these categories are foreign to Islam.[47] They attempt to show how it is that Islamic law covers every aspect of life and society. Obviously, the desire to live a theocentric life and create a just society is admirable and resonates with all Christians seeking to embody a "God-entranced vision of all things."[48] But it is important that Christians laboring among Muslims come to understand the juridical lenses through which Muslims view the world, versus the theological lenses typically used by Christians for evaluating religious worldviews. Once a certain level of understanding of the Muslim worldview is achieved, Christians will then be better equipped to properly apply the tools of biblical and systematic theology in their evaluation of Islam. The goal of that evaluation should be to demonstrate why it is that Islam's impulse to frame all of human life and society entirely in legal categories fails to appreciate the comprehensive nature of creation, the fallen nature of humanity, and the proper role of law in God's plan for redeeming people from all nations. Law is important in the story of redemption and in the biblical worldview, but it is not the sole means in the biblical economy for transforming society or living a life that is pleasing to God. Additionally, anyone desiring to live a life pleasing to God and in accordance with his law must first experience the life-giving power of regeneration through the Spirit. Otherwise, all law keeping is futile.

---

[47] They are also foreign to the Bible as this book demonstrates.

[48] This is the title of a small book by John Piper and Justin Taylor on the three-hundred-year anniversary of Jonathan Edwards's death. See John Piper and Justin Taylor, *A God Entranced Vision of All Things: The Legacy of Jonathan Edwards* (Wheaton: Crossway, 2004).

That being stated, Christians ministering among Muslims must be able to articulate a comprehensive view regarding the role of biblical ethics and morality both in their personal spirituality and in society. This is especially true for those discipling believers and planting churches in predominantly Muslim countries. Where churches are planted, local believers must come to properly evaluate their history in light of the biblical narrative and engage their present with the transformative power of the gospel. God's will for their lives is more comprehensive and encompassing than a mere attestation to his unity and submission to his cosmic code of do's and don'ts. The role of missionaries is to bequeath to these believers a heritage of fidelity to Scripture and the tools they need to interpret and apply biblical truth to everyday problems in a faithful and relevant way. They must also be clear that the goal is not to create a "Christian *shari'a*." Christianity has a legal mode for approaching certain issues; however, social justice and communal transformation cannot be solely accomplished through legislative means. Indeed, this conceptualization of human life solely in juridical categories is one of the major differences between Islam and biblical Christianity. Therefore, while realizing the limitations of moral legislation, Christians must be clear that the ethical teachings and paradigms one finds in the whole of the Bible are relevant regardless of time or place.[49] Under the guidance of the Holy Spirit, these believers must be encouraged to engage every dimension of their sociocultural context with the aim of bringing the gospel to bear upon the realms of education, law, business, the environment, human rights, and politics.

Christians would also do well to make clear that the goal of Christian missions in the Muslim world is not the creation of Western democracies. Rather, the goal is God-glorifying and Christ-exalting lives, communities, cities, and nations. Titus 2:11–14 demonstrates well how the moral transformation that Christ renders takes place within God's redemptive plan for all nations: "For the grace of God has appeared, bringing salvation for all people, training us to renounce ungodliness and worldly passions, and to live self-controlled, upright, and godly lives in the present age, waiting for our blessed hope, the appearing of the glory of our great God and Savior Jesus Christ, who gave himself for us to redeem us from all lawlessness and to purify for himself a people for his own possession who are zealous for good works." Thus, the church's mission does include an ethical agenda, but it can only be properly appreciated and applied when seen within the overarching redemptive context of Scripture.

Biblical Israel vs. the State of Israel. Inevitably, all those who labor among Muslims and share the Bible's story with them will be challenged to provide an explanation of the relationship between biblical Israel and the modern State of Israel within the Bible's narrative. This is one of the greatest challenges for Western Christians laboring among Muslims. And it is one

---

[49] Wright demonstrates that though these paradigms are embedded within specific historical and cultural contexts, it is assumed God's people will apply them to the contemporary context. See Wright, *Old Testament Ethics*, 321–25.

of the greatest barriers to Muslims accepting the gospel, particularly Arab Muslims. The difficulty lies in the creation of the State of Israel in 1948, and is complicated by the fact that most Christians fail to distinguish between biblical Israel and the modern political state. Modern Israel is not identical with biblical Israel, and speaking about them as if they are identical creates confusion. Christians must differentiate between the sense of "Israel" in the Bible and the use of "Israel" as a referent to the modern political state.

For Muslims who come to accept Christ, it is imperative that they view themselves as true children of Abraham by virtue of their faith in Abraham's seed, Jesus (cf. Luke 3:8; Gal. 3:7). And in order to accomplish this, they must locate their acceptance of the gospel squarely within God's redemptive plan for all nations. Successful accomplishment of this will be, in large part, contingent upon the extent to which they are able to appropriate Israel's faith and history as their own faith and history, and in a way that does not create a superior attitude toward the Jewish people. This will require a deep fidelity to the Scriptures and a keen analysis of one's culture and worldview in light of them.[50]

Finally, a word of caution. One might be tempted to use a number of the resources mentioned throughout this essay in order to construct philosophical arguments against Islam. There is a place for that, particularly on the campuses of Western universities and in the media, but this type of approach is generally ineffective for evangelizing Muslims and can create a certain animosity that obscures gospel comprehension. This is especially true in the Muslim world where the use of critical scholarship to examine one's faith is foreign. Even if this type of approach were effective in creating a critical attitude towards Islam, this is not the ultimate goal. The goal is the proclamation of the gospel through a faithful telling of the grand biblical narrative. It alone has the power to subvert the story told by Islam and convey the life-giving message of the gospel. And the best way to achieve that is to allow the Bible to have narrative control in any discussion with Muslims. This ensures that they understand God's message and can respond to his Son.

---

[50] For a balanced investigation into the relationship between Jews and Arabs in the Bible and redemptive history, see Tony Maalouf, *Arabs in the Shadow of Israel: The Unfolding of God's Prophetic Plan for Ishmael's Line* (Grand Rapids: Kregel, 2003).

Chapter Seventeen

MISSION TO HINDUS

J. B. Snodgrass

INTRODUCTION

The contributors of this book hold to a common confession: the Christian Scriptures give the true story of the world. In its narrative of creation, fall, redemption, and restoration, the Scriptures tell us about the origins of humanity and the world; the reason for the evil, pain, disorder and evil that surround us; the redemption that Christ Jesus provides in the midst of that evil, pain, and disorder; and a future in which the world will be made whole again. This is the foundation for the Christian mission and indeed drives the Christian mission. Christian mission to Hindus is particularly challenging because they, unlike Muslims or postmoderns, for example, have no one "story" of the world. Hindus pride themselves in the fact that their religion has no founder, no definitive dates or events to mark its beginning. They revel, in other words, in the absence of one overarching story into which they would be forced to squeeze all their beliefs and practices. Religious diversity comes quite naturally to Hindus. Perhaps a story will help to make the point.

In his book *The Argumentative Indian*, the noted Indian economist Amartya Sen tells how he, though raised a Hindu, eventually came to be an atheist. As he grew up, he found that his innate skepticism "seemed to mature with age." Despite the assurances of his Hindu grandfather that he would one day "find" his religion, he eventually came to flatly deny the existence of God. "I told my grandfather, some years later, that he had been absolutely wrong. 'Not at all,' replied my grandfather, 'you have addressed the religious question, and you have placed yourself, I see, in the atheistic—the Lokay-ata—part of the Hindu spectrum!'"[1]

Here Sen makes the rather surprising claim that belief in God is optional for a Hindu. And lest we think that the grandfather was merely offering some folksy, anecdotal acceptance to a wayward grandson, it should be pointed out that Sen's grandfather was a Hindu scholar. K. M. Sen was considered an authority on Hinduism, the author of a seminal work on the subject. He was even able to reference by name the particular atheistic "school" of Hinduism. While an atheistic Hindu is certainly not the norm, we are nevertheless left with the startling fact that one does not *have* to believe in God to be a Hindu. As is clear from the story, the realm of Hinduism provides ample room for people of various—even opposing—worldviews.

Of all the major world religions, Hinduism has proven to be the most difficult to define. It is remarkably diverse. It is so diverse, in fact, that some commentators have claimed that Hinduism should be considered a "parlia-ment" of religions as opposed to a single religion.[2] There is, however, a unity to be found within Hinduism. Beneath all the perplexing paradoxes, there are a few common threads that can guide us toward a typical Hindu worldview. The reader should therefore bear in mind that this chapter brushes the topic of Hinduism with broad strokes. We are not after an exhaustive description of the Hindu landscape, but rather a portrait of the typical Hindu worldview. Familiarization with this portrait is vital as we pursue the mission of God among Hindu peoples.

To begin with, how does one define Hinduism? What does it mean to be a Hindu? The confusion regarding the term *Hinduism* reaches back to the origin of the word itself. The word *Hindu* was originally a geo-political term. It was the Persian rendering of the Sanskrit word for river, *sindhu*. The river to which the old Persians were referring was the Indus River in present-day Pakistan, which served as a border between the Persians and the people of India. The Persians called the people who lived on the other side of the river "Hindus."[3] Hindu*ism*, then, was simply the term given to the religion of those people. The name, along with the idea that the name refers to a single reli-gion, stuck. The problem, however, is that the Western concept of a "religion," requiring as it does a somewhat unified doctrine, creed, and practice, has been superimposed upon a geographical location—the Indian subcontinent.

Hindus themselves are somewhat reluctant to define Hinduism, as they mostly refuse to distinguish between what is "true" Hinduism and what is not. Monotheists, polytheists, and agnostics are all counted as Hindus. A man may worship any god he chooses, or no god at all, and still rightly (though perhaps a little grudgingly in the latter case) be called a Hindu. Given the staggering variety of beliefs and practices within Hinduism, it is clear that

---

[1]   Amartya Sen, *The Argumentative Indian* (London: Penguin Books, 2005), 46.

[2]   See H. L. Richard, "New Paradigms for Understanding Hinduism and Contextualization," *Evangelical Missions Quarterly* 40:3 (July 2004), 308–15.

[3]   John Keay, *India: A History* (New York: Atlantic Monthly Press, 2000), 57.

what we mean by the word is not anything like what we mean by Christianity. There is no Apostle's Creed in Hinduism, no test of orthodoxy to which a good Hindu can appeal.

There are indeed vast differences among the various religious traditions of Hinduism. And yet, there is unity, even religious unity, in Hinduism that is based on more than just geography. The rather uniform appearance of Hinduism throughout the subcontinent is striking. From the familiar red streak in the part of a woman's hair to the fruit and flowers strewn at the feet of stone idols, there is a common religious culture that is recognizable throughout the Hindu world. As one Indian commentator noted, "While Hindu religious beliefs and practices are multiform, the Hindu religious outlook is very unitary. Wherever they come from, the Hindus will hold the same view of the deity, express the same views about religious life, and put forward the same apologia for their religion."[4] This distinctive "religious outlook" forms the basis for the Hindu worldview. Rather than identifying with a single religious tradition, Hinduism is built upon a unique attitude toward religion in general.

This Hindu attitude is characterized by a generosity toward diverse religious beliefs alongside a strict adherence to a uniform code of behavior. For the most part, Hindus are content to allow for differences in religious opinion as long as everyone abides by the Hindu social structure. Interestingly, the Sanskrit word translated as "heretic" refers not to one who holds unorthodox beliefs, but to a person who violates Hindu social mores.[5] In the world of Hinduism, what you do is more important than what you believe. This very central truth is encapsulated in the Hindu concept of *dharma*. For the Hindu, "a difference of metaphysical doctrine need not prevent the development of an accepted basic code of conduct. The important thing about a man is his *dharma*, not necessarily his religion."[6]

DHARMA

When asked about his religion, a Hindu will most often respond with reference to his *dharma*. While the nearest English equivalent of *dharma* is probably "religion," its true meaning touches on a broader family of ideas. It includes within it the ideas of "order," "duty," "law," and "ethics," among others.[7] *Dharma* is the very notion of social order.[8] A Hindu's *dharma* dictates everything—his social standing, his marital possibilities, his familial responsibilities, and even, though this practice is much diminished from former times, his career. For the Hindu, dharma provides a framework for

---

[4]   Nirad C. Chaudhuri, *Hinduism: A Religion to Live By* (Delhi: Oxford University Press, 1997), 136.

[5]   Ibid., 148.

[6]   K. M. Sen, *Hinduism* (London: Penguin Books, 2005), 30.

[7]   Gavin Flood, *An Introduction to Hinduism* (New York: Cambridge University Press, 2007), 11.

[8]   Wendy D. O'Flaherty, *The Origins of Evil in Hindu Mythology* (Berkeley: University of California Press, 1980), 94.

life. The outlines of this framework are seen most clearly in the Hindu caste system.

While scholars heavily debate the origins and the meaning of the caste system, its presence and pervasiveness are undoubtedly powerful in Hindu society. The Sanskrit word translated as caste is *varna*, meaning "color." Whether or not the color in question refers to race has been the subject of much debate; the important point is that *varna* is a means of separating people into discrete categories. Within each of the castes there is a virtual galaxy of smaller divisions known as *jatis*. The *jatis* are the local manifestations of the broader outlines of the castes. In addition to the concept of caste, the system of *dharma* further divides life into stages, or *ashrama*. These too are categorized into discrete sections, and one's duties and lifestyle vary as a result of one's stage in life. Together with *varna*, *ashrama* completes the picture of one's *dharmic* identity. Each person is born into his or her particular *dharma* and, outside of the changes in *ashrama* according to age, this identity is immutable.

Generally speaking, then, adherence to one's *dharma* is the fundamental socio-religious concept of Hindu civilization. For a Hindu, right religion boils down to the proper practice of one's *dharma*, not the correctness of one's faith. Hindus are much more concerned with orthopraxy than orthodoxy. It is in the context of *dharma*, and only in that context, that the Hindu will be truly strict and exclusive in his thinking. With regard to his beliefs, on the other hand, the Hindu is nothing if not broad.

THE THREE "RELIGIONS" OF HINDUISM

As we have seen, Hinduism is more of a particular attitude toward religion than one specific religion. Religious diversity is a fundamental part of the Hindu identity and stretches back to its earliest traditions and texts. Numerous theological and philosophical tributaries flow into the Hindu worldview. Among all the sources that converge in Hinduism, however, there are three major streams of religious thinking that ultimately shape and guide its flow. While some Hindus may identify more strongly with one of these three religious traditions, they are under no compulsion to choose any one to the exclusion of the others. Most Hindus will have a rough familiarity with the major elements of all three of these "religions." These familiar elements protrude from their respective traditions like islands pushing up out of the sea. Hindus know those islands well, but they remain largely indifferent to the textual and ritual depths that lurk beneath. That is the exclusive domain of the privileged (i.e., Sanskrit-literate) few. For the rest, they are free to draw upon the accessible parts of each of the three religious traditions as the need or occasion arises.

Vedic religion. The *Vedic* tradition is the oldest of the three major Hindu religions. It is founded upon the *Vedas*, the ancient Sanskrit texts that are the most highly revered Hindu scriptures. This collection of hymns, speculative philosophy, and ritual ordinances is believed to be unauthored and eternal. Virtually all the religious traditions within Hinduism appeal to the *Vedas* as their ultimate source of spiritual legitimacy. Indeed, some kind of reference or relationship to the *Vedas* is considered by some scholars to be a "criterion of being Hindu."[9]

While the *Vedas* are technically regarded with the highest reverence, the writings themselves are, for most Hindus, distant and unfamiliar territory. The priestly *Brahmins*, with their exclusive command of Sanskrit, are the true keepers of the *Vedas*. The religious reality constructed by the *Vedas* centers upon these *Brahmins* and their mediatory role in the rituals and sacrifices. Within this reality the emphasis is entirely upon the ritual itself. The priests are exacting in their worship—reciting the *Vedic* passages in precise tones and rhythm, meticulously preparing and arranging the offerings, directing the worshippers in their prayers and other ritual actions. The reason for this stringency is that the rituals and sacrifices carry cosmic significance—they carry the power to enact a sort of contract between the worshipper and the divine. In exchange for the proper execution of the prescribed ritual, the god is obligated to hear and respond to the supplicant's request.

Through the proliferation of various rituals, the *Vedic* tradition laid the groundwork for *dharmic* society. The *Vedas*, and in particular the later commentaries on the *Vedas*, prescribed ceremonies for every significant event in life and facilitated the structuring of Hindu society, including the intricacies of the caste system. For a Hindu, every part of life is infused with religious meaning; *dharma* is inescapable. Though the vast majority of Hindus have never read the *Vedas* themselves, they live and breathe the ancient texts as they follow their *dharma*.

Post-Vedic religion. Within the broad categorization of the *Vedas*, there is a group of texts knows as the *Upanishads*. While they are technically considered part of the highest Hindu canon, the *Upanishads* present a picture of reality that is very different from the ritualism of the earlier *Vedas*, and are therefore referred to here as "Post-*Vedic*" Hinduism.[10] The Post-*Vedic* worldview is speculative and philosophical, and rejects the formal rigidity of the *Vedic* system. In some ways, it is an acute reaction to the ritualism of *Vedic* religion. Whereas in *Vedic* religion the priests are considered necessary as mediators between the people and the divine, the *Upanishads* teach that communion with god is an essentially self-centered exercise. Through deep introspection and meditation, one can directly encounter god—the ultimate reality—and finally become one with the power that permeates all of existence.

It is probably this strand of Hinduism that is most familiar in the West. Indeed, it is oftentimes presented to Westerners as "true" Hinduism. The increasingly popular varieties of meditation and yoga, now so conspicuous in the West, arose out of this tradition. However, relatively few Hindus adhere

---

9   Flood, *An Introduction to Hinduism,* 11.
10   See O'Flaherty, *The Origins of Evil in Hindu Mythology,* for a similar three-part division.

strictly to the Post-*Vedic* tradition. The primary importance of this tradition lies in its contribution to the mental landscape of the Hindu world. Specifically, it provides scriptural and philosophical warrant to that most Hindu of religious beliefs—the plurality of the gods.

Though polytheism and image-worship are the most recognizable expressions of Hinduism, they are not simply to be taken at face value or treated as the final word in Hindu theology. Most Hindus hold that, beneath all the different manifestations and incarnations, the true god, the ultimate reality, is one. Somewhat paradoxically, this idea of the oneness of god is the basis for the idea of many gods. That is because, according to the *Upanishads*, god is ultimately indecipherable and unknowable. Furthermore, this god underlies, penetrates, and transcends all things. It is therefore no surprise that this ultimately mysterious and omnipresent reality could express itself in any number of ways. A god like this can appear anywhere and in almost any fashion.[11] This elemental conception of the divine—the absolute mystery, oneness, and immanence of god—is zealously and almost universally held by Hindus.

Bhakti religion. The *Bhakti* path, or the path of devotion, is by far the most popular stream of Hinduism.[12] Turning from the formal rigidity and the sacrifices of the *Vedic* system and the obscurity of the Post-*Vedic*, the *Bhakti* tradition is religion for the common man. The devotees of *Bhakti* pursue a personal relationship with their god. Generally, *Bhakti* followers devote themselves to one of the three major gods in the Hindu pantheon. The candidates for supreme god are Shiva, Vishnu, or, in various forms, the Goddess. In *Bhakti*, the object of devotion becomes almost a monotheistic god for the worshipper.

The source material for the *Bhakti* movement is found in a large body of myths and stories of the gods known collectively as the *Puranas* (meaning "Old"). The most famous of these stories are the *Mahabharata* and the *Ramayana*. In these stories, the two main protagonists (Krishna and Ram, respectively) are revealed to be incarnations of the divine lord Vishnu. These two epics play an indelible role in the lives and beliefs of most Hindus, and typify the texts of the *Bhakti* movement in general. Readers of the *Ramayana*, for instance, are urged to "meditate only on Rama, sing only of Rama, give ear only to Rama's infinite perfections . . . . [I]s there anyone who has worshipped Rama and not found salvation?"[13] Verses like these, found as they are amid epic tales of love and valor, resonate with Hindus far more strongly than the abstractions and speculations of the *Vedas*.

Over the centuries since the writing of the earliest *Puranas*, later writings, including songs and poems, elaborated the *Bhakti* tradition and helped it grow into the main expression of Hinduism. In accordance with this tradition, most

---

[11] H. L. Richard, *Hinduism: A Brief Look at Theology, History, Scriptures, and Social System with Comments on the Gospel in India* (Pasadena: William Carey Library, 2007), 14.

[12] Ibid., 10.

[13] F. S. Growse, *The Ramayana of Tulsidas*, rev. ed. (New Delhi: Motilal Banarsidass, 1978), VII, Caupai 125; quoted in Richard, *Hinduism,* 25.

Hindus will identify themselves as devotees of one god or another (though this will not keep them from patronizing a host of "lesser" gods). The *Bhakti* tradition supplies the most enduring and familiar images of Hinduism—from the smoking incense of a morning *puja* (worship) ritual to the stone gods on display in almost every Indian shop to the widely popular TV serials of the Sanskrit epics. The simple popularity of *Bhakti* has, at times, invoked the scorn of highly educated Hindus. They dismiss the displays of *Bhakti*, including icon-worship, as a lower form of Hinduism. This is a baseless accusation, however, as there is no uniform authority in Hinduism that could approve or condemn these popular expressions as "un-Hindu." For a vast number of worshippers *Bhakti* is, in essence, Hinduism.

WORLDS COLLIDE

In our portrait of a typical Hindu worldview, the major thematic elements are now all present. *Dharma*—the very medium of Hindu life—can be thought of as the canvas upon which the portrait is painted. Each Hindu's portrait will represent the three major traditions—*Vedic*, Post-*Vedic*, and *Bhakti*—along with a host of local and familial beliefs, in varying hues and proportions. Furthermore, little thought will have been given to blending each of these elements together. They are simply present as indispensable, if sometimes incongruous, pieces of the Hindu portrait. The result is a picture—a worldview—that is unique not only to Hinduism, but also to each Hindu.

In comparing this portrait to that of the Christian worldview, the differences become readily apparent. In this last section, we will examine some of the major differences by way of the creation-fall-redemption-restoration pattern. Before plunging into the pattern, however, we need to make a preliminary observation about the Hindu worldview. Perhaps the first and most obvious characteristic of Hinduism is, to return to where we started, the lack of an overarching narrative in the Hindu world. Hindus are comfortable with a multiplicity of answers to life's great questions. This is somewhat of a necessity for them, given the great variety of their revered texts and traditions. There is no single, binding authority within Hinduism. The *Vedas* provide a nominal point of authority, but in the end it is simply that—nominal. A legitimizing appeal to the *Vedas* is an appeal to their status as revered texts, not to any meaning or message that they may teach. That is, a teaching is not correct or useful because it explicitly agrees with the doctrine of the revered texts, but because it refers in some way, however tangentially, to the galaxy of ideas and characters propounded in those texts. As long as they locate themselves somewhere within that galaxy, new teachers and schools become their own locus of authority. The proliferation of modern-day "babas" and "gurus," with their throngs of followers, testifies to this reality.

Religious belief for a Hindu is therefore not a matter of concrete truths or abrupt, life-altering decisions; it is a meandering path through a forest of voices. The Christian claim that there is one answer, one Way, is an outright affront to the Hindu. As one Indian commentator noted, Hindus find the notion of Christ's exclusivity to be a "monstrous perversion of religion."[14] Here then, at the beginning, the paths of Christianity and Hinduism diverge radically. Revealed, exclusive truth is at the very heart of Christianity. The Christian idea of God's Word—delivered by the prophets at many times and in various ways but finally, and unalterably, in the Son—is foreign to the Hindu. Hindus take offense at the idea that any one person or sect could make an absolute claim on truth and divinity. God cannot be confined into one incarnation. For the Hindu, the Christian God is too small.

In reply, the Christian must say that the Hindu conception of god is, in a manner of speaking, too large. Hindus acknowledge that the paths to god are many—indeed infinite. The problem, then, is how to account for the differences in the paths. If the differences are truly substantive, then one way must be more correct than the others. If the differences are merely illusory, as the Hindu contends, then what is the point in following one over another? To say that different—even contradictory—religious expressions are really the same is to say that the very elements that give them their unique character are meaningless. One may just as well worship in any way one sees fit, or in no way at all. Furthermore, if all traditions stand on equal footing, then on what grounds could anyone object to the more unsavory manifestations of Hinduism, like the sexual profligacy of Tantrism or other socially deviant movements? There are no ultimately compelling reasons to deny any school of thought or practice, no matter how socially or morally aberrant, from the claim to be truly Hindu.

Beyond that—and perhaps more importantly—how does one account for the multiple, and sometimes conflicting, manifestations of god? Many of the myths of the gods depict not just their shining virtues but also their vices. This rather troubling fact opens the door to question the very nature and character of god. If the gods are capable of both good and evil, what assurance do we have of their actions and intentions toward us? They may do us good, but they may just as easily do us harm. In the absence of such assurances about the nature and intentions of god/the gods, Hindus are oftentimes compelled to take matters into their own hands. Worship becomes contractual, a fulfillment of certain divine requirements in order to achieve the desired outcome. With the character of the gods open to question there is little to keep Hindu religious practice from becoming this sort of sanctified bargaining.

The Hindu approach to religion, then, suffers from a fundamental difficulty. Their embrace of the ultimate mystery of the godhead—the foundation of their religious liberality—undermines any attempt at positive knowledge about god's nature or character. There are no assurances in Hinduism that god is good or loving. This conception of god stands in stark contrast to the God of the Bible—a God who has clearly revealed himself in his Word. In that Word he leaves no room for doubt as to his goodness and holiness. Tragically, the Hindu has no such assurance.

---

[14] Chaudhuri, *Hinduism,* 148.

Creation. There is no single account of the creation of the cosmos within Hinduism, not even within the original *Vedas* themselves. In fact, they are emphatically ambiguous about the nature of creation, as this hymn from the *Rig Veda* makes clear:

> Who really knows? Who will here proclaim it? Whence was it produced? Whence is this creation?
> The gods came afterwards, with the creation of this universe. Who then knows whence it has arisen?
> Whence this creation has arisen—perhaps it formed itself, or perhaps it did not—the one who looks down on it, in the highest heaven, only he knows—or perhaps he does not know.[15]

The Post-*Vedic* sources contain a great deal of speculation about the nature of reality. Building upon the cryptic passages in the *Upanishads* about the nature of god and the universe, one prominent school conceives of life as a great illusion. That illusion keeps us from realizing that, beneath our experience of the world, everything is just part of the one universal soul, the *Brahman*. While these philosophical conceptions of the nature of god and the world have disseminated widely throughout the Hindu world, they carry little practical weight for the typical Hindu. In terms of everyday relevance, one creation myth in particular has proven to be the most enduring—primarily because of its intimate connection with that hallmark of Hindu *dharma*, the caste system. This myth, found in the *Rig Veda*, describes the ritual sacrifice of the primal god-man, *Purusha*. When he was sacrificed, his body was separated into four parts. These parts, in turn, became the four *varnas*, or castes.

In this myth, caste, and by implication the entire *dharmic* categorization system, garners divine sanction. If origins are a clue to purpose, then this account of creation states first of all that ultimate purpose in life is tied directly to one's *dharma*. Fulfillment of one's *dharmic* identity, in all its roles and responsibilities, is the very purpose for which Hindus are created. This basic fact carries with it some implications that are, from the Christian perspective, troubling. First of all, the divisions that are at the heart of *dharmic* society are divinely ordained. Interestingly, the term *jati*—the subset of caste—is used to distinguish not just among humans but among all manner of beings. The rather startling implication of this fact is that "differences between human castes might be regarded as being as great as differences between different species."[16] Anything close to the biblical doctrine of divine image bearing that applies universally and uniquely to humankind is totally absent from the Hindu texts. Paul's claim that there is neither Jew nor Greek, slave nor free stands in stark contrast to the Hindu doctrine of the inherent, indeed divinely ordained, inequality of peoples. A true brotherhood of believers is a concept foreign to most manifestations of Hinduism.

---

[15] From *The Rig Veda*, trans. W. D. O'Flaherty (London: Penguin Books, 1981).
[16] Flood, *An Introduction to Hinduism,* 59.

Another, and perhaps more troubling, implication is the necessity of evil within the system of *dharma*. In *Vedic* Hinduism, the end toward which *dharma* moves is social—even cosmic—balance. Within this balance, evil is not simply an aberration; it actually has tangible significance as a necessary part of the cosmic order. That is, evil must be present in the universe to ensure this sense of balance. It can therefore literally be the case that one's *dharma* is to do evil.[17] Even within the *Bhakti* tradition, there are myths that reveal the gods intentionally producing, even performing, evil in order to sustain the sense of balance. As we noted above, this explicit, intended inclusion of evil within the created order is a serious difficulty for the Hindu worldview. If evil is inherent in creation, there are no grounds upon which a Hindu could truly and absolutely condemn it. Evil actions, and the consequences they produce, could very well be the will of the gods. Consequently, this idea of balance within *dharma* has a direct impact on the Hindu conceptions of sin and morality, and so to those issues we will now turn.

The fall. For a Hindu, morality varies in accordance with one's *dharma*. Under the idea of *svadharma* (literally, one's "own *dharma*"), each person's responsibilities and duties are unique to his or her caste or stage in life. There is therefore a natural relativity with regard to morality. What is right for a person of the priestly caste may not be, and in most cases emphatically is not, right for a person of a lower caste. While there is a concept of universal *dharma*—a set of ethics that applies to all Hindus in all contexts—*svadharma* has invariably proven to be of greater significance.[18] As one Indian commentator noted in an examination of modern Hindu society, "A man can do no wrong if he acts to protect his *svadharma*."[19]

This commitment to *dharma*, at the expense of other moral impulses, runs deep in the Hindu worldview. In some cases it serves as a sort of religious sanction for mercenary behavior in the interest of providing for one's family. The definite good of accumulating wealth and taking care of one's family, such an essential part of *svadharma*, takes precedence over ethereal moral ideals. Ultimately, it serves to relieve a Hindu of the feeling of individual guilt for moral transgressions. In this, it does not function alone, as the important Hindu concepts of *karma* and reincarnation also contribute to this moral alleviation.

Within the world of *dharma*, *karma* serves as judge and executioner. *Karma* is an impersonal, cosmic force of moral accountancy. For good deeds one accrues good karma; bad deeds produce bad consequences. Rather than the gods, it is ultimately *karma* that monitors and enforces the dictates of *dharma*. *Karma* "decides" the penalty for violations of *dharma*—usually enforced in a subsequent life. Here, in the intersection of *karma* and reincarnation, a Hindu is offered another way out of personal culpability. Any misfortune or evil under which one is forced to suffer (in Hinduism, evil

---

[17] O'Flaherty, *The Rig Veda,* 377.
[18] Ibid., 99.
[19] Pavan K. Varma, *Being Indian* (New Delhi: Penguin Books, 2005), 29.

applies equally to natural and moral badness) could conceivably be reparation for the sins of a previous existence. The Hindu is simply a victim of his circumstances—a receptacle of the inexorable force of *karma*.

The point here is that the Christian notion of personal guilt for sin, particularly sin that offends a holy God, is largely absent from the Hindu worldview. The most common Hindu conception of sin pictures it not as moral transgression but as a mistake of the intellect—simple ignorance, in other words. In *Vedic* thought, sin is conceived of primarily in terms of ritual impurity, not morality. And while the *Bhakti* literature has shown some rare flourishes of personal repentance, "these are outweighed a thousandfold by instances of sin regarded as the fault of nature."[20] Most Hindus would admit a certain amount of sin in their lives, but they would generally deny the fact that they are innately sinful. Indeed, for some schools of Hindu thought, the idea that humans are sinful by nature is positively repugnant. In the end, sin is ultimately not the fault of an individual. Whether attributable to the immutable laws of *karma*, the sins of another life, or the caprice of the gods, for a Hindu the blame for sin inevitably rests somewhere else.

Redemption. Given the ambiguity in the concept of personal sin within Hinduism, there is a corresponding confusion regarding salvation. Exactly what one needs to be saved *from* is something of an open question for many Hindus. The Sanskrit word most typically used for salvation is *moksha*, meaning "release." Like most Hindu religious terms, it carries a bevy of different connotations. It generally refers to release from the cycle of reincarnation, though there are also various folk conceptions of heaven and hell (these are always conceived of as impermanent). In positive terms, it refers to some kind of union with the divine, whether it is conceived as the impersonal *Brahman*, or a personal god like Shiva.

In reaction, perhaps, to the lack of clarity surrounding the question of the hereafter, Hindus have a strong affinity for the things of this world. As one rather cynical Indian commentator put it, "As to the notion of salvation, it is wholly unreal and unattractive—a mere talking point, as indeed the verbiage about it shows. Salvation is never the object of the religious observances and worship of the Hindus. The main object is worldly prosperity."[21] While this is surely an overstatement, it nevertheless highlights the strong vein of worldliness that runs throughout Hinduism. The Hindu scriptures give explicit sanction to seeking the pleasures and wealth that life has to offer. As one Indian commentator noted, "Hinduism must be the only religion that expressly includes the fulfillment of physical desires, and the pursuit of prosperity, among the supreme aims of life."[22] Coming, as it does, from the Hindu scriptures, this worldliness is not perceived negatively. On the contrary, its inclusion in scripture gives it a sanctified status. For a Hindu, it is simply appropriate, even religious, to seek wealth and pleasure in life. This need not

20 O'Flaherty, *Rig Veda*, 7.
21 Chaudhuri, *Hinduism*, 9–10.
22 Varma, *Being Indian*, 65.

distract one from seeking salvation. Indeed, in some cases pursuing wealth and pleasure, within the context of one's *svadharma*, may be the very path to salvation.

Traditionally, Hinduism has recognized three different paths toward salvation: the Way of Works, the Way of Knowledge, and the Way of Devotion. These paths roughly correspond to the three religious traditions. The Way of Works refers primarily to the religious system prescribed by the *Vedas*, the Way of Knowledge to the meditation and asceticism of the Post-*Vedic* tradition, and the Way of Devotion, naturally, to the *Bhakti* tradition of heartfelt worship of a specific god.

The final way, the Way of Devotion, is by far the most popular among Hindus. As stated above, salvation for a devotee is union with a personal god, made possible by divine grace. This grace can ultimately overcome even the reach of *karma*, essentially freeing a devotee from the world of *dharma*. Most Hindus of this persuasion are incredibly committed in their devotion: fasting regularly, following fastidious rules about diet and behavior, and stirring up deep emotion toward their god. So deep is this devotional passion that some of the literature of this tradition is explicitly erotic in its depiction of the relationship between the worshipper and the divine.

In its pursuit of a personal reunion with the divine, the *Bhakti* path shows some obvious parallels to Christianity. The differences, however, remain profound. Outside of a rough exterior resemblance, *Bhakti* parts with Christianity over a most basic element—the central element in any grace-based system of devotion—the identity and character of the Savior. Unlike the suffering Christ, Hindu gods are worshipped in their opulence. According to some myths recorded in the *Puranas*, they are even worshipped in their vices. Many of the pictorial representations of Krishna, the most beloved manifestation of Vishnu, depict him arrayed in finery, surrounded by a veritable horde of beautiful, doting maidens. Hindus regard this gilded splendor as natural to divinity. There is no notion of God as a humble, suffering servant. Absent also is the idea of God as substitute—bearing the punishment of his people. In almost every Hindu conception of salvation, god is the object, not the subject. That is, god is the one being pursued, not vice versa. Whether through sacrifices, righteous deeds, or meditation, or even—and this is subtle—the fires of devotion one is able to summon up, the effort in salvation is always on the side of the saved, not the savior. The Hindu gods do not seek and save that which is lost; nor do they die for sinners. Here, as with all comparisons between Christianity and other religions, the key turns upon the person and work of Jesus Christ. For a Hindu, Christ on the cross is as unthinkable as it is unnecessary.

Restoration. For the most part, eschatology—a concern about the end times—does not play a major role within Hinduism. The only notable myth involving the end of the world comes from the *Puranas* and conceives of history as four successive *yugas*, or ages. Each of the *yugas* consists of a vast number of years, and they proceed from a primal state of perfection in the first age to a world of deprivation in the last. According to this cosmology, we are presently in the final age—the Kali *Yuga*—and are thus headed toward the consummation of these ages, when the universe will be destroyed by the final incarnation of Vishnu and, after several million years, be recreated. This cycle repeats itself throughout all eternity. This endless progression is purposeless; it is simply the lord's caprice, his *lila*, or "play."[23]

While this view of the end of time may be considered restorative in the sense that it is an eventual return to the initial golden *yuga*, it cannot be considered complete. The Kali *Yuga* will come again, as it will throughout all eternity, carrying with it the need to be destroyed and recreated. Perhaps most troubling, from a Christian perspective, is the utter lack of purpose. While the God of the Bible will ultimately and finally restore good out of a love for his creation, Hinduism offers no such assurance as to the intentions of the Creator. The universe simply is, and will continue to be, and the reason is ultimately arbitrary. Needless to say, this incompleteness, this generosity inherent in the vast turning of ages, insulates the Hindu from a sense of urgency regarding his eternal state. For many Hindus, theirs is not the expectant hope of a bright and final hereafter but the endless return of that which has gone before.

THE MISSION OF GOD TO HINDUS

As we have seen from the discussion above, Hindu beliefs come in many shapes and sizes. Hindus feel no compulsion to fit their beliefs into one all-encompassing cosmic narrative. In the life of a typical Hindu, the three different streams of religious tradition coalesce with the code of *dharma* in a seamless river of existence. This way of life is not only distinctively Hindu but also, it should be noted, distinctively Indian. The geographical situation of Hinduism has changed little since the time of the old Persians. The vast majority of Hindus in the world still reside on the Indian subcontinent. With a few exceptions, almost all Hindus that live outside of the subcontinent trace their lineage there. Hinduism is not a missionary religion. While some of the ideas of Hinduism have spread to the Western world, the Hindu writings and traditions take little to no account of those who are not born Hindu. For those who live and die outside of the world of dharma and caste, the Hindu gods are mostly silent.

The God of the Bible, on the contrary, is explicit in his intentions toward the nations—including Hindu peoples. His Son died to ransom a people for himself from every Hindu tribe, jati, and language. Today, the Indian subcontinent is home to the largest concentration of lostness on earth, over a third of the world's unreached population—above 1.4 billion people.[24] The great need in this vast harvest field is more laborers—laborers who know how Hindus

---

23 Flood, *An Introduction to Hinduism*, 113.
24 International Mission Board, "Global Status of Evangelical Christianity: Unreached People Groups by Region, July 2009," Global Research, IMB; http://www.imb.org/globalresearch/

think so that they can effectively communicate the gospel. Laborers who can tell the pursuer of Krishna about the God who pursued us, even to the point of suffering and death. Laborers who can convince the high-minded priest that the Lamb of God is the final, perfect sacrifice for our sins. Laborers who can cut through the mists of philosophy and meditation with the clear testimony of the living, personal God of the universe. Laborers who can point Hindus to the purpose of history and the consummation of the ages, when Jesus himself will return to judge the living and the dead. Laborers who can see, in other words, all the ways that the gospel of Jesus Christ answers the great questions Hindus have asked for thousands of years. It is in the hope of equipping those laborers that this chapter has been written.

---

downloads/thismonth/2009–07%20GSEC%20Unreached%20People%20Groups%20by%20 Region.pdf.

Chapter Eighteen

MISSION TO BUDDHISTS

Kyle Faircloth

INTRODUCTION

Human existence is inextricably intertwined with suffering and, therefore, also with human attempts to endure, escape from, or vanquish suffering altogether. Many think that if only they can find the source of suffering, its root cause, then perhaps they can dig it out and finally find peace for their weary hearts. Buddhism is a bold attempt toward this endeavor. Buddhism, in its beliefs and practices, is about nothing if it is not about suffering.

Christians who seek to minister to Buddhists rightly reject Buddhist teaching, but they sometimes also wrongly demean those who call themselves Buddhists. We must not allow this to happen, nor must we forget that ultimately we are concerned with Buddhists themselves rather than Buddhism *qua* Buddhism. In seeking to minister to Buddhists, therefore, Christians must find an immediate and significant point of contact in the identification of a common problem—the problem of suffering. This point of contact allows Christians to approach Buddhists in humility as fellow sufferers, inviting them to come with us along the true path to peace.

In this chapter, we will focus on the biblical narrative of creation, fall, redemption, and restoration, comparing and contrasting it with Buddhism and showing the insufficiency of Buddhism as a salvific system. Buddhism, however, is rather diverse, so it would not be helpful to run it through this thematic filter indiscriminately. Instead, this chapter will focus on Theravada Buddhism because it is considered to be the most "orthodox" of all the branches.[1] Known as "the Way of the Elders," Theravada Buddhism is the oldest form still practiced today, and its basic philosophical core runs through all the different variations.[2]

CREATION

In this beginning. It all began, as it always does, with a small wind. This was no ordinary wind, but one moved by the *karma* of living beings. The beginning was simply one of an infinite number of beginnings. It began, like all the others, when the time of nothingness came to a close and the time of creation was set in motion. This current universe will follow the same cosmic cycle as those that came before it; the *Kalpa* of Creation, the *Kalpa* of Duration, the *Kalpa* of Dissolution, and the *Kalpa* of Nothingness.[3] Within the universe, there are multiple layers of existence. There are gods, angels, ghosts, demons, people, and animals that exist as several of these beings at different periods of time. The universe expands and contracts, which causes these beings to exchange places, depending on exhaustion of a lifespan or merit.

In *this* beginning, when the winds of *karma* began to move once again, a being came into existence known as a Brahma (a higher being). He existed in his palace for a long time until he became discontent and cried out, "Oh, if only some other beings would come here!"[4] At that time, other beings, from the exhaustion of their lifespan or merit, fell into the Brahma palace as companions for him. The Brahma, upon seeing this, thought to himself, "I am Brahma, the Great Brahma, the Conqueror, the Unconquered, the All-Seeing, the All-Powerful, the Lord, the Maker and Creator, Ruler, Appointer and Orderer, Father of All That Have Been and Shall Be. These beings were

---

[1] World religion scholars often speak of Theravada Buddhism in contrast to Mahayana Buddhism, viewing them as the two main branches of Buddhism. Mahayana can be further divided, including the sects of Pure Land, Zen, Shingon, and Tibetan Buddhism. Other scholars, however, argue that it does not make sense to speak of two branches of Buddhism because Theravada is a monastic tradition and Mahayana is not; therefore, the two are not comparable phenomena. In theory, therefore, a Buddhist could be both Theravada and Mahayana. For an example of the former view, see Winfried Corduan, *Neighboring Faiths: A Christian Introduction to World Religions* (Downers Grove: IVP, 1998), 220–50. For an example of the latter view, see Paul Williams, "Buddhism: A Historical Overview," in Christopher Partridge, ed., *Introduction to World Religions* (Minneapolis, MN: Fortress, 2005), 188–94.

[2] This includes the teachings of *Anicca*—nothing is permanent; *Dukkha*—existence is suffering; *Anatta*—there is no personal soul, as well as the *Four Noble Truths* and the *Noble Eightfold Path*.

[3] A *kalpa* is used to measure each of the four periods of time in the cycle of a universe. The length is demonstrated through the use of similes. For example, "It is at least the time required to take away all the mustard seeds stored in a castle of one cubic *yojana* (7.4 cubic kilometers) if only one seed is removed every hundred years." Akira Sadakata, *Buddhist Cosmology: Philosophy and Origins* (Tokyo: Kōsei Publishing, 2004), 96.

[4] *The Long Discourses of the Buddha: A Translation of the Digha Nikaya*, trans. Maurice Walshe (Boston: Wisdom Publications, 1995), 76.

created by me."[5] Then, these new beings looked to the Brahma and thought, "That Brahma, . . . he made us, and he is permanent, stable, eternal, not subject to change, the same forever and ever."[6]

The ignorant creator. This story, from the *Digha Nikaya*, shows that this "creator" was not always a Brahma, but simply fell into this position as the result of previous lives from a previous universe. Also, he created as a result of his unrest, discontent, and worry. There is another story later in the Buddha's teachings that tells about a monk who, by his great concentration, was able to make the Brahma's world appear before him. He then asked the Brahma, "Friend, where do the four great elements—earth, water, fire, air—cease without remainder?"[7] The Brahma answered simply by stating how great he was. Three times the monk asked this question until the Brahma pulled him aside and admitted he did not know the answer, but he did not want to lose face in front of his angels. He then reproved the monk for looking for the answer to this question beyond the Lord Buddha.

What these stories seek to illustrate is that this Brahma acted out of selfishness and unrest; he is foolish and certainly not all-knowing—he is an ignoramus. Walpola Sri Rahula writes, "Man's position, according to Buddhism, is supreme. Man is his own master, and there is no higher being or power that sits in judgment over his destiny."[8] Wan Petchsongkram, in *Talk in the Shade of the Bo Tree*, quoted a monk from Sri Lanka who took this teaching to its extreme. This monk said, "The teaching of the church is to reverence and trust in this God, but Buddhism teaches that we should annihilate and conquer this God at all costs."[9] Feeling confident in his position, he continued by stating, "Kill him, kill him! Why should we do so? Because God has created to suffer, created an evil world, which proves that he is stupid."[10] Based upon the teachings of the Buddha, this monk concluded that people should not trust this creator and they should do all that is necessary to keep him out of their lives completely.

The problem of suffering, or the problem of evil, is perhaps the biggest stumbling block for a Buddhist to believe in God. It is difficult for their minds to reconcile an all-good Creator with a suffering creation. Chao Phya Phraklang was the minister of foreign affairs in Thailand in the mid-1800s, when Protestant missionaries began to enter the country. Because he was responsible for all the foreigners, he had countless philosophical conversations with missionaries over his thirteen-year career. When he retired, he wrote a book concerning his thoughts on these conversations. Here is one of his conclusions:

---

[5]   Ibid.
[6]   Ibid.
[7]   Ibid., 178.
[8]   Walpola Sri Rahula, *What the Buddha Taught* (Bangkok: Haw Trai Foundation, 2005), 1.
[9]   Wan Petchsongkram, *Talk in the Shade of the Bo Tree*, trans. and ed. Frances E. Hudgins (Bangkok, 1999), 50.
[10]   Ibid.

If we were to hold with those who believe in God the Creator, it should follow that (the impartial justice of God) would make all men and animals equal in life and similar in nature, which is not the case. . . . If we say that God made these, we must regard Him as unjust, partial, and ever changing; making those suffer who have never done anything to deserve suffering, and not giving to men in general that average of good and bad fortune.[11]

According to Buddhism, God is in need of help just as much as humankind is. God is equated with ignorance (*avijja*), and at most deserves our pity. As Bhikkhu Buddhadāsa says, "God as *creator* is known in Buddhism under the term '*avijja*'. This means the lack of knowledge, or ignorance. Ignorance is the power of nature which is the cause of all existing things and as such the cause of suffering."[12] Many Buddhists either believe that God is a physical being who is ignorant of the truth and, therefore, must be avoided, or they believe these stories are simply a personification of the primary problem of mankind—ignorance.

Unanswered questions. Buddhists have concluded that though he is not malevolent, God did an evil thing by creating. He created out of ignorance, and he can provide no solution to the dilemma of suffering. According to Buddhism, questions about God, creation, and one's purpose in life are irrelevant. History was a mistake and can only be overcome by enlightenment to the truth.

Once, a disciple named Mālunkyaputta approached the Buddha with the ultimatum that he would only follow the Buddha if he answered his questions about the universe and existence. The Buddha responded, "Mālunkyaputta, if anyone says: 'I will not follow the holy life under the Blessed One until he answers these questions such as whether the universe is eternal or not, etc.,' he would die with these questions unanswered by the Tathāgata [the Buddha]. . . . Because it is not useful, it is not fundamentally connected with the spiritual holy life."[13] As far as the Buddha was concerned, if one is to cease suffering and escape from evil, then the answer is found in moving away from God. Salvation, or "enlightenment," is found outside of God—it is found in oneself.

THE FALL

Sweet earth. The Brahma and his angels lived together in self-luminous delight for a very long period of time. At some point, the universe began to expand again and some of the beings from the Brahma world that had passed away were reborn in this world. At that time, this world was completely dark and everything was covered with water. "Neither moon nor sun appeared,

---

[11] Henry Alabaster, *Wheel of the Law* (London: Trubner and Co., 1871; reprint, Whitefish, MT: Kessinger Publishing, no date given), 40–41.

[12] Bhikkhu Buddhadāsa, "Christianity and Buddhism" Sinclaire Thompson Memorial Lecture, Fifth Series. Given in Chiang Mai, 1967, 53.

[13] Rahula, *What the Buddha Taught*, 14.

no constellations or stars appeared, night and day were not distinguished, nor months and fortnights, no years or seasons, and no male and female, beings being reckoned just as beings."[14] For another long period of time, these self-luminous beings hovered over the waters in delight. At some point, earth began to spread out along the waters. "It looked just like the skin that forms itself over hot milk as it cools. It was endowed with colour, smell and taste. . . . It was very sweet, like pure wild honey."[15] One of the beings, who was greedy in nature, saw the pleasing color and smelled the savory scent, and dipped its finger into the earth and tasted it. It was so taken with the flavor that for the first time craving arose. "Then other beings, taking their cue from that one, also tasted the stuff with their fingers. They too were taken with the flavour, and craving arose in them."[16] They could not stop eating the tasty earth, and as a result they lost their self-luminance causing the sun and moon to appear and the reckoning of time began as the world re-evolved.

Craving: the ultimate sin. As the story continues it tells how the bodies of these beings became more and more corrupted as they ate the soil, then mushrooms, then creepers, and finally rice that grew upon the earth. The ultimate result of this corruption was the formation of the fleshly bodies of male and female. The story explains, "The women became excessively preoccupied with men, and the men with women. Owing to this excessive preoccupation with each other, passion was aroused, and their bodies burnt with lust."[17] Morals declined steadily so that there was stealing, killing, and sexual activity. This is why humans find themselves in such a predicament today.

This story harmonizes with the creation story in that it attempts to pinpoint the cause of suffering as one basic sin—craving. Rahula says, "It is this 'thirst,' desire, greed, craving, manifesting itself in various ways, that gives rise to all forms of suffering and the continuity of beings."[18] The reason we continue to suffer is because we continue to be, and we continue to be because we continue to crave for life. According to Buddhism, the fall is implicit in the very fact that we exist. As Winston King wrote, "The '*fall*' of man, according to Buddhism, was his '*fall*' into individual sentient being."[19] The Buddha said, "That formation—what is its source, what is its origin, from what is it born and produced? When the uninstructed worldling is contacted by a feeling born of ignorance-contact, craving arises: thence that formation is born."[20] The only way to cease suffering is to cease being, and the only way to cease being is to cease craving.

[14]   *The Long Discourses*, trans. Walshe, 410.
[15]   Ibid.
[16]   Ibid., 410.
[17]   Ibid., 411.
[18]   Rahula, *What the Buddha Taught*, 29.
[19]   Winston King, *Buddhism and Christianity* (London: Allen & Unwin, 1963), 49, quoted in John Davis, *The Path to Enlightenment* (London: Hodder & Stoughton, 1997), 75.
[20]   *The Connected Discourses of the Buddha*, trans. Bhikkhu Bodhi (Boston: Wisdom Publications, 2000), 922.

Many lives. Speaking to his disciples, the Buddha said, "I declare, monks, that actions willed, performed and accumulated will not become extinct as long as their results have not been experienced, be it in this life, in the next life or in subsequent future lives. And as long as these results of actions willed, performed and accumulated have not been experienced, there will be no making an end to suffering, I declare."[21] People are now ruled by the effects of *karma* because of craving. Rahula defines *karma* saying, "It means only 'volitional action,' not all action. Nor does it mean the result of *karma* as many people wrongly and loosely use it. . . . *Karma* never means its effect; its effect is known as the 'fruit' or the 'result' of *karma*."[22] *Karma* is any volitional action, whether good or bad. Regardless of whether or not the action was good or bad, *karma* occurred. Saeng Chandra-ngarm breaks this down further explaining, "An act can be classified as good (wholesome), evil (unwholesome) or neutral." He then mentions four factors of *karma*, mental drive, choice, action, and karmic result, and then says, "An act is 100% good if all the four factors are good."[23]

Because of this definition of *karma*, Buddhists do not understand sin in the same way as Christians. They can understand *doing* a sin, but they have difficulty grasping that they *are* sinful beings. They would think perhaps, within their last action, three of the factors of *karma* were good, so really, that action was only 25 percent bad. In the whole scheme of things, 75 percent good is not so bad. Depending on the amount of one's good and bad fruit of *karma*, one can be reborn in this world as an animal, ghost (spirit), woman, or man. One can also be reborn in one of the many hells or heavens.

The Buddha taught that "those cruel sinners who, from a desire of [worldly] life, commit bad deeds, will sink into the dreadful hell which is full of dense darkness and great suffering."[24] There are 136 hells with numerous creative ways of punishing wrongdoers.[25] For example, Marlane Guelden wrote that Buddhist hell scenes "depict ghosts in various hells as emaciated and deformed, being thrust headfirst into a pot of boiling molten iron, speared by guards, or running individuals whose bodies are on fire."[26] For the sin of adultery, the punishment is even more creative:

> Each sinner must endure sharp fiery thorns to reach his or her lover at the top of the tree. A man is goaded by guards with spears, by vicious dogs and pecking birds as he tries to reach his female lover. But when he reaches the

[21] *Numerical Discourses of the Buddha: An Anthology of Suttas from the Anguttara Nikāya*, trans. and ed. Nyanaponika Thera and Bhikkhu Bodhi (Walnut Creek: Altamira Press, 1999), 269.

[22] Rahula, *What the Buddha Taught*, 32.

[23] Saeng Chandra-ngarm, *Buddhism and Thai People* (Chiang Mai: Ming Muang Printing, 1999), 8.

[24] "Great good-fortune," *The Group of Discourses* (Sutta-nipāta), vol. 2, trans. K. R. Norman (Oxford: The Pali Text Society, 1992), 31, quoted in Sadakata, *Buddhist Cosmology*, 44.

[25] *Three Worlds According to King Ruang: A Thai Buddhist Cosmology*, trans. Frank E. Reynolds and Mani B. Reynolds (Berkeley: Asian Humanities Press, 1982), 62.

[26] Marlane Guelden, *Thailand: Into the Spirit World* (Singapore: Times Edition, 1995), 50.

top, she is whisked away and placed at the bottom of the tree to begin her fruitless climb.[27]

Just as Buddhism teaches there are many hells, there are also a multitude of heavens. It is not difficult to be reborn in one of the heavenly realms. Indra, the god of heaven (different from Brahma, the creator), once explained how a certain being was able to be reborn in heaven. He said, "This deva in a former life was a cowherd out in the fields who once shared his food with the other herders. That virtuous act earned this reward for him."[28] Neither hell nor heaven, however, is viewed as an eternal punishment or reward. Instead, either place only lasts until all the accumulation of volitional action is experienced. In other words, it depends on the amount of fruit of *karma* one has built up through previous lives.

Therefore, heaven is not the highest goal. The highest goal is to negate *karma* altogether. Chandra-ngarm says, "Karmic energy can be neutralized and rendered impotent by the power of Enlightenment."[29] When a person ceases craving for being as well as non-being, and simply is or is not, then they negate *karma*, and are able to gain enlightenment. Enlightenment is redemption.

REDEMPTION

Glorious truth. During the time that the beings in this world lost their self-luminance, causing the sun and moon to appear, truth moved through the universe and filled the whole world with blazing light. "Yet there was no eye to see the light, no ear to listen to the truth, no mind to perceive its meaning; and in the immeasurable spaces of existence no place was found where the truth could abide in all its glory."[30] Though sentient beings existed with sense perception, they struggled with pleasure and pain, hatred and love, so that no place was found in them where truth could abide.

> Men broke down under the burdens of life, until the savior appeared, the great Buddha, the Holy Teacher of men and gods. And Buddha taught men the right use of sentiency, and the right application of reason; and he taught righteousness and thus changed rational creatures into human beings, just, kind-hearted, and faithful. And now at last a place was found where the truth might abide in all its glory, and this place is the soul of mankind.[31]

The Buddha attained the truth and was, therefore, able to point others to this truth so that they might attain it as well. The Buddha was the first Enlightened One and the archetype for others to follow. Being enlightened

---

[27] Ibid., 52.

[28] Bonnie Pacala Brereton, *Thai Tellings of Phra Malai: Texts and Rituals Concerning a Popular Buddhist Saint* (Tempe: Arizona State University, 1995), 196.

[29] Chandra-ngarm, *Buddhism and Thai People*, 9.

[30] Paul Carus, *The Gospel of Buddha* (New York: Cosimo, 2007), 228.

[31] Ibid., 229.

to the truth is a process, and there is no urgency: "Righteousness is the place in which truth dwells, and here in the souls of mankind aspiring after the realization of righteousness, there is ample space for a rich and ever-richer revelation of the truth. This is the Gospel of the Blessed One. This is the revelation of the Enlightened One. This is the bequest of the Holy One."[32] The Buddha is a savior in that he shows others how they must be saved, but he does not save them himself. His teachings provide the thread of revelation to the truth, but it is up to the individual to follow it.

Oneself is one's own redeemer. Redemption is a two-stage process. The first stage was the Buddha's enlightenment and his willingness to preach the truth to others (*Dhamma*). The second stage is one's willingness to accept this revelation and apply it to one's own life. As Buddhadāsa says, "The primary Redeemer is therefore the Enlightened Teacher and the real redeemer is none other than the traveler himself."[33] Redemption in Buddhism has nothing to do with atonement because there is no one to whom to be reconciled. As the Buddha taught, "Evil is done by oneself alone, by oneself is one defiled. Evil is avoided by oneself; by oneself alone is one purified. Purity and impurity depend on oneself; no one can purify another."[34]

Within his *Four Noble Truths*, the Buddha provided a systematic path towards enlightenment. He first said that life is filled with suffering, imperfection, impermanence (*Anicca*), emptiness, and insubstantiality (*Dukkha*). Second, the Buddha said these things come from a thirst or a craving for life: "And what is the origin of suffering? It is craving, which brings renewal of being. . . . Craving for sensual pleasures, craving for being, and craving for non-being. This is called the origin of suffering."[35] So how does one escape this vicious cycle? The Buddha's third *Noble Truth* is known as cessation. If people *desire* to get out of the cycle of suffering and rebirth, then they must cease *desire* altogether. The Buddha said, "It is the . . . fading away and ceasing, the giving up, relinquishing, letting go, and rejecting of that same craving. This is called the cessation of suffering [*Nirvana*]."[36] The fourth *Noble Truth* is basically known as the path, or more popularly known as the *Noble Eightfold Path*. By following this path, people will learn how to cease their craving and, therefore, cease suffering by ceasing to be.

The delusion of "I." Because the only way to cease suffering is to cease being, the Buddha taught that the idea of a personal soul is false (*Anatta*). In reality, there is no "mine" because there is no "I." As Buddhadāsa said, "The matter of 'I' and 'mine,' ego and selfishness, is the single essential issue of Buddhism. The sense of 'I' and 'mine' is the one thing that must be purged

---

[32] Ibid., 230.
[33] Buddhadāsa, "Christianity and Buddhism," 81.
[34] *The Dhammapada*, trans. Gil Fronsdal (Boston: Shambala, 2005), 44.
[35] *The Middle Length Discourses of the Buddha: A Translation of the Majjhima Nikaya*, trans. Bhikku Nanamoli and Bhikku Bodhi (Boston: Wisdom Publications, 2005), 135.
[36] Ibid., 135.

completely."[37] As noted above, the ultimate goal is to cancel out *karma* altogether. Strangely enough, this means that one *should not* not believe in a personal soul any more than one *should* believe in a personal soul. Rahula says, "According to the Buddha's teaching, it is as wrong to hold the opinion 'I have no self' . . . as to hold the opinion 'I have self', . . . because both are fetters, both arising out of the false idea 'I AM'."[38]

The teaching of *Anatta* raises the question, who is it that is reborn in another life or eventually attains *nirvana* if there is no personal soul? This question is explained through a concept known as Conditional Genesis. Rahula says that everything is relative, "interdependent and interconnected, and nothing is absolute or independent; hence no first cause is accepted by Buddhism. . . . Conditional Genesis should be considered as a circle, and not as a chain."[39] In Buddhism, there are no questions of free will or determinism because neither exists. Instead, everything is simply an effect of a previous cause. Phraklang said that "it may be compared to the seeds of plants which sprout and grow, and produce more seed; can the succeeding tree and seed be said to be the same as the original tree and seed?"[40] A person is simply made up of five aggregates—matter, mind (not spirit), perception, volition, and consciousness—and it is these "forces" which are carried into the next life, because the individual does not actually exist. John Davis says that it could be compared to the impact of billiard balls upon each other.

> While nothing is transferred upon impact between one ball and the other, the second ball is set in motion (karmic law), by the first and the second ball can in turn change the course and direction of a third with no transference of the "condition" . . . but there is no silk thread of continuity, which would link the individual pearls of "personhood" on the string of subsequent existences.[41]

Redemption occurs by negating the effects of *karma* upon the Five Aggregates of being. As the Buddha said to one of his disciples, "'If, Ānanda, there were no kamma [*karma*] ripening in the sense-sphere realm, would there appear any sense-sphere becoming?' 'Surely not, Lord.'"[42] The final result is *nirvana*.

RESTORATION

End times. When the *Kalpa* of Duration begins to wane, people will forget the teachings of the Buddha. As a result, morals will decline steadily so that people no longer share their property with the needy, and covetousness and

---

[37] Buddhadāsa Bhikku, *Heartwood of the Bodhi Tree: The Buddha's Teaching on Voidness* (Chiang Mai: Silkworm, 2004), 5–6.

[38] Rahula, *What the Buddha Taught*, 66.

[39] Ibid., 54.

[40] Alabaster, *Wheel of the Law*, 44.

[41] Davis, *The Path to Enlightenment*, 56–57.

[42] *Numerical Discourses*, trans. Thera and Bodhi, 69.

hatred will increase. In the beginning people had thousand-year life spans, but as they became more and more corrupt, their life spans decreased little by little until they lived only a hundred years. Toward the end of the cycle of Duration, the sins of people will become so bad they will begin to commit incest and they will be promiscuous as if they were no more than mere animals. As a result, people will only have ten-year life spans, and "for those of a ten-year life span there will be no word for 'moral,' so how can there be anyone who acts in a moral way?"[43]

During the time of those who have ten-year life spans, there will be a "sword-interval" of seven days. People will mistake each other for wild beasts and "sharp swords will appear in their hands and, thinking: 'There is a wild beast!' they will take each other's lives with those swords."[44] There will be some, however, who will not want to kill or be killed. These few will run to the jungle and hide in caves while those outside "will die to the last of them in countless numbers."[45] At the end of seven days, those who survived will emerge from their hiding places and will rejoice upon seeing each other saying, "Good beings, I see that you are alive!"[46] From this humble beginning they will completely embrace wholesome morals so that they live together in harmony and their life spans will increase to 80,000 years.

A new earth and the next Buddha. In the midst of this eschatological sermon, the Buddha gave a very curious prophecy. It seems that he was not the last Buddha, but another will come who will do even greater things than he.

> And in that time of the people with an eighty thousand-year life-span, there will arise in the world a Blessed Lord, an Arahant fully-enlightened Buddha named Metteyya, endowed with wisdom and conduct, a Well-Farer, Knower of the worlds, incomparable Trainer of men to be tamed, Teacher of gods and humans, enlightened and blessed, just as I am now. . . . He will teach the Dhamma, lovely in its beginning, lovely in its middle, lovely in its ending, in the spirit and in the letter, and proclaim, just as I do now, the holy life in its fullness and purity. He will be attended by a company of thousands of monks, just as I am attended by a company of hundreds.[47]

A story exists in later Buddhist writings about a saintly monk name Phra Malai, who by his great concentration and merit was able to visit the heaven of Indra. In his palace, Indra built a pagoda that housed a relic of the Buddha, and celestial beings often went to pay homage to the relic. After Phra Malai gave homage to the Buddha relic, he sat with Indra and observed the different beings as they came to worship at the pagoda. Phra Malai was excited because Metteyya was due to arrive that day as well. After the monk observed twelve different deities worship at the pagoda, Metteyya finally arrived. He

---

43 *The Long Discourses*, trans. Walshe, 401.
44 Ibid., 402.
45 Brereton, *Thai Tellings of Phra Malai*, 213.
46 *The Long Discourses*, trans. Walshe, 402.
47 Ibid., 403–4.

was "surrounded by a retinue of an infinite number of celestial gods and goddesses."[48]

When Metteyya finished worshipping, he went over to greet Phra Malai. He asked Phra Malai what the situation was like in the human realm, to which he replied that for the most part "those who sinned were great in number."[49] Mettayya responded by giving a message to the people. If they wanted to be reborn during the time that he, Mettayya, would be enlightened as a Buddha: "Those who wished to meet him should listen to the recitation of the entire *Vessantara Jātaka*—all one thousand verses—in one day and one night. In addition, they should bring offerings of one thousand candles, incense sticks, flowers, and other gifts to the temple."[50] The *Vessantara Jātaka* is the story of the previous life of the Buddha before he was born as Siddhartha Gautama, the one who became the Buddha. According to this message, if one follows through with all that Mettayya said, then "all his wishes will be fulfilled . . . . In the future they will attain *nibbaña*."[51]

During the time of 80,000-year life spans, the Mettayya will come to the human realm in order to receive enlightenment. The corrupted earth will be remade as a "torrent of celestial rain will pour down every half-month. Cascading down at midnight, it will strike the surface of the earth, cooling it and fertilizing it with its essence. The continent of Jambu will then appear, flourishing with vegetation."[52] It will be a time of utopian bliss as "creatures of every kind will be full of affection for one another . . . . There will be only constant joy and tranquility."[53]

Mettayya will be perfect in every way when he attains enlightenment, and he will be able to transfer his great merit to all those who live during this time. Because in his millions of past lives he practiced generosity and morality, everyone's bodies will be glorious. Because he once gave his eyes to a beggar, everyone's eyes will glow with light and no one will be blind. Because he gave his own body until there was nothing left, "all beings will be graceful and without flaw. Those who were crippled will be healed."[54] Ultimately, the Mettayya says, "I will use my extraordinary wisdom as a weapon to sever completely the bonds that entrap beings, and I will free them from these shackles . . . . Then they will enter the abode of *nibbāna* through my accumulated merit."[55]

Nirvana. As great as this utopian society will be, it is still not the final act according to Buddhist teaching. *Nirvana* is.[56] The Buddha said, "There is a

---

[48]   Brereton, *Thai Tellings of Phra Malai*, 9.

[49]   Ibid., 10.

[50]   Ibid.

[51]   Sommai Premchit and Amphay Doré, *The Lan Na Twelve-Month Traditions* (Chiang Mai: The Toyota Foundation, 1992), 78.

[52]   Brereton, *Thai Tellings of Phra Malai*, 214.

[53]   Ibid., 216–17.

[54]   Ibid., 218.

[55]   Ibid., 221.

[56]   Sanskrit: *nirvāna*; Pali: *nibbāna*.

realm that is not earth, nor water, nor fire, nor air. It is not this world, nor the other world, neither sun nor the moon. It does not come by birth, nor does it go by death. It is simply the end of suffering."[57] As long as one exists, then one will suffer. Even in the time of bliss when people live to be 80,000 years old, there will still be death as well as sadness for those who are left behind. Even joy will cause sadness because at some point the joy will end and it will be replaced with a longing for joy—suffering. The only answer to this dilemma is to experience nothing and be nothing. Davis says, "Nirvana for the Buddhist is described not as a place, but as a state of being, or perhaps a state of non-being. To be in Nirvana is literally to be extinguished. There will be no birth, or re-birth, no attachment, no desire, no ignorance, no passion or anger, nothing. Nirvana is not a place; it is a 'stateless-state,' an unreal reality."[58]

Nirvana may sound like nothing more than an annihilationist view, but because the Buddha taught that there is no such thing as a personal soul, *nirvana* is simply the final absorption into reality. As Rahula notes, "Nirvāna is definitely no annihilation of self, because there is no self to annihilate. If at all, it is the annihilation of the illusion, of the false idea of self."[59] Because *nirvana* is defined in this way, people do not have to wait until they die to experience a *nirvanic* state. *Nirvana* can be experienced here and now through mindfulness. In fact, true mindfulness is *nirvana*, because true mindfulness is voidness. Mindfulness is best illustrated through the practice of *Vipassana* meditation. The purpose of this exercise is to train the mind to be empty and in so doing, gain insight into the truth of impermanence. As Ayya Khema says, "The great renunciation that arises in meditation is to drop all thoughts. When there's nobody thinking, there's no ego confirmation."[60] It is in these moments that one experiences a taste of *nirvana*.

Restoration in Buddhism is not really restoration. There is no first cause so there is no person to whom to be restored, therefore, there is no former glory or former perfection to which to return. There is only what is—suffering (*dukkha*), and what could be—no suffering (*nirvana*).

CONCLUSION

No hope. A Westerner reading this chapter about Buddhism is likely to be exasperated at Buddhism with its Eastern categories and logic. How can there be no first cause? Where did *karma* come from? How does *karma* determine what is good and bad if it is nothing more than cause and effect? How was good and bad determined in the first place? How can one save oneself if there is no such thing as self? How does Mettayya fit into all of this since the core of the Buddha's teaching is, "Be islands unto yourselves, be a refuge unto

---

[57] *Buddhist Scriptures,* ed. Donald S. Lopez Jr. (Victoria: Penguin Group, 2005), 3.
[58] Davis, *The Path to Enlightenment,* 95.
[59] Rahula, *What the Buddha Taught,* 37.
[60] Ayya Khema, *Being Nobody, Going Nowhere* (Boston: Wisdom Publications, 2001), 4.

yourselves with no other refuge."[61] Even more maddening is the Buddha's refusal to answer these questions.

Buddhism, it seems, creates much undue suffering, therefore causing the very thing it seeks to eliminate. Bruce Little writes, "If one believes that the elimination of suffering is an absolute in itself, then any means will be acceptable to that end."[62] When Prince Siddhartha Gautama began his journey toward enlightenment as the Buddha, he left his wife and child behind. On the night he left, "he stood at the door, and longingly, lovingly continued to look at his child, until his thoughts showed him his error. 'How can I continue to live thus,' he reflected; 'how can I live, loving my wife and child, and at the same time escape the evils of circling existence?'"[63] Ultimately, love is evil. It does not matter that Gautama's wife and child had to suffer because Gautama saved himself. In the end, this is what everyone must do—cause suffering in a lonesome pursuit for self-deliverance. There is no room for neighbor love or altruism because according to Buddhism it does not actually benefit anyone, especially the doer.

Though fascinating and complex, Buddhism leaves one with little or no hope. At funerals, monks hold up four fans and chant the words that are written on them. Sitting on their knees with hands folded reverently in front of their faces and incense smoke burning their nostrils, grief-stricken people listen to the monks chant these words: "Gone never to return. Asleep never to awake. There is no resurrection. There is no escape." There is no hope.

Hope. It does little good to attempt to show Buddhists the apparent contradictions within their belief system. Often, where the Western mind sees contradiction, the Asian mind sees harmony. We may think their belief system is irrational, but this assumes that "rational" is the ultimate objective. In their minds they strive to be reasonable (in the ordinary sense of the word, not rational in the philosophical sense of the word). When a Westerner encounters an apparent contradiction, his goal is to immediately deduce which is true and which is false. The Asian mind, however, is primarily concerned with relationship, or holism. Nothing exists in isolation and can only be defined within its context. As Richard Nisbett notes, "The principle of holism, in contrast, indicates that a thing is different in one context than in another and the principle of change indicates that life is a constant passing from one state of being to another, so that to be is not to be and not to be is to be."[64] Instead of focusing on the apparent contradiction, Asian holism seeks to find the truth in A as well as in not-A.

When ministering to Buddhists, Christians will find little benefit in a "theology as logical martial arts" approach. Instead, they are well served to draw

---

[61]   *The Long Discourses*, trans. Walshe, 404.

[62]   Bruce Little, *A Creation-Order Theodicy: God and Gratuitous Evil* (Lanham: University Press of America, 2005), 183.

[63]   Alabaster, *Wheel of the Law*, 127.

[64]   Richard Nisbett, *The Geography of Thought: How Asians and Westerners Think Differently ... and Why* (New York: Free Press, 2003), 176–77.

the Buddhists into the Christian Scriptures, narrating to them the true story of the world, and inviting them to believe and receive. In so doing, we can begin to answer their questions about suffering and yet at the same time admit that we cannot answer comprehensively. We can share why we believe God is omnibenevolent, omniscient, and omnipotent even in the face of evil and suffering. We can share how suffering is not evil in itself, but in relation to God there is great value in suffering. On this middle ground we can introduce Mary as both virgin and mother, Jesus as both God and man, and ourselves as both sinful and just. It is also here that we find the Father, Son, and Holy Spirit as three separate persons, yet one God, who by suffering gave our lives purpose.

Kazoh Kitamori said, "The pain of God means that the love of God had conquered the wrath of God in the midst of the *historical* world deserving his wrath. Thus the pain of God must *necessarily* enter the historical plane as a person."[65] History, and the suffering therein, suddenly become something beautiful in Christ. Life has purpose and there is hope. As witnesses to the suffering of Christ, our pain is turned into something fruitful. Only in the biblical understanding of creation, fall, redemption, and restoration is there hope. A place exists where truth abides in all its glory, and that place is in Jesus Christ.

---

[65] Kazoh Kitamori, *Theology of the Pain of God* (Eugene: Wipf and Stock, previously published by John Knox Press, 1965), 34.

Chapter Nineteen

MISSION TO ANIMISTS

R. L. Calvert and David R. Crane

INTRODUCTION

Animism pervades the world in which we live and minister. Animistic beliefs and practices may be found in every region of the world, including the United States and Europe, and they may be observed even among the adherents of every major world religion. Gailyn Van Rheenen and others have noted that 40 percent or more of the world's population is impacted by animistic thinking.[1] In light of the pervasive impact of animism on today's world, this chapter aims to provide a brief definition of animism, an assessment of where and how it may be found, and a delineation of its false salvific system in comparison to the biblical narrative.

What is animism? British anthropologist Sir Edward Burnett Tylor, in his study with pre-literate societies, is often credited with coining the term "animism."[2] The word is derived from the Latin *anima*, meaning "breath" or "breath of life." He postulated that primitive cultures had a simple definition of religion being a belief in spiritual beings. This included a belief that non-living objects have life, personality, and even souls. Tylor used the term *animism* not so much as a technical term developed from a comparative religion viewpoint, but more as a descriptive term used to distinguish a deep

---

[1] Gailyn Van Rheenen, *Communicating Christ in Animistic Contexts* (Pasadena, CA: William Carey Library, 1991), 25.

[2] Edward Burnett Tylor, *Primitive Culture*, 7th ed. (NY: Bretano's, 1924; London: John Murray, 1871), II, 2. In actuality, the eighteenth-century German physician and chemist Georg Ernst Stahl coined the word *animism* to describe his theory that the soul is the vital principle responsible for organic development. Since the late nineteenth century, the term has been mainly associated with anthropology and the British anthropologist Sir Edward Burnett Tylor.

spiritualism from a materialistic philosophy. Tylor's classic definition (1873) focuses on a religious adherent's belief in the spirit world, explaining that "animism, in its full development, includes the belief in souls and in a future state, in controlling deities and subordinate spirits . . . resulting in some kind of active worship."[3]

Despite this accepted basic definition, there is still much debate concerning the notion of animism.[4] It is sometimes referred to as a "tribal religion." However, while it is certainly found among specific tribes worldwide, it is also true that many non-tribal European and American peoples employ various aspects of animism in a "non-tribal" fashion. Others refer to animism as a "primitive religion" even though it is quite complicated, inclusive, and pervasive throughout the contemporary world. Allen R. Tippett, therefore, is correct to refer to the term "animism," as a "term of convenience to provide a frame of reference for our discussions."[5] He maintains that the term

---

[3] Edward B. Tylor, *Religion in Primitive Culture* (London: John Murray, 1970), 11.

[4] Among biologists and psychologists, *animism* refers to the view that the human mind is a nonmaterial entity that nevertheless interacts with the body via the brain and nervous system. As a philosophical theory, *animism*, usually called *panpsychism*, is the doctrine that all objects in the world have an inner or psychological being. Others view animism not as a belief in a spiritual being(s) but a belief in a supernatural force. R. H. Codrington, in *The Melanesians*, made the first serious study of impersonal spiritual powers called *mana*. He described *mana* as a supernatural force behind all human activity that acts for good or evil and is imperative to possess and control; Codrington, *The Melanesians* [Oxford: Clarendon, 1891]. The British anthropologist, Robert R. Marett, rejected Tylor's theory that *all* objects were regarded as being alive, thus advancing the idea of *mana*. Marett thought that primitive peoples must have recognized some lifeless objects and probably regarded only those objects that had unusual qualities or behaved in some seemingly unpredictable or mysterious way as being alive. He held, moreover, that the ancient concept of aliveness was not sophisticated enough to include the notion of a soul or spirit residing in the object. Primitive peoples treated the objects they considered animate as if these things had life, feeling, and a will of their own, but did not make a distinction between the body of an object and a soul that could enter or leave it. Marett called this view *animatism* or *preanimism*, and he claimed that animism had to arise out of animatism, which may even continue to exist alongside more highly developed animistic beliefs (Marett, "Animism," *Encyclopedia Britannica* [1932], 1:975; *The Threshold of Religion* 2nd ed. [London: Methuen, 1909, 1914]). French sociologist, Emile Durkheim, in *The Elementary Forms of the Religious Life* (London: G. Allen and Unwin, 1915), held that *animism* was also too advanced for primitive cultures conceiving the concept of *totemism* as the essence of primitive thought. British anthropologist, Sir James George Frazer, in his book, *The Golden Bough*, argued that the term *animism*, the belief in spirits, was too abstract and advanced to be man's first religion. He concluded that magic preceded religion because it helped man to live in this world by obtaining food, blessing the family, cursing the enemy, warding off curses from others, etc. (Frazer, ed., *The Golden Bough: A Study in Magic and Religion* [New York: Macmillan, 1922]). Later, anthropologist Bronislaw Malinowski, in *Magic, Science, and Religion*, would further the thought that magic was pre-animistic (Malinowski, *Magic, Science, and Religion* [Garden City, NY: Doubleday, Anchor Books, 1954]). There are others who are calling for a "new animism." They understand their worldview as one of a community of living persons, expressing mutual respect and engaging in communication in which only some of whom are human (Graham Harvey, *Animism: Respecting the Living World* [New York: Columbia University Press, 2005].

[5] Alan R. Tippett, "The Evangelization of Animists," *Let the Earth Hear His Voice: International Congress on World Evangelization*, ed. J. D. Douglas (Minneapolis, MN: World Wide Publications, 1975), 844.

"animism" can be examined because of sufficient universal aspects that will permit a comparison between the worldview of the animist and that of Biblical Christianity.[6]

Perhaps Gailyn Van Rheenen's definition best captures the way this chapter speaks of animism. Van Rheenen summarizes animism as "the belief that personal spiritual beings and impersonal spiritual forces have power over human affairs and, consequently, that human beings must discover what beings and forces are influencing them in order to determine future action and, frequently, to manipulate their power."[7] This chapter will utilize Van Rheenen's definition as the working paradigm for animism, treating animism as a religious system that (1) focuses on belief in the spirit world, and (2) is characterized by the quest to control one's life in light of the spirit world.

Animism is most well known as a feature of African Traditional Religions (ATR).[8] However, as we pointed out above, animistic belief and practice is not limited to those people who are adherents of polytheistic tribal religions. It influences the adherents of the major world religions and even those who might consider themselves irreligious. Steyne, in his classic book *Gods of Power: A Study on the Beliefs and Practices of Animists*, notes that there are four broad levels of animistic influence. The first level is dominated by animism reflecting polytheism, pantheism, and deism. The second level has significant effect on the religions like Folk Catholicism, Folk Islam, and African Traditional Religions. The third level has no constant animistic practices, but the practices surface when the adopted religion fails to address the felt needs usually involving a desire for power, success, healing, happiness, or protection. The fourth level involves orthodox practice, but the piety is only a form of trying to impress the spirit world in order to gain felt needs.[9]

Further, animism is not limited geographically to Africa or Asia. Animistic beliefs and practices are found throughout the Western world.[10] It can be seen any time a person consults the horoscope in the local newspaper, wears a rabbit foot for good luck, or "knocks on wood" to avoid misfortune. Further, Western literature, cinema, and television portray and sometimes advocate animistic beliefs and practices. Take, for example, television series such as *Buffy the Vampire Slayer* and *Charmed*, or books such as the *Harry Potter* series.

In light of the manifold influence of animism on the global community, evangelical Christians are well served to craft a robust biblical response.

---

[6]   Ibid., 845.

[7]   Van Rheenen, *Communicating Christ in Animistic Contexts*, 20.

[8]   African traditional religions usually believe in one supreme creator god who is distant and uninvolved with daily life. Some also hold to lesser gods or other deities. Other deities could fall under the category of dead ancestors, capricious spirits or lesser gods, and life forces that tend to be immaterial.

[9]   Philip M. Steyne, *Gods of Power: A Study on the Beliefs and Practices of Animists* (Columbia, SC: Impact International Foundation, 1990), 46.

[10]   Van Rheenen, *Communicating Christ in Animistic Contexts*, 27.

Steyne notes that Western theologians have been occupied primarily with historical issues, while Asian, Africa, and Latin American theologians are being confronted with how to deal with issues more relevant to them in the arenas of current social, economic, and political problems in a mesh of spiritualism or animism.[11] Even the African church, which deals directly with animism on a daily basis, often keeps one foot in Christianity and one in their traditional beliefs. This dualism is reflected by Emeka Onwurah, for example, who writes, "Most Africans tend to uphold two faiths. They maintain the Christian faith when life is gay and happy, but hold to the indigenous faith when the fundamentals of life are at stake."[12]

This chapter, therefore, seeks to facilitate an understanding of animism and how it conflicts with biblical Christianity. We will compare the Bible's cosmic narrative to the animistic story of the world, exposing animism as a false salvific system that cannot give account for creation, fall, redemption, or restoration.

AN ANIMISTIC VIEW OF CREATION

Christian Scripture begins by claiming, "In the beginning, God created the heavens and the earth" (Gen. 1:1). While it is typical for Westerners to begin by speaking of God's creation of the physical world, sometimes those who work with animistic peoples prefer to begin by speaking of the creation of the spirit world: angels (Gen. 19:1), cherubim (Gen. 3:24), heavenly hosts (Ps. 148:2), seraphim (Isa. 6:2), archangel Michael (Jude 9), and the fall of Satan and his demons (Job 1:6–7; 38:6–7; Isa. 14:12–15; Ezek. 28:11–19; 2 Cor. 11:14; 1 Tim. 3:6; 2 Pet. 2:4; Jude 6; Rev. 12:7–9).[13] This does not in

[11] Steyne, *Gods of Power*, 169.

[12] Emeka Onwurah, "The Quest, Means, and Relevance of African Christian Theology," in *African Christian Studies,* 4:3 (November 1988), 6. This Christian-Animist syncretism is treated in Paul G. Hiebert, R. Daniel Shaw, and Tite Tienou, *Understanding Folk Religion: A Christian Response to Popular Beliefs and Practices* (Grand Rapids: Baker, 1999).

[13] A full discussion or thorough listing of the numerous verses concerning angels and fallen angels (demons) is beyond the scope of this chapter. The authors recognize that there is some controversy concerning the application of the Isaiah 14 passage, and even the Ezekiel 28 passage, to the fall of Satan, referred to as "the anointed cherub" in the Ezekiel passage, especially if compared to the Luke 10:18 passage. The Isaiah passage is directed to the king of Babylon, more than likely Sennacherib (705–681 BC). There are some scholars who only consider this passage to be highly figurative language about a pompous king who considered himself to be a god or equal to Yahweh. There are other scholars who view the Isaiah 14 passage as one who, at least, describes (some say literally and others view this figuratively) the fall of Satan. This view has been held historically since Tertullian (AD 160–230), as well as by Origen, Augustine, Gregory the Great, Jerome, and Thomas Aquinas. Even Calvin adhered to the fall of Satan although he did not use the Isaiah 14 passage. The Ezekiel passage is directed to the king of Tyre, more than likely Ethbaal III (591–572 BC). There are some scholars who only view this passage as figurative language describing a prideful king (some say comparing him to Adam, but that view has many problems as well) who viewed himself as a god or equal with Yahweh. This view has some difficulty explaining the passage, "You were in Eden, the garden of God" (Ezek. 28:13, NASB), even if one thinks this is a comparison to Adam—usually in light of the next passage that says,

any way negate God's creation of the physical world. Instead, it begins with an item of great interest to animists—the creation of unseen beings.

Those who seek to minister to animists must understand both the animistic view and the biblical view. They will find both similarities and differences. Many animistic Africans believe that God created the heavens and the earth and all their contents.[14] Most animists in Africa and Asia have a concept of a high God who created all things. Steyne observes, however, that the high God of animism tends to be deistic in nature and involved only minimally in human affairs. Some animists believe that one high God can only be reached through other spirits in the chain of command under him. They would understand high-God attributes such as Creator, Provider, and Judge, but they would not address the one high God as Father or one personally involved with man's daily life.[15] Others, however, do not view the high God as distant. Peter Sarpong maintains that many animists feel the Supreme God is close to them, and that the apparent distance is a consequence of the respect that the African has towards those in authority. If God is great, then surely he must be approached through intermediaries.[16] Steyne points out that the animist has many avenues for talking to the one high God. One of those avenues is lesser gods and another is helping spirits. These are entreated through sacrifices, rituals, ceremonies, or a religious expert. Some animists worship a plurality of gods while others worship the one true God through the lesser gods, ancestors, or helping spirits embodied within objects, places, or animals.

Others view these lesser divinities as self-sufficient, able to act independently of the high God. They are thought to have the same attributes as the high God, but are only accorded special spheres of concern. They tend to be arbitrary and capricious as they bring man either success or failure. They are thought to have human appetites and passions and must be placated with different kinds of offerings and sacrifices. Household gods, ancestor spirits, and

---

"You were the anointed cherub who covers, and I placed you there. You were on the holy mountain of God; You walked in the midst of the stones of fire" (Ezek. 28:14, NASB). The authors reject J. W. McKay's view that Isaiah or Ezekiel had taken their ideas, material, or passages from pagan cultures like Ugaritic myths of the Dawn goddess, Palestinian myths of Baal, or Greek myths of Phaethon. See R. Laird Harris, Gleason L. Archer, and Bruce K. Waltke, eds. *Theological Wordbook of the Old Testament: Vol. 1* (Chicago: Moody Press, 1980) 217, no. 499. It is better to view that this material was taken from a pre-creation viewpoint of the fall of Satan. The authors realize the Isaiah 14 passage may be forced a bit to conform to the fall of Satan view; however they still believe both passages are references to Satan, the one who was influencing or motivating the human king(s) to do his bidding. The Ezekiel 28 passage is unmistakable in its reference to the fall of Satan. See Sinclair B. Ferguson, David F. Wright, and J. I. Packer, eds. *New Dictionary of Theology* (Downers Grove: IVP, 1988) 20–21, 196–98; See also John F. Walvoord and Roy B. Zuck, eds. *The Bible Knowledge Commentary OT* (Colorado Springs: ChariotVictor Publishing, 1985), 1061, 1282–84.

[14]   Tokunboh Adeyemo, *Salvation in African Tradition* (Nairobi, Kenya: Evangel Publishing House, 1979), 19.

[15]   Steyne, *Gods of Power*, 74.

[16]   Peter Sarpong, "Synod for Africa," *World Mission* (March 1994): 25.

fetishes would also fall in the category of lesser gods.[17] John S. Mbiti uses the term "living dead," while Healey and Sybertz use Mbiti's term to point out that these "benevolent ancestral spirits are the link between the living and the "Supreme Being."[18]

Moreover, some animists also hold to the belief that the spirit world was created with the good spirits as man's helpers and the evil spirits as the destroyers of man constantly seeking to distress mankind.[19] The good spirits are to be enlisted to provide special protection while the evil spirits are to be feared.[20] The entire life of these animists is focused on the spirit world and all its actors within. Each of the spirits, totems, and fetishes will get special attention by certain rituals, ceremonies, or sacrifices in order to assure they are appeased.

AN ANIMISTIC VIEW OF THE FALL

Christian Scripture teaches that man was created in harmony with his Creator God until he disobeyed and was driven from the Garden of Eden to be separated from God (Gen. 1:26–3:24; Isa. 59:2). Likewise, many animistic myths and oral traditions tell about the fall of man and the separation of heaven and earth.[21] Most African stories about a "fall" tell of God withdrawing to heaven because of man doing something wrong rather than man being driven from the Garden of Eden.[22]

The Bible teaches that Eve was deceived by the serpent, who induced her to eat from the tree of the knowledge of good and evil by promising that she would "be like God, knowing good and evil" (Gen. 3:5). Satan spoke through the serpent to tempt Eve to attain what he wanted for himself when he was removed from heaven—to be God in order to choose good and evil (Isa. 14:14; Ezek. 28:11–19; Rev. 12:9).[23] Eve, likewise, sinned by attempting to set herself up as autonomous and sovereign.

Just as Eve sought to be autonomous, so the animistic person also desires to be god and control the world that affects him.[24] Animism does not teach its adherents to look for ways to obey and please the one true God, but instead to compel, entreat, and coerce their god to do their will, not the will of their god.[25] The animist is constantly seeking to manipulate the one true God, the lesser gods or deities, the ancestral spirits, and the other spirits in order to

---

[17] Steyne, *Gods of Power*, 74–76.

[18] Joseph Healey and Donald Sybertz, *Towards an African Narrative Theology* (Nairobi, Kenya: Paulines Publications Africa, 1996), 211.

[19] Steyne, *Gods of Power*, 78–79.

[20] Osadolor Imasogie, *Guidelines for Christian Theology in Africa* (Ibadan, Nigeria: University Press Ltd., 1986), 75.

[21] Adeyemo, *Salvation in African Tradition*, 25.

[22] Healey and Sybertz, *Towards an African Narrative Theology*, 63.

[23] See the note on footnote 13.

[24] Steyne, *Gods of Power*, 46, 171.

[25] Ibid., 38.

harmonize his life and control it. In part, the animist seeks to manipulate the gods because of his fear of the gods, spirits, angry ancestors, and human enemies.[26] This desire for control and manipulation is in keeping with five foundational beliefs of animism: holism—that all the universe is interconnected whether physical, material, or spiritual with no distinction between sacred or secular; spiritualism—that spirituality is the essence of life with everything in the physical realm being influenced by the spiritual realm and vice versa; dynamism—that a life without power is not worth living because one must have access to it to control or manipulate the spirit world; communalism—that the individual does not matter but only the community comprised of the living as well as the departed ancestors, called the "living dead," where harmony and unbroken relationships are imperative;[27] and fatalism—that the position, place, and status of animists have been pre-determined by some external, supernatural force that can be accepted, hindered, or thwarted, but with severe consequences for the latter.[28]

Christian Scripture teaches that God cursed the serpent, Eve, Adam, and the ground because of their disobedience to God (Gen. 2:16–17; 3:14–19). God told Adam that the penalty for disobedience, sin against God's laws, was death (Gen. 2:16–17). The apostle Paul reaffirms this truth, stating that "the wages of sin is death" (Rom. 6:23). Therefore God's intended harmony was broken by Adam and Eve's sin. Through them, death entered the world.

Animists, however, see sin and death in a different light. Among some of the African stories, death is portrayed as an accident or mistake. The blame is usually laid on the people themselves, on animals, and, in some cases, on spirits or monsters. Death represents a separation from human beings and from God. Most animistic death stories do not refer to personal sin, but blame outside forces. Some of these forces are evil and therefore not in harmony with nature.[29] This disruption of "harmony" between the one high God and nature is reflected by Yusufu Turaki when he observes that there are two main issues that disrupt cosmic harmony in an animistic setting. The first is the unpredictable attitudes and behavior of the agents of the spirit world. The second is any breach in the fellowship or relationship between people and their benevolent spirits caused by either sins of omission or commission.[30]

Among many animists, there is no individual responsibility for personal actions. As a result of an animist's belief that he is an extension of the spirit world, he concludes that all share the responsibility. This would include the corporate family and the tribe. An animist believes he is being acted upon by spirits and powers beyond his control. Since he believes that he is basically a good person abiding by all the customs and taboos, he is free from any

---

[26] Hiebert, Shaw, and Tienou, *Understanding Folk Religion*, 87.

[27] Steyne, *Gods of Power*, 58–62.

[28] Yusufu Turaki, *Foundations of African Traditional Religion and Worldview* (Nairobi, Kenya: WordAlive Publishers Ltd., 2006), 40–42.

[29] Healey and Sybertz, *Towards an African Narrative Theology*, 206.

[30] Turaki, *Foundations of African Traditional Religion and Worldview*, 44.

wrongdoing. Even if for some reason he does break some custom or taboo he will visit the ritualistic expert in order to discern who is actually responsible.[31]

Animists do not consider their sins of omission or commission to have been committed against the one high God. The animist believes that sin is chiefly an offense against one's neighbor and is punishable here and now.[32] The traditional African animist view is that evil does not come from God or a broken relationship with God, but from a break in relationships with the ancestors or with the living.[33] This uncertainty in the relationships with these spiritual beings causes the animist to be constantly motivated by fear.[34] The animist does not trust these spiritual beings, because of their whimsical and capricious nature, and seeks to control or manipulate.[35] This fear affects the way the animist views relationships and evaluates events in his life.

Many animists, especially African animists, think the greatest human need is to counter the effects of witchcraft because the worse possible scenario is to be cursed or bewitched.[36] When faced with bad circumstances, the animist typically will not examine himself to see what he may have done to cause the events, nor even look at his environment for a way to bring about a more favorable outcome. Instead, he seeks to ascertain who cursed him and for what reason. He will then work for ways to remove the curse, rather than look for ways to change the circumstances.

THE ANIMIST SEES NO NEED FOR REDEMPTION

The apostle Paul makes clear that through Adam's sin, all have sinned and all die as a result of that sin (Rom. 5:12). Furthermore, because man has sinned against holy God, he is helpless (Rom. 5:6), is a sinner (Rom. 5:8), and is an enemy of God (Rom. 5:10). As a result of man wanting to become like God, he disobeyed God by eating from the fruit of the tree of the knowledge of good and evil (Gen. 2:16–17; 3:5–6).

As discussed in the previous section, the animist does not view himself as a sinner against the one high God. When sin is committed against other living humans or those viewed as the living dead (ancestors), the animist can purchase the services of a religious specialist, perform a ritual act himself, use a charm or fetish, or observe taboos to rectify any erring on his behalf. There is no need, as far as he is concerned, to be redeemed from any sin committed against the one high God.

The animist does not think that the high God is concerned with redeeming mankind. John S. Mbiti notes that there is not a single myth in the animistic African Traditional Religions that attempts a solution or reversal of the loss

---

[31]   Steyne, *Gods of Power*, 67.
[32]   Adeyemo, *Salvation in African Tradition*, 66.
[33]   Healey and Sybertz, *Towards an African Narrative Theology*, 218.
[34]   Steyne, *Gods of Power*, 77.
[35]   Van Rheenen, *Communicating Christ in Animistic Contexts*, 22.
[36]   Healey and Sybertz, *Towards an African Narrative Theology*, 218.

of man's original state with God.[37] He maintains that man has just accepted the separation between him and the one high God. He concludes by declaring that these traditional religions do not offer a way of escape or a message of redemption.[38]

The animist has no need to be redeemed because he desires more than anything to control his own destiny.[39] The animist is concerned about acquiring power for himself to provide rain for animals or crops, blessing in relationships, success in life's endeavors, protection from sickness or evil, or just personal aggrandizement.[40] This power can come from the spiritual beings or forces. R. H. Codrington first described this impersonal force as a Melanesian phenomena called *mana*.[41] Gailyn Van Rheenen has noted that this aspect of a power force or life force is called various names, *toh* in Indonesia and *baraka* in the Muslim world.[42]

The Animist Has No Need for Restoration

The Lord Jesus Christ's declaration to Martha that "I am the resurrection and the life" (John 11:25) is the crowning statement of victory over death, the grave, hell, and Satan. By believing in Christ, we may receive the benefits of his victory (John 11:25–26). The apostle Paul declared as "most important" among Christians that "Christ died for our sins according to the Scriptures, that He was buried, that He was raised on the third day according to the Scriptures, and that He appeared to Cephas, then to the Twelve. Then he appeared to over 500 brothers at one time" (1 Cor. 15:3–6, HCSB). Paul continued to declare that all in Adam died, so all who place their total trust in the Lord Jesus Christ would be made alive (1 Cor. 15:22). Paul also mentions the fact the creation groans to be free of the slavery to corruption while the apostle John affirms this world will be made new (Rom. 8:20–22; Rev. 21:1). All these verses presuppose a linear view of time, a view in which history has both an origin and a destiny.

The animist, however, does not view time as linear but circular.[43] He believes that all of life is spiritual, that there is no distinction between the natural and the supernatural, and therefore that death only changes the form or

---

[37] John S. Mbiti would contend that the term *animist* is inadequate and should be abandoned in relation to African Traditional Religions. John S. Mbiti, *African Religions and Philosophy* (New York, NY: Frederick A. Praeger, 1969), 8. Others maintain that the African Traditional Religion belief system is animistic. Richard J. Gehman, *African Traditional Religion in Biblical Perspective* (Nairobi, Kenya: East African Educational Publishers, Ltd., 1989), 29.

[38] Mbiti, *African Religions and Philosophy*, 128–29.

[39] Steyne, *Gods of Power*, 171.

[40] Ibid., 38–39.

[41] Codrington, *The Melanesians*, 191.

[42] Van Rheenen, *Communicating Christ in Animistic Contexts,* 21. Others have found similar concepts in other cultures (Marett, *The Threshold of Religion,* 108–113; Gehman, *African Traditional Religion in Biblical Perspective*, 85–87).

[43] Van Rheenen, *Communicating Christ in Animistic Contexts,* 34–35.

the essence of a person. Some African animists believe death is annihilation and others believe it is a transition. Some view death as a separation of the material body—the flesh—from the immaterial part—the spirit or soul—that continues to live on.[44] This would lend to John S. Mbiti's view of the departed ancestors as the "living dead" in his book *Concepts of God in Africa*.[45]

This cyclical view of history gives rise to such beliefs as karma and reincarnation. The animist has no need for a resurrection because the departed are not dead or gone, just transformed. Most animists do not have any doctrine of the resurrection of the dead or of the consummation of all things. Some believe in "partial reincarnation" where the dead are "reborn" in certain children. Others hold to a transmigration of souls where the spirits of some people are reborn into animals. Yet others believe that a soul cannot be destroyed neither can it grow.[46] Nonetheless, in all of these cases, the common factor is a cyclical view of time, life, and existence.

Moreover, animists believe there is no punishment for those in disharmony with the one high God, the lesser deities, or ancestors. Nor do they believe there are any rewards for good living. The majority of Africans do not expect any form of judgment in the hereafter.[47] The majority of African people claim that God punishes people and rewards them only in this life. Richard J. Gehman points out a major consequence of this belief: there is no hope of fellowship with God.[48] There is nothing awaiting them when they die, for sin is chiefly an offense against one's neighbor and is punishable here and now.[49] The Maasai tribe in East Africa does not believe there is an afterlife. Once a person is dead, that is final.[50] There is no reward, no punishment, no judgment, and no hope.

CONCLUSION

Theologians, missiologists, missionaries, and indeed the entire Christian world can no longer afford to ignore animism. Believers must be able to address animistic beliefs and practices in a way that is theologically sound and missiologically savvy. Paul G. Hiebert calls for believers to develop a holistic theology that takes into account the "spirit world" or what he refers to as the "excluded middle."[51] This theology would include the biblical account of God in history and his personal dealings with mankind on a daily basis. Further, it would detail his constant love, provision, healing, and protection

---

[44] Adeyemo, *Salvation in African Tradition*, 61.

[45] John S. Mbiti, *Concepts of God in Africa* (London, UK: SPCK, 1970).

[46] Adeyemo, *Salvation in African Tradition*, 67.

[47] Ibid., 64.

[48] Richard J. Gehman, *Who Are the Living-Dead? A Theology of Death, Life After Death, and the Living-Dead* (Nairobi, Kenya: Evangel Publishing House, 1999), 25–26.

[49] Adeyemo, *Salvation in African Tradition*, 66.

[50] Healey and Sybertz, *Towards an African Narrative Theology*, 205.

[51] Paul G. Hiebert, "The Flaw of the Excluded Middle," *Missiology: An International Review*, vol. X (January 1982): 35–47.

for those who have rejected this world and its religious systems, having placed their trust in Jesus Christ as their Savior and Lord. Such a theology must be informed by a comprehensive and robust explication of biblical teaching on the Holy Spirit as well as Satan and his minions. Building such a theology will better equip Christians to bring them to a saving knowledge of the Lord.

Animism fails to acknowledge sin or its consequences. This belief system is completely destitute of any offering of redemption or restoration. A thorough understanding of animism will also assist believers in rejecting any animistic practices in their own faith, whether one is a missionary in an exotic locale or a pastor dealing with New Age doctrine or popular superstitions in the United States.

Chapter Twenty

MISSION TO POSTMODERNS

J. D. Greear

INTRODUCTION

The most difficult culture for which to contextualize the gospel is one's own. I had to serve as a church planter for two years overseas in a Muslim country to learn that reality. The same rigor applied to contextualizing the gospel for a foreign culture must be applied to contextualizing the gospel for each new generation of Western culture. Modern Western culture is the most rapidly changing culture yet to appear in history, with seismic culture shifts emerging nearly every decade.[1] Thus, those who do Christian ministry the same way their childhood churches did it will find themselves wielding decreasing influence in a culture increasingly foreign to them.

The most common descriptor of Western culture is "postmodern." Western postmodernism has a rich, albeit confusing, philosophical history. My interaction with postmodernity, however, comes more from it being the cultural milieu in which I minister than a theory expounded in the academy. I currently pastor a church steeped in a postmodern context. The Summit Church exists in Raleigh-Durham, a cityplex ranked by *Forbes* magazine to be "the #1 educational hub in America" and the top spot in the country for start-up tech industries, attracting highly educated people from all over America and the world. My congregation is largely comprised of college students and young professionals, many of whom are not from Christian backgrounds. Postmodernism is the air that we breathe in Raleigh–Durham.

---

[1]   See Leonard Sweet, *Soul Tsunami* (Grand Rapids: Zondervan, 1999), 17–18, 75–76.

The first difficulty in reaching postmoderns is defining what exactly post-modernism is. There seem to be as many definitions of postmodernity as there are analysts of postmodernity! I am not going to attempt an original description here. Rather, from a practical perspective, I'll suggest four main dimensions of postmodernity that present an opportunity for the gospel, and then offer some reflections on how the gospel meets those opportunities.[2]

THE POSTMODERN MILIEU

There is a vacuum of authority in postmodern thinking. This first dimension is the one most often noted about postmoderns. Postmoderns are wary of truth claims presented as true for all peoples in all places of all times. There are at least two reasons for this; one is technological and the other is philosophical. Technology has made the world "flat" now (to borrow the phrase made famous by Thomas Friedman), and on a regular basis we are exposed to people of other cultures, religions, and worldviews. Furthermore, many American cities are now a collage of various people groups. A common way to avoid conflicts that arise from distinctions in worldviews is to say each worldview is valid for the "world" out of which it arose. To approach others this way, it is believed, communicates respect and humility toward those with a different perspective than us.

Philosophically, religion is no longer seen as belonging in the category of objective truth. Immanuel Kant, late in the eighteenth century, made a distinction between "facts" and "values."[3] Facts, he said, are scientifically verifiable realities that are objectively true (e.g., "the English channel is west of France"). Values are personal preferences that are only subjectively true (e.g., "it feels hot in here"). Religion was put into the latter category, so that religions have come to be seen as subjectively helpful but not objectively true.

As this idea developed, experience and observation came to be seen as more certain avenues to truth than revelation. Our observation and experience certainly did not need to submit themselves to any revelation from God; they were authorities unto themselves.

Later postmodern philosophy brought into question the idea that *anything* could be known as objectively certain. Our perceptions of scientific evidence were proven to be just that—perceptions. Darwin once famously said that a

    [2] I am indebted to several men who have really shaped my thinking on these things, most notably Tim Keller, pastor of the Redeemer Church of New York City and David Powlison, author of numerous books on Christian counseling, such as *Seeing with New Eyes: Counseling and the Human Condition Through the Lens of Scripture* (Phillipsburg: P&R, 2003). A number of the ideas in this chapter show the marks of his influence. I will try to direct the reader to some of his most helpful sources throughout.
    [3] See Immanuel Kant, *Critique of Pure Reason*, ed. Eric Watkins, trans. Werner S. Pluhar (Cambridge: Hackett Publishing, 1999).

scientific man should have "no wishes, no affections, a mere heart of stone."[4] Theorists like Michel Foucault, Jacques Derrida, and Richard Rorty demonstrated that such objectivism was not possible.[5] Our reading of the evidence often says more about us than it does actual reality. All each of us has is perception of truth, not knowledge of truth. This loss of authority is the most important quality of postmodernism, and all the other qualities ultimately derive from this one.

Postmoderns look to each individual to determine his own truth. According to postmodernism, we cannot correct others' perceptions because to do so we must draw solely from our own perspective, which is, by definition, no better than anyone else's. Michel Foucault said that evaluating the perceptions of others by your own was not only arrogant, but an attempt to gain power over others. Each group, he said, interprets reality in a way that is favorable to them. To claim to have "the truth" is to assert power over others.[6] Thus, postmoderns believe it is the individual, or the local community, that is best suited to establish the truth for themselves.

While postmoderns desire spirituality, they see organized, institutional religions as unnecessary to the pursuit of spirituality. Much to the surprise of many agnostics, the technological and scientific advancements of American culture have not led to a decreased belief in "God." Quite the contrary, there are more signs of spirituality now in America than at any point in her history. In the 1980s the first of the *Megatrends* (ed. John Naisbitt) books came out, which analyzed trends in Western culture.[7] Naisbitt observed that for the last one hundred years science and technology had attempted to explain away any need for the supernatural, the thought being that the more science accounts for the world, the less religious we will be inclined to be. Naisbitt's observations, however, suggested the opposite, namely that there was a growing religious backlash against that trend. Modern people were becoming more religious, not less.

Peter Roszak, the acclaimed sociologist, noted the same thing. He said that trying to cut all supernatural or mysterious elements out of a human's existence would be like trying to put a cork in Old Faithful. You might be able to stop the eruptions of Old Faithful for a little while, but don't think you have seen the last of Old Faithful! In the same way, the desire for spirituality in the human spirit is just too strong to be repressed. Human beings will find a

---

[4] "Letter 2122, C. R. Darwin to T. H. Huxley," July 9, 1857. See http://www.darwinproject.ac.uk/darwinletters/calendar/entry-2122.html.

[5] Michel Foucault, *The Archaeology of Knowledge & The Discourse on Language* (New York: Vintage, 1982); Jacques Derrida, *Dissemination,* tr. Barbara Johnson (Chicago: UCP, 1983; Richard Rorty, *Philosophy and the Mirror of Nature* (Princeton, NJ: PUP, 1979).

[6] Michel Foucault, "Truth and Power," in Michel Foucault, *Power/Knowledge: Selected Interviews and Other Writings,* ed. Colin Gordon, 1972–1977 (New York: Pantheon, 1972), 109–33.

[7] John Naisbitt, *Megatrends: Ten New Directions Informing Our Lives* (New York: Warner, 1985).

way to worship, whether that worship is directed to God, romance, a political agenda, or the pursuit of money.[8]

This does not mean that participation in organized religion has gone up, however. Quite the contrary, while pop-spirituality is on the rise, organized religion is on the decline. Americans are inventing spiritualities, both "Christian" and non-Christian in origin, quite apart from any organized religion. Organized religions are often seen as *un*helpful in the pursuit of an individualized spirituality. Rather, they are instruments of power, created by one group to establish their superiority over others and to thrust their preferred worldview onto all.

Postmoderns recognize that the world needs healing and believe that it is their responsibility to facilitate it. Most young postmoderns see the world as a place of inequality and injustice, on the brink of environmental and economic collapse. Capitalism, corporations, and consumerism are now seen as the biggest threats to world health and peace. It has become very fashionable to participate in societal healing efforts. You can see this in how companies now advertise their products. Corporations want to be seen as "green friendly" and as giving back to their world. Volunteerism and charitable work are very much in vogue. Let us now see how the gospel of Jesus speaks uniquely to these situations.

HOW THE GOSPEL SPEAKS TO POSTMODERNISM AND THE IMPLICATIONS FOR HOW WE DO MINISTRY

We must help our culture see that all worldviews, including the postmodern ones, are truth claims. Postmoderns believe that claims to absolute truth are arrogant and are "power plays." However, the only way to be able to assert that all truth claims are relative is by assuming you know that no one worldview has found all the truth. This assumes the very knowledge that postmoderns disallow in others and can be every bit as much the "power play" they so disdain in religious truth claims.

Let me illustrate this principle through an Indian parable I heard in college:

> Three blind men encountered an elephant, each running into a different part of the elephant. The one who touched the body of the elephant said, "The elephant is like a wall." The one who touched the trunk said, "The elephant is like a snake." The one who touched the tusks said, "The elephant is like a spear." The moral of the story is that no one blind man had the whole picture, so they should all be open to what each of the others added to the picture. Each of them was right in what they saw; but each of them was wrong to argue that what he saw was the whole picture. In the same way, no one religion has the full picture of God. We should be open to the wisdom

---

    [8] See Tim Keller, Psalm 63, "The Search for Transcendence." Available at http://sermons. redeemer.com/store/index.cfm?fuseaction=product.display&product_ID=17024&ParentCat=6; see also Tim Keller, *Counterfeit Gods* (New York: Penguin, 2009), ix–xxiv.

of other religions, because it is only through our collective wisdom that we can approximate real truth.

Lesslie Newbigin, a missionary to India, said in his book *The Gospel in a Pluralist Society* that he was unsure how to answer that parable until he realized that in telling the story, the narrator himself assumed he saw the whole elephant. The only way to claim that each blind man only saw a part of the elephant was because the narrator himself was not blind and could see the whole elephant. Thus, he was claiming to be able to do the very thing he was telling everybody else they could not do.[9] Thus, all truth claims are exclusive, even the claim that all truths are relative. The claim that all truth is relative excludes any truth that would claim to describe "the whole elephant." The relativist truth claim can be just as arrogant, dogmatic, and intolerant, and can be used to justify power assumptions as much as any other truth claim.

Furthermore, postmoderns often claim that religious viewpoints are culturally situated, meaning that the only reason that Christians believe in Christianity is because they are from Christian-culture countries; the only reasons Muslims are Muslims is because they were born in Muslim lands, etc. This can be applied to the postmodern, too, however! Likely, the main reason that the postmodern sees all truth is relative is because they were born into a postmodern, Western society. Why should their religious viewpoint alone be so unique as to apply to all peoples of all cultures in all places?

Since all truth claims are culturally situated and have the potential to lead to arrogance and power plays, relativism not excluded, we must ask which truth claim is the most well-substantiated and which produces the most peace-loving, inclusive attitude toward humanity. The gospel of Jesus stands unique on both accounts. The truth of the gospel is not based on the observations of men, but on the revelation of God in history, specifically in the resurrection of Jesus Christ. This claim should be evaluated on its own merits, not weighted for or against by the cultures from which it has originated. Furthermore, as will be demonstrated below, the Christian truth claim not only is the most humble truth claim, but also is the most peace-loving and inclusive toward humanity.

We must demonstrate that the gospel is the most humble and inclusive of all truth claims. The Christian truth claim is the most humble of truth claims. It is not founded upon the wisdom of men (1 Cor. 1:27–31) but upon the revelation of God. Such revelation was not given as a reward for either righteousness or ingenuity. Peter's claim that Jesus was the only Savior for all mankind was followed up by Luke's acknowledgment that the apostles were "unlearned and ignorant men" (Acts 4:13, KJV). Peter's claim that Jesus was the only way rested on the fact that Jesus had risen from the dead and his power had made the lame man walk (Acts 4:10).

[9] Lesslie Newbigin, *The Gospel in a Pluralist Society* (Grand Rapids: Eerdmans, 1999), 9–10.

The gospel leads to peace and inclusion more than any other truth claim. All "religions" distinguish which people are acceptable from those who are not, those who are good from those who are bad. Even secularism has its way of distinguishing the "good" from the "bad." A very strict, albeit unstated, moral code exists among many postmoderns. There are the "enlightened" and the "unenlightened," the "tolerant" and "intolerant," the "greedy" and the "socially conscious."

All religions, except Christianity, teach that it is what you do, not do, or who you are that makes you acceptable. The gospel teaches that it is not who you are or what you have done that forms the basis of your acceptance, but what Christ has done for you. This leads to an acceptance of others who are not like us, because Christ accepted us when we were unlike him. It also leads to love for others, even those who do not like us, because Christ gave himself for us when we cared nothing for him. History bears this out. Numerous examples could be given of how Christianity has led to the removal of societal barriers of all types (race, gender, class, socio-economic level, age, etc.). Perhaps the best example, however, comes from the newly formed gospel communities of the ancient Roman Empire.

Rodney Stark, in his book *The Rise of Christianity,* notes that one of the things that made Christian communities unique in the ancient world was the harmony that existed among the different races and classes of people.[10] Ethnic tension ran high in the new Greco-Roman urban centers because, for one of the first times in history, communities of different origins were thrust together. In churches, however, the varying ethnicities got along and treated each other respectfully. Churches were some of the only places in the Roman Empire where one could find peace among the multiethnic groups living together in the city. Their reasoning was that Christ was not raised as a Jew or a Greek but as the Lord of all humanity. Therefore, all races were essentially one in him. Why has the gospel produced the most loving, inclusive communities ever known? Because, as Tim Keller often puts it, ultimate reality for the Christian is a Man on the cross loving people who do not love him and giving himself for people who did not agree with him.

Effective preaching to postmoderns will have the ring of both boldness and humility. Christians preaching to postmoderns must speak both with the apostolic boldness that comes from the certainty that Jesus rose from the dead and with the humility that comes from knowing that we did not come to this knowledge because of our moral or intellectual superiority but because of God's gracious revelation.

A good example of this is, again, the apostles' preaching. The first-century world into which Peter first preached the gospel was much like our postmodern world—a very spiritual, pluralistic society. All the peoples Rome had conquered had their own gods. Rome created "peace" between the conquered peoples by allowing each to have their own gods, but they allowed no one

---

[10]   Rodney Stark, *The Rise of Christianity* (San Francisco: HarperCollins, 1997), 160–61.

to claim their god was superior to all the other gods.[11] The idea was that the claim that one god was superior would lead to the assumption by the people of that god that they should be superior, even free of Rome's rule.

The Roman Pantheon housed statues of all the various gods. An emblem of Caesar stood on top of it. The message of that building was "to each his own, as long as you acknowledge that Caesar functions as supreme Lord." The apostles' preaching incensed Rome not because it introduced a new god to worship. What would one more god be among the thousands of others? What challenged Rome was the apostolic insistence that Jesus was the only way. At one point the Roman Emperor Severus decided that the Christians had been persecuted for too long, so he declared that he would sanction the Christian religion by adding a statue of Jesus to Caesar's Pantheon. The Christians did not rejoice that they had finally received state recognition. Rather, they insisted that Jesus be taken out of the Pantheon. They insisted he could never be just one among the gods, but the Lord of lords.

While our preaching should ring with apostolic certainty, it should also exude humility. We must, like the apostles, present ourselves as weak, fallible, "earthen vessels" to whom God has graciously revealed himself, as those who "cannot but speak of what we have seen and heard" (Acts 4:20). Often, our tone belies the content of our message. Bombastically belittling and dehumanizing those who do not agree with us will immediately (and unnecessarily) turn off a postmodern audience. Our communication must entail respect for those who disagree with us. *We must preach to people as people with God-given dignity, because this is not a war of theories but a war for hearts!* Perhaps a helpful question we should often consider when we preach is, "Am I trying to argue my position or win my hearer?"

Those who preach the gospel to postmoderns should strive to make their preaching as conversational as possible. Any "preacher voice" is likely to be a turn-off, as it communicates both institutionalism and a lack of authenticity. Furthermore, creative alliteration and neatly packaged structure will probably detract from the ability of the message to connect with the audience. Talk to unbelievers from the pulpit as if they are across a coffee-shop table from you. Our preaching should have a *tone* that says, "I am a sinner to whom God has revealed himself. I stand only by the grace of God. I believe this is his word, and this is how I am trying my best to apply it."

Paul's admonition to Timothy in his second letter to him is a perfect prescription for postmodern preaching, "The Lord's bond-servant must not be quarrelsome, but be kind to all . . . with gentleness correcting those who are in opposition, if perhaps God may grant them repentance leading to the knowledge of the truth, and they may come to their senses and escape from the

---

[11] Erwin Lutzer, *Christ Among Other Gods: A Defense of Christ in an Age of Tolerance* (Chicago: Moody, 1997), 27–60. See also Tim Keller, "No Other Name," sermon on Acts 4. Keller's thoughts on the unique nature of Christianity in a pluralistic world have been a great source of help to me. See also his sermon on the exclusivity of Christ from 1 John 4:1–10 (available through www.redeemer.com) and *A Reason for God* (New York: Penguin, 2008), 20.

snare of the devil, having been held captive by him to do his will . . . preach the word" *(2 Tim 2:24–26; 4:2;* NASB, emphasis added).

We must be committed to the expository teaching of the storyline of the Bible. As demonstrated above, postmoderns suffer from the loss of two things: a source of authority and a grand narrative uniting all of human existence. Thus, our preaching must present the Bible as the one, authoritative story of Jesus Christ and his plan for the earth. Let us break that apart:

Our preaching must demonstrate the authority of the Scriptures. In seminary I learned that there are four main stages in the act of God's revelation to mankind:

1. The truth conceived in God's mind;
2. The revelatory event itself (e.g., God giving the Ten Commandments on Mt. Sinai; Jesus teaching on the mountain; Peter's sermon, etc.);
3. The record of that event in the text of Scripture;
4. The interpreter or interpretive community.

Various Christian "traditions" place the locus of authority in various stages.[12] The mystical traditions say the authority is in the first stage, the truth as conceived in God's mind. The mystics believe that they encounter God directly and that these firsthand revelations of him are the most correct and most true. (This category includes a wide range of people, including many Quakers, Pentecostals, the neo-orthodox, and any number of churches influenced by the New Age movement.)

Many of the modernistic traditions say the truth is best discovered in the actual revelatory event, the second stage. The Bible, if anything, is a record of revelation, not the revelation itself. It is what Jesus actually did and said, not what is recorded, that needs to be discovered. Modernists thus give great weight to historical pursuits like "the Jesus seminar" (wherein scholars try to find out what Jesus *really* said), textual criticism, or archaeological discovery.

Postmoderns say the authority is *in* the fourth stage, the interpreter or interpretive community. Following the lead of the Reader Response theorists such as Foucault and Rorty (even though postmoderns often do not realize they are following their lead), they assume that we can never really know truth certainly. All we have is our interpretation. Brian McLaren, whose book *A New Kind of Christian* elaborates on the shape he believes Christianity must take in postmodernity, once told me that the problem with the doctrine of inerrancy was that it was itself an interpretation of Scripture, and no one could assume their interpretation was infallible. Thus, he said, the Bible may be inerrant, but we cannot teach it as such to others, because we are thrusting our interpretation on others. The emphasis in postmodern Christian

---

[12] For more on this, see R. C. Sproul, *Scripture Alone* (Phillipsburg: P&R, 2005), 21–24, 121–74. To hear how this affects preaching, see Mark Driscoll's talk "Preaching and Teaching Jesus from Scripture," available at http://mrclm.blogspot.com/2006/12/mark-driscoll-preaching-and-teaching.html. Driscoll gave a helpful breakdown of how different traditions of Christians fall back on one or another source of authority. This breakdown, in some ways, follows his.

communities is often not in digging into the text to try and determine what the author actually meant when he wrote the words—what is more important is what it means to me or my community. Ironically, postmoderns are joined in this category by Roman Catholics, who believe the Magisterium's interpretation of the Word trumps even the Word itself. In other words, what the church says the Bible says is more important than what the Bible itself says.

The Bible points us *to* the third stage, the Bible itself, as the correct locus of authority. Second Timothy 3:16 says that it is the words of Scripture that are "breathed out" by God, and 2 Peter 1:20–21 says that it was what the prophets wrote that was "carried along" by the Holy Spirit. Scripture considers itself to be a better interpreter of what God is saying than archaeology, our mystical experiences, or our interpretive traditions. This is not to say, of course, that there is any contradiction between what the Bible says and the actual events the Bible recounts. Rather, the Word itself is the final authority for determining God's truth. We teachers are only humble servants of that Word, always submitting our understanding of God, his truth, and even the revelatory event itself to the text of Scripture. The Bible is to be read "in community," but this does not mean that the community assigns "meaning" to a text. The community is beneficial in that it employs many minds to measure the traditional interpretation against the Word itself. The final authority is always in the Word.

To teach the Bible this way provides the authority postmoderns are missing while at the same time demonstrating the humility postmoderns admire. Sermons that sound like "life coaching" sessions or "practical tips for living" and are not grounded in Scripture often do not appeal to the postmodern audience. They demonstrate neither authority (as they are not grounded in God's revelation) nor humility (as they sound like I believe everyone should heed my insights for living). I recently received a letter from a highly educated young adult who had begun attending our church. He told me that ours was the first church he had really attended. He said that he had visited a few churches growing up, but he always felt like the pastor was offering his own insights on living. He told me, "When I come to church, I think I at least should hear what the Bible says about my life. I do not yet believe the Bible, but I am interested in what it has to say about me. I come to your church because you seem to offer very little of your own opinions and most of what you say I can see right in the Word." He went on to say, "I need you to help me discover whether or not Jesus rose from the dead. I need to figure that out now, because as I see it, if he rose from the dead, then that will change everything about my life—who I marry, what career choices I will make, and how I will spend my money. I need you to help me discover that now."

Our preaching must expose the grand narrative of Scripture. Western pastors often teach the Bible as if it were a collection of vignettes about great men and women whose examples we should emulate, or as a sourcebook of wisdom on how we can make our lives work. We treat the Bible as if its main subject matter was *us.* Jesus said, however, in John 5:38–39 that the whole Bible was really about *him,* not us. That means if we preach the main point of a passage as being something about our lives, I have still missed the *main* point of the passage. Bible passages are not intended, primarily, to fill in some missing piece in the story of our lives, but to show us that we must rewrite our stories in terms of God's story. The Bible was not primarily intended to explain to us what we should do for God, but to point us to what God was doing for us in Christ.

Take the popular Old Testament story of David and Goliath. The teaching usually goes like this: "Like David, we have giants in our lives. Through the power of God, we can knock them down like David did!" The *main* point of the David narrative, however, was not simply the ability of one man to defeat in this life every giant that comes against him, but that David, a young Jew, hated by his brothers, went out and defeated a giant who had completely immobilized Israel, and through his victory all of Israel was saved, even though they did not lift a finger to help him! Then all Israel shared in his victory. In this way, David was pointing us to Jesus. Because Jesus, the "ultimate David," has conquered the "giant" of our separation from God, we do not have to worry as much about other so-called giants, like cancer or vocational failure. Through Jesus' work, no longer does death really defeat us or personal failures devastate our sense of personal worth!

Another example would be the Old Testament story of Joseph. Sermons on Joseph often follow this pattern: "You are experiencing difficulty. Look at Joseph! He went through tough times, but it all worked out in the end for him. Thus, if you trust God, you also will get out of your prison and be crowned with success and reward." The main point of the Joseph story, however, is not that we see our lives as similar to Joseph's, but that we see Joseph as a picture of Jesus. Just as Joseph was a man who was hated and unjustly betrayed by his own brothers, but then rose from the prison to rule the world, saving them and the whole world in the process, so was Jesus. Because Jesus, the "ultimate Joseph," has been victorious to save us from the real destruction of being separated from God, we are victorious in him *even* if we die in prison.

It is the "bigger picture" of the Bible that most connects with a postmodern audience.[13] Postmodernism primarily suffers from the loss of a metanarrative (an overarching story) that explains all of life and ties it together. When we preach each story of the Bible as if it is simply an example for us to emulate, we reduce the Bible to a collection of self-help techniques. Our audience simply fits "Christian" principles into their idolatrous, self-centered stories.

Postmoderns have lost the centrality of God in the universe and replaced it with the centrality of themselves. It is the preaching of the gospel that reverses that. It is only when we teach people to trade their self-centered story

---

[13] There are several books that can help frame a particular biblical story within the overall framework. Especially good are: Graeme Goldsworthy, *According to Plan* (Downers Grove: IVP, 1991); Craig Bartholomew and Michael Goheen, *The Drama of Scripture* (Grand Rapids: Baker, 2006), and the vastly underrated John Sailhamer, *NIV Compact Bible Commentary* (Grand Rapids: Zondervan, 1994).

for the story of God that we can truly be "preaching the Word." Preaching the gospel means teaching people to put Jesus back in the center of the universe where he belongs and to trust what he has done and can do on our behalf. What we should be *exposing* from the Bible is the Gospel!

We need a new way of explaining sin beyond simply "thou shalt not." Many have noted that one of the most difficult things for postmoderns to grasp is the reality of sin. Sin assumes a standard of right and wrong that post-moderns *prima facie* reject. So presenting sin as the breaking of certain "thou shalt nots" often meets with an immediate disconnect. Tim Keller has suggested that we need a broader way of presenting sin to postmodern people, one that may be more nuanced and philosophical than simply declaring the "thou shalt nots," but just as biblical.[14] Sin, Keller says, is fundamentally idolatry: valuing something more than God or defining ourselves by something other than God. Rather than beginning our explication of sin with Exodus 20 (the Ten Commandments), we begin in Genesis 3.

Everyone has a "functional god." The first sin (in the Garden of Eden) was our decision that the fruit of a forbidden tree and the knowledge it promised was more necessary to our lives than the presence and approval of God. Paul calls that original sin of mankind "idolatry": they worshipped and served the creature rather than the Creator (Rom. 1:23). You may ask, "How was Adam and Eve's eating of the forbidden fruit worship? I do not see them bowing down or paying homage to the tree." Adam and Eve worshipped the tree because they thought having a certain type of knowledge would make them happier than God would. They "worshipped the tree" as an all-satisfying object rather than God, and thus traded the "glory of the invisible God" for an earthly substitute. That is the essence of all sin: we substitute something for God, deeming it more central to our identity than the glory and pleasure of God. Perhaps it is money, a career achievement, a reputation, or sexual pleasure. Whatever it is, we believe we cannot live without that thing and would give up anything else for it. That thing becomes a "functional God" to us.

The first effect of our disobedience was a sense of our nakedness. Before they sinned, Adam and Eve were naked; it just did not bother them. After the fall, however, their sin gave them a sense of shame about that nakedness. The early church fathers said that prior to sin Adam and Eve's nakedness did not bother them because they were "clothed" in the love and acceptance of God. Their sin left them (and us as their descendants) with a sense of nakedness—exposure, guilt, and shame. We believe that we are not lovable as we are. We feel naked and exposed.

Everyone has a "functional savior." What did Adam and Eve do with that sense of nakedness? They covered themselves with fig leaves. Humanity

---

[14] For further reading on this topic, see chapter 10 of Keller's "The Problem of Sin," in *The Reason for God* (New York: Dutton, 2008), 159–73. See also Keller's *The Prodigal God* (New York: Penguin, 2008), 29–72. Both the terms "functional gods" and "functional saviors" have been popularized of recent by Keller. See, for example, Keller's article, "Gospel-Centered Ministry," available at http://www.stevekmccoy.com/reformissionary/2005/07/tim_keller_arti.html.

after them has been on a quest to cover their nakedness—to find that acceptance and satisfaction that they had previously known in the presence of God.

Whatever we choose to provide us with that sense of covering is called
a "functional savior." Attempts at salvation can take religious or irreligious
forms. Religious attempts at salvation are based on the belief that *if* we
become a "good" person, God will accept us. Religious salvation is based
on works-righteousness: *if* we change, *if* we obey, *then* we will be accepted.

Irreligious forms of salvation function on the same works-righteousness
basis as does religious salvation; irreligious salvation just does not see God
as part of the solution. Instead of seeking God's approval, one believes that
satisfaction is found in something else: the pride of accomplishment, the
approval of others, some material reward, etc. We might believe our success
in business or athletics, our physical beauty, our ability to be a good parent,
our moral behavior, or our racial identity makes us worthy of respect and
approval. We might believe a life of luxury or sensual pleasure constitutes
"completion." Whatever thing we look to for soul satisfaction or for personal
worthiness is our "functional" salvation. Søren Kierkegaard encapsulated all
this by saying that sin is ultimately finding our identity in anything but God.[15]
As Keller notes, whereas declaring to postmoderns that they are rule-breakers
often falls on deaf ears, explaining to them that they have found their identity, worship, and functional salvation in something besides God more readily
connects.[16]

Our evangelism must prioritize relational engagement. As noted previously, postmodern people have become wary of institutions. Thus, they are
less likely than ever to respond to strangers, whether those strangers take the
form of people knocking on their doors or mailouts in their mailboxes. For
this reason, even the traditional "seeker service" is less effective today than it
was twenty years ago. Megachurch seeker services are still effective for the
unchurched with a Christian background, but less so for the post-Christian
members of society, who grow proportionately each year. Effective evangelistic churches among postmoderns have a certain "rawness" to them. The
preacher is not as polished, and there is more time for interaction (whether
through prayer, communion, worship, or question and answer). The effect is
that the church appears as a community of real people experiencing something
genuine together. Large churches can accomplish this in a number of ways,
ranging from effective small group ministry to multi-site church campuses
and new church plants. This is not to suggest that "performance-oriented"
churches will not continue to reach lots of people and grow very large in the
days to come, just that those who most effectively engage postmoderns will
emphasize relational engagement of its members with non-believers.

---

[15] Sören Kierkegaard, *Sickness Unto Death*, 1849. See discussion in Keller's *The Reason for
God*, 162–64.

[16] See Keller, "The Gospel in All Its Forms," http://www.christianitytoday.com/le/2008/
spring/9.74.html?start=4.

The most effective evangelistic churches will be both "attractional" and "incarnational."[17] Attractional churches emphasize the Sunday morning experience. Their Sunday morning program is of the highest quality and is designed to attract interested people into the service. Incarnational churches look at its services as a way to empower its members to take Jesus into the community. Both have biblical precedent. Jesus taught five thousand men at once with a creative bread-and-fish illustration. He spent other time empowering his twelve disciples to be the incarnation of his hands and feet after he was gone. Effective evangelistic churches will be both attractional and incarnational. Members will be empowered to know unbelievers in the community, earn their trust, and bring them into the community to hear the gospel.

Our gospel presentation must address issues of global, social, and physical healing. Finally, effective ministry to postmoderns will address the issues of global, social, and physical healing that postmoderns crave. Christianity provides the only real answer to the problem of global deterioration and suffering. Jesus' plan of salvation was not simply to redeem souls out of a hopelessly damned creation, but to bring resurrection and healing to the whole creation. In the final chapter of Revelation what we see is not a group of Christians being evacuated off of earth and into heaven, but a city coming down from heaven to earth. Jesus' resurrection was just the "firstfruits" of the resurrection of the whole world. Ultimately, just as Jesus' actual body was raised from the dead, so creation itself will be reborn and renewed (Ps. 96:1–4; Isa. 65:17–25; Rom. 8:20–23).[18]

The other worldviews competing for the attention of postmoderns do not satisfactorily address the problem of global suffering. The evolutionist's worldview says that the violence in the world is the natural, unchangeable order of things; Buddhism and Hinduism teach an escape from the physical world into the spiritual. Islam says that the physical world is simply a testing area to see who is worthy of heaven, and at "the last day" God will destroy the world; all those who are saved will adopt the Arabic language and culture. By contrast, the gospel alone offers redemption for the physical world. Christ was raised in a physical body, which means (in contrast to Eastern religions) that matter matters to God. Christ ended suffering through his death on the cross, which means that (in contrast to evolution) the suffering of the world is an aberration of the created order, not natural to it.

The ministry of Jesus and the apostles was characterized by "signs" of that coming global and cultural healing. Jesus' miracles in the Gospels pointed to this progression. They were called signs, meaning they pointed beyond themselves to something greater and more important. Jesus' miracles

---

[17] These terms are commonly used to mark a distinction between how "traditional seeker churches" (like Bill Hybels' Willow Creek) and newer postmodern churches see the church and the role the Sunday morning gathering should have in evangelistic efforts. For more on this, see Ed Stetzer, *Planting Missional Churches* (Nashville: B&H, 2006), 161–69.

[18] N. T. Wright offers some helpful discussion on this in his *Surprised by Hope* (New York: Harper, 2008), 3–12, 79–92. Many of Wright's conclusions I find to be objectionable, but his presentation of the work of Christ in its larger cosmic purpose has been very helpful.

were not merely random acts of kindness or magic tricks to prove his power. He didn't prove he was the Son of God by levitating, catching bullets in his teeth, or freezing himself in a block of ice for six months. Those things might have proved the point that he was the Son of God, but his miracles were more than mere demonstrations of power. His miracles had a message. *He healed blindness. He stopped storms. He fed the hungry.* His miracles showed that his mission was to reverse the curse caused by sin. As Tim Keller has noted, "Jesus' miracles did not show off the naked fact of Jesus' power, but revealed the redemptive purpose of His power."[19] We often think of Jesus' miracles as a suspension of the natural order, but they were quite the opposite. They were a *return to* the natural order. Miracles demonstrated in physical form the message of the gospel.

The apostles' ministry followed the same pattern. Many of their "signs" were miraculous, as with Philip who preached in Samaria. It was said that there was "much rejoicing" in Samaria because of the message Philip preached and the signs that he did (Acts 8:7–8). Some were not supernatural, as Tabitha's loving service of making clothes for her community (Acts 9:36–39). Effective ministry to postmoderns will substantiate the verbal proclamation of the message with signs demonstrating its contents. Christians should not preach that the earth is simply a sinking *Titanic* off of which we are rescuing people for heaven. The earth is indeed a sinking *Titanic*, but one which God intends to raise. Like Jesus and the apostles, we should give pictures of that resurrection in the communities to whom we are preaching. To effectively reach postmoderns, we should find the places of greatest pain in our society and immerse ourselves in the lives of the suffering, demonstrating the generosity and healing power of the gospel.

The radical generosity of Christians and our love for Christ and joy in the midst of suffering will most likely be the most compelling signs of the gospel for postmoderns. As Francis Schaeffer famously argued, love is "the final apologetic."[20] Our lives should pose questions to those that are watching.

Many people today say that since postmoderns typically show more resistance to "evangelism by strangers," our witness should follow the pattern of 1 Peter 3:15, that we "always be ready to give a defense to anyone who asks you for a reason for the hope that is in you" (HCSB). We should no longer be the aggressors in witness, it is said, but be ready to respond. That overlooks the crucial fact that Jesus' command to us was to *go* and be his witnesses. We are never to wait for unbelievers to come to us to ask questions. We are to go to them and proclaim a message that answers a question they may not have known to ask. What Peter is saying in 1 Peter 3:15 is that we are to live in such a way that our lives *beg* a question from the people that are watching, not that we are simply ready to talk about our faith when people are curious. Our

[19] I heard Keller say this in his talk at the Resurgence Conference, 2006, "Being the Church in Our Culture." Available at http://www.theresurgence.com.

[20] Francis A. Schaeffer, *The Church at the End of the Twentieth Century* (London: Hodder & Stoughton, 1970), 189.

lives are to be so characterized by radical generosity, and we are to display such joy in the midst of suffering, that people are simply befuddled and have to ask us how it is possible.

The way Paul and Silas handled themselves in Acts 16 effectively demonstrated the beauty of the gospel to the cynical Philippians and raised the questions about the gospel that Paul was able easily to answer. It was when the Philippian jailor saw their interminable joy after being beaten and their wild generosity (in that they would rather stay and witness to him than take their freedom), that he asked the question, trembling, "What must I do to be saved?" Christians who are not regularly getting those kinds of questions from postmodern people may not be living the gospel-demonstrating life that Paul and Silas were. Even with a lifestyle witness we should be the aggressor. We should be seeking to preach the message by the radical way in which we live.

We should not overlook that the greatest sign of the kingdom is a healthy local church. Ephesians 3:10 says that God's "multi-faceted wisdom" would be made known to the rulers of the world through the local church. Local churches are God's demonstration community, putting the gospel on display. *Koinonia*—members simply loving each other—is itself the most compelling sign of the kingdom of God given on earth! When local churches are places of great diversity (race, age, and economic class), they demonstrate the cultural healing of the gospel. When they organize their members to testify to the gospel from house to house as they minister in the streets to the city's greatest needs, they put on display the generosity of the gospel.

Finally, our preaching of the gospel to postmoderns should address the world's need of healing. A great example of this is a new approach to sharing the gospel offered by James Choung of InterVarsity Ministries. Choung suggests replacing the most popular evangelistic presentation of the previous generation, "The Four Spiritual Laws," with four circles. Those circles represent the following:

- We were designed for good
- We are damaged by evil
- We are restored for better
- We are sent together to heal

Choung's presentation presents the gospel according to the four major biblical movements: *creation, fall, redemption,* and *restoration.* It shows how the gospel addresses society's problems and not just our personal feelings of dissatisfaction. This approach also demonstrates that our decision to follow Jesus is not simply a matter of returning to personal piety, but it also includes a call to be involved in the mission of God. It emphasizes discipleship, not just a quick decision. This is not only a more fully biblical presentation of the gospel; it is also a more relevant presentation for contemporary Western culture, which is asking the question of what "earthly good" a "heavenly gospel" can do. (Unfortunately, Choung's presentation has one glaring shortcoming: it leaves the centrality of God out of the gospel. That can be seen in the presentation's first point: "We were designed for good." This is, of course, true, but even more importantly we were designed for *God*. The *result* of our rebellion against God is that our world is marred by destruction and evil. The fruit of our living for God is that we live in peace and harmony with each other and our world. The root of those problems, however, is that we have rejected God's rightful rule and flouted his glory. This aside, however, Choung's idea to include the issue of global healing and the Christian's commitment to it in the gospel presentation contextualizes the gospel for postmoderns in a helpful way.) Our presentations of Jesus will be most effective if they do not focus only on what Christ can do for the individual, but what he can do for the world as well.

CONCLUSION

Postmodernism proposes unique challenges to Christianity, but this is no cause for despair! The New Testament was actually written in the context of a world that had much in common with our postmodern milieu. A return to the New Testament style of ministry and historic apostolic methodologies is more than sufficient to meet the challenges supplied by the reigning gods of the postmodern age.

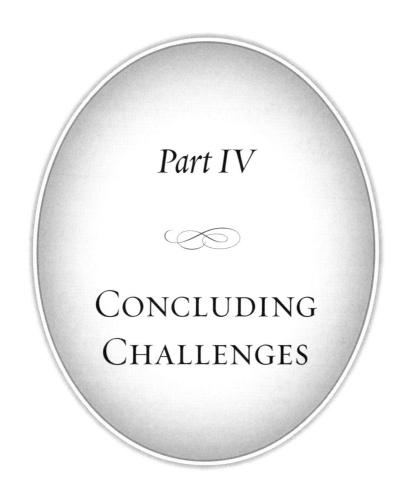

Part IV

CONCLUDING
CHALLENGES

Chapter Twenty-One

A THEOLOGICALLY
DRIVEN MISSIOLOGY

Bruce Riley Ashford

T he first chapter of *Theology and Practice of Mission* set forth the
basic storyline of Scripture, portraying God's mission to redeem for
himself a people who will be a kingdom of priests to the praise of
his glory, who will bear witness to his gospel and advance his church, and
who will dwell forever with him on a new heavens and earth.[1] This unified,
coherent, and divinely inspired narrative reminds us—the church—that we
are called to be ambassadors for the God who created us and purchased us
with the blood of his Son. Further, embedded in this narrative are the classic
doctrines of the Christian faith that shape and form the church's ministry and
mission.

Indeed, one of the most significant challenges facing churches, agencies, and missionaries today is the imperative to allow Christian doctrine to
shape their actual ministry practices. Although our evangelical churches have
declared their belief that the Christian Scriptures are *ipsissima verba Dei*, the
very words of God, our declaration is not always consistent with our actions.
In reality, we sometimes ignore Scripture when forming our strategies, methods, and practices. It is as if we are saying that what we believe about God is
important, but how we practice those beliefs is not.

If we are not careful, these fissures between belief and practice will derail
our mission and render our evangelical theology impotent. A faulty doctrine

---

[1]   This chapter is a revised version of "A Theologically Driven Missiology for a Great Commission Resurgence," originally published in Chuck Lawless and Adam W. Greenway, eds., *The
Great Commission Resurgence: Fulfilling God's Mandate in Our Time* (Nashville: B&H, 2010),
177–207.

of God, for example, will lead us to a wrong definition of success. A poor hermeneutic will lead to an aberrant definition of God's mission and of our mission. A misguided soteriology neuters our attempts at evangelism and discipleship. A reductionist ecclesiology will result in anemic churches that fail to disciple their members or reach their communities. In order to foster a healthy mission, therefore, we must seek carefully, consciously, and consistently to rivet missiological practice to Christian Scripture and its attendant evangelical doctrine.[2]

In other words, sound doctrine must take the "driver's seat" in our missiology. In the following pages, this chapter will provide summaries of the classical loci of Christian theology along with practical examples of how each one may be brought to bear upon the church's practice in general and upon missiology in particular.

REVELATION

Our evangelical churches believe that Scripture is written by men divinely inspired and is God's revelation of himself to man.[3] In contrast to certain theologians who view Scripture as a merely human *construction* devoid of divine revelation, we believe that Scripture is given supernaturally by God; indeed, it is the very breath of God (2 Tim. 3:16). And unlike other theologians, who see Scripture as a merely human *witness* to divine revelation, we believe that Scripture is *ipsissima verba Dei*, the very words of God.

Because the Christian Scriptures are indeed the very words of God, we will want to shape our strategies and methods according to its teachings. And while, for most evangelicals, this might seem to be a yawningly obvious observation, we must pay careful attention in light of the fact that we sometimes *do not* allow the Scriptures to inform and shape our evangelism, discipleship, church growth, and church planting. We sometimes speak loudly about inerrancy, while undermining that same conviction by our practices.

One cannot craft a truly evangelical missiology by means of proof-texting. Many of the practical ministry challenges waiting to be met are not explicitly addressed in isolated passages of Scripture. In the absence of clear statements on some particular methodological or strategic initiative, we must call forth the deep-level principles in the Bible and allow them to speak with propriety and prescience to the issue at hand. Further, as our global, national, and

---

[2] Thom Rainer's *The Book of Church Growth* is an example of one missiologist's conscious and careful reflection on the connection between theology and missiology. He devotes one-third of the book to showing how each locus of systematic theology comes to bear upon church growth principles and practice. Thom Rainer, *The Book of Church Growth* (Nashville: B&H, 1993), 71–168.

[3] See, for example, the doctrinal confession of the Evangelical Theological Society: "The Bible alone, and the Bible in its entirety, is the Word of God written and is therefore inerrant in the autographs. God is a Trinity, Father, Son, and Holy Spirit, each an uncreated person, one in essence, equal in power and glory." http://www.etsjets.org/about, accessed 3 December, 2010.

cultural contexts change from era to era, our missiology must be reworked and rewritten afresh for every generation.

Nor can we craft our missiology without taking into account general revelation. While God provides certain knowledge (e.g., the Trinity, the incarnation, and salvation by grace through faith alone) through special revelation alone, he provides other (non-salvific) knowledge through our human faculties. It is God himself who created us with the capacities for reason and imagination. Therefore, we benefit from studying history, philosophy, linguistics, anthropology, sociology, marketing, and other disciplines. In other words, God is the giver both of Scripture and of the created order, and the two are not in conflict with one another. When properly interpreted, they are shown to agree.[4]

How, then, might a missiologist view such extra-biblical disciplines as history, philosophy, anthropology, sociology, and marketing? How are they to be positioned in light of Christian Scripture? Here are four ways that they might be helpful:[5]

First, extra-biblical disciplines may be helpful for the apologetic task of pointing to God's existence and some of his attributes (Rom. 1). We may make ontological, teleological, cosmological, and moral arguments for the existence of one God, based upon what we may learn in philosophy, anthropology, sociology, or other disciplines.

Second, knowledge from these disciplines may be helpful for proclaiming the gospel and planting churches in a contextually appropriate manner. Reading widely in history and current affairs, for example, helps us to understand the cultural and social contexts of those to whom we minister. Cultural anthropology and sociology may also be helpful in studying the way God's image-bearers live in their diverse contexts, assisting us in the task of contextualization. Linguistics and communication theory are helpful in showing us how to proclaim the gospel across linguistic and cultural barriers.

Third, these disciplines are sometimes useful in illustrating theological truths. One might illustrate such concepts as God's love and fatherhood, or man's sin and its consequences, through the use of insights gleaned from anthropology and sociology.

Fourth, they may be helpful in subverting false theologies. We may use philosophy and the social sciences to defend the truth, goodness, and beauty of the gospel, in response to those who attack us. We may use them to "take

---

[4]   This is not to say that theologians and natural or social scientists never disagree. Often they do, but the disagreement is not found in any inherent conflict between Scripture and the natural world, but rather in theologians' and scientists' interpretations of the two. Either group might err, and either group is therefore subject to correction. To sharpen the point, our will is bent toward idolatry, and therefore our attempts at interpreting Scripture and the natural world will be affected by our idolatry. God's grace, by his Spirit and Word, corrects our interpretations of both Scripture and nature. For further reflection, see John M. Frame, *Apologetics to the Glory of God* (Phillipsburg, NJ: P&R, 1994), 22–26.

[5]   For further reflection on the relation of theology to other disciplines, see David K. Clark, *To Know and Love God: Method for Theology* (Wheaton: Crossway, 2003), 259–317.

the roof off" of opposing worldviews, philosophies, and religions, showing them to be unable to deliver what they promise.[6]

This, then, is a very limited exploration of how the doctrine of revelation comes to bear upon the church's practice.[7] In shaping our missiology according to revelation, we must beware of at least two dangers. The first is to allow the insights gleaned from general revelation (in particular, anthropology, sociology, and business marketing) to take the driver's seat in missiology. The second danger, however, is to give theology the driver's seat and demand that no other discipline be allowed a seat.[8] To do so, I believe, is to reject the great gift that God has given us in allowing us to study and interact with his good world.

GOD

The doctrine of God is central to all of the church's life although, ironically, we seem to have difficulty allowing this doctrine to drive our practice. How does such a lofty and majestic doctrine speak to concrete and even mundane practices? How do God's Trinitarian nature, his creativity, and his sovereignty affect our strategies and methods?

God as Trinity. God is Triune. This truth is revealed by Scripture (Matt. 3:16–17; 28:19) and has been taught by the church across the ages. But what does this doctrine have to do with missiology? One oft-overlooked example of the relevance of Trinitarian doctrine for missiology is hermeneutics and cross-cultural communication. The task of proclaiming the gospel across cultures is no longer limited to international missionaries, as church planters and pastors in North American contexts are now confronted with a diverse array of cultures and subcultures. Countless books, articles, and essays on cross-cultural communication and contextualization have been written, but many of these publications fail to recognize that the success of this enterprise rests squarely on the shoulders of the triune God.

Kevin Vanhoozer makes this point, arguing that the Trinity is not only the foundation for a faithful hermeneutic, but also a model of accomplished communication. The triune God is God the Father (the one who speaks), God the Son (the Word), and God the Spirit (the one who illumines and guides and teaches); God the Father speaks through his Son, and we as humans are

---

[6] Francis Schaeffer spoke of "taking the roof off" of a person's worldview in order to reveal its unliveability. For a brief description, read Bryan Follis, *Truth with Love: The Apologetics of Francis Schaeffer* (Wheaton: Crossway, 2006), 40–42. Also see James W. Sire, *The Universe Next Door: A Basic Worldview Catalog*, 3rd ed. (Downers Grove: IVP, 1997).

[7] This chapter provides further reflection on Christian Scripture below, under the doctrine of the Spirit.

[8] This former danger is perhaps the greater challenge at the present moment. Evangelicals have discovered and put to use many concepts gleaned from business marketing, anthropology, psychology, and other disciplines. The problem, however, is that many of the theories and practices recommended within these disciplines arise from, and are shaped by, false worldviews and therefore are at odds with the gospel and its implications.

enabled to hear and understand that communication by his Spirit. The Trinity is a demonstration that accomplished communication is possible.[9] In communicating across cultures and subcultures, the North American or international church planter is assured that the gospel can accurately be communicated precisely because of the God who called him to do so.

God as Creator and King. As creator, God brought into existence the world in which we now live, and it is a *good* world (Gen. 1–2). God's world is ontologically good and—although it is morally corrupt as a result of the fall—we may use any and all aspects of God's world to bring him glory. A robust doctrine of creation emphasizes the biblical teaching that God created man in his image and likeness (Gen. 1:26), endowing him with spiritual, moral, rational, relational, and creative capacities. It does not ignore the cultural aspect of our Christian witness, but it encourages us to bring the gospel to bear upon all aspects of the created order, including the arts, the sciences, and the public square.[10] It urges us to live out the implications of our faith in the midst of multiple callings—workplace, family, church, and community.[11]

Our salvation includes being remade into the image of our Creator (Col. 3:10) and conformed to the image of the Son (Rom. 8:29) who is himself *the* image of God (Col. 1:15). The gospel, therefore, affects all aspects of man in the image of God, and these aspects ought to be used to minister in God's world for his glory.

Finally, the doctrine of creation reminds us that God claims sovereignty over every tribe, tongue, people, and nation—over every type of person who has ever lived throughout the span of history and across the face of the globe. In short, a biblical doctrine of creation teaches us to use every aspect of our created being to give God glory in every dimension of human culture and across the fabric of human existence, among every tribe, tongue, people, and nation.

God and his name. God the Creator, in all of his blazing glory, stands at the center of the universe. He is the fountainhead of all truth, all goodness, and all beauty. And the increase of his glory and his kingdom is God's ultimate goal and man's ultimate purpose.[12] Scripture describes how God does all that he does for the sake of his name, for his renown, for his glory. He created

---

[9] See Kevin J. Vanhoozer, *Is There a Meaning in This Text?* (Grand Rapids: Zondervan, 1998), 455–68.

[10] Abraham Kuyper, the famous theologian and former prime minister of the Netherlands, is perhaps best known for his work on this aspect of our Christian witness. See Abraham Kuyper, *Lectures on Calvinism* (Grand Rapids: Eerdmans, 1931); Peter Heslam, *Creating a Christian Worldview: Abraham Kuyper's Lectures on Calvinism* (Grand Rapids: Eerdmans, 1998).

[11] A concise and helpful treatment of vocation is Gene Veith, *God at Work: Your Christian Vocation in All of Life* (Wheaton: Crossway, 2002), which is based on Martin Luther's sermons and teachings on the topic.

[12] Jonathan Edwards, in his *The End for Which God Created the World*, gives the most well-known and extended reflection upon this doctrine. Technically, *The End* is the first part of a two-part book by Edwards entitled *Two Dissertations*. See *Two Dissertations, Ethical Writings*, ed. Paul Ramsey, *The Works of Jonathan Edwards*, vol. 8 (New Haven: Yale University, 1989). It should be noted, however, that it is not only Reformed Christians who would affirm this doctrine.

man for his glory (Isa. 43:7) and chose Israel for his glory (Isa. 49:3). God delivered Israel from Egypt for his name's sake (Ps. 106:7–8) and restored them from exile for his glory (Isa. 48:9–11). He sent our Lord Jesus Christ so that the Gentiles would give him glory (Rom. 15:8–9) and then vindicated his glory by making propitiation through his Son (Rom. 3:23–26). He sent the Spirit to glorify the Son (John 16:14) and tells us to do all things for his glory (1 Cor. 10:31). He will send his Son again to receive glory (2 Thess. 1:9–10) and will fill the earth with the knowledge of his glory (Isa. 6:1–3; Hab. 2:14). Indeed, all of this is "so that at the name of Jesus every knee should bow . . . and every tongue should confess that Jesus Christ is Lord, to the glory of God the Father" (Phil. 2:10–11, HCSB).

One implication of this for mission is that we have the great joy of proclaiming that God's goal to be glorified enables man's purpose, which is to be truly satisfied. The Psalmist writes, "God, You are my God; I eagerly seek You. I thirst for You; my body faints for You in a land that is dry, desolate, and without water" (Ps. 63:1, HCSB). Man's deepest thirst turns out to be resonant with God's highest goal for him. The road toward pleasing God and giving him glory and the road toward knowing deep happiness are not two roads; they are one. The message we bring to the nations is one of profoundly good news.[13]

Another implication is that if our ultimate goal is God's glory, then we are set free from unbridled pragmatism. Our ultimate goal is to please God, not to manipulate or coerce professions of faith, church growth, or church multiplication. And so we are directed away from the temptation to engage in evangelism and discipleship that subverts the gospel or the health of the church, and we are free to proclaim the gospel God's way and leave the results to God.

God's mission. Finally, and this point will be expanded upon at a later time, mission finds its origin in God. Mission is God-centered, being rooted in God's gracious will to glorify himself. Mission is defined by God. It is organized, energized, and directed by God. Ultimately, it is accomplished by God. The church cannot understand its mission apart from the mission of God.

CHRIST

It is said that a Hindu once asked E. Stanley Jones, "What has Christianity to offer that our religion has not?" Jones's answer: "Jesus Christ."[14] Indeed, Jesus Christ, central to Christian belief and practice, is the driving force in our missiology.

Jesus Christ is supreme. Jesus Christ is pre-eminent—all things were created by him, through him, and for him (Col. 1:16). It is only through him

---

[13] For further reading, see John Piper, *Let the Nations Be Glad: The Supremacy of God in Missions*, 2nd ed., rev. and exp. (Grand Rapids: Baker, 2003). This thesis about God's glory and man's happiness runs throughout Piper's theology of mission.

[14] Paul Borthwick, *Six Dangerous Questions* (Downers Grove: IVP, 1996), 48.

that man is saved (Acts 4:12) and only through him that the church is built (Matt. 16:18). It is in Christ, writes Ajith Fernando, that "the Creator of the world has indeed presented the complete solution to the human predicament. As such it is supreme; it is unique; and it is absolute. So we have the audacity in this pluralistic age to say that Jesus as he is portrayed in the Bible is not only unique but also supreme."[15]

Scripture in its entirety proclaims none other than Christ himself. Both the Old and New Testaments are Christocentric—Christ is the axis of the testaments, the linchpin of the canon. The purpose of the Scriptures is to present Christ (Luke 24:27). The central promise of the Old Testament is that God would send the Messiah (Gen. 3:15). Directly connected to that promise is the further promise that this Messiah would win the *nations* unto himself and indeed reconcile *all things* unto himself. From Genesis 3 onward, we see the triumphant march of God to fulfill that promise in the crucified and resurrected Jesus who will come again and bring with him a new heavens and a new earth where his redeemed will live in his presence.

He has commissioned us to make disciples of all nations. From his supreme authority comes the commission Christ has given his church (Matt. 28:18–20). We proclaim this Great Commission, but sometimes we overlook the particulars of the command. In the first phrase, "All authority has been given to Me in heaven and on earth" (HCSB), it is made clear that the follower of any other lord must repent and follow Jesus, and do so on the basis of the supreme authority of the Lord of the universe. He has authority over Satan, evil spirits, the forces of nature, the human race, and indeed all of the created order. We go in confidence, even as we pray for a resurgence in Great Commission theology and practice.

Next, our Lord gives the imperative, "Go, therefore, and make disciples of all nations, baptizing them in the name of the Father and of the Son and of the Holy Spirit" (HCSB). In this command, we are instructed to make *disciples*, and not merely professions of faith. Moreover, we are to do so through baptism (and therefore in the context of his church) and in the name of the triune God (who alone can save), teaching believers to obey everything he has commanded us.

The missiological implications of this are manifold, but two demand our attention. First, the "commands of Christ" are contained in the *Christian Scriptures*. There is no true evangelism or discipleship apart from the proclamation of the Word of God. Any other tools that we may use, such as philosophical apologetics or Qur'anic points of contact, are preliminary and are for the sole purpose of initially engaging that person with the Word of God, recognizing that evangelism and discipleship come solely through communication of the teaching of the Christian Scriptures.

Second, the commands of Christ are not limited to those statements in the New Testament in which Jesus speaks in the imperative. Indeed, the entirety of Christian Scripture, including Old and New Testaments, teaches us what

[15] Ajith Fernando, *The Supremacy of Christ* (Wheaton: Crossway, 1995), 262.

God has done through Christ. "All Scripture is inspired by God" (2 Tim. 3:16, HCSB), and hence also bears the insignia of Christ. Our evangelism and discipleship, therefore, will include the clear teaching of the entire canon of Scripture.

In the final phrase of Matthew 28:20, our Lord promises, "And remember, I am with you always, to the end of the age" (HCSB). This promise is our confidence; we go under the authority of Christ and in the very presence of Christ. *Missiology is at its heart Christological*, and there is perhaps no better picture of this than in Revelation 5:9–10, where the Lion of the Tribe of Judah receives the worship of the nations: "You are worthy to take the scroll and to open its seals; because You were slaughtered, and You redeemed [people] for God by Your blood from every tribe and language and people and nation. You made them a kingdom and priests to our God, and they will reign on the earth" (HCSB).

Missiology is also inextricably linked with suffering. Just as the Lion of Judah suffered as the Lamb who was slain, we are called to be willing to suffer on behalf of the gospel. Paul hints at this "missiological suffering" when he writes, "Now I rejoice in my sufferings for you, and I am completing in my flesh what is lacking in Christ's afflictions for His body, that is, the church" (Col. 1:24, HCSB). There is a sense in which Paul's suffering makes up what is lacking in Christ's suffering, and the only thing lacking is Christ's sufficient renown among the nations.[16] Thus, we now proclaim his name to all people, living in anticipation of his Second Coming when he will be worshipped in his splendor as the king of the nations.

HOLY SPIRIT

Christians acknowledge that Father, Son, and Spirit live in eternal and unbroken communion with one another. The unified nature of their fellowship lies not only in their shared attributes and perfections but also in their shared mission. The triune God's mission is equally the Father's, the Son's, and the Spirit's. Though the persons of the Trinity may play different roles, they nonetheless are working as one. Scripture presents the Spirit as he who empowers us for mission (Acts 1:8) and gives us the words to say in time of need (Matt. 10:17–20). It is he who convicts souls (John 16:8–11) and grows the church both in number (Acts 2:14–41) and in maturity (Eph. 4:7–13). Again, the application of this doctrine is significant.

The Spirit reveals. Throughout the ages, Christians have recognized that God reveals himself through his Word by his Spirit. Indeed, the human writers of Scripture wrote as the Spirit moved them (2 Pet. 1:21) so that Paul could make clear that all Scripture is *theopneustos*, or "God-breathed," and is "profitable for teaching, for rebuking, for correcting, for training in righteousness" (2 Tim. 3:16, HCSB). Scripture is the very breath of God.

---

[16] For further reflection on missiological suffering, see Piper, *Let the Nations Be Glad*, 71–107.

This teaching has manifold and serious implications for our missiology. For example, there are entire people groups who are oral learners unable to read Scripture. Christian workers must (1) make every effort to communicate the Scriptures orally to them even though they are not able to read the Scriptures on their own; (2) equip those same oral learners to share the gospel and build the church even while they are unable to read the Scriptures; (3) pray for and support those who work in Bible translation; (4) pray for Bible translation movements just as we pray for church planting movements; (5) pray for, and work toward, the development of literacy among the leaders of these people groups;[17] and (6) pray, work, and even fight to have the Scriptures translated accurately.[18]

The Spirit empowers, convicts, teaches, and illumines. The Spirit empowers us to proclaim the Word (1 Thess. 1:5; 1 Pet. 1:12), to pray effectively (Rom. 8:26), and to have power over the forces of evil (Matt. 12:28; Acts 13:9–11). He convicts of sin, righteousness, and judgment (John 16:8–11). He teaches all things (John 14:26) and opens the eyes of our hearts that we might understand (1 Cor. 2:12; Eph. 1:17–19). With this in mind, we must not rely exclusively on our human efforts such as communication models, demographic studies, or people-group profiles. Rather, our mission in any context should be undergirded by prayer, in reliance upon the Spirit who will enable us to interpret the Scriptures rightly and bring understanding and conviction to our audience.

The Spirit gives gifts and enables fruit. The Spirit gives gifts to each person (1 Cor. 12:11) and enables believers to bear fruit (Gal. 5:22–23). This truth suggests that church planting is probably best done in teams, as the multiple members of a team use their spiritual gifts together, and bear fruit together in the context of Christian community.[19] The result is that those who are watching will see more clearly what Christ intends for his church. It also suggests that a new convert can immediately be considered a "new worker," a part of the team, as he is surely already gifted by the Spirit and capable of bearing fruit. Immediately he can give testimony to Christ and edify the believers.

---

[17] Some missiologists reject the call to translate the Bible for, and thereby introduce literacy to, a society of oral learners. This rejection, however, is misplaced. Although cultures have a fair degree of internal consistency, they are always changing because of either internal developments or external introductions. Change is not bad in and of itself. While the missionary does not seek to be colonial (seeking to export Western culture) or to build his missiology upon Darwinist anthropology (seeing Western culture as inherently farther along on the evolutionary scale), he does seek to be a change agent by introducing the gospel immediately and the written Scriptures eventually.

[18] Some Bible translators, in their desire to provide contextualized translations, have mistranslated the Scriptures and in so doing have undermined doctrines central to the gospel. For example, some translators working in Islamic contexts have sought to remove the phrase "son of God" from translations in an attempt not to offend Muslims. However, to do so is to remove a central biblical teaching and to neuter the gospel itself.

[19] For further reflection on a "team model" for international church planting, see Daniel Sinclair, *A Vision of the Possible* (Waynesboro, GA: Authentic, 2006).

The Spirit restrains. The Spirit works providentially, restraining evil (2 Thess. 2:6–7). After the fall, sin entered the world with devastating consequences. Man's relationship with God, with others, with the created order, and even with himself were broken. Sin fractured the world at all levels. It is only by the restraining power of the Spirit that the world is not an utter horror. This is a grace that God has given to the entire world, a common grace that allows us to act and interact in family, workplace, and community. It is a grace that allows us to use our relational, rational, and creative capacities, even though they are distorted by sin and are bent toward idolatry.[20]

MAN

Apart from the Christian Scriptures, one cannot make sense of humanity. Absent the Christian doctrine of God and the *imago Dei*, one cannot account for the unique nature, capacities, and ends of human existence.

Man's creation. Inevitably, other worldviews tend toward either enthronement or denigration of humanity, unable to strike a proper balance.[21] Scripture, however, strikes a balance, making clear that man has both a great humility and a great dignity. His great humility, on the one hand, is that *he is not God*; indeed, he is created for the express purpose of worshipping God. His great dignity, on the other hand, is that unlike the animals and the rest of the created order, *he is created in God's image*.

At creation, man possessed a fourfold excellence in his relational capacity. He was in right relationship with God, with others, with the created order, and with himself. He experienced *shalom*—a universal human flourishing, a right ordering of things, a divine peace. It was in this state of *shalom* that God instructed man to work the ground, to change and even enhance what God had made. Further, he instructed man to multiply and fill the earth. Man, therefore, is made to be both productive and reproductive.[22]

Man's fall. After the fall, however, man experienced the cataclysmic consequences of his rebellion; he was no longer in right relationship with God, with others, with the created order, or with himself. Beginning with Adam and Eve, every member of the human race has taken up arms and rebelled

---

[20] For further reflection, see Michael S. Horton, *Where in the World Is the Church?* (Phillipsburg, NJ: P&R, 2002).

[21] Naturalism is exemplary in this respect. On the one hand, the atheists of the humanist manifestos enthrone man, speaking of him as if he is a god. On the other hand, contemporary pagans such as Peter Singer denigrate man, speaking of him as a mere animal. "By 2040," Singer writes, "it may be that only a rump of hard-core, know-nothing religious fundamentalists will defend the view that every human life, from conception to death, is sacrosanct." Peter Singer, "The Sanctity of Life," *Foreign Policy* (Sept/Oct 2005), 40.

[22] G. K. Beale views the Great Commission as the fulfillment of God's original command to fill the earth. According to Beale, Adam was to expand the Garden of Eden, which is presented in Genesis as a temple, and thereby expand God's presence "to the ends of the earth." Therefore, in the Great Commission, "Jesus is empowering his followers . . . with spiritual empowerment to do what Adam and others had failed to do" (G. K. Beale, *The Temple and the Church's Mission* [Downers Grove: InterVarsity, 2004], 199).

against God. The aftermath has been devastating, with sin wreaking havoc across the entire fabric of human life. Man's sin has caused a deep and pervasive distortion of God's good creation.

Because of the fall, our relationship with *God* is broken. We are serial idolaters, enemies of God, seeking goodness and happiness on our own, apart from him. We are *homo incurvatus in se*, or man "turned in on himself" (Luther) and, thus, are not "fully alive" (Irenaeus).[23] Our wills are bent toward sin; we are dead in our trespasses (Eph. 2:1). As a result, we must recognize that such idolaters need something deep and powerful in order to be saved. In other words, if man is corrupted by sin "through and through," then salvation is not a matter merely of intellectual assent. Therefore, we must avoid reductionist methods of evangelism and discipleship. We must proclaim the gospel according to the Scriptures as we seek to see God break up the ground of hard hearts.

Second, our relationship with *others* is broken. Rather than being marked by unbroken love and service, our relationships are marked by interpersonal and societal ugliness. There is hardly a more easily proven fact than human badness—consider the abuse, divorce, rape, war, incest, gossip, slander, murder, and deceit that abound. The church should take note that her mission includes the modeling of a more excellent way; a watching world should know us by our love for one another (John 13:35). Our life together, in mutual love for one another and Christ, is a sign of God's kingdom, a foreshadowing of the unbroken harmony that we will experience on a new heavens and earth.

Third, our relationship with the *created order* is broken; rather than unbroken harmony and delight, we experience pain and misery. This brokenness of the created order provides an opportunity for the church to minister. Natural disasters are signposts that point to the brokenness of the natural order. We can use this signpost to proclaim the gospel, by teaching the gospel according to the Scriptures. In other words, we do not simply tell hurting and suffering people, "Jesus loves you." In addition, we describe how the world was created without such evil, that such evil entered the world because of sin, and that one day there will be a new heavens and earth where there is no more sin and no more evil. We also act upon the privilege of ministering to the physical needs of our fellow image-bearers, demonstrating the love about which we speak.

Fourth, we are alienated even from *ourselves*. This alienation is another signpost that points to the brokenness of God's good creation. Again, we can use this signpost to declare the gospel. Take, for example, the despair that many experience at the apparent meaninglessness of life. The person who despairs may be an American materialist, a Thai Buddhist, a philosophical

---

[23] Luther argues that man is *incurvatus se*, "curved in on his own understanding." See Jaroslav Pelikan, ed., *Luther's Works* (St. Louis, MO: Concordia, 1955–1986), 25:426. For Irenaeus, there is no "complete" or "perfect" man without the Spirit. Christ, through his incarnation, bestows the Spirit and enables man to be truly alive. See Dominic Unger, trans., *Against Heresies* (New York: Paulist Press, 1992), 5.6.1 and 5.9.2.

nihilist, a victim of sexual abuse, or merely a person who senses that his life lacks meaning and purpose. The gospel answers this concern by showing man that he is created in the image of God, that his purpose in life is to glorify God, and that this purpose is not at odds with his own deepest satisfaction. Happiness, in its deepest and most profound sense, comes from being conformed to the image of the Son (Rom. 8:29), who himself is the image of God (Col. 1:15).

In light of man's pervasive and holistic corruption, we are driven to minister to every aspect of man in every dimension of his world. We must work hard, therefore, to bequeath to the churches we plant a vision for the deep, broad, and powerful impact that the Christian faith can and should have on the various socio-cultural dimensions of life. We may use all of our human capacities to minister to man in the wholeness of his humanity. We may seek to glorify God in the arts, the sciences, education, and the public square, as well as inside the four walls of a church meeting. We must teach our children to devote their intellectual and creative capacities to Christ, and not merely their spiritual and moral. We must teach them that "pastor" and "missionary" are not the only honorable callings for a godly child; science, education, law, and journalism are also honorable callings. In so doing our churches will bear witness from within every arena of human society and culture.

SALVATION

The doctrine of salvation receives as much attention as any of the classical loci of Christian doctrine. It is central to missiological method, and yet ironically, we have a difficult time making a "full connect" between the doctrine and our methods and strategies.

The redemption of man. Salvation is God's work from beginning to end (Ps. 3:8; Heb. 12:2). At the beginning, we see God's hand in election, the gracious decision by which he elects man to salvation. We see God's hand also in calling man back to himself (Gen. 3:9), and in calling preachers who are an instrument of others' salvation (Rom. 10:14–15). God is also at work as man repents and places faith in Christ. Man is converted as God regenerates him, renewing his inner man, and imparting eternal life to him.

Salvation is by grace alone, through faith alone, in Christ alone. We seek to form missiological practices that recognize all aspects of God's work of salvation. Because of the limited scope of this chapter, I will choose only a handful of the many facets of soteriology and give a limited exposition of their implication for missiology.

We must recognize that it is God who calls. In the *ordo salutis*, we see God drawing men unto himself (Gen. 3:9; Luke 15:1–7). While we will never have sure or final knowledge of whom God is drawing unto himself, we may pray that God will bring across our paths those men and women whom he is drawing unto himself. These may very well be men and women through whom he will declare his glory to an entire city or people group. We may pray for particular people, asking God to begin drawing them unto himself. We do evangelism God's way, without compromising sound biblical theology, and leave the results to God who calls.

We must call non-believers to repentance and not merely mental assent. We must work hard to form evangelism and discipleship practices that recognize the entire salvific process. One of the most oft-ignored aspects of salvation is repentance. Therefore, we seek to form testimonies, gospel presentations, Bible-study sets, and sermons that call men to repentance rather than merely to mental assent. This means that men must turn their backs on false saviors, repudiate tribal gods and witch doctors, reject their belief that the Qur'an is God's revelation and that Muhammad is his prophet, cease to worship in spirit temples and ancestral shrines, turn their back on the worship of sex, money, power, and other metaphorical idols.[24]

We must preach salvation by grace through faith in Christ, and do so in a way that is faithful, meaningful, and dialogical. We must work hard to preach justification by grace alone, through faith alone, in Christ alone. We must do so in a contextually appropriate manner, communicating faithfully, meaningfully, and dialogically. We do so *faithfully* by remaining true to the authorial intent of the biblical writers and *meaningfully* by communicating in such a way that the audience understands our message in the way we intend it.[25] We must be very careful, as we face cross-cultural and cross-linguistic

---

[24] This doctrine of repentance, premised upon the Lordship of Christ and crucial to biblical teaching about salvation, disallows "insider movements" (IM) as a mission strategy for reaching Muslims. Proponents of IM say that such movements contain Muslim background believers who choose to remain within Islam as a means of reaching Muslims. IM proponents say that this type of contextualization allows the convert to overcome significant barriers. Further, they argue that Christ does not require a convert to change his identity or religion, and that he is free to reinterpret passages of the Qur'an so that he does not have to renounce it as a whole. Finally, many IM proponents seem to see Islam as similar to OT Judaism and therefore not inherently opposed to the gospel. In response to the IM movement, and in light of biblical teaching on the lordship of Christ and the necessity of repentance, we argue that IM ideology transgresses biblical bounds and misunderstands the nature of Islam. Islam is a religion custom-built to subvert and overthrow orthodox Christianity. Its Arian Jesus and doctrines of *tawhid* and *shirk* make clear that the worst possible sin for a Muslim is to believe in the Christian doctrines of Trinity and incarnation. Although Muslim background believers face persecution and even death, and although we understand that it will take God-given courage to stop attending the mosque and confessing that Muhammad is God's prophet, we must reject IM strategy because of its subversion of the doctrines of lordship and repentance. For two insider descriptions of IM, see Kevin Higgins, "The Key to Insider Movements: The 'Devoted's' of Acts," *IJFM* 21 (Winter 2004): 155, and Rebecca Lewis, "Promoting Movements to Christ within Natural Communities," *IJFM* 24 (Summer 2007): 75.

[25] For a concise and helpful discussion of the concepts of "faithfulness" and "meaningfulness," see David J. Hesselgrave and Edward Rommen, *Contextualization: Meanings, Methods, and Models* (Pasadena: William Carey, 2000), 199–211. Perhaps this is the best place to comment on the current debate about using the term "Allah" in Bible translations in Arab contexts. Sometimes the term Allah is the most appropriate word for the deity, as it predates Islam and is the only serious term used to refer to God. See Irfan Shahid, "Arab Christianity before the Rise of Islam," in *Christianity: A History in the Middle East*, ed. Habib Badr (Middle East Council of Churches, 2006), 441–42. Christians may use the term, therefore, but must consciously,

challenges, to work hard not only to rightly divide the Word, but also to proclaim the Word clearly.

In addition we proclaim the gospel *dialogically*.[26] The gospel must be proclaimed and embodied. There is an ever-present danger that Christian preachers, missionaries, and communities will equate the gospel with a cultural context, the consequence of which is devastating. In an attempt to communicate the gospel meaningfully within a culture, and in an attempt to affirm whatever in a culture can be affirmed, Christians find it easy to lose sight of the effects of depravity on that same culture. The gospel stands in judgment of all cultures, calling them to change. It does not condemn all of a culture, but it is always and at the same time both affirming and rejecting.

For example, a married Hindu-background believer will cease to have his primary relationship with his mother, and it will now be with his wife. This is contrary to Hindu tradition. A married Muslim-background believer will cease beating his wife. When an Animist-background believer comes to Christ, he may see eventually that the Bible answers but also reframes his questions about "power." The gospel answers that Jesus Christ has defeated Satan and his forces, but the gospel also reframes the animist's worldview by teaching him that he need not constantly be in fear, that he need not constantly think in terms of "power."

When a Buddhist background person is confronted with the gospel, he may see "shame and honor" as the central categories in life. The Bible affirms those categories, but adds a new set of questions about guilt, sacrifice, and forgiveness. If the gospel loses this prophetic edge, it loses its power. Much has been made about contextualization, but often the discussion emphasizes the need to make the gospel meaningful while neglecting or de-emphasizing the need to teach it faithfully and dialogically. To do so, however, almost ensures that one's proclamation will distort the gospel and one's church plant will not adequately represent the gospel.

We must beware of mechanical or magical understandings of salvation. One of the greatest hindrances to missions is the tendency to present a "magical" or "mechanistic" view of salvation.[27] We must correct the tendency to view salvation as mere mental assent, mere verbal profession of faith, or mere repetition of a prayer of salvation. If a person holds to such a reductionist view of salvation, he will have a wrong goal: the maximum number of people who have prayed a prayer or made a verbal profession. Further, he will give false assurance of salvation to men who are not saved, and a false testimony to the church and the broader community. Third, he will create methods of

---

carefully, and consistently define the term according to Christian Scripture, just as John did in using *logos* and as Moses did in using *elohim*.

[26] For a concise and helpful discussion of the dialogical nature of contextualization, see David K. Clark, *To Know and Love God: Method for Theology* (Wheaton: Crossway, 2003), 99–131.

[27] I owe this idea to a conversation I had with Greg Turner, a long-time mission leader in Central Asia.

evangelism that are reductionist and harmful to the progress of the gospel and the planting of healthy churches.[28]

We must beware of both reductionism and complexification. One who holds to a mechanical or magical understanding of salvation will likely create methods of evangelism, discipleship, leadership training, and theological education that are reductionist to the extreme, that misunderstand what we are saved *from* and what we are saved *for.* Another, however, may run the opposite risk of crafting methods that are unnecessarily complex. The tendency is to attempt to dump one's historical, systematic, and philosophical theology on the new convert's head. Instead, he needs to be taught the gospel in a manner that he is capable of understanding and reproducing in his present context. We must resist, therefore, the twin errors of reductionism and complexification.

We must make sure that our methods are grace– and gospel-centered. Because only the gospel saves, our methods should be gospel-centered. Since salvation is by grace through faith, our methods should center on grace. Take, for example, various methods of "obedience-based teaching" which are popular in international missions.[29] Although we must teach obedience, these methods can quickly become legalistic and works-oriented if "obedience to Christ" is not carefully and consistently put in the context of what Christ has already accomplished through his death.

It is not that obedience-based teaching is inherently legalistic or works-oriented. The point is merely that teaching "obedience to Christ" can be lifeless legalism that does not differ essentially from Islam or any other works-based religion. It is not only justification which comes by grace through faith, but sanctification also.

We must learn how to disciple. One of the significant challenges any pastor or church planter faces is how to create an environment in which the church makes robust disciples of its members. Discipleship is the process of being conformed into the image of Christ and therefore involves much more than a weekly Bible study. Discipleship at its best is immersion in the life of a healthy local church, and when such a church does not yet exist, discipleship is best accomplished through deep relationships formed with whatever believers the disciple might know.

---

[28]   Many proponents of insider movements (IM) in Islamic contexts hold to an overly privatized and reductionist view of salvation which leads to a warped and reductionist ecclesiology. IM proponents promote a "churchless Christianity." However, the persecuted believers of the New Testament baptized, gathered together for worship, and refused to recognize Caesar as a god. Theirs was not a churchless Christianity. Although the (commendable) aim of IM proponents is to help new converts maintain familial and communal connections, they undermine the role of the church in nurturing faith, building community, and bearing witness to the kingdom. It is my hope that this treatment of IM does not appear to be insensitive to the massive challenges that Muslim background believers encounter as they face persecution and even death.

[29]   One prominent paradigm for obedience-based teaching is George Patterson, *The Church Multiplication Guide* (Pasadena: William Carey, 2002). Another is Ying Kai, *Trainers: Establishing Successful Trainers,* 2nd ed. (Ying Kai, 2005).

Americans who seek to plant churches outside of the deep South of the USA will likely find themselves in non-Christian, pre-Christian, and post-Christian contexts. In such contexts, the church planter confronts the massive challenge of discipling a person who has little or no knowledge of the Bible or Christ, and little or no experience watching others live their lives in a truly Christian manner.[30] In such instances, we find it particularly urgent and necessary to allow a robust soteriology to inform our discipleship.

Such a soteriology demands several responses. First, we must teach the entire redemptive narrative, refusing to teach isolated passages of Scripture divorced from their context. We teach the broad sweeping redemptive story, beginning at creation, leading through to the first coming of Christ, and concluding with his second coming and the new heavens and earth. We do not need months or years to do this; it may be accomplished in fifteen minutes, in an hour, or in a twenty-lesson Bible study set. Second, we must teach biblical commands regarding Christian living. Often, this is accomplished by what some missionaries call "obedience-based teaching," which expounds biblical imperatives for the disciple, and does so (optimally) in the context of the gospel of grace set forth in the redemptive narrative discussed above. Third, we must model what we teach by practicing "life-on-life" discipleship. Such discipleship is not accomplished merely by information dissemination. We must roll up our shirtsleeves and get involved in people's lives, eating with them, laughing with them, and weeping with them. We must *show* a man what it means for him to love his wife and children, *show* him what it means to carry himself with the grace and love of Christ, and *show* him how to remain faithful in the midst of adversity.

In sum, the doctrine of salvation is a most precious doctrine, displaying for us the salvation that we have found in Christ Jesus, to the glory of God the Father. It is our responsibility and high privilege to proclaim that gospel in a manner worthy of our Lord. Whatever we model for new believers we disciple and for churches we plant will likely be copied for generations to come; therefore nothing less than the purity of the gospel and the health of the church is at stake.

---

[30] Church planters face many additional challenges, especially in persecution-heavy environments. The disciple who publicly professes faith in Christ faces the possibility of losing his job and family and perhaps even his life. He must decide how (and how soon) he will make public his faith in Christ. He may deal with second thoughts about his faith and must do so without the support network of his family and community, and without having been given a biblical upbringing. In one Middle Eastern country, our workers ask fearful new converts to list the two hundred people they know best—family, friends, colleagues, etc. Once these new disciples have come up with a list of two hundred friends and acquaintances, our workers ask them to pick five names of those who are least likely to kill the new disciple if he shares the gospel. Armed with those five names, the new disciples begin to share their faith. For further reflection on discipleship in persecuted contexts, see Sinclair, *A Vision of the Possible*, 139–57.

THE CHURCH

Missiology is inextricably intertwined with ecclesiology; one cannot be discussed properly without the other. It is probably for that reason that there are so many controversial issues at the intersection of the two disciplines. At the beginning of this section, we will give a cursory overview of some of the main themes of ecclesiology. This concise biblical ecclesiology will give us a "place to stand" as the latter part of the section will speak to some significant and controversial ecclesiological issues in contemporary missiology.

Being the church. Scripture does not give a dictionary definition of the nature of the church. What it does instead is provide images and analogies that help us to understand the nature of the church. The church cannot be defined apart from its relationship to God, which is evident especially in the following three images.

In 1 Peter 2:9–10, the church is described as the *people of God*, reminding us that we are God's possession, and that we are a community rather than a collection of individuals. Second, Paul instructs us that we are the *body of Christ*. Sometimes he uses this image to refer to the church universal (Eph.; Col.) and sometimes to the church local (Rom.; 1 Cor.). This image helps us to understand that we are many members but one body (unity and diversity) and that each of us belongs to the other members of the body (mutual love and interdependence). Third, we are the *temple of the Spirit*. Our body is a temple of the Spirit (1 Cor. 6:19); we are living stones built into a spiritual house (1 Pet. 2:5). This image evokes not only the memory of Christ who "tabernacles" with us, but also the idea of relationship. We are held together by the Spirit.

As the church fathers and the Reformers reflected upon the Scriptures, they came to identify the church with certain marks. The fathers spoke of the church as being one, holy, catholic, and apostolic. We are *one*, in that we are indwelt by the same Spirit. We are *holy*, in that we seek to allow as members only those who profess faith in Christ and show visible signs of regeneration. We are *catholic*, in that the gospel is universally available for all people, in all places, at all times. We are *apostolic*, in that we hold to the same gospel proclaimed by the apostles. Moreover, the Reformers noted that the church is marked by the right preaching of the *gospel*, the right administration of the *ordinances*, and a commitment to church *discipline*.

These marks, however, are not exhaustive. There are many ways we can describe the church. For example, as John Hammett has pointed out, the church (1) is organized and purposeful; (2) is primarily local; (3) is, by nature, living and growing; (4) is centered on the gospel; and (5) is powered by the Spirit.[31]

The Scriptures teach that the church is composed of regenerate members (1 Cor. 5:11). This belief is the center of Baptist ecclesiology, and is directly

---

[31] John Hammett, *Biblical Foundations for Baptist Churches* (Grand Rapids: Kregel, 2005), 67–77.

linked to the purposes of the church.[32] While, on this side of eternity, we will never know for sure the state of another person's soul, we may keep diligent watch over the church, discipling and disciplining toward the goal of faithfulness and holiness.

Doing church. The Scriptures speak of churches that met in houses (Rom. 16:5) as well as house churches that were connected to one another as city churches (Acts 13:1). Further, the Scriptures speak of these churches, together, as a sort of regional church (Acts 8:1) and the church universal (1 Cor. 1:2). The universal church includes believers both living and dead; is not synonymous with any one institution, denomination, or network of churches; and is not entirely visible at any time.

The way that the church functions is a direct outworking of what the church is. Scripture gives us specific guidance as to how we are to live as the church. The church is defined by its relation to Christ, and therefore its members are actually connected to one another. Our union with Christ connects us not only to God but also one to another.

This relational dimension is evident especially in the Eucharist and in the "one another" commands. For example, we must live in harmony with one another (Rom. 12:16; 15:5), forgive and bear with one another (Col. 3:13), and not pass judgment on one another (Rom. 14:1). We must admonish and encourage one another (1 Thess. 5:14), care for one another (1 Cor. 12:25), and comfort one another (2 Cor. 13:11). Perhaps all of the many "one another" commands could be summed up in 1 Thessalonians 5:15: "Always pursue what is good for one another and for all" (HCSB).

These commands, which are given to all of the members of the church, show that we are all responsible to one another and ultimately to Christ. The church is congregational (Acts 6:3; 13:2–3; 15:22), recognizing the congregation as the human authority but Christ as the ultimate divine authority. We follow Christ as he leads the church.

This understanding is not at odds with the appointment of pastors, to whose leadership we submit unless for doctrinal or moral reasons their leadership is rescinded. Scripture teaches that the church has two leadership offices, the bishop/elder/pastor and the deacon. The officers are chosen by the congregation (Acts 14:23). The bishop/elder/pastor must be able to administrate (bishop), teach and nurture (pastor), be mature in the faith (elder), and meet the requirements laid out in Scripture (1 Tim. 3; Titus 1). The deacon is a servant (Acts 6:1–6) and must meet the requirements laid out in Scripture (1 Tim. 3:8–13). Pastors, in particular, are to equip the saints for the work of ministry (Eph. 4:11–12).

---

[32] Ibid., 81. See also J. D. Freeman, "The Place of Baptists in the Christian Church," in *The Baptist World Congress: London, July 11–19, 1905, Authorised Record of Proceedings* (London: Baptist Union Publication Department, 1905), 27; Justice C. Anderson, "Old Baptist Principles Reset," *Southwestern Journal of Theology* 31 (Spring 1989): 5–12; and Mark Dever, *Nine Marks of a Healthy Church* (Wheaton: Crossway, 2000), 136.

The church's ministries are manifold and may be summarized in five categories. Hammett points out that these five ministries may be seen together in Acts 2:42–47. Those ministries are teaching, fellowship, worship, service, and evangelism.

Ecclesiology and missiology. It is difficult to overstate the significance of ecclesiology for Christians in general and for missiologists in particular. We must agree with Mark Dever, who writes:

> The enduring authority of Christ's commands compels Christians to study the Bible's teaching on the church. Present-day errors in the understanding and the practice of the church will, if they prevail, still further obscure the gospel. Christian proclamation might make the gospel audible, but Christians living together in local congregations make the gospel visible (John 13:34–35). The church is the gospel made visible.[33]

In the coming decades, at least four issues will continually surface at the intersection of ecclesiology and mission, demanding theologically sound and missiologically savvy answers to (1) what counts as a *church*; (2) how to evaluate *house* churches; (3) how to plant *indigenous* churches; and (4) how to remain faithful to biblical ecclesiology and at the same time pray for church planting *movements*.

Bible study or church? One of the first questions that a fledgling church planter often faces is "When does a group of believers become a church?" This is another way of asking, "What are the marks of the church?" In the previous section, we affirmed the patristic and Reformation marks of a church.

There is, however, yet another challenge which causes us to inquire about the true marks of a church once again. That challenge is world evangelization. This is the case today as our churches and missionaries seek to bring the gospel to, and plant churches among, every unreached people group in God's creation. In an eagerness to do so, though, some well-intentioned missionaries have counted as churches some groups that are not churches. For example, Bible studies or small clusters of believers who know one another are sometimes improperly counted as churches.

So, how do we know when a group has become a church? First, we should say that churches can be placed legitimately on certain spectrums, such as mature and immature, healthy and unhealthy, developed and undeveloped. A group of believers can be a church without being a fully developed, mature, or healthy church. Second, we must affirm certain minimum standards in order for a group to qualify as a church. There must be a group of baptized believers, consciously committed to one another under the headship of Christ, partaking of the Lord's Supper. They may or may not have a pastor, but at the very least must be praying for the Lord to raise up among them a pastor. Such a group may be called a church even if it is a very small group.

---

[33] Mark E. Dever, "The Church," in Daniel L. Akin, ed., *A Theology for the Church* (Nashville: B&H, 2007), 767.

Church in a house? The church is not a building; the church is the people of God, the body of Christ, the temple of the Spirit. We do not need a temple because we are the temple. Therefore, where the people meet is less significant, perhaps, than we tend to think. In many of the contexts in which we are seeing the gospel go forth and churches planted, conversion to Christianity is illegal—and therefore the purchase of a building is also illegal. In these cases, of course, a church meets in a house. This raises two questions.

Is a house church un-evangelical? Is it in some way an inferior type of church? It absolutely is not, although believers in the United States might tend to think so. A church is a church, no matter where it meets. It has the same nature, and is held to the same standards, as any other church. There is precedent in the Scriptures for churches meeting in a house (Rom. 16:5), and such churches are never treated as inferior. A house church is, in every sense of the word, a church. A church is a church, whether it meets in a wooden chapel, a brick auditorium, or a neighborhood home.

Is "house church" then the superior model for church? Those who are involved in house churches are sometimes tempted to speak as if churches that meet in houses are superior in every way. This is not the case. While a church in a house might tend to better fulfill one of the ministries of the church (e.g., fellowship), it might also tend to lag behind in another ministry (e.g., teaching).[34]

An indigenous church? Much ado has been made, in the past century, about the "indigenous" church. Henry Venn, Rufus Anderson, John L. Nevius, Roland Allen, and others have argued for a church that is self-supporting, self-governing, and self-propagating, and few evangelicals would disagree, at least in principle.[35] Based upon our doctrine of the church, especially our views on regenerate membership and congregational rule, we affirm these principles. In practice, however, we struggle to implement what we believe.

Concerning *self-support*, often our stateside churches subsidize overseas pastors and fund overseas churches in a way that undermines the health of those same pastors and churches. While it is acceptable to give special gifts for specified needs, we must be careful with other types of well-intended financial offerings. Supporting national pastors tends to sever accountability between the pastor and the church, and supporting national churches on a regular basis can foster the mind-set that an expensive building is necessary for a church to be formed. Setting a finance-heavy model for church

---

[34] Wolfgang Simson is a leading house church proponent and influential missiologist who argues that house church is a superior model. A fair-minded and helpful Baptist response to Simson's argument is James A. Atkinson, "House Church: A Biblical, Historical, and Practical Analysis of Selected Aspects of Wolfgang Simson's Ecclesiology from a Southern Baptist Perspective," Th.M. thesis, Southeastern Baptist Theological Seminary, May 2006.

[35] Max Warren, ed., *To Apply the Gospel: Selections from the Writings of Henry Venn* (Grand Rapids: Eerdmans, 1971); R. Pierce Beaver, ed., *To Advance the Gospel: Selections from the Writings of Rufus Anderson* (Grand Rapids: Eerdmans, 1967); John L. Nevius, *The Planting and Development of Missionary Churches* (Hancock, NH: Monadnock, 2003); Roland Allen, *The Spontaneous Expansion of the Church* (Grand Rapids: Eerdmans, 1962).

life and church multiplication will unnecessarily hinder or kill the spontaneous expansion of the church. Short-term help, in this instance, may handicap long-term growth.

Concerning *self-governance*, the churches we plant must submit to the leadership of Christ, who is their Head. We must not, unintentionally, set up a hierarchy with the church planter (or the mother church or the church planting agency) as the "Pope." Long and Rowthorn describe the missiological context in which Roland Allen proclaimed the need for an indigenous church: "In missionary work overseas, concern for 'traditions' made missionaries reluctant to hand over real responsibility to indigenous leaders and often confused the Tradition of the gospel with the particular traditions of the church and society from which the missionaries came."[36] We must love and care for, exhort and admonish, and even hold them accountable, but we must not control the congregations that we plant.

Concerning *self-propagation*, we must consciously seek to plant churches who understand their responsibility to reach their own people group. We must plant sound, healthy churches that will grow over the long run and not just in the short term, and we must remove anything that unnecessarily hinders the growth and multiplication of the church. They must not see the Westerner as the "key" to the evangelization of their people group; they must see that they have the God-given privilege of winning their own people. It is, in fact, appropriate that we lovingly allow the churches we plant to grow without being dependent on us.

Church planting movements? In recent days, much has been said about church planting movements (CPM), and rightly so. David Garrison defines a church planting movement as, "a rapid multiplication of indigenous churches planting churches that sweeps through a people group or population segment."[37] Evangelicals have been praying for and working toward the birth of CPMs among the unreached people groups of the world, but there is much work left to be done to ensure that our methodology is driven by the Scriptures. It must be biblical theology that gives church planting methodology its starting point, trajectory, and parameters.

Of the many substantial missiological issues that cluster around CPM theory, two must be treated. The first issue relates to *CPM as a goal*. Our ultimate goal, above all others, is the increase of God's glory and kingdom; no goal that we have should subvert this goal. For this reason, we are concerned not only with rapidity of multiplication, but also with the purity of the gospel and the health of the church.

On the one hand, if the church multiplies rapidly but is not healthy, the long-term picture is bleak. An inordinate emphasis on rapidity will likely lead to reductionist methods of evangelism and discipleship and a reductionist view of the church that will harm the church in the long term and actually

---

[36] Charles Henry Long and Anne Rowthorn, "The Legacy of Roland Allen," in *International Bulletin of Missionary Research* 13.2 (April 1989), 67.

[37] David Garrison, *Church Planting Movements* (Midlothian, VA: WIGTake, 2004), 21.

curb its growth. On the other hand, if the church is doctrinally pure but not seeking to multiply, the long-term picture is also bleak. Maybe it would be better to say that a church cannot be doctrinally pure without praying for, and working toward, the healthy and rapid growth of God's church.[38]

The second missiological issue is *leadership development*. The rapid reproduction of the church will lead to challenges in leadership identification and development. If multiple churches are planted in a short period of time, they are faced with the question of how soon a believer might be recognized as an elder. Further, in a context where the church is persecuted, how might elders train for pastoral ministry? In addition, how will they be discipled if they are not able to read? These are not hypothetical scenarios—they are church planting situations faced globally at any given time. We must take seriously the biblical teachings concerning the church, discipleship, and elder qualifications and work hard to apply them in challenging situations such as the ones listed here.[39] A Great Commission Resurgence assumes first a Great Commission *church*.[40]

THE END TIMES

Eschatology, as much as any other doctrine, undergirds the theory and practice of mission. Indeed, "all of Christian theology points toward an end—an end where Jesus overcomes the satanic reign of death and restores God's original creation order."[41] The doctrine of the end times is broad-ranging,

---

[38] A final note regarding CPM as a goal: CPMs are not the only worthwhile missiological accomplishment. In Hebrews 11, we read of men and women of great faith whose reward was not a CPM; instead, their reward was torture, destitution, affliction, and martyrdom (11:35b–38). Many faithful workers who labor in prayer and in deed, hoping with all that is within them to see a CPM, never see the birth of a CPM. This does not mean that their labor is in vain. If they have labored for the glory of God, then he is pleased with their efforts. Rodney Stark, in fact, shows how it took several centuries of faithful witness for an obscure and marginal "Jesus movement" to become the dominant religious force in the Western world. Rodney Stark, *The Rise of Early Christianity* (San Francisco: Harper SanFrancisco, 1997).

[39] These are only a few of the methodological issues connected to the doctrine of the church. The challenges are many and though they are not easily met, we may conclude with J. L. Dagg that, "Church order and the ceremonials of religion, are less important than a new heart; and in the view of some, any laborious investigation of questions respecting them may appear to be needless and unprofitable. But we know, from the Holy Scriptures, that Christ gave commands on these subjects, and we cannot refuse to obey. Love prompts our obedience; and love prompts also the search which may be necessary to ascertain his will. Let us, therefore, prosecute the investigations which are before us, with a fervent prayer, that the Holy Spirit, who guides into all truth, may assist us to learn the will of him who we supremely love and adore" (J. L. Dagg, *Manual of Church Order* [Harrisonburg, VA: Gano, 1990], 12).

[40] This chapter mentions only a few of the methodological issues connected to ecclesiology. Not only are there many more issues, but each of the issues are raised within numerous different civilizational, cultural, and social contexts. Further, the answers to our questions are not always presented in an immediately clear manner in the Scriptures. We must do the hard work applying biblical principles to concrete situations.

[41] Russell D. Moore, "Personal and Cosmic Eschatology," in Akin, *A Theology for the Church*, 858. Moore writes, "In Scripture the eschaton is not simply tacked on to the gospel at

and therefore this section will address only three aspects of this doctrine, followed by pointing the way toward a missiological appropriation.

The great divide. The Christian Scriptures instruct us about death, heaven, and hell. To be concise to the extreme, we may say that death entered the world because of sin (Rom. 5:12) and is a tool of Satan (Heb. 2:14–15). It is appointed to man once to die, and then the judgment. After death, he enters into either eternal damnation or eternal bliss. Eternal torment waits for those who die apart from Christ (Matt. 5:22; 8:12), while eternal bliss is the reward of those who are in Christ (Rev. 21:2–4).

This is a difficult doctrine, but a necessary one, as it is clearly taught in the Scriptures. Furthermore, it is a great motivator for the Christian and for the church. The Christian must hold three truths together in tension: (1) there is no name other than Christ by which men are saved, and all men who die apart from Christ abide in eternal torment; (2) countless millions of people have practically no access to the gospel, many of whom could search for days, weeks, and months, and never find a Bible, a Christian, or a church; and (3) we, as believers, have the awesome privilege and responsibility of proclaiming to them the good news. More to the point, those of us in the United States have greater financial and personnel resources to proclaim the gospel than Christians in any other part of the globe or at any other time in history.[42]

If we apprehend and affirm these three truths, we should find it difficult to remain apathetic. Once we hold these truths in tension, we are faced with a decision: will we act on their implications? Many people have never heard the gospel; without Christ they will go to Christless eternity; we are able to take the gospel to them. Our response likewise tends to fall into one of three categories: (1) we may change our belief system by rejecting the biblical teaching that salvation comes through Christ alone in order to ease our conscience; (2) we may simply ignore these truths, so that our conscience may rest more easily; or (3) we may take these truths to heart by working to take the gospel to the nations. This latter choice means building Great Commission churches and seminaries, raising up believers who will take the gospel to the nations, and praying for and supporting those who go.

The nations. The Scriptures also reveal, as a point of focus, the destiny of the nations. The teaching of Christian Scripture is that the gospel will be proclaimed to the whole world: "This good news of the kingdom will be proclaimed in all the world as a testimony to all nations. And then the end will come" (Matt. 24:14, HCSB). But the point is not merely that the gospel will be *proclaimed.* The further point is that the gospel is *powerful to save*

---

the end. It is instead the vision toward which all of Scripture is pointing—and the vision that grounds the hope of the gathered church and the individual believer. In the face of death, we see faith, hope, and love. This is what we mean when we speak of Christian eschatology—the study of the last things or ultimate matters."

[42] This, of course is changing, as the Christian faith is experiencing explosive growth in certain areas of sub-Saharan Africa, East Asia, and South America. Increasingly, these regions of the world will have more personnel resources for engaging the unreached people groups of the rest of the world. See Philip Jenkins, *The Next Christendom* (Oxford: Oxford University, 2002).

worshippers from among all people: "Worthy are You . . . for You were slain, and purchased for God with Your blood men from every tribe and tongue and people and nation" (Rev. 5:9, NASB).

The ingathering of the nations is not an add-on to Christian doctrine; it is at the heart of God's promises. The central promise in the Scriptures is that God would send Messiah, and directly connected to it is the promise that Messiah would win the nations unto himself. God put his Son on the cross in order to purchase the nations. The ingathering of the nations is not an issue merely for the missiologists to write about, for professional missionaries to care about, or for churches to nod toward during a special missions offering emphasis. Rather, it is central to all who are Christian because it is central to the work of Christ.

We are to be instruments in God's hands as he makes clear to the world that he is not a tribal deity. He is the Creator, King, and Savior of the nations, and we will not know him in his full splendor until we know him as the King of the nations.

The new heavens and earth. Finally, the Scriptures declare God's promise of a new heavens and a new earth. Peter instructs us to "wait for new heavens and a new earth, where righteousness will dwell" (2 Pet. 3:13, HCSB). John sees a vision in which there is a new heaven and a new earth, where there remains no pain or tears (Rev. 21). Although this teaching does not get much airtime in evangelical circles, it is no insignificant doctrine. Indeed, it is the doctrine of creation come full circle. The God who gave us the good creation of the Genesis narrative is the God who will give us a new heavens and a new earth.

In this new universe, God's image-bearers will experience neither sin nor its consequences. No longer will we use our rational capacities to speak false-hoods, or our creative capacities to construct idols. Never again will we use our relational capacities to suppress others and promote ourselves, our moral capacities to slander, rape, or murder. No longer will we live in an environment where tsunamis and floods destroy or where pollution poisons the ground and air. Never again will there be war or rumors of war.

Instead, we will live in unbroken relation with God, with others, with the new universe, and with ourselves. We will be "man fully alive," man worshipping God in spirit and truth. Indeed, but what does this doctrine of a new heavens and earth have to do with the mission of the church? Of the many implications, here are three.

First, as noted earlier, we may use our God-given human capacities to glorify him in human culture, as a sign of what the new heavens and new earth will be like. We may teach our children that it is honorable to be an artist (writer, composer, singer, painter, graphic designer, etc.), a scientist (biologist, chemist, physicist, sociologist, anthropologist), or a participant in the public square (journalist, lawyer, politician, ethicist, educator). In so doing, we will see God glorified from every conceivable dimension of human society and culture. Second, we may seek to glorify God in all of our callings.

May we speak and live the gospel in all of those contexts so that the glory of God is not limited to the four walls of a church building, but instead is broadcast across every square inch of his universe.

Third, we may demonstrate that if there is anyone who should care about God's good creation, it is the evangelical Christian. We do not care about it inordinately, or in the wrong way, but we do care. We have a different motivation than do most "environmentalists." We recognize the creation as *God's* good creation. We do not take the gift that God has given us and trash it recklessly. This is an insult to the God who made it and gave it to us to have dominion over it.

In the doctrine of the end times, therefore, we confess that the promised Messiah has come, and he will come again to win the nations unto himself and to reconcile all things unto himself. He will do this because he loves the world (John 3:16–17). In his first coming, he provided the firstfruits of that redemption, and in the second coming he will provide the consummation of it.

We find ourselves living between those two comings, and the ramifications of this are multiple and significant. We must proclaim the gospel not only in Jerusalem, Judea, and Samaria, but also to the ends of the earth (Acts 1:8). We must also seek to glorify him in every facet of creation and culture, and in all of our multiple callings. Our worship of God should not be limited or reduced to what happens once a week on Sunday mornings. Moreover, we look toward, and hope for, the day when we can join the chorus around the throne and declare, "The Lamb who was slaughtered is worthy to receive power and riches and wisdom and strength and honor and glory and blessing!" (Rev. 5:12, HCSB).

CONCLUSION

One of the most significant imperatives facing the church today is to ensure that her evangelical theology drives her actual ministry practice, that sound doctrine fosters healthy missiology. This chapter has been an attempt to join the conversation, drawing attention to the great doctrines of the Christian faith and some of their implications for our missiological strategies, methods, and practices. May we seek carefully, consciously, and consistently to rivet missiological practice to Christian Scripture and its attendant evangelical doctrine and, in so doing, bring glory to Christ who gave us both the doctrine and its attendant mission imperative.

Chapter Twenty-Two

A CHALLENGE
FOR OUR CHURCHES

Daniel L. Akin and Bruce Riley Ashford

INTRODUCTION

M ission finds its origin in God. It is God-centered rather than man-centered, being rooted in God's gracious will to glorify himself.[1] Mission is defined, organized, empowered, and directed by God. Ultimately, it is accomplished by God. The church cannot understand her mission apart from the mission of God. The purpose of this book, therefore, has been to provide a basic biblical-theological framework and trajectory for understanding God's mission, the church's mission, the church's mission to the nations, and the connection between those three concepts.

The present chapter hopes to build on this framework and trajectory by challenging churches, mission organizations, and other Christian institutions to be ever-vigilant and faithful in heeding the Christian mission as set forth in Christian Scripture. Toward this end, this chapter delineates five crucial factors for the success of Christian mission as we move forward together in reaching the nations with the gospel. Our mission must be one that is (1) set forth in the Christian Scriptures, (2) based upon God's mission, (3) focused on the nations, (4) focused on this nation, and (5) centered on the gospel.

---

[1] This chapter is a revised version of "An SBC Vision for Fulfilling the Great Commission," an essay to be published in Larry McDonald and Matthew Queen, eds., *A Passion for the Great Commission: Essays in Honor of Alvin L. Reid* (Nashville: CrossBooks, Fall 2011).

A MISSION SET FORTH IN THE CHRISTIAN SCRIPTURES

The character of God underlies Christian mission. In the Bible's opening act of creation, we learn that he is a God of life and love. In the aftermath of the fall, we find that he is still a God of life and love, setting in motion his plan to redeem his image-bearers and restore his creation. This same God gave the Great Commission, empowered the early church of Acts in her mission, and empowers us in ours. Our knowledge of these teachings, indeed our confidence in them, stems from the narrative set forth in the Christian Scriptures. If we cannot trust the Scriptures, we have nowhere to turn for a trustworthy word about God and his character, or the church and her mission.

Evangelical churches confess that the Scriptures are the very words of God. Time and again, the Scriptures claim to be the word of God. The Scriptures are inspired, or literally "God-breathed" (2 Tim. 3:16). For this reason, the words of Scripture are more sure even than Peter's eyewitness experience of our Lord's life and ministry (2 Pet. 2:16–21). This doctrine of inspiration is foundational. Because the Scriptures are inspired, we confess that the biblical autographs are perfect (Prov. 30:5–6), meaning that they are without error. Christian Scripture is infallible—it will not lead us astray (Ps. 19:7). It is inspired in the whole and not merely in the parts (Rom. 15:4), as given in the autographs (2 Pet. 1:21). God has given us the Scriptures through the pens of human authors (2 Sam. 23:2) who used human language (Matt. 4:4). In other words, the Bible is the Word of God written in the words of men. Moreover, it is sufficient to instruct us concerning life and salvation (2 Tim. 3:15), sufficiently clear for us to comprehend (Ps. 119:105), and sufficiently powerful to convict sinners and deliver the good news of God's salvation (Heb. 4:12). Finally, the Scriptures are Christocentric: the purpose of Scripture is to present Christ (Luke 24:44–49). Christ himself stands at the center of the Scriptures—he is the linchpin of the canon and the towering actor in the drama of history.

This is our confession. Although it may be treated as intellectual leprosy in the academy, and although modern and postmodern socio-cultural currents are diametrically opposed to it, we stand firmly upon this doctrine. Other issues pale before this one. The doctrine of Scripture is a "watershed" of theological conviction, and its significance reaches across the whole of the Christian mission.[2] When we lose conviction concerning God's Word, we will surely feel the effects in other doctrines and in the life and practice of the church. If we lose our way in relation to the Scriptures, we will lose our way in Christology and

---

[2] This is the point Danny Akin makes when he writes, "We must never forget that the 'war for the Bible' is not over and it will never end until Jesus returns. Launched by Satan in the Garden of Eden, 'has God said' will continue to be under assault, and we must be ever on guard and ready to answer those who question its veracity and accuracy." Daniel Akin, "Axioms for a Great Commission Resurgence" (Wake Forest, NC: Southeastern Baptist Theological Seminary, 2009), 10.

soteriology. If we do not have a sure word from God, we will soon lose our mission.[3]

A Mission Based Upon God's Mission

In an attempt to organize the biblical teaching concerning Christian mission, this book has offered three "golden threads" of mission. The first thread is the *mission of God*, woven throughout the biblical narrative of creation, fall, redemption, and new creation. The biblical narrative reveals that the uncreated triune God created this world from nothing. God created and fills a good world with his image-bearers from whom he will make a kingdom of priests. This world reflects God's glory and points continually to him. God's first image-bearers, however, sinned against him, setting themselves up as autonomous, and in so doing, they alienated themselves from God, each other, and the rest of the created order. As a result, they and we are dead in our trespasses, and the good world God created is marred by the ugliness of sin, the consequences of which are far more pervasive than we might typically imagine.

In the aftermath of man's rebellion, God immediately promised to send a Savior, one born of a woman, one who would redeem the nations and restore God's good world. Indeed, from the third chapter of Genesis onward, the Scriptures bear witness to the triumphant march of God who accomplished the redemption he promised through the Savior he sent. The Savior came, was crucified to cancel the debt that we could not pay, rose from the dead, and is seated at the right hand of God the Father. Further, he will return again, bringing with him a new heavens and earth, where the redeemed of the nations will worship him forever and ever.

The second thread discernible in the biblical narrative is *the church's mission*. The church finds itself between the third and fourth plot movements in redemptive history, between the time when he sent his Son to purchase redemption and the time when he will have gathered the redeemed of the nations and created the heavens and earth anew. We bear witness to the sent One, to glorify him in both word and deed. Just as he will return one day to receive the worship of the redeemed and to restore his good creation, so the church's mission includes both redemptive and creational aspects.[4] In its redemptive aspect, the church bears witness to the gospel in word and

---

[3] For further reflection, we commend Paige Patterson, "Beyond the Impasse: Fidelity to the God Who Speaks," in Robinson B. James and David S. Dockery, eds., *Beyond the Impasse? Scripture, Interpretation, and Theology in Baptist Life* (Nashville: Baptist Sunday School Board, 1992), 149–68, and David S. Dockery, *Southern Baptist Consensus and Renewal: A Biblical, Historical, and Theological Proposal* (Nashville: B&H, 2008), 16–57. The Patterson chapter is helpful in exposing how an errant view of Scripture issues forth in an errant mission. The Dockery chapter is an extended argument that, for Baptists, Scripture, global missions, and cooperation go hand in hand. None can be separated from the others.

[4] It is fitting that the book of Revelation encapsulates both the redemptive and creational aspects. Revelation 5 speaks to the redemption of men and women from every tribe, tongue,

deed so that she may be an agent of grace to a lost and perishing world. In its creational aspect, the church works out the implications of the gospel in every dimension of society and culture. In so doing, it provides a sign of the kingdom that has been inaugurated and will come in all its fullness in the *parousia*.

The third thread is *the church's mission to the nations*. Throughout the Scriptures, God makes clear that he will glorify himself among the nations. In Solomon's prayer, for example, we learn that God will make known to the nations his great name, his strong hand, and his outstretched arm. In Psalm 67, we learn of a God who will make his salvation known among all the nations and to whom all the peoples of the earth will give their praise. In Matthew's gospel we find our Lord commanding us to take the gospel to the nations, while in Luke's we find him promising that his name will be preached to all nations. Finally, in Revelation, we are given a glimpse of those redeemed worshippers from among every tribe, tongue, people, and nation (Matt. 28:16–20; Luke 24:46–49; Rev. 5, 7). These passages and numerous others make clear God's mission to redeem worshippers from every people and nation in his good creation.

God has woven these golden threads deeply into the biblical tapestry. To remove any of the three threads is to distort the overall picture: God's mission—to win the nations and to restore his creation—frames the church's mission. The church's mission, in redemptive, ethical, and cultural aspects, frames the cross-cultural and cross-linguistic aspects of her mission.[5] Mission, therefore, begins with God and culminates in God. He organizes, energizes, and directs it. The danger is that we lose sight of this, thereby divorcing missiology from theology, and thence making the church's mission in our own image, which is nothing less than idolatry.

A MISSION FOCUSED ON THE NATIONS

An awkward tension. Reflection upon the biblical narrative makes it clear that our mission efforts often fall short. Revelation 5 serves to illustrate the point. This chapter portrays perhaps the most breathtaking and glorious

---

people, and nation, while Revelation 21–22 speaks to the restoration of God's good creation, as he provides a new heavens and earth.

[5]   By this, we do not mean that our international missionaries will pay the same attention to a cultural mandate that they will to their evangelistic mandate. It is our opinion that most mission agencies and most missionaries should focus their energies on evangelism, discipleship, and church planting, and in particular on church planting among unreached people groups. However, the churches that we plant should seek to glorify God in every conceivable manner among their people group (UPG). These churches' efforts, therefore, would optimally include efforts to work out the implications of the gospel in every dimension of their respective cultures. Further, we would note the significant contribution of certain mission agencies who place considerable emphasis on aspects other than church planting and on audiences other than UPGs. We think of agencies such as the International Institute of Christian Studies, which specializes on sending Christians professors into universities and seminaries around the world.

vision in all of Scripture. In it, God gives a vision to John, the disciple whom Jesus loved, who was being held captive in his old age on the island of Patmos. In the midst of the vision, John saw the four living creatures and the twenty-four elders prostrate before the Lord, singing a new song, saying: "You are worthy to take the scroll, and to open its seals; for You were slain, and have redeemed us to God by Your blood out of every tribe and tongue and people and nation, and have made us kings and priests to our God; and we shall reign on the earth" (5:9–10, NKJV). And again, together with all of heaven, they were singing with a loud voice: "Worthy is the Lamb who was slain to receive power and riches and wisdom, and strength and honor and glory and blessing!" (5:12, NKJV).

In this passage, which reveals to us the consummation of God's redemptive purposes, we note two truths in particular. First, we note that there is something so profoundly true, so deeply good, and so strikingly beautiful about our God that he finds for himself worshippers among every type of person on the face of the earth. He brings his salvation not just to every continent, and not merely to every nation-state, but also to every "tribe and tongue and people and nation"—to every people across the span of history and to the farthest reaches of the globe. In doing so, he makes clear that he is superior to all other "gods" and that he is intent upon winning the nations to himself. This is no footnote to redemptive history. It stands front and center. God killed his Son in order to redeem the nations. In the words of our Lord, "This gospel of the kingdom shall be preached in the whole world as a testimony to all the nations, and then the end will come" (Matt. 24:14, NASB).

Second, we learn that this salvation comes through Christ alone. John tells us that the creatures and elders sing to the Lamb: "You were slain, and have redeemed us to God *by Your blood*" (Rev. 5:9, NKJV, emphasis added). Salvation is wrought by the shed blood of the Lamb of God. For this reason, Luke describes him as the chief cornerstone of the church and writes: "Nor is there salvation in any other, for there is *no other name* under heaven given among men by which we must be saved" (Acts 4:12, NKJV, emphasis added). In this vein, Paul writes "through *[Jesus Christ]* we have received grace and apostleship for obedience to the faith among *all nations* for His name" (Rom. 1:5, NKJV, emphasis added). For this reason we sing: "There is a fountain filled with blood, drawn from Emmanuel's veins, and sinners plunged beneath that flood lose all their guilty stains."[6]

But we must not allow these two points to stand alone. We must place beside them two striking realities. The first reality is that there are several billion people who have little or no access to the gospel. They could search for days and months and years and never find a Bible or a Christian or a church. The second reality is that American churches possess great financial and personnel resources, and therefore clearly are able to take the gospel to

---

[6] William Cowper, "There is a Fountain," in *The Baptist Hymnal* (Nashville: Convention Press, 1991), 142.

the nations. Yet there are those who have never heard the gospel. The question we all must ask is, "Why?"

Here is the bottom line: If we believe that salvation comes through Christ alone, and if we know that two billion people have little or no access to the gospel, then we are faced with a dilemma. Either we build Great Commission churches and accomplish the task that God has given us, or we force the Lord to plow around us to accomplish his will. Indeed, the Lord will accomplish his will. The question before us is, "Will we be found in his will or watching from the sidelines in disobedience?" We are hopeful it will be the former.

Five clear challenges. As we fulfill our mission to the nations, we face many decisions, including the five following challenges.

With a limited number of missionaries, to which parts of the globe do we send missionaries? It is our conviction that the established church should make a concerted effort to send missionaries to unreached and unengaged people groups, those who have little or no access to the gospel. As we mentioned above, there are vast stretches of the globe (Asia and Africa in particular) where there is no church capable of reaching its own people. Our churches must take the gospel to these people groups. This mission to unreached and unengaged people groups, however, must include not only "reaching" but "teaching," not only evangelism but full-orbed discipleship. Further, the church should continue to find ways to minister in the mission fields that are not considered unreached or unengaged, but where the believers have not yet been discipled or equipped to further the mission.

When we send our workers to the unreached and unengaged, what are we sending them to do? Should they primarily preach the gospel? Feed the hungry? Heal the sick? It is our belief that, ultimately, we are sending missionaries to make disciples by means of *planting churches* (and training indigenous church planters) that will preach the gospel, feed the hungry, and minister to the sick. It is these churches, and not primarily the cross-cultural missionaries, who will preach the gospel and work out its implications in all aspects of their society and culture: in their families, workplaces, and communities. God works primarily through his church; therefore, he would have us to extend his kingdom by means of his church.[7] We seek to plant churches whose immediate goal is to plant other churches until there is a cascading chain of churches planting churches. Indeed, we hope to see churches planted within walking distance of every house in the world.

When we plant these churches, how will we ensure that we do so in a way that is biblical and appropriate to their respective contexts? How can we

---

[7] In Matthew 28:18–20, we are commanded to make disciples of all nations. If we are to "make disciples" of the nations, we must do so through the planting of churches, because discipleship can only be fully accomplished through the local church. For further biblical-theological treatment of the mandate and implementation of church planting, see John L. Nevius, *The Planting and Development of Missionary Churches* (Hancock, NH: Monadnock, 2003); Roland Allen, *Missionary Methods: St. Paul's or Ours* (Grand Rapids: Eerdmans, 1962); and David Hesselgrave, *Planting Churches Cross-Culturally: North America and Beyond* (Grand Rapids: Baker, 2000).

guarantee that we are not planting American churches on Iraqi, Nigerian, or Vietnamese soil? In brief, the answer lies at the intersection of three imperatives. First, we must preach the gospel and plant churches *faithfully*, in a way that conforms to the Scriptures. In a phrase, we seek to plant healthy, biblically-defined churches. Second, we must preach the gospel *meaningfully*, using words and categories and teaching styles that enable the hearer to understand the gospel in the same way that the preacher intends it. Third, we must preach the gospel and plant the church *dialogically*, in conversation with the host culture as national believers prayerfully seek to allow the gospel to critique the very language and categories of their own culture. If we will hold these three imperatives in tension, we have good reason to hope that the churches arising from native soil will be biblically faithful and appropriate to their contexts.

How may our American churches fulfill their calling to the nations? First and foremost, we must find ways to build mission into the DNA of our churches. Mission is not a sometime "ministry" of the church; it is at the heart of who she is. This means that in our preaching and teaching ministries we need to trace the message of mission throughout the Scriptures and publicly invite our members to commit a summer or two years or even a lifetime working among the nations. In our community ministries, we need to reach out to the immigrants, foreign exchange students, and other international people who live in our cities. In our mission ministries, we might seek to adopt an unreached people group as the church's own and then seek the guidance of seasoned missionaries on how to proceed in ministering to that people group.[8]

How might our seminaries and colleges assist our churches in fulfilling our calling to the nations? They may do so by not divorcing theology from missiology and by not quarantining missiology to a lonely corner of the campus. Theology may be the "queen of the disciplines," but it will be a distorted theology indeed if it is not forged in the fire of mission. We must be careful to teach the books of the Bible and the classical theological loci with reference

---

[8]   This provides a natural opportunity for partnership between a local church, missionaries, and national partners (unless there are not yet any national believers and churches). When an American church embarks upon mission trips without such a partnership, there are three potential pitfalls. First, the church will have limited insight on how to make their work fit within a broader long-term strategy. Second, the church often will find itself crafting the trips primarily according to what is best for the local church team rather than what is best for the people group to whom they are ministering. Third, the church will be tempted to focus too much on certain *perceived* needs of the nationals and, in so doing, create an unhealthy dependency upon the American church. For a church's short-term mission trips to be truly strategic, they must be part of a long-term field-based strategy in collaboration with missionaries and (if a national church exists) with seasoned national partners. George Robinson has addressed all three of these issues in *Striking the Match: How God Is Using Ordinary People to Change the World through Short-Term Missions* (Franklin, TN: E3 Resources, 2008). Also, see Robert J. Priest, ed., *Effective Engagement in Short-Term Missions: Doing It Right!* (Pasadena, CA: William Carey, 2008).

to the biblical narrative and God's missional character.[9] In so doing, we will find ourselves teaching about God with reference to his missional heart. We will teach about the church in relation to her missional calling. We will teach about the end times in light of the ingathering of the nations. Some institutions will need to be careful not to allow their missions department and missions professors to be viewed as second class citizens. Other institutions that more naturally emphasize missions must take care to ensure that their missional zeal is buttressed by sturdy theology. In riveting theology to mission, we will produce students who can build and sustain Great Commission churches.

A MISSION FOCUSED ON THIS NATION

We must confront the brutal facts. In Matthew 28:18–20, Jesus commands us to make disciples of *all* nations. This includes our own nation—the United States of America—and yet the truth is that we are failing to meet the challenge. While the population of our nation increases, the population of our churches has not kept pace. While the United States becomes increasingly diverse, many of our churches have remained mostly middle-class, mostly white, and mostly declining churches.[10] This is a painful truth, and to ignore this fact is the worst form of denial.

It is not as if our churches have not tried to reach their own towns and cities. Many of them have worked hard to reach their cities, and many of them have more or less succeeded. But the truth of the matter is that we are losing the battle. Our nation is becoming increasingly post-Christian, and we are not stemming the tide. Perhaps one of the reasons that we are losing the battle is that we are "aiming at" a culture that no longer exists. The SBC, for example, built its programs and its personality, if you will, in the 1950s. However, we find ourselves in a socio-cultural context that varies significantly from that of sixty years ago. Many of our churches no longer have the luxury of communicating the gospel within a city that has basically one culture. Instead, they find themselves communicating across numerous cultural and subcultural divides.[11]

In years past, many of us found ourselves ministering in regions heavily influenced by Christianity, but now we often do not. Many, if not most, of

---

[9]   Russell D. Moore makes this point in "Theology Bleeds: Why Theological Vision Matters for the Great Commission, and Vice Versa," in *Great Commission Resurgence*, Chuck Lawless and Adam W. Greenway, eds. (Nashville: B&H, 2010), 103–20.

[10]   For statistics on the SBC's decline, see Ed Stetzer's commentary on Lifeway's research, http://www.edstetzer.com/2009/06/new-sbc-data.html#more. Accessed 10 December 2010.

[11]   One particularly helpful treatment of ideological diversity in the United States is Gertrude Himmelfarb, *One Nation, Two Cultures* (New York: Vintage, 2001). Himmelfarb argues that the United States is a divided nation. On the one hand, there is a religious culture that has common categories for discourse and common convictions on ethical issues. On the other hand, there is an elite culture that is very permissive on moral issues and does not share the religious culture's moral language and categories.

our neighbors had sufficient knowledge of the biblical narrative to be able to understand "sermonese," but now they do not. In a previous era there were common categories for moral discourse, but now these categories are less and less common. There was a day when we were able to build our churches by inviting people to church events, but now we find it hard to do so. So how do we conceive of the task of communicating the gospel effectively to the various cultures and subcultures of our own country? How can we create and implement a missiology that will enable us to win the lost, make disciples, and plant churches in an increasingly larger array of American sociocultural contexts? In a nutshell, how can we build missional churches and a missional convention?

Our mission must be cross-cultural. The United States is increasingly multi-cultural, multi-ethnic, and multi-linguistic, as immigrants from around the world now live in our own cities and suburbs. Many of the tribes, tongues, and peoples of Revelation 5 are right here on our doorstep. Further, there is a dizzying variety of subcultures within the broader American culture, each with their own distinctive beliefs and ways of life. Many of them do not have even a basic understanding of Christian worldview or vocabulary. *Churches and pastors in the United States must take their own cultural contexts as seriously as missionaries take their international contexts.*

We must seek to understand the cultures and subcultures around us so that we can preach the gospel *faithfully* and *meaningfully* within the framework of our neighbors' cultural and social contexts, and plant churches that are at home in the culture. We must preach the gospel *faithfully*, allowing it to be defined and delimited by the Scriptures. We must also preach the gospel *meaningfully*, so that the hearer understands the gospel in the same way that the preacher intends it. The concept of the gospel might be foreign to them, but we may communicate it in language and constructs that are not. In doing so, we are able to preach the gospel clearly within the framework of the audience's cultural, subcultural, and situational contexts.

The way we preach the gospel affects the way the audience receives it. Many church planters, pastors, teachers, and authors have pointed out that if evangelical churches are to be missional, they must make changes in their preaching. Many of us, for example, have become accustomed to ministering in the Bible Belt in the mid-to-late twentieth century, to a population who had some (or much) knowledge of the biblical narrative and often possessed a common language for moral discourse. But in the twenty-first century, we find ourselves in a context where many people have little or no knowledge of the Scriptures or Christian language. How do we communicate the gospel effectively in this situation? Tim Keller is one church planter who has written extensively on this challenge.[12] He argues that:

---

[12] Tim Keller is the founding pastor of Redeemer Presbyterian Church in New York City, New York. Keller founded the church in the late 1980s, and since then has seen the church grow to more than 5,000 in attendance (in addition to 5,000 sermon downloads per week), most of whom were unchurched before finding Redeemer. More significantly, perhaps, is the fact that

- The missional church avoids "tribal" language, stylized prayer language, unnecessary evangelical pious "jargon," and archaic language that seeks to set a "spiritual tone."
- The missional church avoids "we-them" language, disdainful jokes that mock people of different politics and beliefs, and dismissive, disrespectful comments about those who differ with us.
- The missional church avoids sentimental, pompous, "inspirational" talk. Instead, we engage the culture with the gentle, self-deprecating, but joyful irony the gospel creates. Humility + joy = gospel irony and realism.
- The missional church avoids ever talking as if non-believing people are not present. If you speak and discourse as if your whole neighborhood is present (not just scattered Christians), eventually more and more of your neighborhood will find their way in or be invited.
- Unless all of the above is the outflow of a truly humble-bold gospel-changed heart, it is all just "marketing" and "spin."[13]

To Keller's admonition, we would add this clarification. We are not proposing to give up biblical-theological language, the very grammar and vocabulary of our faith. Instead, we are proposing to speak to those who are gathered in such a way that they can understand the gospel. We do so precisely so that we can draw them into the biblical world, where they will find a better set of categories for understanding God and his world as well as a deeper and more profound vocabulary for speaking of those things.

Our mission must be multi-faceted. In addition to proclaiming the gospel from inside of the four walls of a church building and in addition to community outreach programs and door-to-door visitations, we must continually remind ourselves and our congregations that everything we do matters to God. Drawing upon Martin Luther's concept of *vocatio*, we must teach that every believer has the privilege and responsibility of bringing glory to God in each of his callings: family, church, workplace, and community. The workplace, in particular, is an oft-neglected calling in which we are given an almost unparalleled opportunity to bring God glory and to love our neighbors.[14]

Further, God has given us the ability and responsibility to work out our faith in the various spheres of culture, including especially the arts (e.g., literature, music, movies, visual art), the sciences (e.g., biology, physics, chemistry, sociology, anthropology, psychology), the public square (e.g., law, politics, economics, journalism, moral philosophy), business, and education.

Redeemer's church planting center has facilitated over 100 church plants. In January 2007, *Outreach Magazine* named Redeemer the top "Multiplying Church" in America. See http://outreach-magazine.com/docs/25innov_JA07.pdf.

[13] Tim Keller, "The Missional Church" (June 2001), http://www.redeemer2.com/resources/papers/missional.pdf. Also, this material is explained in Tim Keller and J. Allen Thompson, *Church Planter Manual* (New York: Redeemer Church Planting Center, 2002), 224–25.

[14] The best brief introduction to Luther's treatment of calling is Gene Veith, *God at Work: Your Christian Vocation in All of Life* (Wheaton: Crossway, 2002).

For the gospel-minded Christian, there is no room for indifference or hostility toward these aspects of human culture. We are not given the option of abdicating our responsibility to glorify God across every square inch of his good creation.[15] Instead, we are called to engage the culture arising from the society in which we live and minister, critiquing and developing it according to God's Word. In so doing, we sow the seed of the gospel throughout every dimension of our cultural context, providing a sign of God's kingdom.

Our mission must be all-encompassing. Not only is our task cross-cultural and multi-dimensional, but it also stretches across the geographic and demographic spectrum. We must reach both the small towns *and* the great cities of the United States. While evangelicals have been moderately successful in reaching the South, we have been even less successful in reaching the great cities of the Northeast and the West. We recognize the strategic nature of urban involvement and seek to heighten our involvement in the largest, least churched, and most influential American cities. Urban centers such as New York, Washington, D.C., Boston, and Los Angeles are the nerve centers of North American socio-cultural activity, having massive influence on our continent and across the globe, and yet they are among the least churched cities in America.

We must reach both the down-and-out *and* the cultural elite. Our churches have often been fairly effective at reaching the upper and lower middle classes in the Bible Belt, but often we have not reached the cultural elite or the poor and disenfranchised. In reaching those who are "down and out," we must be prepared to build churches that intentionally minister in the inner cities, are willing to embrace those with HIV, and are happy to include those who may never be able financially to contribute in a significant way to the church. When we minister to these men and women, we recognize that they are God's image-bearers and deserve our love and attention every bit as much as anyone else.[16] In reaching those who are the cultural elite, we must intentionally reach out to artists, scientists, philosophers, moral and political movers, and many others. In so doing, we are "swimming upstream," ministering to those who in turn may have significant ability to influence our society and culture for the sake of the gospel.

---

[15] Among the most helpful books treating Christianity and culture are D. A. Carson, *Christ & Culture Revisited* (Grand Rapids: Eerdmans, 2008); Michael S. Horton, *Where in the World Is the Church?* (Phillipsburg, NJ: P&R, 2002); and T. M. Moore, *Culture Matters* (Grand Rapids: Brazos, 2007). Carson's text is a meta-level theological treatise on the Christian's place in culture, while Horton's text is a popular level, practical treatment of the church's role in its cultural context. Moore's monograph is a concise, intermediate level manifesto for Christian cultural engagement. David Dockery's treatment of Christian higher education exemplifies the outworking of our faith across the various dimensions of culture. David Dockery, *Renewing Minds: Serving Church and Society through Christian Higher Education* (Nashville: B&H, 2008).

[16] In the gospels, we learn that the most "religious" people, the Pharisees, were able only to attract people just like them. They circled the world in order to find one convert. However, Jesus attracted all kinds of people: tax collectors, prostitutes, lepers, etc. Jesus, not the Pharisees, must be our model.

We must build churches that do serious-minded student ministry, both for youth and college students. Student ministry might be the closest parallel to international missions, as student ministers must learn to speak the gospel into various youth cultures that have their own beliefs, vocabularies, narratives, and heroes. It will be a good day indeed when an increasing number of our churches' student ministries are known more for sound doctrine and genuine cultural savvy than they are for cutesy Bible studies and superficial cultural gimmickry.[17] Moreover, we pray that the day comes when more of us seek, consciously and consistently, to win our nation's college campuses to Christ. In the classrooms of our American universities sit the students who are the future of our nation and in many cases the future of our churches, as well as international students who are the future of their nations and of their nations' churches. We must make student ministry a priority in our churches, even during those times when it seems not to bear spiritual fruit and even during those times when it does not make sense financially.

Our mission must center on church renewal, church planting, and cooperation. Our mission will not succeed without healthy churches. This requires, first and foremost, an emphasis on church renewal. We must always be renewing and reforming. This is the only way to ensure that our churches are sound in their doctrine, consistent in their evangelism, intentional in crossing cultural and linguistic boundaries, and contextual in their cultural forms. It is only from the wombs of healthy churches that we might see a church planting movement that is capable of reaching our own country. It is only healthy churches who will faithfully and meaningfully proclaim the gospel of our Lord and build churches across cultures and sub-cultures, languages and races, vocations and dimensions of culture, cities and suburbs, rich and poor, young and old.[18]

Second, our mission requires aggressive and intentional cooperation in church planting. The churches we plant must be sound in their doctrinal orientation, contextual in their cultural forms, and aggressive in their evangelistic and mission orientation. In order to make this work, we need renewed commitment from those with whom we partner.[19]

Third, our mission will not fare well if it is not cooperative. This includes local church cooperation with other churches, networks, seminaries, mission

---

[17] This is not to degrade the solid student ministries in many of our churches. There is a revival of interest, in our churches, for theologically sound and culturally savvy student ministry.

[18] Many resources are available to help pastors and their congregation work toward church health, of which we mention the following three. First, IX Marks ministries offers a website, a journal, and books on the topic of church health: http://blog.9marks.org. Second, Thom Rainer has authored more than a few helpful books dealing with church health and growth. Thom S. Rainer, *The Book of Church Growth* (Nashville: B&H, 1993); with Eric Geiger, *Simple Church* (Nashville: B&H, 2006); with Daniel L. Akin, *Vibrant Church* (Nashville: Lifeway, 2008). Third, see Ed Stetzer and Mike Dodson's recently published *Comeback Churches* (Nashville: B&H, 2007), a study of 300 revitalized churches.

[19] In our denomination, the SBC, this means renewed commitment from our churches, local associations, and state conventions.

agencies, and other organizations. The daunting nature of our task demands that if any of these entities are unwilling to fulfill their missional calling, then healthy churches will find other entities with which to cooperate in order to fulfill the calling God has given them. We must be willing and able to take on this God-given calling.

A MISSION CENTERED ON THE GOSPEL

Paul warns the Corinthians about the danger of factional battles within the church; this warning also applies to seminary communities, mission agencies, and other similar entities and organizations. Sometimes the battles we fight are unnecessary and/or they are waged inappropriately. Often, unnecessary battles are waged because a group of people is excited about a particular idea, movement, or tradition. They begin to condescend or castigate, and they seek to exclude anyone who does not share their ideas, emphasis, jargon, or agenda. The idea, movement, or tradition becomes a virtual test of orthodoxy.[20]

Some unnecessary wars stem from a doctrine of "separation" (sometimes known as the doctrine of non-fellowship). This doctrine is based upon such passages of Scripture as Amos 3:3: "Can two walk together, except they be agreed?" (KJV). For some Christians, this doctrine means merely that we should separate ourselves from worldliness. For others, it means that we should separate ourselves from those who do not separate themselves from worldliness. Still others, however, would disallow fellowship (and sometimes friendship) with those who differ from them in any matter of theology (e.g., the particulars of one's position on the rapture), physical life (e.g., preference in apparel or music), or social life (e.g., one's friendship with a controversial person or preacher). The result is a flattening of all theological and practical categories as if they are of equal weight and importance. For a time, I (Bruce Ashford) walked in Independent Baptist circles where such "third degree separation" is practiced. Although I admire many of these men and am thankful for what I have learned from them, this doctrine is one of the primary reasons I left those circles.

Al Mohler has proposed that the hospital emergency room provides an apt analogy for how we might handle doctrinal and practical differences.[21] Those who are reading this chapter might have had opportunity to see the goings-on of the "triage" unit of an emergency room. In triage, the doctors and nurses determine the priority of the diseases and injuries that will be treated. Shotgun wounds are treated before ankle sprains, and seizures before bunions. This is because certain diseases and injuries strike at the heart of one's well being, while others are less life threatening.

---

[20] We owe this point to John Frame. See his booklet *Studying Theology as a Servant of Jesus* (Reformed Theological Seminary Bookstore, 2000), 18.

[21] See R. Albert Mohler Jr., "Has Theology a Future in the Southern Baptist Convention? Toward a Renewed Theological Framework," in *Beyond the Impasse?* ed. Robison B. James and David S. Dockery (Nashville: B&H, 1992), 91–117, and R. Albert Mohler Jr., "The Pastor as Theologian," in *A Theology for the Church*, ed. Daniel L. Akin (Nashville: B&H, 2007), 930–32.

Pastors, theologians, and missionaries would benefit from the same sort of triage. When deciding with whom we will partner and in what way, and when deciding which battles need to be fought and in what way, it is helpful to distinguish which doctrines are more primary and which are less so. Primary doctrines are those that are most essential to Christian faith. Without believing such doctrines as the Trinity, the incarnation, and salvation by grace through faith alone, one's belief is not Christian.

Secondary doctrines are those over which born-again believers may often disagree, but which do not strike as closely at the heart of the faith. Two examples are the meaning and mode of baptism, and gender roles in the church. Disagreement on these doctrines does significantly affect the way in which churches and believers relate to one another. For example, although Presbyterians and Baptists may evangelize together and form close friendships, a Baptist and a Presbyterian could not plant a church together precisely because of their differences on church government and on the meaning and mode of baptism. Some secondary doctrines bear more heavily on primary doctrines than others.

Apart from primary and secondary doctrines, there are those that we can call tertiary. These are doctrines over which Christians may disagree and yet keep the closest of fellowship between networks, between churches, and between individual Christians. An example of a tertiary doctrine would be the timing of the rapture.

This does not mean that we avoid controversy at all costs. As one theologian pointed out, lack of controversy is either a sign of theological death or theological maturity.[22] We hope to avoid the former and strive for the latter. Nor does this mean that we view secondary or tertiary doctrines as insignificant. "A structure of theological triage," Mohler writes, "does not imply that Christians may take any biblical truth with less than full seriousness. We are charged to embrace and to teach the comprehensive truthfulness of the Christian faith as revealed in the Holy Scriptures. There are no insignificant doctrines revealed in the Bible, but there is an essential foundation of truth that undergirds the entire system of biblical truth."[23] It does, however, mean that we can have close fellowship with those who differ from us on tertiary issues but decreasing levels of fellowship when we disagree on secondary issues. The upshot of this whole discussion is that we must avoid the liberal extreme of refusing to admit that there are such things as primary doctrines, as well as the fundamentalist extreme of elevating tertiary issues to the status of primary importance.

Numerous spats center on method and practice. In such cases, it is wise to ask whether the practice at hand is based upon biblical command, apostolic precedent, or local tradition.[24] If it is based upon biblical command, then there

---

[22] Clark Pinnock, "A New Reformation: A Challenge to Southern Baptists" (New Orleans: NOBTS, 1968), 3.

[23] R. Albert Mohler, "A Call for Theological Triage and Christian Maturity," http://www.albertmohler.com/commentary_read.php?cdate=2004–05–20.

[24] By "apostolic precedent," we mean those practices of the apostles that are described in the New Testament. Some apostolic precedent is to be imitated (e.g., church planting) while other

is no question that it must be obeyed. If it is based on apostolic precedent, then it demands our attention but nonetheless is not a biblical injunction. We pay close and careful attention to apostolic practices, but some of those practices were contextual (such as taking missionary trips in wooden boats without electricity) and may be modified for today. If it is based on local (non-universal) traditions that have been handed down from believers in times past, we may respect those traditions and seek to understand why they were formed and whether they might be helpful for us today, but we are not beholden to them.

Distinguishing between essentials and non-essentials, and managing to keep missional partnerships without compromise, is not easy. We must pray for God's wisdom in doing so. "We need to recognize," writes David Dockery, "that in essentials of the Christian faith, there is no place for compromise. Faith and truth are primary issues, and we stand firm in those areas. Sometimes we confuse primary and secondary issues. In secondary issues and third-level and fourth-level issues, we need mostly love and grace as we learn to disagree agreeably. We want to learn to love one another in spite of differences and to learn from those with whom we differ."[25] But distinguish we must. We cannot allow ourselves to be sidetracked, or worse, shipwrecked, because of unnecessarily heated or extended argument over secondary and tertiary issues. For the sake of the billions who have never heard the gospel, we must rid ourselves of fundamentalist infighting that distracts from, and contradicts, the proclamation of the gospel.

CONCLUSION

Mission finds its origin in God, being rooted in God's gracious will to glorify himself. God himself defines, organizes, empowers, and ultimately accomplishes Christian mission. Based upon this truth and the confidence it engenders, we seek to glorify God in every manner conceivable, and to proclaim and embody the gospel by every means possible, making it readily accessible to every tribe, tongue, people, and nation. Our task is daunting, considering that opposition to the gospel has never been more formidable than in the twenty-first century. The magnitude of our task, however, is matched and exceeded by the magnitude of our biblical convictions: that God is a missionary God; that a central theme in the Scriptures is God's desire to win the nations unto himself; that since the coming of his Son, God has chosen that all saving faith be consciously focused on Christ; that the church's task in each generation is to proclaim the gospel, make disciples of the nations, and bring God glory in every conceivable manner; and that God has promised and will secure the final triumph of his gospel, even to the ends of the earth.

---

apostolic practices are neutral and context-specific, not necessarily applying to us today (e.g., writing on parchment with large letters).

[25] David S. Dockery, *Southern Baptist Consensus and Renewal: A Biblical, Historical, and Theological Proposal* (Nashville: B&H, 2008), 144.

Name Index

SUBJECT INDEX

SCRIPTURE INDEX